The Greenbelt Cooperative:

Success and Decline

by

Donald H. Cooper

and

Paul O. Mohn

PUBLISHED BY THE CENTER FOR COOPERATIVES

The Center for Cooperatives was established by the California Legislature in 1987 as a center in support of research, education, and extension activities to "advance the body of knowledge, concerning cooperatives in general and address the needs of California's agricultural and nonagricultural cooperatives . . ."

The Centers objectives are to promote:

- EDUCATION. The Center offers formal and informal educational programs to those involved in cooperative management and develops teaching materials for all levels of interest.

- RESEARCH. To help the state's cooperatives reach their objectives, research is conducted on economic, social, and technical developments. A practical aspect of this research: the provision of competitive research grants, and studies for government agencies on how cooperatives can help achieve public policy objectives.

- OUTREACH. The Center informs the public on cooperatives and their significance to the economy of California.

Located on the University of California, Davis campus, the Center is a University-wide academic unit. Its teaching and research resources are drawn from interested professionals from all University of California and state university campuses, other colleges and universities, as well as sources indigenous to the cooperative business community.

The Center is prepared to receive gifts and contributions from the public, foundations, cooperatives, and other like sources and has established an Endowment Fund.

TABLE OF CONTENTS

ABOUT DONALD H. COOPER

Resident of Greenbelt, Maryland, the "cooperative town", from October 1, 1938 to October 15, 1946.

Participation in the Greenbelt Cooperatives:

One of the first 50 members (stockholders), Greenbelt Consumer Services, Inc., February 1940.

Elected to Board of Directors, Greenbelt Consumer Services, Inc., and served from November 24, 1943 to September 26, 1945. While on the Board, served as vice president and as chairman of the Education Committee.

Committee on Functions and Procedures for the GCS Co-op Congress, 1954.

Elected Chairman, Supervisory Committee, from July 10, 1956 to June 3, 1958.

Elected to Board of Directors, from June 3, 1958 to May 17, 1968. While on the Board, served as vice president from June 1958 to July 1959, as secretary from July 1959 to June 1967, on Executive Committee form 1962 to 1967.

Appointed to Ad Hoc Committee to Review Congress Structure, 1970.

Employed as Membership and Education Coordinator (and as a corporation vice president), from October 1977 to December 1979.

Elected delegate at large, GCI Delegate Assembly, various years.

Appointed to Bylaws Revision Committee, 1987.

Chairman, Delegate Assembly Ad Hoc Futures Committee, 1988.

Employed as secretary to the Board of Directors, from April to December 1989.

Board of Directors and secretary, Greenbelt Health Association, 1940-1941.

President, Greenbelt Cooperative Publishing Association, 1943.

Editor, *Greenbelt Cooperator*, 1938-1940, 1942; and business manager, 1945.

Other cooperative participation:

Elected to Board of Directors and as secretary, Cooperative Institute Association, 1967. Served on teaching staff at five annual Institutes.

Information specialist and management specialist for rural electric and rural telephone cooperatives, Rural Electrification Administration, U.S. Department of Agriculture, 1950-1967.

Board of Directors, International Cooperative Development Association, 1964-1965.

Short-term advisor on cooperative organization and structure, Commonwealth of Puerto Rico, San Juan, Puerto Rico, 1966.

Cooperative specialist, National Rural Electric Cooperative Association, Washington, D.C., 1967-1977.

Organization and management specialist (for electric cooperatives) on assignment from NRECA to the National Electrification Administration, Quezon City, Philippines, 1973-1977.

President, Cooper Consultants, Inc., preparing proposals and reports for rural electric cooperatives in Indonesia, Costa Rica, Philippines, etc. 1980-1983.

Lee – This book will not bea money-maker for the Center for Cooperatives or for the University – but should be good reading for those who get the book in their hands.

— Don Cooper

ABOUT PAUL O. MOHN

From 1968 through 1991 Mohn was active in Greenbelt Cooperative Services and its successor organizations, four as Speaker of the GCS Congress and eleven as Chairman of the Board.

During that period he also served on the boards of other cooperatives including: the National Consumer Cooperative Bank, now the National Cooperative Bank; Mid-Eastern Cooperative, a consumer goods wholesaler; the Cooperative League of USA, now the National Cooperative Business Association; and the Cooperative Savings Credit Union. He also served on the Central Committee of the International Cooperative Alliance.

He continues to serve on the board of the American Bowling Congress, a national bowling organization of over 3 million members and served as its President in 1985-86. He also continues to serve as President of Cooperative Travel Services.

He established, for Puerto Rican cooperatives, a Management and Board Development Program and served as its Director for three years. He is co-author of *Boards of Directors of Cooperatives* and for many years conducted seminars for directors of cooperatives in Canada in conjunction with his colleague of long standing, Dr. Leon Garoyan of the University of California. He has conducted numerous board audits and provided other consultative services for cooperatives in the USA and other countries throughout the world.

He conducted an annual international conference for board chairmen of cooperatives for several years, in conjunction with the University Center for Cooperatives, University of Wisconsin. From 1983 to 1989, he was a Visiting Fellow in the Centre for Cooperative Studies, University College Cork, Ireland. Here he co-authored a number of publications on boards of directors and financial management of cooperatives with Dr. Garoyan. They also conducted several seminars each year aimed at improving the proficiency of boards of cooperatives.

He is a Past President of the International Association of Cooperative Educators. In 1984, he was one of the two U.S. delegates invited by Centrosoyus, USSR, to attend their Quadrennial Congress.
He is a graduate of Kansas State University, earned an M.S degree at Mississippi State University, and pursued further graduate work at Oregon State University and the University of Maryland. He is a graduate of the American Management Association's Management Course. Until recently he was a member of the National Association of Corporate Directors.

Lee —
Without your initiative this book would never have been published. You've been a true solid friend for these many years. As we wind down our active life in co-ops it is indeed fitting that we each had a part in, perhaps, our last publication.
Paul O. Mohn

vii

AUTHORS' PREFACE

Taping interviews and assembling records for this book began in 1986, anticipating publication for Greenbelt Cooperative's 50th anniversary in January 1990. Shortly thereafter, it became apparent that the Cooperative was heading into serious trouble and there might not be any 50th anniversary to celebrate. The writing project was put on hold.

Not until after the decision of the bankruptcy court and the transfer of SCAN, the Cooperative's remaining business enterprise, to control by the Danish Export Credit Council did publication of the Greenbelt Co-op story again appear practical.

The temporary Co-op Food Store in Greenbelt, Maryland opened October 5, 1937 with 24 shoppers and first-day sales of $11.45. By February 1968, Greenbelt Consumer Services, Inc., was operating 23 co-op supermarkets and as the nation's largest consumer-owned cooperative had annual sales of $42.5 million. Sales reached $56 million in 1976. Co-op membership reached 138,000 in 1987.

As of December 1, 1989, under a Chapter 11 bankruptcy order, Greenbelt Cooperative became a paper organization with no operating outlets, an estimated 12,000 members, and no cash assets.

What happened to this "wunderkind" of the cooperative movement in its half-century of growth and collapse? Are there lessons to be learned? What were Greenbelt Co-op's strengths and weaknesses? Did it have a significant impact on the marketplace? What did it contribute to the consumer cooperative movement? How did it affect the communities where it offered goods and services? What did it do to the lives of its members, its employees, and especially its leaders?

If a cooperative is people working together to provide themselves goods and services, who were the men and women who built this Greenbelt model? What did they do right? What did they do wrong? What factors were beyond their control?

The story of the Greenbelt Co-op is not so much a record of business statistics as of personalities and human emotions. In a cooperative, members supposedly work together, why then was there so much divisiveness in this one? Yet, at the same time, there were those who did cooperate, who did carry on in the face of frustration, who gave of themselves far more than a "fair share".

We hope you will enjoy reading about this human drama, as much as we enjoyed writing about it and as much as many of us enjoyed living it.

INTRODUCTION

During the Franklin Delano Roosevelt administration, largely with the efforts of Eleanor Roosevelt, a model town called Greenbelt was established in Maryland. Operated by a government agency, it evolved into cooperatives for housing, food, and goods and services.

Out of this beginning, Greenbelt Cooperative Services, Inc., was founded.[1] At the beginning it included a food store, service station, a barber shop, a pharmacy, a movie theater and a few other stores. There was no private enterprise competition within Greenbelt.

Over the years GCS expanded into other geographical areas of the Washington, D.C. metropolitan area and Baltimore. With mergers it also moved into the Norfolk/Hampton, Virginia area; Westminster, Maryland; and Chicago, Illinois.

From its beginning as a tiny conglomerate, it evolved first into a predominantly food cooperative with pharmacies, service stations and furniture (SCAN) stores. By this time the barber shop, movie theater and others had been sold or closed. In the mid-1970s it became predominantly a retail furniture cooperative. In 1983 its only business was SCAN.

GCS survived many crises in its fifty-year history. Sadly, it also failed to capitalize on a number of key opportunities. Finally, a circumstance largely beyond its control (lowered value of the dollar to the Danish kroner) and a questionable decision to 'take' a prolonged strike combined to bring the member-owned business to an ignominious end.

The impetus for consumer cooperation in the U.S. developed during the great recession of the 1930s. As early as the 1970s consumer cooperatives worldwide were beginning to experience difficulties. By the mid-1980s, consumer cooperatives with few exceptions, were facing serious problems. Some, like the strong Scandinavian cooperatives, underwent major reorganizational changes, closed smaller and older stores, and jettisoned previous flagship manufacturing operations. Others, such as the large New Castle Consumer Cooperative in Australia shut down altogether.

Smaller one or two store cooperatives, on the other hand, continued to flourish. Evidence of this can be seen in the Westminster and Greenbelt cooperatives which once again resumed their independence after GCS closed its food and service station operations in 1983. This book is written to

---

[1] GCS became Greenbelt Cooperative, Inc. in 1979. Reference to the cooperative throughout is GCS.

provide a chronicled history of GCS, in order to learn something from its experience that might aid others in avoiding some of the mistakes and pitfalls experienced by GCS.

The book is divided into two parts. The first part is about people and the part each played in shaping the growth and decline of the cooperative. The second part focuses primarily on business decisions and the financial results during Greenbelt's history.

To achieve the exciting detail found in Part I, Don Cooper, the senior and major author, spent months pouring over board minutes, annual reports, the house organ for members, taped interviews, and many other documents. In fact, he went through well over 100 storage file boxes in his quest to develop the smooth flowing chronological history.

Part I details the people, the emotions of this decision making, as well as the ecstasies and agonies of the many who explained the success and failures of their cooperative. The senior author fills in many of the details left out of Part II because, in fact, Part II is meant to be generic and impersonal while Part I is meant to be humanistic.

Part II is written to give the reader a broad picture of Greenbelt's growth, performance, philosophies, planning and decision making. It also provides the reader with graphs depicting comparisons within the cooperative and with a competitor. A few names are included because of their very significant contribution, but generally the two chapters in Part II are about the cooperative as a business.

Some of the interpretations and conclusions in Part I are the opinions of the junior author. These opinions are based upon 18 consecutive years in a leadership portion in GCS, May 1968 to May 1972 as Speaker of the Congress and May 1972 to May 1986 as a Board member. Of those 14 years on the Board, 11 consecutive years were served as Chairman. Most of the opinions expressed were discussed with a number of long time leaders and others familiar with GCS and cooperatives to elicit their views before putting the ideas and opinions on paper.

Interestingly, one or the other of the two authors served in a leadership position in GCS continually from June of 1958 through May of 1986. The senior author served on the Board from November 1943 until October 1945. However, neither served on the Board at the same time.

The appendices provide more detailed data and information to support commentary and figures of the text.

Appendix A. Lists of the directors who served on the GCS Board and their years of service.

Appendix B. Identifies a number of accomplishments during the Cooperative's 50 year history.

Appendix C. Over the years GCS was involved with a large number of organizations. Appendix C lists those which were jointly owned with others and those of which were significant to GCS as a member.

Appendix D. Chronologically lists the historical highlights of the Cooperative.

Appendix E. As noted in Chapter XXI. much planning took place in GCS. Excerpts from one such exercise is herein included because it clearly identifies serious problems and suggested solutions, solutions the Board chronically postponed.

The genesis of GCS was 1937, although it did not become an incorporated cooperative until 1939 with the Board elected in January of 1940. The cooperative grew and expanded over the years, changing from a mini-conglomerate to primarily a food operation and finally, in 1983, exclusively a retail furniture cooperative until under a Chapter 11 court approved "plan" it became a shell organization with no facilities, virtually no assets and no paid staff.[1]

---

[1] See Appendix D for a chronological listing of historical highlights.

PART I

HISTORICAL GROWTH AND DECLINE

I. BEFORE GREENBELT

Out of the Great Depression of the early 1930s came a tide of cooperatives. Most of them were small, unplanned responses to economic needs. A few survived and grew. Before Greenbelt, the Washington, D.C. area already felt the stirrings of people who tried to improve their daily living by pooling their purchases. Most of the consumer cooperatives in the Nation's Capital started as neighborhood or church-based buying clubs.

My wife, Evelyn, and I joined one of these in 1935 a few months after we arrived in Washington from the west coast to take a Government job at $105 a month. This buying club was in the Mt. Pleasant area, where we took turns buying produce by the crate or basket from the wholesale markets by the Potomac River and carting our purchases to the Congregational Church at the corner of 14th and Columbia Road NW. We did this once a week and in the church basement we divided the produce and other wholesale purchases we had ordered and received our change from the advance payment. It was a cooperative, although we did not recognize it at the time.

Similar groups sprang up about the same time in other neighborhoods. Dr. Leroy A. Halbert ("Pop" Halbert), in an unpublished manuscript, "Reminiscences of a Co-operator", credited the start of "self help co-operatives" to several persons employed in the U.S. Department of Agriculture and other Government agencies. He named Jacob Baker, Udo Rall, and Walter Krimont as three who persuaded Harry Hopkins, the national administrator of unemployment relief, to help them organize needy people into groups who could "earn their own support and avoid the name of being on relief".

A group called the Washington Consumers Club, organized chiefly in the Consumers Division of the Department of Agriculture, is credited by Halbert as being "the germ out of which practically all the consumer co-operators in Washington got started". The Halberts joined one of these co-op buying clubs organized in Takoma Park by Simon and Sarah Newman. The Newmans subsequently became long-time, respected leaders in Rochdale Cooperative and then in the Greenbelt Cooperative after the two organizations merged.

Halbert started study groups about cooperatives which attracted from one to two hundred people to monthly meetings at the Congregational Church in the Mt. Pleasant area. Among them were Ed Knapp, David H. Scull and others who later became well known leaders in the Greenbelt Cooperative and other cooperative endeavors.

The Washington Consumers' Club set up a contract department which arranged for its members discounts on purchases of milk deliveries, fuel oil, books, clothing, furniture, and other goods and services. By 1936, seven well established buying clubs had sprung from the study groups and the Washington Consumers Club. Participants realized savings of from 8 to 10 percent on their purchases, and part of the savings were used to buy and keep in stock in basement homes canned and packaged goods most commonly used.

The next step came with a decision by a number of the buying clubs to combine their purchases. They agreed on Dave Scull to hire a truck once a week and deliver the orders. New members and purchases increased so fast that a vacant store space was rented as a sort of warehouse, where sorting and weighing could be done and the accounts maintained. This put the groups within striking distance of having a co-op store.

In July 1937, some of the numerous buying clubs opened Rochdale Stores, Inc. at 1412 Wisconsin Avenue NW, in the Georgetown section of Washington. The enterprise lost money and was near to closing the small store by a year later. Following an emotion- laden meeting, a campaign for new members, more capital, and greater sales got underway, and there was improvement enough for survival -- barely. There was realization that any very small store was handicapped by inability to buy wholesale in large quantities and by a limited variety of items on the shelves.

Members opened a second grocery on October 1, 1940 at 2513 14th Street NW. It also operated at a loss at first. By the end of 1942, Rochdale Stores could pay a 3 percent dividend on its stock but there was not enough left over for a patronage return.

In 1936, Principal John P. Murchison, teaching a class on consumer cooperation at a Works Progress Administration night school, started a co-op store at 38 P Street NE. Before it closed in 1941, it had 250 "colored" families as members, did a business of about $1,000 a week, paid both dividends and a patronage refund, and liquidated without a loss.

Another "black" co-op enterprise which, with help from friendly "white folk", achieved some success was the Frederick Douglass Buying Club. Mr. and Mrs. Harry L. Terry started the buying club in their basement in March 1941. A savings to consumer-members was said to be better than 19 percent, and that could be possible because this was an entirely voluntary project with no operating costs. Merchandise was bought under the full benefit of wholesale prices that Rochdale Stores provided.

In July 1944, the Frederick Douglass group merged with Rochdale Stores, converting its $6,338 in stock to Rochdale shares at par. It brought with it also $1,480 in surplus accumulated during its operation as a buying club. Rochdale bought land and built a store at 2101 Alabama Avenue SE for the neighborhood in 1945. The buying club had served only its members. The store sold to the general public as well.

There was also a small co-op store on Benning Road, run by Consumers Services, Inc. This became part of Rochdale Stores, Inc., in August 1945.

Rochdale Stores paid dividends on its shares, usually 3 or 4 percent, and there were patronage refunds some years. Under the managership of James M. Dunaway, a new store was started in Fairlington, Virginia in January 1946. Another branch store had been started in Bethesda - Chevy Chase, Maryland, on the northwest edge of Washington. That was in October 1944.

This very small chain of co-ops grew but was hampered by top-heavy staffing, overstocking of slow-moving goods through tie-in selling forced by the wholesalers, and by increasing competition from A&P.

At about the time the first small co-op food store opened, another small group organized a cooperative gasoline station. Because neither the District of Columbia nor Virginia at that time made any provision for incorporation of consumer cooperatives, this enterprise called itself Konsum, Inc., organized under the regular Virginia corporation law.

It had a first station in 1937 at 2110 Virginia Avenue NW in Washington. This was replaced in 1940 by a new station at 26th and Virginia Avenue NW on property which had been purchased by Co-operators' Properties, a Maryland corporation created for obtaining that site for the station. Konsum also had for a short time a second service station on Sherman Avenue NW which lost money. Rationing of tires and gasoline during the war cut into the Virginia Avenue station's sales to the point where it had only $3,234 net worth to show for over $14,000 paid-in working capital. However, by January 1947 when Konsum was consolidated with Rochdale, increase in value of the land had wiped out the loss. The property was finally disposed of some years later following the merger of Rochdale Cooperative and Greenbelt Consumer Services, Inc.

When William H. Petri became manager of Rochdale Stores in March 1948, he closed the Benning Road and Bethesda - Chevy Chase stores and sold the Frederick Douglass store. Dispensing of stock and equipment at a heavy depreciation saw losses soar to $25,888. However, the Georgetown store earned $5,300 and the 14th Street store $2,387 in 1948. In 1949 while Florence E. Parker was president of Rochdale, steps were taken to wipe out the losses. A court order approved reorganization of what had been two heavily indebted Rochdale organizations -- one in D.C. and one in Virginia -- into Rochdale Co-operative, Inc., with shares which would have the value of only the property behind them. Losses amounting to $87,453 from the reorganization were simply absorbed by the shareholders of the two earlier Rochdale organizations.

The land and building for a supermarket at Falls Church, Virginia, on Broad Street was purchased by Rochdale Cooperative, Inc. for $276,723 -- considered a bargain at that time. That was in 1956. The Falls Church supermarket prospered as a consumer-owned cooperative and became a well accepted community institution. When Rochdale Cooperative merged with Greenbelt Consumer Services, Inc. in February 1959, its leaders and staff -- especially Manager Petri, Robert P. Gowell, and Edith Christianson, who directed the membership program -- played major roles in what became the area's and the nation's biggest consumer cooperative.

Outside the Washington, D.C. area, two other consumer cooperatives organized and grew -- and later merged with Greenbelt Consumer Services, Inc. to become part of that story.

In the fall of 1937, something unusual was beginning to happen in Westminster, county seat of Carroll County, Maryland, about a 2- hour drive north of Washington. A group of farming families struggling to pull themselves out of the Great Depression found common ground to share with a cluster of nearby college professors. There was nothing new about cooperation among farmers. For generations they had come together to pull their proverbial oxen out of ditches, thrash each other's wheat, husk corn, raise barns, and buy farm supplies cooperatively. Southern States Cooperative was and still is an important part of the rural community in Carroll County.

When some of these families decided to share in an experiment to buy groceries together, the Westminster Consumers Cooperative came to life. It started as a buying club on Saturday mornings in the sunroom over the Rhinehart family's garage. Ruth and Carroll came back from a tour of European cooperatives in the summer of 1937 under the leadership of Jack and Anne McLanahan. They were impressed with the story of the 18 Rochdale weavers who started the pioneer cooperative store on Toad Lane.

Carroll Rinehart's older brother Harry already was buying some of his groceries from Eastern Cooperative Wholesale in New York. Soon more and more neighbors were coming to the farmhouse on Taneytown Road to split up the cases of canned goods into their individual orders. By May 1939, the 11 original families had multiplied into the Westminster Consumers Cooperative Club. The CO-OP label had special appeal, offering a first experience with consumer information labels to tell the contents, exact weight, and the red, blue, or green quality labels.

The first small store was on Longwell Avenue across from where the post office is now. The move was made in October 1942, but growth of the co-op soon required a larger and better location, at 43 East Main Street. At first all the work was done by volunteers. After the move, Ruth Rinehart became the co-op's first manager at $15 a week. By the end of 1947 the co-op had 374 members and averaged weekly sales of $1,337, and it was time to move again. The following year brought another stage of growth in a move to a small supermarket in a new building adjacent to the Westminster municipal parking lot.

With reluctance, the pioneers accepted the realization that this was no longer just one big co-op family "playing store". The happy days of the early years are recounted with nostalgia in a publication, "50 Years of Service" put together by Phil Grout and published by the Carroll County Co-op Foundation, Inc. in 1987. It is charming reading and tells many heart-warming incidents about the cooperative's founders, too numerous to list here.

Two names, however, have to be mentioned. One is that of John Brown, who was manager of the Westminister store from 1950 to 1957 and then built a career with the Greenbelt Cooperative until his retirement in 1984. The other is Solomon L. Hoke, prominent Carroll County farmer who was president of the Westminster Cooperative at the time it merged with Greenbelt Consumer Services, Inc. in 1956 and then for several years served as a director on the Board of GCS.

Three hours drive south of Washington and east of Richmond, Virginia, a committee of individuals from the National Committee for Aeronautics and the Hampton Institute explored the feasibility of organizing a consumer cooperative in the Peninsula area of Hampton Roads. During December 1947, the organizing committee hired a temporary manager named Paul Walk, who had been recommended by the Cooperative League of the USA.

Dave Goldenbaum was the first president of the cooperative that was launched, and Rudolph Schubert was hired as general manager. The board of directors and members of the founding committee raised $33,000 in shares with a par value of $10. With these funds the Peninsula Cooperative Association, Inc. purchased the lease and inventory of a Rich food store in the Southampton district of Elizabeth City County.

"The store was an instant success," remembers Chris Malami, chairman of the board of directors from 1960 to 1967, "and its profitability enabled us to pay a five percent dividend on stock shares plus a three percent patronage rebate." Another supermarket and three book and record stores were opened as sales volume and net margins increased.

Sales continued to climb and income held at a fairly stable level until 1960 when the book and records stores began to show losses which ate into the margins earned in the supermarkets. By this time total sales reached $4 million for the year. When Schubert left for an assignment in India, William Petrie was hired as general manager and stayed until 1966.

The book and record stores were closed when losses became a continuing drag. On advice of Robert Gowell, head of the Greenbelt Cooperative's SCAN furniture stores, Peninsula Cooperative opened a Scandia furniture store in 1965 which earned a satisfactory net margin. During 1966, the two supermarkets began to operate in the red, with losses which amounted to $131,182 for that year. Petrie left at this time. A replacement did not work out well, so the board appointed Checchi and Company (then managing Greenbelt Consumer Services, Inc.) to restore profitability. With this shift, Peninsula came up with substantial net earnings the next year. By consenting vote of the membership, Peninsula affiliated with the Greenbelt Cooperative in 1968.

These, then, were some of the strands of the fabric that held together many tens of thousands of people -- some strongly, some tenuously -- in the experiment of running their own business.

II. HOW IT ALL STARTED (1937-1939)

Most dedicated cooperators hold that the way to a consumer-owned co-op is generally through a buying club. A few economy-minded people in a neighborhood, church, union, or college campus, pool their purchases of groceries or other big-margin items to get wholesale or discounted quantity-sale prices. They take turns sharing the work of buying and dividing the purchases into the individual orders, and return to each member his share of change from the estimated amount paid in advance. If the venture is satisfactory and more consumers join, a store may be planned and opened when enough capital can be secured.

Greenbelt was different. Key people in the federal government's Resettlement Administration, which planned and built Greenbelt as a low-income community, believed in the usefulness of cooperatives. And the Filene Foundation, a philanthropic fund created by the Boston department store entrepreneur Edward A. Filene, offered to play fairy godmother to provide services for families moving into the New Deal town.

However, with store structures in place and the necessary initial funding and start-up management offered, it was the people themselves -- the families in the community -- who organized and built and paid for the cooperative, Greenbelt Consumer Services, Inc. (GCS).

The first families moved into completed houses in the autumn of 1937. It would be a year before the town was filled. A food store and other shops would be required during this period of community growth, because Greenbelt was several miles from the nearest shopping area and a dozen miles from Washington, D.C., with no public transportation assured at first.

Anticipating the need for shopping facilities, the Resettlement Administration had explored options for the town's commercial center. Government operation of the community's stores was ruled out. Planning officials found a lack of interest among retail firms in opening stores in an experimental, government housing project for low-income renters. Widespread criticism of the Greenbelt "boondoggle" included a prediction that it would be a failure.

In this climate, the Filene Fund agreed with the Resettlement Administration to provide stores and shops for the difficult start-up period with the prospect that the resident families themselves could take over the enterprise after meeting certain conditions. To that end the Fund administrators, through a subsidiary known as the Consumer Distribution Corporation (CDC), created a Maryland entity incorporated as Greenbelt Consumer Services, Inc. (GCS) on

September 1, 1937. The directors of CDC served as the board of GCS until the member-owned cooperative was organized and took over on January 1, 1940.

This first board included: R. N. Benjamin, president of the Pennsylvania Farm Bureau Federation; Percy S. Brown, president of Consumer Distribution Corporation; Herbert E. Evans, vice president and later secretary of CDC; Clark Foreman, chief of the power division in the government Public Works Administration; and Flint Garrison, president of Garrison-Wagner Co. Two Greenbelt residents were added during the summer of 1938.

The first families moved into their new Greenbelt homes September 30, 1937. Two days later a temporary, makeshift store began selling necessities to the newcomers. This served until construction progress and additional consumer families made possible the opening of the first regular food store on December 15, in time for the community's first Christmas. Meanwhile, the auto "filling station" already had been in operation for several days.

Strictly speaking these were not yet cooperative enterprises owned by members. But the contract which the Filene affiliate signed with the Resettlement Administration assured consumer ownership and control as soon as the town's housing was filled and at least half of the families became members of a cooperative to take over from Consumer Distribution Corporation.

All through the transition period, the stores and services in the shopping center operated as if they were customer-controlled. Percy C. Brown, president of CDC, and Herbert E. Evans, vice president, spent a great deal of time in Greenbelt during that first year. They made sure the stores and services met local needs. They also encouraged organization of groups for learning economical buying techniques and consumer protection, and they facilitated the formation of the cooperative which would take over GCS.

The CDC-appointed board for GCS selected Robert E. Jacobsen to be the first general manager. R. M. Templeman supervised the food store, with Sulo Laakso, Cumly Richie, Henry Little, and George Hodsdon comprising the staff. On March 12, 1938, Laakso stepped into the position of food store manager. James Dunaway ran the auto service station when it opened and until Jimmie Porter assumed the position in March. In May, Thomas B. Ricker became station manager.

There were frequent shifts in personnel with the opening of other shops as the town's population increased.

Dry cleaning and laundry service on a pick-up basis got underway by the end of 1937. A full-service drug store with a lunch counter opened its doors April 21, 1938 under the supervision of Robert Jacobsen and with Frank L. Purdum as the first pharmacist. The following day saw the addition of the first barber shop, with Michael Juliano as manager and barber number one. The completed community theater building was used for plays by the Greenbelt Players on May 6, and GCS began showing movies September 21. This, by the way, is believed to be the first movie theater in the United States owned and operated by a cooperative.

During the summer of 1938, GCS opened a variety goods annex to the drug store, in anticipation of enough population growth to launch a complete variety store in space already provided and waiting. Soon afterwards GCS also opened a news and tobacco shop at the bus depot, a shoe repair shop, and a beauty parlor. The service station included a facility for auto repairs.

For a touch of nostalgia, look at some of the prices of goods and services offered by GCS in its advertisements in the town's weekly newspaper, the GREENBELT COOPERATOR.

In the food store:
    butter 37 cents a pound
    milk 11 cents a quart
    eggs (medium) 38 cents a dozen
    rice 2 pounds for 9 cents
    sugar 10 pounds for 51 cents
    cornflakes (13 ounce package) 10 cents
    rolled oats (20 ounce carton) 8 cents
    coffee 25 cents a pound.

At the service station:
    gasoline 12 cents a gallon
    lubricating job 49 cents
    CO-OP label tires $6.80 to $8.85.

Movie prices were 30 cents for adults and 15 cents for children. Haircuts were 35 cents with no tipping. You could buy garden gloves for 15 cents a pair and a 16-inch, 5-blade lawn mower for $6.95 (the kind you pushed -- remember?) at the variety annex to the drug store.

Prices, especially those in the food store, were a matter of concern to Greenbelt families, none of whom earned more than $1,800 a year at that time. The income limit defined the government project as housing for low-income families. Periodic price checking with other stores in nearby locations marked the formation period of the Cooperative, and throughout the later years this became a routine protection for shoppers at GCS supermarkets.

A checklist made March 2, 1939 and published in the Greenbelt weekly newspaper compared the prices of 50 national brand items selected at random by the food store committee of the Cooperative Organizing Committee (C.O.C.). Shopping their list in two nearby chain supermarkets and then in Greenbelt's food store, they found a total of $7.73 in store A and $7.75 in store B, compared with $7.83 at their local store. The 8-cent or 10-cent difference was important to families on limited budget, so prices on CO-OP label items were listed then alongside comparable standard brands to show the savings that could be had by selective shopping. Even at this early date it became obvious that Greenbelt's one independent food store would have to compete on prices with the large-volume chain stores in Berwyn, College Park, and Washington, D.C.

Comparative pricing was just one of the many consumer education activities which kept Greenbelters busy during the Cooperative's formative months -- and for years after as it reached the status of a regional supermarket chain.

With encouragement from the GCS Board, from the Greenbelt Citizens' Association, and from the Co-op Advisory Committee, women formed consumer discussion groups throughout the community. These are worth some elaboration because they were so successful and had such a positive impact on the character of the Cooperative.

The origin of these groups sprang from a Co-op Advisory Committee appointed by the Greenbelt Citizens' Association when that organization and the town itself were less than 3 months old. Herbert Evans, of CDC, met with the Committee January 4, 1938 at the home of Mr. and Mrs. Peter A. Carroll. Evans advised that the Committee could "effectively keep a record of all constructive suggestions and investigate all types of merchandising practices" in preparation for the cooperative to be formed. He urged a plan "to visit leading Washington stores and bring back a report on quality, quantity, and brands which the consumer-shopper is able to secure for a specific sum of money".

Five women volunteered and brought back a list the next week for the manager of the Greenbelt store to use in adjusting stock carried and prices. At their next meeting, the women opened, tasted, tested, and compared various brands of peas, peaches, canned milk, and string beans. A Mr. Genung, former vice president of the Great Atlantic and Pacific Tea Co., met with them and provided advice on testing and background on the canning and food merchandising businesses.

From this beginning the shopping group expanded and soon announced the following findings in the town newspaper:

"1. Labels do not give much information.
2. Price is not an indication of quality or value.
3. Brands are not an indication of quality or value.

4. Size of can does not determine actual food content.

5. Some sizes in cans vary so imperceptibly as to be mistaken one for the other but actually contain one or two ounces less in content.

6. Some merchandise not highly publicized may be very good in quality.

7. Merchandise bought in bulk runs cheaper than packaged merchandise."

The shoppers concluded that "the consumer should know the quality he buys for the price he pays". In the year 1938, that should have read "she" because nearly all the shopping was done by women. That was before sexual equality became an issue. These Greenbelt women, who were becoming a strong foundation for the Greenbelt Cooperative, were among the leading advocates for U.S. standards in labeling and for stronger government control of safety and quality in foods and other consumer products.

Some of these neighborhood discussion groups met as often as once a week, and attendance varied from six to a dozen women. Working together with GCS personnel they conducted several town-wide meetings. One on March 4, arranged by Miss Ollie Hoffman and food store manager Laakso, brought in an audience of 300 women to hear a presentation on meat inspection and beef grading by B. F. McCarthy, head of the U.S. Department of Agriculture's meat inspection office. This was an amazing response in a community which at that time numbered less than 500 families. There were 150 women and a few men at a meeting 2 weeks later to discuss grade labeling and consumer information on canned and packaged foods. Mrs. Linden Dodson led this meeting and obtained passage of a resolution forwarded to Eastern Cooperative Wholesale and the American Canners Association. This statement supported grade labeling where appropriate and information about contents.

A food and cosmetics products display for price and quality comparison, prepared by a committee working with Mrs. Bertha Maryn, attracted 120 shoppers early in the summer.

Among other successful projects was the establishment of effective milk inspection in Prince Georges County, following complaints by dairy customers. Mrs. Carnie Harper headed this effort.

By July 20, 1938, there were 15 of these neighborhood consumer discussion groups and they formed a Greenbelt Chapter of the National Federation of Consumers. From here on, the groups identified themselves as the Better Buyers' Club, and became an essential and highly regarded part of Greenbelt Consumer Services.

Each weekly edition of the town newspaper during this period carried news of what the women's shopping groups were doing as well as extensive information on consumers' interests and about cooperatives.

The CDC-appointed Board for Greenbelt Consumer Services distributed brochures to each new family on arrival, defining a cooperative and describing the plan for turning the community's stores into a member-owned cooperative.

On December 5, 1937, just 2 months after the first families began moving into the new town, a public meeting in the school auditorium launched the campaign to form a cooperative to own and operate the stores that would be serving the community. Wallace Campbell, at that time the editor of CONSUMER COOPERATION, published by the Cooperative League of the U.S.A., "told the fascinating story of European cooperatives in a brief and concise manner, bringing the cooperative movement up to date, from the time of the Rochdale, England, pioneers in 1844 to Greenbelt in 1937." This was how the fledgling town newspaper (a producer cooperative already in operation by volunteers) reported the meeting. Herbert Evans described the role of the Filene Foundation in helping the proposed cooperative get on its feet. Community Manager Roy S. Braden welcomed the townspeople and speakers, and "suggested that in the near future Greenbelt might serve as a model to the world-famous European cooperatives."

Prophetic words, which came to reality in the next years as not only co-op leaders but government officials and leaders in all walks of life came from all over the world to see the Greenbelt example.

The Greenbelt Citizens' Association had appointed a Citizens Advisory Committee on Cooperatives to learn how cooperatives worked, talk with GCS board members and personnel, and prepare a report on how appropriate the CDC proposal would be for the residents of Greenbelt. Chairman of the Committee was Peter J. Carroll. The other members were; George D. Berkalew, Mrs. Louis M. Bessemer, Mrs. Velma A. Brewer, Howard C. Custer, Mrs. Harry A. Falls, Mrs. Bertha Maryn, Mrs. Jean R. Nance, Mrs. Irvin B. Reamy, and Mrs. Alexander Schwarz.

The Committee's report was submitted to the public meeting of the civic body April 4. It proposed that at a meeting which all citizens were urged to attend, a Cooperative Organizing Committee be elected. This new Committee would be representative of the whole town, four members to serve for a year and five only until October 1938 when their places would be up for election again -- at a time when the town's housing would be filled. Each member would assume a specific responsibility in the overall function of planning and supervising the conversion of the stores from Filene Fund sponsorship to a member-owned, nonprofit cooperative.

Residents in attendance adopted the report and nominated 20 candidates. At a public meeting April 11, an even larger crowd elected: Peter J. Carroll, Henry

Little, Dr. Linden S. Dodson, Bertha Maryn, Thomas R. Freeman, Charles E. Fitch, William R. Poole, Reed P. Maughn, and Fred Wilde. When the Committee (immediately designated as the C.O.C.) met 2 days later it named Carroll chairman. The Citizens' Association resolution specified that the C.O.C. hold open meetings at least once a month, and report its progress to each meeting of the Association.

An example of the work undertaken by the C.O.C. was the April meeting in connection with the opening of the drug store. Two hundred and fifty residents showed up (out of a total population of 450 families) to discuss with GCS spokesmen preferred kinds of merchandise and operating policies. Printed forms invited requests for specific items and brands. At the meeting and in the 7 months that followed, buying tips including brand comparisons helped consumers do their shopping.

During the summer and fall of 1938, volunteers on C.O.C. subcommittees built a team totaling 40 or 50 men and women. To explain what a cooperative could do for the community and to promote its formation, the C.O.C. volunteers worked closely with the Better Buyers women and with GCS personnel. The weekly newspaper boosted these efforts with reports and editorial comments, along with occasional negative letters to the editor.

There were some residents who were critical of the rush to form cooperatives in Greenbelt. Some frowned on the monopoly position of GCS stores, some mistrusted the idea that the local people could manage their own businesses, and others viewed cooperatives as socialist. (Later we will note that Senator Joseph McCarthy, of Wisconsin, claimed cooperatives were subversive and included several GCS leaders on his infamous list of 57 -- or was it 92, or 165 -- "known Communists".)

Nevertheless, support for GCS and for cooperatives in general proliferated and strengthened. Greenbelt boasted a cooperative nursery school and kindergarten, credit union, cooperative health care association, and cooperatively owned newspaper. The community still has [in 1991] a food market and a service station that were part of GCS but now are operated by a locally owned cooperative, Greenbelt Consumer Cooperative, Inc. Except for the health association, the other cooperatives also are operating successfully today, and in addition, Greenbelt Homes, Inc. is one of the nation's outstanding cooperative housing stories.

Coming back to the summer of 1938, GCS developed strongly enough to advise shoppers to save their receipts for a possible patronage refund at the end of the operating year. And the C.O.C. began planning for the issuance of stock in the proposed cooperative.

An article in the July 6 GREENBELT COOPERATOR explained that: "Any person going into business has to invest a certain amount of working capital in it, and that is what a cooperative group must do. A certain part of the needed amount may be borrowed, and it has proved the most sound policy to do as little of it as possible, and to insist that each member contribute his part to the financing."

As the Citizens' Association had determined in the spring, a second election for C.O.C. members came up after 6 months, when all the housing projects units were filled. Several hundred residents attended the October 10, 1938 meeting and elected Howard C. Custer, Paul Dunbar, Walter Volckhousen, George Fair, Reed P. Maughn, and Joseph F. Loftus to fill the vacancies. The new group of nine then named Volckhausen to be chairman. Earlier, the CDC had added two members of the C.O.C. -- Carroll and Dodson -- to the GCS Board of Directors, in preparation for the prospective conversion to local ownership.

A month after the C.O.C reorganization, the newspaper printed an extra edition to announce November 16 as the start of the subscription acceptance for membership, with a minimum requirement of one $10 share.

Explanation is needed at this point about why the Greenbelt Cooperative became and remained for many years a stock corporation. The Maryland corporation law recognized only farmer producer cooperatives -- no other kind until 1978 when GCS was able to persuade the State legislature to change the law to accommodate the needs of consumers who wanted to incorporate themselves in cooperatives.

By the end of 1938, 373 Greenbelters representing 323 housing units had signed up for membership shares of stock. The target would be 443 homes and at least $5,000 for the down payment to CDC.

GCS sales increased as the town's housing units filled. On the first anniversary of the food store, the GREENBELT COOPERATOR noted that the day's sales amounted to $2,089 and compared that to the $11.45 total for 24 customers on the opening day in 1937.

All operations for the first full year (1938) showed a net loss of $6,627. This was not at all surprising for the start-up period and only 2 months' operation with all homes occupied. The food store, accounting for about 60 percent of the total sales figure, had smaller dollar and percentage losses for each successive quarter. Indeed, in the first quarter of 1939 it showed a net margin. For the entire year of 1939, GCS turned out a net margin of $5,858.

Laakso took over the position of general manager in March when Jacobsen returned to Minneapolis to run a family business after the death of his father.

The town's weekly newspaper paid high tribute to the Jacobsens following a community dance in their honor:

"Besides supervising the formation and operation of all our stores, managing the drug store, assisting the Cooperative Organizing Committee, and exemplifying the unselfish and untiring devotion typical of outstanding cooperative leaders...Bob found time for many community activities, including service on Greenbelt's first Town Council.

"Mrs. Jacobsen, too, contributed...assisting in the formation and direction of the Women's Gym Classes, and helping in the work of the Community Church, the Baby Clinic, the Girl Scouts, and the Better Buyers Club." In picking up the management of GCS, Laakso brought with him 16 years experience in both chain stores and cooperatives.

By the end of March 1939, the C.O.C. had signed up 485 members for the Cooperative, but only 99 had paid the full $10. The others had pledged to pay at least $1 a month. Planning began for anticipated conversion of GCS in the fall.

An important part of that planning was the programing of information to reach householders who knew little or nothing about cooperatives and those who held a negative attitude about them.

This was a continuing effort carried on by the CDC representatives working through the GCS Board and store managers, by the consumer discussion groups which became the Better Buyers, by the C.O.C., and by the community newspaper. A key figure in the campaign was Miss Ollie Hoffman, serving as education director for GCS. When she left Greenbelt after the Cooperative became a reality, she was featured in the town's newspaper as one of Greenbelt's Hall of Outstanding Citizens:

"Holder of no public office, maker of few public speeches, she has been nevertheless one of the leaders of community thought and action....In fostering the Gum Drop Co-op (by children in the elementary school) she insisted upon staying in the background; let the youngsters run the show and develop true responsibility ....Her work with the Better Buyers has been distinguished by lack of the falsetto enthusiasm so often found in cooperative education....by encouraging others to think and act for themselves Miss Hoffman has set an example that might well be more generally emulated by community leaders."

The more visible leadership in developing a cooperative community came from young men and women who had some experience in college campus or farmer co-ops, credit unions, and neighborhood or office buying clubs. An examination of the early years in Greenbelt shows overlapping of the most active leaders. Many of the founders of the Greenbelt Cooperative also served as movers and shakers in the Health Association, credit union, nursery school, newspaper, Citizens' Association, and other community organizations.

In addition to leaflets, neighborhood (block) meetings, exhibits, posters, and use of the newspaper, the cooperative leadership arranged a number of special events. One of these was a dinner and program in September 1938 put on by the C.O.C. and GCS for 140 officers of Greenbelt's many organizations. Herbert Evans, CDC vice president, explained the objectives of the Filene Fund in sponsoring stores for the community's shopping center, the relationship with GCS, and his hopes for creation of a successful cooperative venture by the local citizens. There were encouraging responses from many of the organizations represented. Earlier in that same week, the C.O.C. had attracted a large attendance to a public meeting to hear Anders Hedberg, director of Kooperativa Forbundet and of Luma, in Stockholm. He described the consumer cooperative movement in Sweden, where one-third of the population were members at that time and cooperatives handled 60 percent of the retail trade.

In February 1939, the C.O.C. and GCS, together with the Greenbelt Health Association, held a most successful 2-day Cooperative Institute. Widely known speakers, panel discussions, entertainment, and a dinner prepared by store employees and women from the Better Buyers, attracted a large attendance.

Another 6-month election for C.O.C. positions was due in April, as a democratic way to assure that the entire population of Greenbelt could participate in determining how the prospective cooperative would be shaped. The new names were Mrs. Carnie Harper, B. F. Yhnell, and Lester Hayes. J. P. Loftus was re-elected to another term. Volckhausen continued as chairman. George A. Warner replaced Hayes in June.

In preparation for an organizational meeting June 19 of residents who intended to join the Cooperative, the C.O.C. turned its full attention to drafts of tentative bylaws, financial agreement with CDC, management contract, and other required paper work. Copies in advance of the meeting went to every household, and two public hearings before the organizational meeting gave the widest possible input. Francis Lastner, president of the Citizens' Association, chaired this critical meeting. It was a public meeting but only subscribers for shares could vote. The proposed bylaws and financial agreement with CDC won approval with very little change. Evans for CDC found the documents acceptable except for some legal wording.

After a year and a half of hard work and contagious enthusiasm, GCS appeared headed for quick conversion to real cooperative ownership and operation by its customers. The next 6 months, however, turned out to be disappointing in some respects. And continuing after that, organizing and maintaining GCS and other projects and entities, as well, seemed more difficult. Perhaps the early euphoria wore off. Maybe leaders simply exhausted themselves. Some individuals complained that a clique appeared to be running everything in town. Letters to the editor showed more and more criticism.

Disagreements at meetings were sometimes bitter and on occasion led to threats and even blows. At one Citizens' Association meeting, a belligerent citizen engaged in an argument with Volckhausen, came up to where he was speaking and struck him. The attack was very brief. Volckhausen's strong and well known pacifist views made any physical encounter one-sided.

Attendance at meetings dwindled. Referring to a meeting of the Citizens' Association, the local newspaper said, "The sparse attendance was too evident in the large meeting room". A second Cooperative Institute in October 1939 was reported as "too meager for the welfare of the projected cooperative....None of the prominent personages invited indicated any emotions at the failure of the local townspeople to realize a sense of responsibility in the face of the impending formation of their own cooperative enterprise".

And most threatening for the C.O.C. and those devoted to activating the CDC commitment to turn the stores over to local ownership, subscribers were not completing payment on their $10 shares of stock. By the end of October, there were 536 subscribers to membership, representing more than half of the homes in town, but only 310 shares were fully paid. Cash on deposit to meet the required payment to CDC was only $3,918.

With a January 1, 1940 deadline established in the contract between the Resettlement Administration and CDC for the town residents to decide whether they wanted locally owned cooperative stores, a crisis loomed. The C.O.C. debated the interpretation of the word "members" in the contract, and decided that anyone who had signed up to purchase a share of stock could be considered a member. Further, the enterprise now had enough net margin so that possibly some of that could be used to fill out the required payment of $5,000.

The C.O.C. voted 6-2 to proceed with transfer of GCS to a member-owned cooperative.

Much remained to be done within a 2-month time frame. A score of volunteers went from door to door seeking completion of payment on $10 shares. The C.O.C. sat down with the CDC board and Resettlement Administration officials to work out financial and legal details of the transfer.

And -- the residents of Greenbelt needed to have a final input on the proposal.

Supporters and those in opposition wrote letters to the editor of the paper and voiced their views at Citizens' Association meetings. One rather nasty contention exploded over "niggers being allowed to shop in our stores, and to sit at the lunch counter in the drug store". This was 1939, before the civil rights days, and at that time no blacks lived in the community.

Here is how the GREENBELT COOPERATOR reported the meeting, which was chaired by the newly elected president of the Citizens' Association, Joseph Bargas:

"The only interruption came when George O'Brien asked [about] barring Negroes from Greenbelt stores. Booed by several members of the audience, Mr. O'Brien threatened to 'knock the teeth out' of one of them who sat near him.

"Mr. Carroll secured the floor amid the confusion which followed, saying 'This is America, and our Constitution guarantees equal treatment for all of us. I am surprised to see the race issue brought up here.'

"Heavy applause greeted Mr. Carroll's reply and a similar statement made by Mrs. Peggy Arness."

I was in the audience and scribbled a note for myself at the time that she said, "I am from the deep South, but I want you to know that we don't all feel race prejudice there, and certainly not here and especially not in a cooperative."

Unfortunately, O'Brien happened to be commander of the Greenbelt Post of the American Legion. The incident at the meeting stirred up feelings that caused some dissension within the Legion post and in the community, but the vote of confidence at the meeting had cleared the air on the position of the Cooperative.

C.O.C. Chairman Volckhausen called a meeting for December 12 to take final action on the proposed bylaws of the new Cooperative and on the financial agreement with CDC for acquisition of the stores. Drafts of these documents had been delivered to all subscribers to membership prior to the meeting. This was a public meeting, but only subscribers to shares could vote.

These first bylaws, besides insuring the cooperative character of the association, governed such major matters as the qualifications and privileges of membership, the issuance of patronage returns, the election of directors, the conduct and frequency of membership meetings, responsibilities of the board of directors, how patrons could become members, interest on share capital, disposition of savings, and the setting up of protective reserves.

The financial agreement provided for repayment of the CDC investment of about $40,000 in the local stores over the remaining 8-year period of the lease, with clauses protecting the Cooperative from obligation to make excessive payments during periods of poor net margins and clauses protecting CDC in case of poor management of the Cooperative or failure on the part of the Cooperative to fulfill its obligations under the agreement.

The $40,000 represented $10,000 in stock at par value, issued to CDC at the time that it incorporated GCS under Maryland law, plus a $30,000 loan at 4 percent interest. The agreement specified payment as follows:

1. Upon formation of the Cooperative: all sums received by the Cooperative Operating Committee as payments on subscriptions for shares of stock in the Cooperative.

2. Quarterly: all sums received during the preceding quarter in payment or partial payment for capital stock of the Cooperative.

3. Annually: payments totalling at least $5,000, except that in no case should the payment be more than 50 percent of the Cooperative's net savings for the year. Under the agreement, the Cooperative reserves the right to make payments in excess of those stipulated therein.

To protect CDC, there were the following provisions:

1. Until the obligation is paid, the Cooperative agrees not to undertake any new enterprise or invest more than $500 in capital assets without the prior approval of the CDC, except where greater expense is necessitated for repair or replacement of capital assets.

2. In the event that the Cooperative fails to show a net saving for any 6-month period or fails to make payments as agreed, CDC is granted the right to take over the management of the Cooperative to the extent of placing its own employees in control to direct the business and to make changes which CDC regards as necessary. Such rights of control are granted only under the following conditions:

a. That CDC will be responsible for all debts arising and actions taken during the period of its control.
b. That operations during the period of management by CDC will be in keeping with the cooperative character of the debtor as expressed in its charter and bylaws.
c. That no rights of the membership of the Cooperative shall be suspended except the right of actually directing the management.

d. That while under the control of CDC, the Cooperative will not be required to pay CDC more than the sum of
      (1) One-half the net saving of the period;
      (2) All payments received on capital stock subscriptions;
      (3) The amount of defaulted payment, if any.

e. That in the event control is assumed because of impairment of its capital investment in the Cooperative, CDC will return control within a month after the end of the second consecutive quarter during which the Cooperative shows a net saving.

f. That in the event control is assumed because the cooperative fails to make payments as agreed, control will be returned within 3 months after payments in arrears are made.

To protect both parties, the agreement provided audit of the books at least semi-annually by a certified public accountant acceptable to both. Further, that the books would be kept open to inspection at all reasonable times.

The solicitor's office in the U.S. Department of Agriculture had already reviewed the documents and given tentative approval. This was a prerequisite for transfer of the lease on the store buildings.

At the December 12 meeting, stockholders and subscribers for shares gave their approval after careful review and discussion.

The holiday period was a busy time for the C.O.C., in ironing out final details with CDC, for Farm Security Administration officials (which had replaced the Resettlement Administration by that time), and for the local store managers.

The retiring Board of GCS met December 29, 1939 to wind up the details of the transfer. It found the transition at this time to be "feasible and desirable". It made the necessary changes in the Maryland charter and replaced its original bylaws with those approved at the December 12 meeting. It retired shares of stock owned by CDC, and then approved issuance of 303 shares of voting stock and 40 shares of nonvoting stock to paid-up members of the new Cooperative. Finally, the retiring Board set January 2, 1940 as the date for the organizational meeting of paid-up subscribers.

III. LEARNING TO BE A COOPERATIVE (1940-1944)

Putting together a locally owned consumer cooperative took 2 years of hard work, even with initial financing and management in place. But on the night of January 2, 1940, about one-third of the 600 subscribers to membership shares met in what the weekly newspaper reported to be "considered by many as being the most important meeting in Greenbelt's history".

The members at this first meeting elected nine directors from 18 nominees to serve as the Cooperative's first Board. When the winning nine met on January 9, the president and vice president of CDC, which until then held all the stock in GCS, accepted the resignations of the old directors who had been appointed by CDC and declared the newly elected nine directors to be the legal Board.

The new Board then ratified all actions which the CDC-elected Board had taken to effect the transfer. The reorganization still was not legally complete. It had to await the filing of necessary amendments to the articles of incorporation with the Maryland Tax Commission on January 18.

The birth date of the Greenbelt Cooperative therefore can be January 2, 9, or 18, 1940. Or, perhaps, December 15, 1937 when the food store opened its door with the announcement that it proposed to be a consumer-owned cooperative as soon as the town's residents were prepared to take it over.

The initial directors were: Walter R. Volckhausen, Howard C. Custer, Sherrod E. East, Fred C. Wilde, Dr. Joe W. Still, Mrs. Carnie Harper, Mrs. Bertha Maryn, Joseph Loftus, and Earl J. Swailes. The new Board named Volckhausen to be president, with East as vice president, Still as secretary, and Swailes as treasurer. Each director took on a specific assignment as well as a share in the overall responsibility.

Priority decisions crowded the Board's agenda. In a Saturday evening meeting which lasted well into the early morning hours of Sunday, the Board took the following steps:

-- Voted to retain Sulo Laakso as general manager.
-- Discussed a patronage refund on receipts which shoppers had saved during 1939, and voted to present this for decision at a first annual membership meeting to be held February 7. The auditor's report would be ready by then.
-- Agreed on wording for a membership application form. This included agreement to forego proxy voting which Maryland law provided but which seemed out of place for a cooperative in a small compact community.

-- Approved the design for a stock certificate.

-- Determined a schedule of semi-monthly meetings of the Board.

-- Made arrangements for development of operating policies for the Cooperative with clear definition of obligations and authority of the Board and the general manager.

-- Determined to put together rules of procedure for the Board.

All the decisions at this meeting were unanimous, after thorough discussion. The Board was off to a strong start.

Operating and financial figures for GCS also appeared strong. An audit report by Louis Englander, of the Cooperative League Accounting Bureau, certified the following balance sheet as of December 31, 1939:

Assets	
Current assets	$31,791
Investments in cooperatives	807
Leasehold	8,400
Fixed as (net after depreciation)	8,328
Deferred charges	5,073
Total assets	$54,399

Liabilities and Capital	
Current liabilities	$15,896
Long-term debt (owed to CDC)	35,000
Total liabilities	$50,896
Capital:	
Stock outstanding	$3,430
Reserves	73
Total capital	3,503
Total liabilities and capital	$54,399

Sales for 1939 totaled $346,142. The net margin was $5,858. Of this amount, $1,570 went to CDC to make up the shortfall in cash from subscriptions for stock in meeting the $5,000 initial obligation in taking over the enterprise. Allowing for reserves, the Board was able to recommend a patronage return amounting to $2,000.

Stockholders at the February 7 membership meeting approved the patronage refund, after lengthy debate. It amounted to 1.5 percent return on purchases.

Opposition centered around two points. Some members contended that patrons who had not already bought shares should not benefit from the refund. Responses pointed out that in a cooperative a patronage return represented an overcharge above the cost of doing business and should go back to the purchasers in proportion to the total amount of purchases. And further that for those not yet members the refund would be applied to purchase of a share of stock and thus build membership.

The other objection was more technical. While GCS produced a net margin for 1939, there remained a net loss from the start-up period. The creation of a "leasehold" of $8,400 as an asset on the balance sheet, to be paid off within the 8 years remaining on the lease, would wipe out that deficit. This had the approval of CDC and the Department of Agriculture, as well as the auditor. It won membership approval.

February 24 was designated as the closing date for turning in the bundles of store receipts. As it turned out, very few of the paid-up stockholders asked for a cash return. Almost the entire $2,000 helped pay for shares of stock and provided an additional margin of operating funds for the Cooperative.

About 100 members received their stock certificates at the February 7 meeting. After that certificates were mailed out.

That meeting included two other important decisions. There was a vote to have GCS join the Eastern Cooperative League and the Eastern Cooperative Wholesale. That clearly aligned GCS with the organized cooperative movement. The other action was membership ratification of the final wording of the Cooperative's bylaws.

These first bylaws set a pattern. Despite the many changes and rewrites in the 50 years that followed, essential protections endured until the last several years, guaranteeing the GCS cooperative identity and democratic control by its members. The bylaws cited the Rochdale principles as the overall guidelines.

Here are notes on a few provisions that indicate what the Greenbelt cooperative pioneers had in mind:

-- The purpose shall be to promote the economic welfare of its members and patrons by utilizing their united funds and efforts for the purchase, distribution, and production of goods and services of good quality; to associate itself with other cooperatives for mutual aid; and to advance the consumers' cooperative movement.

-- Membership would be open to any Greenbelt resident and to any nonresident except persons whose aims and purposes are contrary to GCS or other cooperatives.

-- The authorized share capital was set at $60,000, divided into $20,000 Series A voting stock and $40,000 Series B nonvoting stock, each with a par value of $10 per share.

-- Membership required purchase of one $10 share of Series A voting stock, but additional share holdings were limited to Series B nonvoting stock. This fulfilled the "one member -- one vote" principle.

-- No one could own more than 20 shares, a maximum investment of $200, in order to prevent undue influence on policy or operations by one or a very few persons with large investment in GCS. This limit had to be lifted upward later when GCS began to expand.

-- The initial dividend rate was set at not more than 3 percent, but this, too, was raised later to a maximum of 6 percent to attract needed capital.

-- Members who wanted to sell their shares would have to offer them first for repurchase by GCS at a price not to exceed the lesser of par value or book value. This provision would eliminate incentive to buy shares for speculation and also avoid stock falling into possession of persons unfriendly to the Cooperative.

-- Dividends on shares would take precedence over patronage refunds, in recognition that return on capital was an accepted requirement of doing business.

-- Provision was made for reserves out of net savings, as a protection and to make possible embarking on special projects.

-- The provision for patronage refunds called for a membership vote, on recommendation from the Board. Refunds would go to nonmembers for application toward a membership share of stock.

-- The initial quorum called for 25 percent of the membership but this was reduced as GCS grew in size and expanded outside of the town. The war emergency also cut into attendance at meetings.

-- Election of nine directors was, of course, to be by secret ballot. Instead of majority vote, the first bylaws called for election by the Hare system of proportional representation. This was quite a fad in Greenbelt at the time and provoked much controversy. Supporters pointed out that giving each voter the opportunity to cast a ballot showing a rating from first to last choice for each candidate permitted minority viewpoints to be represented in the final selection. They saw this as more democratic than giving all power and control to the candidates representing a majority position. Opponents called the system confusing and time-consuming, and stated that its results fragmented boards with resulting dissension and inability to reach decisions. After some years and many public arguments, proportional representation was discarded in favor of majority voting.

-- Conflict of interest and relationship between the Board and the general manager were defined so as to discourage any director from taking advantage of his elected position for personal gain and from "playing store".

George A. Warner, in his book GREENBELT: THE COOPERATIVE COMMUNITY, called these bylaws "a perpetual monument to the members of the Cooperative Organizing Committee, particularly to those who served on its bylaws subcommittee -- Joseph Loftus, B. P. Yhnell, and Bob Volckhausen."

Volckhausen already had been cited in the weekly newspaper's Hall of Outstanding Citizens:

"....Time after time his persistence, his labor, and his understanding of the problems involved have readily overcome official inertia and technical obstacles that were supposed to be insurmountable in the time provided. His grasp of the legal and accounting details involved in the organization of the Cooperative has been acknowledged by outstanding lawyers and accountants. His determination that every document and proposal approved by the Committee should be for the best interests of the Cooperative has caused him to drive himself to studies and labors that were all out of proportion to what might be expected of anyone in his position...."

The ensuing months saw the Board grappling with all the problems that go with a new business -- an entire shopping center, in this instance -- and a new organization. Priority attention had to be spread to cover the need for satisfying the widening range of demand for goods and services, increasing sales in the stores, boosting membership and purchase of shares for more adequate capitalization, and providing education and training in cooperative principles and practices.

There were committees to help with all this, but Board and committees alike had to cope with criticism and complaints from those residents who took a less than enthusiastic approach to cooperatives. Equally difficult were some dedicated cooperators who insisted on their own various individual agenda.

Several problems that confront any business came up for attention during the first year of GCS as a cooperative. The Board, in seeking to establish policies and practices that would be widely accepted, turned to the membership for some answers. This could be done easily in 1940 because the membership was still around the 500 level, the service area was small enough for walking from one end to the other, and quarterly meetings enabled everyone to contribute opinions.

The town newspaper commented editorially about three questions, on May 9, under the heading "Co-op Policy":

"The first item was clearly presented as a problem in labor relations. Wages of the two barbers have been considered inadequate even though they topped union standards. Despite this the barber shop was shown to be losing money by a small margin. The membership present, with but two exceptions, voted a five-cent increase for haircuts, after being told in floor discussion that this was a clear and simple issue of whether the customer-owners were willing to take money out of their own pockets to pay better wages. If private-profit business will look at Greenbelt Consumer Services it will see that the co-ops are putting into practice the fair labor and wage policy they talk about."

In the other two matters, the members present at the meeting advised the Board to invest $3,500 from net margins toward opening a variety store rather than pay that amount in higher patronage returns at the end of the year; and to continue advertising in the local paper rather than use circulars.

In later years, as membership grew and spread geographically, Board and management had to make decisions of this sort without turning to the membership for guidance -- but the imprint of early experience lingered. There were always a few advocates of participation by members in making decisions.

Income, as for the barbers mentioned above, was one factor in high employee turnover in all GCS activities -- though later studies suggested that employee (and leadership) turnover rate was not out of line with other enterprises. For the Cooperative in the early Greenbelt years, transportation from other communities posed hiring difficulties. The war years escalated the problem due to labor shortages and to rising wages and prices.

GCS sought to ease personnel problems with training programs. Selected employees from the food store were sent to short-term trade association programs for retail sales and marketing. Some at supervisory levels, as well as directors and other membership leaders, attended the annual Summer Institute offered by the Eastern Cooperative League and training courses offered by the Rochdale Institute. This kind of educational experience kept GCS leaders and top-level personnel in touch with other organizations in the cooperative movement for many years.

One spinoff of special training and operating experience for store personnel was additional turnover as some moved to manager level jobs in co-op stores in other parts of the country. The Greenbelt experience earned a valued reputation within the cooperative movement, and in the profit sector, too. In September 1940, Sulo Laakso left Greenbelt to accept a district managership for a chain of 40 supermarkets in New England. The GCS Board replaced him with George Hodsdon, who had been assistant general manager.

During the last months of 1940, the GREENBELT COOPERATOR found need to condemn shoplifting and minor vandalism in the stores, but sales increased and net margins improved. Total sales for the year came to $376,872, and net margins amounted to $9,667. That made possible a Christmas bonus for employees, repayments ahead of schedule on the loan to CDC, and a patronage return of 3.85 percent. This was after paying the dividend on shares of stock. Not bad for the Cooperative's first year of business!

The balance sheet as of December 31, 1940 looked like this:

Assets	
Current assets	$35,649
Cash on hand and in banks	18,206
Merchandise inventories	17,258
Investment in cooperatives	3,191
Leasehold	7,350
Fixed assets (net after depreciation)	10,339
Deferred charges	2,570
Total assets	$59,099

Liabilities and Capital	
Current liabilities	$17,042
Long-term debt (owed to CDC)	25,996
Total liabilities	$43,038
Capital:	
Stock outstanding	$6,694
Net margin (for dividends, patronage refund, taxes, reserves)	9,366
Total capital	$16,060
Total liabilities and capital	$59,099

Membership interest continued high during this period. The quarterly meeting in November 1940 drew an attendance of 300, aided by the offering of an unique smorgasbord prepared by member volunteers.

Toward the end of the year, GCS had opened a full valet shop which included shoe repairing, and had started a garage service in what had been the firehouse adjacent the service station. On January 16, 1941, the variety store opened in the last vacant space in Greenbelt's shopping center.

During this first year, the membership began the tinkering with bylaws which continued as a preoccupation year after year. A split in terms of office for directors so that five would be elected at one time and four the next added some stability in the Board. Some years later the one-year term of office gave way to staggered 3-year terms to discourage any change in the majority at a single election. Another change strengthened the role of the Auditing Committee, elected by the members, so that it became sort of a watchdog. This concept continued through the history of the Cooperative (as the Review and Evaluation Committee in more recent years).

Ripples from the war in Europe reached into Greenbelt as armies of Hitler and Mussolini pushed their conquest further and further. In February 1941 came the announcement that 1,000 additional houses would be built in the town to accommodate defense workers who were taking new jobs in the Washington area.

President Volckhausen, who had been reelected to the GCS Board, alerted members that the increased population would require expansion of the Cooperative's facilities and therefore "we must strengthen its capital structure. This can be accomplished through the sale of additional shares, increased patronage, and more sale of CO-OP label products on which the margin is higher than on nationally advertised goods we also carry in our stores."

Another apparent priority would be a strengthened information and educational program about cooperatives and Greenbelt Consumer Services. There were then -- and for the full life of the Cooperative -- education and membership committees by one name or another. In this particular period just before and during the influx of new residents who had no previous experience with cooperatives, the store advertising in the town's newspaper provided educational messages about the co-op way of doing business. News and editorials also helped the educational effort. Aimed directly at newcomers were neighborhood get-acquainted parties by knowledgeable members of the Cooperative. GCS published a 6-page booklet telling about all the community's cooperatives, and this went to the new homes and was also available in the stores.

The year of 1941 was a tough learning period for GCS, with some bright spots and some discouraging incidents.

Most patrons who received refunds let the full amounts accumulate toward additional shares. Only $985 was claimed in cash. Also, purchase of shares increased so that by April the Cooperative could claim 771 paid-in-full members.

It is disconcerting, however, to leaf through the minutes of Board meetings in late 1940 and 1941 and see how many pages were given over to listing approval of individual memberships, of shares of stock to be issued, and of repurchase of shares and payment of patronage refunds which had been pledged toward shares. This went on for much too long a time before the

Board decided that voting on each individual transaction was a waste of time.

And the membership for too long a time looked upon investment in GCS shares of stock as something like a credit union or savings account, where money could be withdrawn whenever needed. The board's practice of accepting all shares offered for repurchase encouraged this attitude, and the result endangered the Cooperative's cash position. On the other hand, directors feared residents would not risk the purchase of shares without the buy-back assurance. Few members in these years had experience with stock investments.

General Manager Hodsden pointed out to the Board in December 1941 that studies in the food marketing field showed a required investment of about $30 for each family in the neighborhood of the store. Board Members Tessim Zorach and Denzil Wood then proposed a bylaws amendment setting a minimum investment of $30 for members requesting repurchase of shares unless moving out of town. This was approved at the following membership meeting.

Another lesson was learned when the spring quarterly meeting in 1941 opened with a quorum but had to adjourn when too many members left after the door prizes were given out. This led, later, to a reduction of the quorum from the unrealistic 25 percent of the membership written into the first bylaws. As membership grew and the war years brought pressures of women working away from home and transportation difficulties, quorums were further reduced from time to time, over the protests of those who saw such action as not in the democratic tradition.

During these spring months of 1941, some of the early enthusiasm and euphoria of the new organization began to wear thin. Not only did attendance drop off at membership meetings but also at Board meetings. Too many meetings and the late hours of their duration produced fatigue and frustration. Frank Lastner, after replacing Volckhausen as president in August 1941, had to remind directors "meetings have been starting late because of the lack of a quorum while those who came on time are forced to while away their time waiting." Minutes of Board meetings in these months record fewer written reports than before, and often no report at all from key committee chairmen.

A close reading of minutes suggests a tendency to postpone decisions on controversial items on the agenda. Inability or unwillingness to take prompt action is found from time to time all through the history of the Cooperative's Boards, but this hesitancy in 1941 marked a change from the 1940 enthusiasm.

Also noticeable was the large number of trips for meetings, conferences, and training courses. These were important for maintaining contact with other cooperatives and for learning how to improve performance. And the cost of each trip was low, running in the $10 to $50 range. Even so, this came at a time when store margins were being squeezed and scheduling pressures caused absences and failures to prepare reports.

Pressures on the directors then and at later intervals caused frequent turnovers on the Board. This was recognized as a weakness, and from time to time remedial measures were tried. At a membership meeting in May, there was a proposal to pay directors $2 per meeting, but absence of a quorum held up any action until a later date. Another try at easing pressure on directors and active volunteers was a proposal to hire a staff member for cooperative education and promotion. This came before the membership meeting in June but was defeated amid declarations that investing the amount of the salary in lower prices and better service would be more useful.

At about this time Volckhausen, who was then president, indicated interest in being a paid supervisor of the education program. Both the general manager and the Board agreed that he was the best qualified of any possible candidates for the job, but after lengthy consideration of the conflict of interest involved, Volckhausen withdrew his name. As noted on an earlier page, Volckhausen, who had been a leading light in Greenbelt's cooperatives from the start, resigned as GCS president in August 1941 and Frank Lastner replaced him.

Changes took place in the stores, too. Thomas Ricker had been appointed assistant general manager by the board in May.

Sales and net margins were satisfactory for the first part of the year, but rising wholesale prices and shortages brought on by the threatening war situation began squeezing margins. One result was an increase in complaints, evidenced in letters to the editor of the GREENBELT COOPERATOR. One of these, reporting great savings in shopping a food market outside the town, prompted the newspaper to make a price survey of its own. This exercise found that the comparison store offered meat graded "good" with prices of course lower than GCS higher quality "choice". Also significant was the finding that the canned goods comparison used nationally advertised brands exclusively. These actually were priced lower in the market which was part of a chain with hundreds of outlets than at the single GCS store. The study by the paper recommended looking at CO-OP brands. The red label items, equivalent in quality to the best national brands priced out at about equal or in a few instances even lower than the national brands. The CO-OP blue label averaged about the same as the chain's "house" brand.

Supporters of the Cooperative also pointed to the patronage refund and to the value of shoppers controlling their own store.

A little later, a professor in marketing research at the University of Maryland conducted a comprehensive survey of shopping in Greenbelt. His students personally interviewed half the residents and found that a large majority shopped at the local facilities and were satisfied with the Cooperative. The study found prices of comparative items about the same. The report was published in the JOURNAL OF MARKETING. But price comparisons remained a controversial matter. This was a problem which persisted as long as GCS operated food markets.

Another test of the Cooperative's labor relations cropped up when union workers struck the laundry which had the contract with the Greenbelt valet shop. The Board and members at a quarterly meeting supported the strikers by withholding the valet shop business, but as the months passed and GCS could find no other laundry to handle the volume through the valet shop, there were second thoughts. When the strike went to the Labor Board for settlement, the Board of GCS decided that holding back the valet shop volume would no longer affect the outcome of the strike. GCS picked up its contract again, and shortly thereafter the strike reached settlement.

Three events near the end of 1941 forced great changes upon GCS. The first was the completion of the 1,000 new houses for defense workers. Newcomers would outnumber the original residents. The GCS Board, together with the general manager, saw that the existing facilities already were at capacity. They began plans for a second food store in the north end of town, where much of the new housing was clustered, and another service station to be located at the edge of town.

The first discussion of expansion had arisen earlier in the year, but at a Board meeting on April 16, 1941, Herbert Evans, of CDC, advised that he saw no possibility of financing additional store space by any government source or by a loan from CDC. He stated further:

"Opening a new food store (at this time) would throw the whole organization back about 3 years, and that the first very important job for GCS is consolidation of services now offered and strengthening the staff and the whole set-up. The date when the newcomers will arrive is still too indefinite to justify even consideration of a new food store."

Evans then spelled out in detail what could be done to utilize existing facilities more efficiently to accommodate more volume.

Almost at the same time, the Farm Security Administration announced that it would begin enforcing its income limitations for renters. This threatened to evict about 300 families who had met the income ceilings when they moved into Greenbelt but had since then acquired better jobs or salary increases. In jeopardy was the leadership corps not only of the cooperatives

31

but of nearly all organizations in the community.

And then Pearl Harbor was bombarded by the Japanese on December 7. Priorities shifted immediately in Greenbelt along with the rest of the country.

During the war years, building materials were not available for new shopping facilities. Wholesale prices climbed, narrowing margins and making consumers unhappy. Gasoline, sugar, butter, and other commodities were in short supply, and GCS resorted to rationing even before that was ordered by the Government. The draft already had taken away some of the community's men, and now the depletion increased, with war-related jobs drawing away many spared from the draft.

Despite difficulties during the year, the Cooperative's sales totaled $450,034, with a net margin of $6,859. That made possible a patronage refund of 1.5 percent for purchases during 1941.

The next year saw an even better operating performance. Total sales for 1942 climbed to $690,157. Net margin came to $34,982, allowing the board to declare a patronage return of 5 percent with the approval of members at the annual meeting. This proved to be the highest profit ratio (net margin to sales) in the Cooperative's long history.

There were worries enough in 1942, but they drew less criticism and gave rise to less heckling than the previous year's difficulties.

The Washington newspapers, which had criticized and poked fun at Greenbelt from the time construction got underway, took space to praise the Cooperative for initiating the rationing of scarce goods. In particular, they expressed amazement that members responded to a plea from the food store manager by selling back about 500 pounds of sugar so it could be shared with other shoppers.

While the Board and general manager searched for ways to provide facilities for serving the new war housing residents at the north end of town, the Federal Works Agency, which controlled these houses, advertised for commercial enterprises to locate there. GCS complained that it had not been notified nor invited to bid. The FWA subsequently withdrew its bid request, acknowledging it had not been in touch with the FSA and was not aware of the GCS lease.

In early spring came word from the Farm Security Administration that it would postpone enforcement of its income ceiling. This was good news for community organizations, including GCS, which feared losing leaders. There were already dislocations resulting from the war. General Manager Hodsdon was called to active duty at the end of March. The Board replaced him by advancing Tom Ricker to the slot. Late in the year the drug store pharmacist and the shoemaker left for military service, and replacing them was difficult.

With more women taking jobs outside of the home and those at home picking up more responsibilities as their husbands went into the services, the Better Buyers Club went into decline and disappeared before the end of the year. Some years after the war its pattern was revived within the Cooperative's educational program. To meet its educational and promotional needs, which had increased with the more-than-doubled population, the Cooperative hired Mary Trumbell. Although she stayed for only a short time, this helped offset the loss of volunteers.

At a later date, Waldo Mott was assigned this responsibility. He told the Board his approach to the co-op education and member relations job would depend more upon individual contacts:

"One of the chief complaints which I have heard is the lack of dependability of volunteer help, not only in relation to GCS but in practically all Greenbelt organizations....we must take the problem into consideration when drawing up a plan of action ....and at the same time to make all possible use of persons who are willing and able. It is important to consider that persons may be enthusiastic about a job for a short period of time but soon lose interest.

"Record keeping is another problem rather neglected....without an accurate record, efforts will be duplicated, improvements will be hard to make....in the past, form letters have been used with questionable results."

For better results, which could be measured in relation to effort, he proposed personal letters and "get-acquainted" home visits even though these would take more time. He also underscored the need for staff training, quoting General Manager Ricker: "An informed membership is a healthy membership and an informed staff is a healthy staff."

He concluded his report to the Board by declaring:

"Many of the complaints and dissatisfactions which have been experienced recently could have been alleviated if the membership and the public had been properly informed."

As the stores became more crowded, the Board met with Farm Security Administration officials to secure a lease for space to accommodate a second, smaller shopping center. Along with this effort, the Board began a drive to raise additional capital. The planning came to grief in September when the War Production Board said "no" to a request for scarce building materials.

A makeshift remedy emerged when GCS secured rental of four row houses on Laurel Hill Road and opened them as the North End Store, January 20, 1943. The community newspaper described it in detail:

"At first you may not be sure you've come to the right place... just a row of houses like so many others. But once inside you'll be glad you've come....Shoppers expressed appreciation for the intimate atmosphere which is possible only in a small store.... bright and cheerful in its four connecting living rooms....in some ways it won't be as convenient as the big store in the center of town. You'll have to carry your basket because there's no room for the carriers...."

All facilities at this time were crowded. The offices of Greenbelt Consumer Services, Inc. were several rooms over the drug store in the shopping center.

At one point the valet shop stopped accepting dry cleaning for lack of space. The barber shop's three chairs could not handle the demand, but there was no room for expansion. But then, keeping three barbers was a problem, too. The GREENBELT COOPERATOR observed during the year that the original barber, Mike Juliano, was still head barber. This seemed unusual with all the other changes that had taken place. He was saluted as "one of the pioneers of Greenbelt".

Eastern Cooperative Wholesale in New York City supplied the food store. By 1943, GCS was the biggest user of CO-OP label canned and packaged goods as well as other items handled by ECW. On Greenbelt's initiative, the wholesale operation and the Eastern Cooperative League, as well, reorganized into three districts. This made possible a warehouse in Philadelphia to serve cooperatives in Pennsylvania, southern New Jersey, Maryland, Delaware, District of Columbia, and northern Virginia. It also gave to the GCS board a stronger voice in operations of both the Wholesale and the Cooperative League.

GCS joined with Rochdale Cooperative of D.C. in exploring the advantages of buying fruits and vegetables direct from farmers in nearby Maryland and Virginia. The two organizations also shared some educational projects and exchanged visits.

Wartime shortages in supplies encouraged ECW to move into some processing. CO-OP label coffee, ground and roasted in the wholesale plant, became a favorite on GCS supermarket shelves for many years. A CO-OP label cigarette did not do as well. A half-page advertisement in the GREENBELT COOPERATOR advised:

"1,000 times NO--but if you insist...The reason your Co-op handles CO-OP cigarettes is because a large number of our consumer-owners ask us. Tobacco is a relative mild form of dope that gives pleasure to some and annoyance to

34

others. [This was 1943!] CO-OP cigarettes will not improve your wind, give you the biceps of a bison, the throat of a songbird or the pearly teeth of a photographer's model. Stubs will not smell more fragrant....but if you must smoke, try CO-OP cigarettes."

A large number of GCS half-page ads in the paper were educational, informing readers about Rochdale principles and the cooperative movement. One quoted Wallace Campbell, then with the Cooperative League of the USA and much later the founder and president of CARE and internationally recognized spokesman for cooperatives, as well as a member of the Greenbelt Cooperative's Delegate Assembly:

"Thru cooperatives the common people with little capital, small savings, buying the goods and services they need from day to day, have created a democracy with more content and more power, with more portent for the new world than all the high flown dreams of economists, politicians and world masters."

Rationing, with its limits on scarce goods and the complications of coupon books, was a burden on Co-op employees as it was to the whole retail trade. GCS personnel and member-owners, however, probably survived the war period's merchandising irritations with better spirit than could be found on average. Membership and management made it clear from the beginning that they would not put up with black markets, hoarding, and under-the-counter shenanigans. Placards on the shelves advised shoppers about supply scheduling, substitutions, the reasons for price changes, etc. Greenbelt's greatest frustration may have been at the service station. The town was a long way from Washington, where most residents worked, public transportation was minimal, and the tight rationing of gasoline, oil, and tires worked an extreme hardship even on car pools.

The Cooperative took a lead in selling war bonds. To meet the quotas GCS set for itself, it offered free movie tickets and free haircuts for purchasers of $10 war bonds. Jack Fruchtman, theater manager, headed several of the drives. One of these drives, shared with the Navy Wives, raised $40,175 in bond purchases.

Frank Lastner gave up the position of GCS president and left the Board at the August 1943 membership meeting. In taking leave of the board, he said:

"Permit me to take this opportunity to thank all of you both individually and as a group for your work and cooperation as fellow Board members. It has been a very pleasant association and I am pleased that so much good work has been accomplished by the Board and management during my tenure of office. I am particularly grateful to you for honoring me with the presidency during the past 2 years.

35

"I also hope that you who remain on the Board and those of you who become directors at this meeting and at later meetings will strive to make GCS a bigger and better cooperative -- one that will serve our people in bigger and better ways. I urge you to bear in mind at all times that ours is now a million-dollar consumers' cooperative and, as such, will be and is looked upon to some extent as the leader in the consumers' cooperative movement."

Lastner also had served 4 years on the Town Council. His induction into the Army left another gap in Greenbelt's pool of leaders. Carl W. Hintz replaced him as the Cooperative's president. After the election and at the end of the meeting, a member questioned lack of a quorum. The dispute which followed was resolved by arbitration which determined that the election was indeed illegal for lack of a quorum. The previous Board and officers were reinstated and gave necessary ratification to actions taken by the "illegal" Board. A follow-up special membership meeting verified the election of all but one of those "elected" at the August 4 "no quorum" meeting. Hintz continued as president.

Total sales for 1943 jumped to $1,001,669, nearly two-thirds of that total achieved in the food stores. The net margin for the combined operations was $31,350. This remained after the board had made payments ahead of schedule on the loan from CDC. After paying dividends on stock and setting aside reserves, there was enough remaining for a patronage refund of 3.125 percent on purchases.

The principal reason for the poorer showing than in the previous year was clearly seen in the operating statistics. Although the general manager had reduced expenses from 23 percent of gross sales in 1942 to 21 percent in 1943, the cost of goods increased from 69.4 percent in 1942 to 72.8 percent in 1943. The Office of Price Administration was holding retail prices, but wholesale prices were allowed to edge upward.

At the annual meeting in February 1944, the membership again made changes in the Board. Fred DeJaeger became president.

By now GCS had 120 employees. The Board already had adopted, with membership approval, a staffing pattern and salary scale. A plan for accident insurance and coverage of hospital costs was the next step GCS took for its employees.

How a grievance committee came to be created gives some insight as to how volatile incidents could become in the Greenbelt community. Lucille Pruitt, a checkout clerk in the Laurel Hill food store, was dismissed for taking 2 days off without approval. She wanted to be with her fiancee who had a short military leave. The store manager, on the other hand, was struggling with trying to meet shopper demands in the midst of the wartime shortage of workers. One member of the Board was a neighbor and friend of the dismissed employee, so the firing became an issue that split the Board and then spread into a community controversy.

Noting the incident here has significance because it was so typical of community life in this cooperative-style town. Personal differences which escalated into disputes that pitted neighbor against neighbor took place in the Citizens' Association, the Health Association (cooperative medical care), and other organizations. Even the Boy Scout troop was troubled with this kind of contention.

The newspaper article announcing settlement of the GCS dispute reported:

" 'This grievance committee to hear complaints and appeals of our employees is something we should have established long ago,' was the comment of Vice President Donald H. Cooper, who made the motion setting up the grievance board last week. 'If both management and employees can have confidence in the ability and fairness of this committee, it can settle potential labor problems in the future before they reach dangerous proportions.'"

In the continuing effort to gain better understanding of the Cooperative, to resolve complaints of shoppers, and to pick up suggestions for better service, the education committee organized a warden system for the nine "blocks" of the town. Henry Walter was picked to construct this network. He broke each area into neighborhoods clustered in the cul-de-sacs that make up the Greenbelt housing pattern. He obtained a knowledgeable GCS member in nearly every group of homes to serve as a volunteer connecting point for the Cooperative.

Although the set-up was informal and flexible, responsibilities of a warden included:

-- Calling on new residents in those 10 to 20 homes to help them become acquainted with Greenbelt and its cooperatively owned stores.
-- Picking up complaints and suggestions about operation of the stores and pass these on to the Board through the Education Committee. And follow through until results are obtained.
-- Passing down to the neighbors information from the Board.
-- Encouraging attendance at the quarterly meetings.
-- Providing neighborhood social evenings, which might include tasting parties, price checking, and consumer education features, as well as refreshments.

The system was never fully completed but served usefully for a time. The idea was revived some years later during the Cooperative's expansion periods. Don Cooper head of the Education Committee and pointed out that "small co-ops have no problem in keeping the customer-member-owners in close touch with operations of the store, but with 1,300 members here in Greenbelt we have to establish a better system of two-way communication between members and their Board and management."

The Education Committee was responsible also for the first small house organ, leaflets about consumer information and cooperatives, and a watch on legislation of interest to consumers and cooperatives. Waldo Mott was for some time doing public relations on the GCS staff and worked closely with the member Education Committee. Merton Trast, personnel director on the staff also helped, a little later.

General Manager Ricker commented at one Board meeting that the Education Committee ought to work on a problem that he described as "members who feel that the Cooperative should offer better goods and services at a lower price than any other business and then pay a bigger refund at the end of the year."

Acting on suggestions from members, the food store installed a case for selling frozen foods. In 1944 this was something of a novelty. Another innovation worked out with the cooperative stores in Washington was CO-OP label bread. This is a good place to note that many years later GCS bought a controlling interest in a bakery -- an interesting story covered in another chapter.

CO-OP label bread was just one of several projects worked out in neighborly fashion with the expanding consumer cooperative groups in Washington and northern Virginia. As related in Chapter I, Rochdale Co-operatives, Inc. had several small food stores by 1944. There were talks about establishing a joint warehouse in the national capital area, but this never reached fruition.

What did develop, however, was the Potomac Cooperative Federation. This was an educational and promotional organization with an office and two paid employees in Washington. Greenbelt members were GCS, the Greenbelt Health Association, and the Greenbelt Cooperative Publishing Association. Volckhausen and I wrote the Federation's first bylaws.

Soon there were 14 member societies -- the number varied from year to year. Financial support came mainly from the three largest organizations: Ohio Farm Bureau Insurance Co. (later Nationwide), Group Health (in Washington), and GCS.

Representation on the Federation's board was related to size of membership and financial support. After a few years, the Board of GCS became dissatisfied with the influence of very small cooperatives in the Federation and with the financial burden. Withdrawal by Greenbelt crippled the Federation and caused bad feelings within Washington area's cooperative leadership. Even so, the Potomac Cooperative Federation persisted, and in 1959 GCS rejoined. The Federation lasted for a few years after that, but closed down when Nationwide trimmed its support.

During the Federation's existence, its contributions were impressive. It offered two training seminars a year; helped find leadership, employees, and support for struggling new co-ops; assisted in public relations and legislative liaison; and provided a forum for the exchange of ideas with weekly open luncheon round tables and a newsletter that went to about 650 co-op leaders.

It is time now to write about events which threatened to wreck the Cooperative. The nine directors who made up the Board differed in their basic views about objectives and policies for GCS. The election system of proportional representation encouraged factions that represented stockholders who were not in sympathy with the Rochdale principles as well as those who upheld them. One Board faction was called idealistic and naive; the other was seen as anti-cooperative. This was a generalized division all through the town of Greenbelt among residents who were at all active in community affairs. Even though 60 percent of the families held voting shares in GCS, a large majority of Greenbelters took no active part in organizations and meetings.

The Board was aware that the drug store and the variety store operated in the red. Net margins from the food store carried the business. By the end of the summer, 1944, several serious problems were emerging or had already become evident.

General Manager Ricker had asked for a 2-year contract. The Board did not oppose that but had taken no action.

An earlier Board had given Fruchtman a 2-year contract to manage the theater. That contract was now responsible for widespread complaints that Fruchtman was making too much money. The bonus percentage of gross income from the theater in addition to salary came to $10,285 for the year -- several thousand dollars more than the general manager's salary. [We have to remember that this was 1944 -- before inflation distorted salaries and costs some years later.] In addition Fruchtman drew a salary as assistant to the general manager. This level of "affluence" was noisily resented by some in this community where the average annual income was closer to $2,500.

The chairman of the Auditing Committee took it upon himself to talk with people in the film booking offices in Washington to learn if some arrangement could be made to give GCS or Greenbelt movie patrons a bigger cut out of showings. The result was higher charges on film rentals for

Greenbelt when booking agents found out the profit margins.

When the manager of the variety store left in September, Ricker told the Board the only way he could get a new manager would be to offer a contract, probably for more than one year. There was already a purchasing contract for the variety store which locked in Butler Brothers as the exclusive supplier. This barred stocking and selling of any CO-OP label merchandise in this store.

Then the drug store manager departed. He was also the full-time pharmacist, so this key enterprise was left with a part-time pharmacist in a town of nearly two thousand families. Maryland law at that time required a registered pharmacist to be on duty for any hours that a drug store could be open. The community faced an emergency situation. The general manager advised the Board that he could find a pharmacist-manager only by offering a long-term contract with a percentage of sales as a bonus in addition to salary if a profit could be produced. The operation had been showing a loss which became more and more serious.

Directors found themselves divided on the question of contracts, and the Auditing Committee jumped into the fray by declaring only the membership body could authorize contracts. Lawsuits were threatened.

At this point the general manager did find a suitable pharmacist-manager, Dr. Meyer Silnutzer, who did not require a contract. The Board authorized his hiring at a higher salary than had previously been paid. An audit found that about $3,000 in merchandise had disappeared during the preceding months, and there had been increasing complaints of rowdy conduct and vandalism credited to a small group of young people who used the lunch counter / soda fountain for a hang-out.

The Board and general manager requested Dr. Silnutzer to clean up the situation. He did just that, tightening up security and firing the young clerks behind the soda fountain who had been for some time serving ice cream and snacks free of charge to their friends. This was not appreciated by some of the younger people. When Halloween came around, the drug store windows took an especially heavy soaping and waxing. This included swastikas and "Jew". Dr. Silnutzer and a "colored porter" were scrubbing the windows next day when the school bus unloaded at curbside. Some in the group began haranguing Dr. Silnutzer and reports afterwards said there were racial taunts. Dr. Silnutzer turned the hose on one of the young men, who responded by striking the manager in the face, breaking his glasses. The son of Dr. Silnutzer, working in the store, then joined the melee. Such confusion followed that when the case came up in court, the judge threw out the complaints filed by both sides, because of conflicting testimony.

In the several days following the drug store incident, the town newspaper reported that "rowdyism in the drug store steadily increased. Insulting signs were scrawled on the doors. The paper carrier serving the Silnutzers 'had orders' not to leave any papers on their porch. On Friday night the Silnutzers asked the police to escort them to their car from the drug store door. Saturday morning the air was let out of their tires."

The family felt it had to leave Greenbelt, and Silnutzer submitted a letter of resignation that said:

"I take this occasion to thank you and the Board of Directors for your whole-hearted support. I want to thank you for the confidence you have placed in me in my very short but conscientious effort to give this community the pharmaceutical service to which it was entitled. Due to the deficiency of recognized police authority I found that my mission was impossible of fulfillment, without jeopardizing my personal dignity, my professional dignity, and my right to the pursuit of life, liberty and happiness...."

So Greenbelt again was without pharmacy services and the cooperative drug store was closed by order of the State inspector -- the second time within a period of 3 months. The GCS Board persuaded a retired pharmacist from a nearby community to serve part time, and volunteers from the Cooperative's leadership provided interim staffing until the general manager could hire replacements.

In a long editorial, the GREENBELT COOPERATOR said of this affair:

"When a community of 7500 is deprived of the services of its only drug store through the action of irresponsible minors, it is no time to fold the hands and murmur 'Boys will be boys'....How many Greenbelt parents know that their high school age boys and girls have been getting free hand-outs at the drug store from their pals behind the counter? Do they know which of their children's friends have acquired reputations with the management and police for 'habitual disorderly conduct' in the drug store, and, since no drastic consequences ensue, that such offenders became heroes in the eyes of their fellows?...Are Greenbelt fathers and mothers concerned that Mr. and Mrs. Silnutzer were goaded by anonymous telephone calls and taunted with filthy names, during the high-schoolers campaign to 'get Silnutzer'?"

THE WASHINGTON DAILY NEWS story about the drug store episode was sympathetic to the Silnutzers but took the opportunity to again lambast the "unusual tie-up...in the superimposed co-op, with a ready-made business...in the Government-owned model town."

The Silnutzer affair took a surprise turn toward a happy ending a few days after he submitted his resignation and was preparing to leave Greenbelt. A delegation of teen-age boys and girls led by Mary Jane Townsend called on the druggist's family, expressed regret over the harassment, and asked Silnutzer to stay on as the drug store manager and pharmacist. The boy who had the altercation with Silnutzer came to him and apologized. The town newspaper praised the young people for this initiative and rejoiced that all appeared to have ended well.

Nevertheless, the Silnutzers left a couple of months later, apparently recognizing some hangover feeling in the community which was uncomfortable. One positive follow-up was better recognition of a need by teenagers to have access to a recreation program to discourage "hanging out" in the shopping center. The Town Council voted money to fix up a basement room as a temporary recreational center. After the war a drive was undertaken and successful in funding a building for young people's activities.

The NEWS, in Washington, D.C., published a series of articles about the problems of Greenbelt and GCS -- the first one, September 18, 1944, bore the heading "Not All Is Green Pastures at Greenbelt: Utopia's in a Turmoil Over Co-ops Vs. Chain Stores". GCS used a full page advertisement in the Greenbelt paper to answer inaccuracies in the NEWS story, and as vice president I met with the city editor of the NEWS to protest the slant of its report on the Cooperative. But there could be no denial of the conflict that prevailed.

As the weeks passed, crisis escalated into crisis. The breaking point came when the Board learned that their general manager, Tom Ricker, was spending part of his time managing a liquor and variety store of his own at Cedar Point, Maryland. Some directors and the Auditing Committee saw this as conflict of interest, especially as the business was tied in with a contract with Butler Brothers, the supplier also under extended contract for the Cooperative's variety store. Adding fuel to the fire were reports that two directors and the part-time attorney for GCS were involved in Ricker's venture.

Max Salzman, chairman of the Auditing Committee, called for a special meeting of the membership. After a stormy executive session of the Board, Ricker agreed to resign. The arrangement provided that he would stay until a new general manager was in place and an inventory could be taken at the time of replacement.

Fruchtman, the theater manager, offered to take over the general manager position and the Board approved, 5-4, but then backed off when three store managers handed in their resignation in protest against Fruchtman as general manager.

Three directors, Volckhausen, Donald Cooper, and Mrs. Carnie Harper (who was new on the Board), went to New York to interview Samuel Ashelman

42

for the vacancy. He was at that time the manager of the Philadelphia warehouse for Eastern Cooperative Wholesale. Of four candidates for the position of general manager, Ashelman was the one selected. The vote by the Board was unanimous.

Of Pennsylvania Quaker descent, Ashelman had lived and worked most of his life in that state. After 2 years at Swarthmore College, he entered the cooperative field as an employee with one of the TVA rural electric cooperatives. Later he returned to Swarthmore for his degree, and then organized a cooperative buying club in the town. The buying club grew enough to open a cooperative food store which became so successful under Ashelman's guidance that an A.& P. store just around the corner closed within 6 months.

During this period, Ashelman took night classes in marketing at the University of Pennsylvania. He also found an opportunity for a trip to Europe to study cooperatives in Scandinavia. On his return he worked for the Eastern Cooperative Wholesale as their trouble shooter, before being advanced to manage the Philadelphia warehouse.

Ashelman started to work for GCS December 11, for a starting salary of $6,000 a year, knowing in advance most of the problems which had to be faced.

The Board of Directors held 36 meetings during 1944. That gives some measure of the year's difficulties.

In the late fall of this year, President DeJaeger skipped six board meetings in a row, and the Auditing Committee suspended another director, Yates Smith, for refusing to attend a crucial Board meeting on short notice. The Auditing Committee also criticized the Board's frequent executive sessions, and at one point called a special membership meeting to oust the Board. Nothing came of this, as the majority of the 324 members who attended the meeting decided to await the next regular election which was due in 2 months.

IV. GROWING UP (1945-1946)

With a new general manager for the Cooperative and a new year ahead, the Board of Directors gave special attention to the auditor's report for 1944. Louis Englander, certified public accountant from the Cooperative League Accounting Bureau, pointed to several aspects of the year's operations which needed correction:

-- Food store expenses increased from 11.1 percent in 1943 to 11.9 percent. The departmental margins were 4.6 percent in 1943 and only 2.8 percent in 1944. The gross margin decreased from 15.7 percent to 14.7 percent. Since the food store represented more than 58 percent of total volume this 1 percent drop means a loss of income of over $6,000.

-- In the drug store the departmental loss was over $4,000 as compared with a gain in 1943 of almost $950.

-- The valet shop showed a departmental loss of over $2,500 as compared with a $300 loss for the previous year.

-- The inventory of the drug store was taken but it was not possible to obtain sufficient information properly to price this inventory.

-- The ratio of inventories to total current assets is increasing -- 56 percent in 1943, 67 percent in 1944.

-- "...your capital certainly should be increased to take care of known future needs....Already you are finding the original equipment installed to be inadequate for present needs, and a program of replacement appears to be imminently necessary."

Ashelman saw that in his first year as the new general manager he must make hard-nosed changes in procedures and staff. The continuing war shortages made any and all remedial steps difficult. A split Board of Directors added to the difficulties.

However, the membership meeting of February 28, 1945 elected five new directors which tipped the balance of control on the Board. The new general manager now had a majority solidly in support of cooperative enterprise. Dayton Hull was elected unanimously as president and introduced a measure of common sense compromise that provided stability on the Board -- an ingredient that was missing during the previous year.

Before this, though, at the beginning of the first Board meeting in 1945, James

A. Flynn, who had been elected a director the previous February, requested time to make a statement. The Board minutes show:

"Mr. Flynn requested that it be recorded in the minutes that he had asked Mr. Volkhausen whether he had refused to take the oath of induction, that Mr. Volckhausen replied that his induction had been postponed but that as a conscientious objector he would have refused to take the oath; and that for this reason Mr. Flynn felt that he could not attend this meeting or any other meeting attended by Mr. Volckhausen." He then walked out of the meeting, but did not resign from the Board. The meeting continued.

This was an omen of more trouble to come. And it did come.

The weekly newspaper for September 14, 1945 reported in its lead story:

"The meeting of the Citizens Association which was called last Monday night to give the 15 candidates for the Town Council a chance to express their views, ended in disorderly fashion with most of the audience walking out when a group seated in the rear of the auditorium refused to obey the chair, and continued to heckle one of the candidates, Walter Volckhausen....

"The meeting began to get out of order when James Flynn took the floor and asked Volckhausen if he would take the oath of allegiance if he were inducted. Volckhausen stated that his stand as a conscientious objector would have prevented him from taking orders from anyone which went against the dictates of his conscience, and that although he had an opportunity to evade his responsibility as a C.O. by accepting a Navy commission teaching mathematics, he had refused to accept it for that reason. Flynn then asked whether Volckhausen had been investigated by the FBI, and on receiving an affirmative answer, asked whether he then admitted being a Communist. Volckhausen explained that he had been cleared by the FBI of any suspicion of being connected with a communist movement.

"At this point, in spite of the chair's repeated requests that he yield the floor, Flynn persisted in his cross-examination, the audience becoming restive when he began to question Volckhausen about his religious beliefs. The accusation of 'Fascist' hurled at Flynn by Irving Rothchild provoked the former into splintering Mr. Rothchild's glasses against his face. After the men were separated, Frank Desmond continued the interrogation, accusing Volckhausen of opposition to the Constitution because he was a conscientious objector. When Volckhausen attempted to explain that his views were allowed for in the Constitution, and were protected by it, the meeting was taken over by the group which had been heckling him. As the chair was unable to restore order, the majority of the audience got up and walked out."

Editor Eleanor Ritchie deplored what had happened, in a front page editorial which said that the "exhibition of personal spite and premeditated heckling was shameful". She noted that, "The feud that was aired on this inappropriate occasion is one of long standing and has already been marked by threats of physical violence, or worse." There were more than the usual follow-up "Letters to the Editor", all but one sympathetic with Volckhausen and angry at the takeover of the meeting by the group of dissidents.

Why this much detail here about a conflict which may appear on the surface to involve personal differences of opinion? Those who lived through Greenbelt's early years with concern about the role of cooperatives in the community realized that the conflict between Flynn and Volckhausen was but one sample of the serious dissension between residents who took the lead in organizing the several cooperatives and those who saw cooperatives as a threat.

Item. During the same week of the disorder at the meeting of the Citizens Association, the newspaper reported:

"A new organization appeared on the Greenbelt scene last Friday night at the American Legion home, when a group calling themselves the Committee of American Voters sent out invitations to a private meeting to decide on the candidates to be supported for election to Town Council."

A slate was agreed upon and a collection was taken to finance the committee's work. The group also voted to study "existing conditions" in Greenbelt Consumer Services, the Greenbelt Health Association (a cooperative), and the GREENBELT COOPERATOR, an independent newspaper published by The Greenbelt Cooperative Publishing Association, Inc., and to take definite action "to eliminate undesirable policies."

Item. A couple of weeks before the Town Council election, five candidates -- Ruth Taylor, David Granahan, Wells Harrington, Walter Volckhausen, and Sherrod East -- announced they were running as individuals but with common agreement on certain objectives. All were well known as active leaders in one or more of the local cooperatives. Listed among their objectives was support for the cooperatives.

Running against them was the slate endorsed by the Committee of American Voters. This slate was elected. Five other candidates, also known for their support of cooperatives simply split off votes.

Item. In mid-October, the newly elected mayor characterized the election as "definitely partisan...between those who think the co-op should run the town and those who do not."

One of the first topics the new Council proposed was an ordinance to see that the public health officer inspect the Co-op stores regularly. (There had been no record of complaints.) Also, to give police authority "by ordinance, to enforce public safety measures particularly in connection with the stores". Police had already been patrolling the shopping center, so the point of this was obscure.

Item. The new mayor, charging that the GREENBELT COOPERATOR "does not bring information of town-sponsored activities to the residents in the proper manner", suggested that the best remedy might be to start another paper. The volunteer staff of the GREENBELT COOPERATOR offered its "gleeful approval" and said they would be glad to give a few tips to help a new paper get underway. And then added the reminder which had appeared at least twice a year that everyone in town was invited to work on the GREENBELT COOPERATOR staff and that the volunteers who did the work controlled its policies. It was suggested that if people who did not like the tone of the paper would just take it over that might be easier than setting up a new one. No new paper appeared, nor did any of the critics show up to work on the staff of the GREENBELT COOPERATOR.

Item. The question of the Cooperative's 10-year monopoly on store space in the shopping center came up again when Tom Ricker, former GCS general manager who had been replaced by Ashelman, proposed building a liquor store in Greenbelt. The Cooperative opposed the proposal, and on this issue 19 of 20 organizations represented at a community meeting agreed. In a town referendum the vote was 4-1 against the proposal, but mostly on the basis of moral disapproval and protection of children rather than on the point of the Cooperative's control of store space.

Nevertheless, Flynn distributed door-to-door circulars saying that the GCS lease on the entire shopping center really was the issue. One leaflet read in part:

"...the issue of a package liquor store is secondary for the reason, should the lease for such a store be issued, does it not follow that other privately owned stores and enterprises will secure leases?

"It has been stated that planning is under way for G.C.S. to operate a new, modern North End Store. This has been promised for the last few years. Why should not the Safeway or A.& P. be allowed to operate this store?

"It was intimated that the present Drug Store would be converted into a Restaurant....I have a proposal with Federal Public Housing Authority to operate a Restaurant and Cocktail Lounge.

"....It is up to folks in Greenbelt to manifest whether or not you desire the blessings of competition."

Item. The Committee of American Voters picked its own candidates for election of directors on the GCS Board in September, and one of them received enough votes under the proportional representation system to be seated on the Board. Control, however, still was held by those closely identified with cooperative activities and growth. The Board continued Dayton Hull as president.

Item. The Committee of American Voters changed its name to the Greenbelt Improvement Association. In November, this group launched a campaign to pull GCS out of its investment in and patronage of Eastern Cooperative Wholesale. This would have ended the sale of CO-OP label products in the local stores. It also probably would have shut down the Philadelphia warehouse, because GCS was the largest retail outlet served.

Spokesmen for this group of stockholders also urged that GCS should withdraw from the Potomac Cooperative Federation.

When the proposal to sever connection with Eastern Cooperative Wholesale was presented at the next quarterly meeting of GCS, members voted it down 528 to 10. A motion to switch from proportional representation voting to a simple majority method also was supported by the Improvement Association faction, apparently in a failure to realize the PR system was what gave them any representation on the Board. Anyway, the motion to change was defeated, but not by a large margin.

Following this November membership meeting, charges of voting irregularities by persons in the Improvement Association group caused the Board to tighten procedures for future meetings.

Toward the end of 1945, leaders of cooperatives making up the Potomac Cooperative Federation put together a proposal for an FM radio station which would be a nonprofit cooperative venture to offer quality programs, promote cooperatives, and provide information geared to consumer education and protection.

This came about partly in consequence of refusal by NBC and CBS to sell broadcasting time to cooperative organizations. This had developed back near the end of 1942. The broadcasting companies explained that cooperatives were controversial, and besides, the cooperative would probably use the programs to build membership.

The question of GCS participation was debated by the Board, with opposition from those who were apprehensive about the amount of the investment and also from vocal Greenbelt residents who looked with disfavor on additional cooperative ventures.

Another divisive issue was the question of whether Tom Ritchie, a director on the GCS Board, should be allowed to resign and be employed on the staff as accountant. The bylaws, as a protection against conflict of interest, required a 1-year interval before a retiring director could be employed on the staff. A vote at a membership meeting, however, could provide an exception. Ritchie did resign, worked for some time on the staff of the Potomac Cooperative Federation, and much later was reelected to the Board. In the summer of 1945, though, the question of whether a director could resign and be employed on the GCS staff was one of many incidents which caused bad feeling in a personal way that was quite typical of life in Greenbelt.

One more contention at about this time helped the Board move toward maturity. Sam Ashelman, the general manager, fired the manager of the variety store after warnings about improvements which were required. William Siegel, the store manager, asked for an appeal before the employees' grievance committee which an earlier Board had created. Ashelman pointed out that a general manager must have the right to hire and fire top staff, with Board confirmation. This was not, he maintained, an employee grievance case.

Members took sides in this matter, as they had in all Co-op staffing problems. After Siegel's dismissal was confirmed, the Board issued a clear statement to the effect that top staffing was not a decision to be made by committees: the members controlled the Board, and the Board was responsible for management through the general manager.

One director, Major Adelbert C. Long, had strong opinions about how GCS should be managed, and devoted much time to spelling out policies and practices he maintained should be followed. A majority of the Board disagreed on some of these proposals, so Long resigned after 4 1/2 months as a director. Thereafter, he took his concerns to membership meetings, to the the town newspaper in "Letters to the Editor", and to residents in door-to-door leaflets over an extended period of time.

In this period of growing up as a cooperative, members elected to the Board were learning that nine directors may have nine different opinions about how the Cooperative should be run. It was pointed out from time to time in orientation sessions that this calls for some willingness to compromise -- or having staunchly supported a proposal and been outvoted, to go along with the majority. Serving on a Board is a joint undertaking, with a lot of give and take. Prima donas do not last long.

Aside from all the dissension, 1945 was a very good year for the Cooperative. There were fewer meetings of the Board of Directors, but attendance improved. Solutions were found for problems.

Shortages in manpower, building materials, and a wide range of consumer goods which had plagued GCS -- and all other commercial enterprises for 4 years -- eased somewhat as the war came to an end. By December the Board and general manager had agreed on plans for a new building on the north side of the shopping center which would house a much larger supermarket, a separate pharmacy, and a lunch room or small restaurant. This replaced earlier planning for construction of a store in the north end of town to replace the makeshift use of four houses there. Application for land lease and permission to build went to the Federal Public Housing Authority.

A very successful stock share drive, under the direction of Herman Ramrus, had raised $53,000 in additional capital for anticipated expansion of facilities to serve Greenbelt.

In October, GCS paid off the last instalment of its $40,000 debt to CDC, well ahead of the 10-year deadline. This improved the balance sheet and helped establish a good credit rating for the Cooperative.

In the last days of 1945, the Cooperative gave the people of Greenbelt a Christmas present. The transportation problem which had accompanied the erection of the defense housing at the north end of town was solved by a bus which toured a circle within Greenbelt for 5 cents. Here was another first for Greenbelt Consumer Services -- a cooperative bus line.

A second bus was purchased some months later so that continuous service could be assured. After a 3-month period of successful operation, GCS obtained a 1-year renewable franchise from the Town Council. This bus service won enthusiastic praise from residents, especially those in the north end of town. They could now ride to the shopping center and back home for 10 cents. At the center, commuters could transfer to the bus service into the District of Columbia and other points outside of town. This had special importance in the period just after the war when gasoline and tire shortages still crippled private auto trips.

Gross sales for the year, covering all operations, totaled $1,162,851. Net margin before patronage returns and taxes came to $28,534. Only the tobacco shop and valet shop failed to produce savings.

The auditor's report showed the following significant comparisons with the previous year:

	1945	1944
Working capital	$79,800	$45,100
Working capital ratio	2.35:1	1.8:1
Percent of inventories to total		
current assets	60%	67%
Ratio of fixed assets and		
investments to capital	34%	50%
Turnover of capital	12.7	17

Comments of the auditor included these:

"Working capital is low, because of the requirements of your check cashing service....Inventory percentages and the actual inventories are considerably higher than they should be.... Grocery turnover is only 9.9, when the average for the larger cooperatives is between 12 and 14."

Results of operations in 1945 permitted payment of a 5 percent dividend on shares of stock and a 2.5 percent patronage refund. Membership at year's end was 1,820. Capital stock totaled $75,078. The GCS staff numbered 113 employees.

Merton Trast, managing the public relations and membership activities for GCS although technically on the payroll of the Potomac Cooperative Federation, worked with volunteers on a wide variety of social and promotional projects. A public dance in January 1946 attracted 500 paid participants. He encouraged the formation of a folk dancing group which later became the Greenbelt Recreation Co-op.

On one evening a week informal discussions open to the public brought one or two dozen people to the Co-op office. Topics included Greenbelt's origins, principles of cooperation, prices and service in the GCS enterprises, shopping tips, the CO-OP label, and anything else proposed by participants. Out of this, a series of cooking classes evolved.

An attractive, 8-page brochure entitled "Our Greenbelt Stores" came off the press in February 1946 and was widely read.

The "Co-op Information Letter", prepared by the Education Committee "to keep members informed about their consumer cooperative business" went into the mail monthly to supplement what could be read in the town newspaper. This was later replaced by "The Greenbelt Consumer", published by GCS "to give Greenbelt residents a reliable guide to best buys, special values, new products and commodity information".

This kind of information became more and more helpful to shoppers during the months of market adjustment that followed the war years when scarcity of goods, rationing, and price controls prevailed and then it continued for some time. Greenbelt was fortunate in being supplied through its own stores with a management fiercely devoted to fairness -- avoiding hoarding, black marketing, price gouging, and favoritism.

By means of advertising and news stories in the town's weekly newspaper, the Co-op's house organ, and signs in the stores, General Manager Ashelman and the store managers announced when shipments of scarce products were expected, which items were overpriced, and possible substitutes.

When President Truman called upon Americans to consume 40 percent less wheat and 20 percent less fats and oils in order to increase shipments to starvation areas abroad, GCS leaders helped organize a local campaign to reduce purchases of these products.

As soon as the Office of Price Administration lifted ceiling limitations in July 1946, there were immediate price increases on products in short supply, especially those in most demand such as beef, butter, sugar, canned milk, orange juice, and soap. Tom Okazaki, food store manager, announced that the Cooperative would limit its price increases to only the markup which had been permitted earlier under OPA regulations or less. This would reduce the Cooperative's gross margin, but this pricing policy would be followed for as long as possible. He noted that wholesale prices were rising erratically, and said that GCS would simply not purchase items that were grossly out of line.

The food store advertisement in the July 19, 1946 GREENBELT COOPERATOR stated:

"A cooperative is in business for service, not to 'make money' out of its customers....The termination of OPA has resulted in general confusion in the business world....Consumers are just beginning to feel the real effect of increases. G.C.S. dislikes seeing price increases and has consistently worked for price controls....Our present policy is to...temporarily refuse to stock items unreasonably high in relations to other items, hoping prices will come down. If the prices do not come down after a temporary period, we will stock the item. However, we will urge you to buy as little as possible."

The use of loss leaders came up for discussion early in 1946, with some members favoring their use to encourage more shoppers to use the Greenbelt store rather than the chain supermarkets offering loss leaders in Washington and the suburbs. GCS decided against loss leaders as deceptive. Years later, when GCS supermarkets had to compete for customers, loss leaders were used.

Early in 1946, a proposal to raise the admission price at the theater by 5 cents was referred by the Board to the membership meeting -- and was voted down.

By the end of the year, however, the price was raised by necessity, along with the price of haircuts, prices in the beauty shop, and for many other services and products.

There were complaints about price increases in general, including some editorial comments in the GREENBELT COOPERATOR during the editorship of Eleanor Ritchie and later.

Some of the complaints about high prices in Greenbelt resulted from a Maryland law which set a floor under the prices of many products sold in drug stores and variety stores. This was called the "fair trade" law by manufacturers who enjoyed the profits guaranteed by the law. The District of Columbia had no such law, so prices could be slashed on high margin products, much to the satisfaction and benefit of shoppers there. Years later, when GCS operated a number of drug stores, it succeeded after a long and bitter battle in persuading the State legislature to abolish the so-called "fair trade" law.

Another difference of opinion that led to much bitter feeling stemmed from the Government's handling of the town. "Tugwell town" as envisioned and created by the planners in the Resettlement Administration was centered around people and community -- a better environment for a better life. The Federal Public Housing Authority, which inherited Greenbelt in August 1945, looked upon the town as just another housing project: rents to be collected, minimum maintenance, a piece of real estate that could be juggled about until the Government could get rid of it.

There was much to feed a sense of unease among residents:

-- A rumor that the Government was considering sale of Greenbelt prompted the Citizens Association to ask the Town Council to appoint a committee to study options for residents in the event of a sale. The Town Council turned aside the   suggestion, with comments that it would be too expensive, would probably be stacked in favor of mutual housing, and that anyway the Council was perfectly capable of making its own study if one were needed.

-- Repainting, repairs and staffing for the town's heating system, financial support for a recreational building (primarily for young people), library improvements, approval of the Cooperative's application for a land lease and permit to build its long-planned new store building -- all these and more had been on hold at the FPHA field office. And then the budget for the town, which had been held up for 2 months, revealed deep cuts when it was released.

-- Residents learned from a story in the WASHINGTON POST that FPHA was about to fire the project manager, James Gobbel, who was also town manager hired by the Town Council. The charge seemed to be his unwillingness to carry out the unrealistic   budget cuts set by FPHA and too much identification with the welfare of the community.

-- Sudden discovery that FPHA had already approved for the Public Roads Administration the right-of-way for the Baltimore /Washington Parkway which would be only 100 feet from Greenbelt houses -- without consultation of any kind with the residents of the town. And at the same time, discovery that FPHA had traded Greenbelt land just across the new highway for a major enlargement to Schrom airport so that it could be used for freight -- again without inquiry of any kind as to its effect on the 1,500 families in the town.

All of these developments had crucial impact on GCS as its 10-year lease on the buildings in the shopping center was due for reconsideration in 1947. The future of the Cooperative was tied to the future of the town.

Leaders and many members of the community's cooperative organizations were interested in some kind of mutual or cooperative ownership of their homes. This would be practical because Greenbelt was made up of row houses [read: town houses in today's terminology] with centralized heating and electric service (no separate furnaces or meters).

Just about all Greenbelt families wanted to stay in their homes when the time came for the Government to dispose of the project. But some saw the sale of the buildings and land as an attractive opportunity to profit in real estate. Many others simply wanted to own their own home free of possible entanglements which they feared in any kind of joint arrangement. A majority of the town councilmen made it quite clear that they opposed mutual housing. Some of the opposition came from the same individuals who had formed the Committee of American Voters nearly a year earlier.

Sherrod East, former director on the GCS Board and former mayor, voiced the complaints and apprehensions of many residents when he wrote a long letter to the editor of the GREENBELT COOPERATOR for the February 22, 1946 issue. He reviewed steps which had led to the threatened dismissal of Manager Gobbel, and criticized the Town Council for foot dragging in facing the ineptness of the FPHA field office.

East made it clear that "whatever is done for Greenbelt has to be based on the particular needs of the community". His stand on the responsibility of the Town Council to face up to FPHA and to let the families of Greenbelt know what was going on, and his support for exploring the possibilities of mutual housing was not an isolated one. David Granahan, president of the Citizens Association, pleaded for unity on the vital issues facing Greenbelt and for "what is best for the whole town". Harry Rhodes, former director of public works in Greenbelt, stated that "people in town believe that the council is giving the people the runaround".

All of the concerns which kept Greenbelt families and their leaders upset were resolved one way or another in the months which followed.

Manager Gobbel left the Government job and FPHA named a replacement. The Town Council was able to pay him some increase in salary which enabled him to continue employment by the town.

FPHA did approve the budget after a 2-month delay. Spokesman for the agency admitted FPHA "was not as well qualified as the council" to determine how funds were to be spent" and hoped "it would all be straightened out next year". Some staff and services were cut, but adjustments were made and the community survived.

Strong protests about the location of the highway led to a realignment that gave 400 feet clearance from the nearest home.

The expansion of Schrom airfield to handle freight on a commercial basis never developed. When the Greenbelt land was sold by the Government the airstrip location was bought for development of a regional shopping center.

On March 28, 1946 the Town Council sat down with the executive committee of the Citizens Association and that body's housing committee to have a look at what could be done to assure the best protection for families who wanted to continue living in Greenbelt following the anticipated sale of the town.

The GREENBELT COOPERATOR reported:

"This meeting was strongly urged at the last Council session by citizens who recommended that the Council take action on the report submitted by the Citizens Association some months ago.

"The Housing Committee was elected at a special public meeting ...last August to consider ways of protecting the interests of residents at the time of the sale of Greenbelt 'scare'. The committee, which investigated the possibilities of mutual housing or other local ownership plans, consists of Thomas Ritchie, chairman; Sherrod East, Cyrilla O'Connor, Ruth Taylor, Merton Trast, Don Cooper and Bob Volckhausen.

"A comprehensive, six-page report was...submitted to the Council on November 12....covered an analysis of the various possibilities for disposal of Greenbelt, the possible effects of each on the community, and an opinion that group control (mutual-local ownership) appeared to offer the greatest protection...."

More than 300 residents attended a public meeting on July 15, 1946 sponsored by the Citizens Association and the Greenbelt Chapter of the American Veterans Committee. They voted to form a Greenbelt Mutual Housing Association and negotiate with the Government for purchase of Greenbelt.

Within a few months, more than a third of the households in Greenbelt had joined the new organization. Today Greenbelt Homes, Inc. is the highly respected mutual housing organization that owns and manages a beautifully maintained community that is still proud of its cooperatives. Leaders from the ranks of GCS helped build Greenbelt Homes and still serve in the leadership of that mutual housing enterprise. Success of the housing venture protected the future growth of Greenbelt Consumer Services, Inc.

Another critical problem came to solution finally, when FPHA signed a lease with GCS for the long-planned new supermarket building in the shopping center. The signing was on November 15, 1946, exactly 364 days after the Cooperative had sent in its application.

Meanwhile, FPHA renewed the GCS lease on the rest of the shopping center after considerable delay. Just before the lease was signed the issue of the Cooperative vs. private profit-making businesses came to a head. The lead article in the September 13 issue of the community newspaper tells the story succinctly:

"In a surprise announcement at Monday's Town Council meeting, Charles M. McCormack, FPHA manager, stated that a commercial bank will be located in Greenbelt in the near future, pending permission from the State Banking Commission.

"The COOPERATOR learned Tuesday that the Prince Georges Bank & Trust Company has applied to the Commission to open a branch in Greenbelt....

"Most surprised, particularly at the speed with which arrangements were made, was Councilman Allen D. Morrison who informed those present Monday that he and eight other residents had been working for nearly a year to organize a bank. This group, Mr. Morrison said, could raise $30,000 overnight, and were on the verge of applying to FPHA for permission to operate in Greenbelt...(but) had held off in the thought that Greenbelt Consumer Services might want to go into the banking business....

"GCS President Dayton Hull informed the COOPERATOR that FPHA has not formally notified them that a bank is being considered for Greenbelt. Such notification is required by the lease between GCS and FPHA, Mr. Hull said."

In a flurry of activity, the Greenbelt Credit Union was asked if it had an interest in opening a bank. GCS inquired of the Banking Commission about requirements for starting a bank, and was informed that although the legal minimum for such an enterprise was $30,000, the Commission would require GCS to have $200,000. GCS, looking at all the potential barriers, declared its lack of intention to go into the banking business.

On April 7, 1947 Prince Georges Bank & Trust opened its Greenbelt branch in space which the Town Council had used for its meetings.
In this way private profit-making enterprise came to Greenbelt.

Much later, Twin Pines Savings & Loan organized with a local ownership and served the town well.

Three weeks after the September 13, 1946 bank announcement, the long smoldering opposition to the Cooperative burst into the open with a Town Council resolution asking FPHA to open Greenbelt to "private enterprise".

Mayor Bauer made the proposal. Councilman Morrison opposed it, saying "nothing good can be accomplished by dissension and stirring up controversies". Town Manager Gobbel expressed the same sentiment. But the resolution passed, stating: "...that as the official body of the town, we believe that the best interests of the Town and of all the residents, would be better served by the introduction of private enterprise, in the Town, to furnish additional stores and also competition to the present cooperative monopoly, and...that the proper authorities of the FPHA be advised of this action...."

Two weeks later the local newspaper headline on the lead story read: "Co-op Stores Held To Half Mile Radius Of Center By New Lease With FPHA." That would seem to have put an end to the unhappiness about the Cooperative monopoly in Greenbelt.

With the renewed lease in hand, including land in the shopping center for the new building, the Cooperative launched another drive for sale of stock shares to raise $200,000 in capital. Dr. James McCarl headed the committee for this successful drive. The initial effort brought in $33,355 in new shares to be added to $26,000 from the previous drive. There were further delays though before construction got underway. In April 1947, consideration was still being given to using available capital for a second shopping center in the north end of town, but nothing came of this much discussed proposal. The new store in the shopping center finally opened November 10, 1948. A surprise problem was dropped in the laps of the general manager and the directors when the Wage Stabilization Board cited GCS for 69 violations in the period prior to Ashelman's acceptance of the general manager position in December 1944. These were unauthorized increases in pay for various employees. Legal penalties could have been as high as $50,000, but Ashelman was able to negotiate the fines down to a total of $1,500, on the basis that the Board at that time was unaware of the violations and the general manager who approved the raises was no longer employed by GCS.

Other happenings at the end of 1946 vied for attention. The GCS Board had joined sponsorship of the experimental cooperative FM radio station in Washington, WCFM. This was a project originating with the Potomac Cooperative Federation (PCF). Volckhausen had by this time been named to head PCF, a move which further displeased those Greenbelters who had decided they did not like anything associated with Volckhausen.

General Manager Ashelman, with Board approval, added a new service to the Cooperative's offerings. Radio and appliance repairs, a one-man service which required no capital investment, proved useful for a while.

Another innovation was a limited stock of shoes for sale in the valet shop. Handling mostly children's shoes, this was designed more as a convenience for local mothers than as a money maker.

When Fruchtman's contract to manage the movie theater expired, he did not renew it, but went into the film booking business in Washington. He continued for a time to assist his replacement at the Greenbelt theater, who was not familiar with the booking system. As 1947 began, management and the Board once more went to the membership for approval of an increase in movie admission prices. The membership voted down the request, but at a later meeting acknowledged the need for an increase on learning the weekly operating loss figure.

A lesson emerged for cooperative boards and managers: If you are going to turn to the membership for decisions, be sure to provide them with enough understandable information so they can know what they are doing.

In August 1946, GCS had 2,000 members, and members' equity in stock shares topped $100,000. At this point the Board earmarked $10,000 as a revolving fund for stock repurchase on request. This ended the cumbersome voting by the Board on each individual request. Because so many members retained their shares and requested more after moving from Greenbelt, the Board resolved to file with the Securities and Exchange Commission for out-of-state sale of shares. Continuing dividends of 5 percent on stock was an encouragement for purchase of shares.

At the end of the year (December 31, 1946), the balance sheet contained these figures:

Assets

Current Assets	$208,852
Cash on hand and in banks	$87,632
Note receivable (E.C.Inc.)	17,190
Accounts receivable	1,759
Investments	19,286
U.S. bond	1,000
Other cooperatives	18,011
Fixed assets	33,369
Deferred assets	7,777
Total assets	$268,485

Liabilities and Capital

Current liabilities	$ 62,328
Capital:	
Capital stock outstanding	$138,980
Reserves	28,918
Net margin (for dividend, taxes, patronage refund)	$ 38,259
Total capital	$206,157
Total liabilities and capital	$268,485

These were the key figures from the operating statement:

Sales	$1,428,586	100.0%
Gross margin	378,700	26.5
Salaries	181,031	12.7
Administration expenses	38,775	2.7
Operating margin	29,461	2.1
Net income	38,259	2.7

The patronage refund was 2.5% on purchases during 1945.

Every co-op leader who has any gray hair remembers the onslaught of the misnamed National Tax Equality Association. Over the years this organization insisted in leaflets, press releases, and speeches that cooperatives do not pay taxes and are therefore unfair to the American way of doing business. Their campaign caught up with Greenbelt Consumer Services as the year 1947 got underway.

The Greenbelt co-op drug store was a member in good standing of the Maryland Pharmaceutical Association, which published a trade journal. Drug Store Manager Si Pearson was surprised to read in THE PHARMACIST an article labeling co-ops a "vastly growing menace", and warning that "these Co-operative retail stores have invaded Maryland....They operate without the payment of taxes and their profits are not subject to an income tax. Moreover,

they enjoy the privilege of borrowing money from the U.S. government
....The question of the continuation of retail cooperatives will likely be
something for our new Congress to consider. Know your representatives in
Congress and make known your sentiments."

General Manager Ashelman, familiar with this sort of dis-information, wrote
to the editor. He noted that one of the Association's members was a
cooperative, incorporated under Maryland's General Business Act, and that it
paid all types of taxes the same as any other drug store, including state and
federal income taxes. He pointed out as a further correction to the article that
although GCS had never borrowed money from the Government, it did have
the same right as any other private business to borrow from the
Reconstruction Finance Corporation.

But the "co-ops don't pay taxes" attacks did not stop there. Two months later
the GCS board was startled to find the Maryland Senate in Annapolis was
about to vote on a bill to impose a tax on the patronage refunds of
cooperatives. Apparently no one ever informed the State Finance Committee
of the Maryland Senate that the Supreme Court had long ago determined that
refunds to patrons on their purchases during the year were not profits, and
therefore not taxable as profits.

A sufficient number of GCS members, along with members of other
cooperatives in the State, telephoned and wrote to key Senators to kill the
measure. With this step the Greenbelt Cooperative leaders tested the political
waters they were to become familiar with as the subsequent years churned up
more legislative tests.

GCS had worked with the farm marketing cooperatives on the tax bill in
Annapolis. Before the month was out, they were adding their strength
through the Potomac Cooperative Federation to a petition by the Cooperative
League of the USA, asking the Federal Trade Commission to question Fulton
Lewis, Jr. about his radio broadcast attacks on cooperatives.

During the spring of 1947, the Maryland legislature considered a state sales tax
of 2 percent. In defense of consumers' pocketbooks, GCS opposed this
measure, in company with consumer organizations and with other retail
businesses. On this issue GCS lost. But members, leaders, and management
continued pressure on other matters of concern to consumers. It had been a
learning experience about the extent to which consumers could influence
legislation.

There were the twin concerns of rising prices and shortages of supply. During
1946-47, prices of meats and especially beef reached such out-of-line
proportions that the Greenbelt Cooperative enlisted in an unrewarding
boycott. Signs at the meat counter in the food store advised customers which

items were not available due to excessive slaughterhouse and wholesale prices, which items were available but not recommended due to high retail price, and suggested substitutes. Shoppers who supported the effort were rewarded with feelings of righteousness, and there was a Congressional investigation of monopoly in the meat supply industry, but prices did not ease off until there was an ample supply moving from farms and ranches to markets.

Some direct control over prices of individual products and services by the Board or the membership had appeal in a cooperative where the consumer is the boss, but management found this increasingly burdensome. At the lunch counter in the drug store members clamored for the continuation of coffee at 5 cents a cup even when the general manager pointed out that the actual cost was 7 cents a cup and that most other lunch counters were charging 10 cents, or 5 cents if ordered with a meal. It was only when 5 cent coffee was shown to lower the patronage refund that pressure eased.

Giving full control over pricing to management was a slow and painful transition.

Management, Board, and membership were showing more maturity as they approached the end of 1946. More and more visitors were coming to Greenbelt to observe how this cooperative was serving its members. Food Store Manager Tom Okazaki, returning from the annual Co-op Institute at Amherst, N.Y., reported that "Greenbelt is considered by others as the utopia of co-ops."

While GCS had taken stands on political issues and had teamed up with other cooperatives, including those in farm marketing, the leadership was finding some difficulty adjusting to expectations in three areas.

When a local rescue squad formed and asked the Cooperative's Board for a $900 donation, the tentative response was to explain that consumer cooperatives did not have "profits" from which discretionary expenditures could be made -- any margins belonged to the members and neither Board nor management could approve donations. This response was not satisfactory to supporters of the rescue squad, and this incident added to the pressure to bring competitive businesses into town. It took a long while to find a workable solution to the problem of requests for donations.

Another issue cropped up when someone representing striking cafeteria workers in Washington asked to put signs and a container for donations in the food store. The manager and Board agreed not to do so because: (a) the store was critically overcrowded since it had been built for fewer than half the current number of customers, and (b) there were many requests of this sort and where should the line be drawn. The result was an attack on the

Cooperative as being not in support of unions. The Cooperative's leaders insisted that they "were so" in favor of unions. Some years later, GCS was the first supermarket chain in the Washington area to sign a union contract. Yet, in the end, it was a long and bitter strike against the Cooperative's SCAN furniture stores that was a factor in bringing the membership organization into bankruptcy court. Much of the fuzziness about the Greenbelt Cooperative's stand reflected the divided opinions of the large membership about what the relationship with union labor should be.

On another divisive issue, race relations, the Greenbelt Cooperative took a more consistent stand over the years. But in this, too, the membership was obviously divided in the early period when no blacks were accepted for occupancy in the Government housing project.

At one point the Potomac Cooperative Federation endorsed the report against segregation submitted by the Committee on Social Relations of the Council of Social Agencies in Washington. The Rochdale Cooperative in Washington agreed to send letters supporting the endorsement to the newspapers. The question of what follow-up GCS would take then landed on the Board's lap, and the response was realistic for the time and place but less than candid.

In a long editorial which may have been ahead of its time (remember this was 1947), the GREENBELT COOPERATOR commented in part:

"...A spokesman...insists that a majority of the members...would not, if polled, endorse active participation in such a campaign .... But every suspicion that a majority of our members do not believe in racial equality and the necessity for the removal of segregation barriers shows the need for an immediate, well planned and long-range program of education and discussion within our co-op.

"As our cooperatives grow we will inevitably be faced more and more with the problems of our attitude toward a great many questions which vitally affect not only our economic but our political life....our cooperative is not fulfilling all of its
functions if adequate provision for such discussion is not made."

In later years, the Greenbelt Cooperative more than made clear its stand against segregation and for racial equality, as we shall see in another chapter.

V. FIGHTING FOR SURVIVAL (1947-1949)

On the national scene, the National Tax Equality Association continued to attack cooperatives with leaflets, canned articles supplied free to magazines and newspapers, speakers, and radio time -- especially Fulton Lewis, Jr. On the local scene, the Greenbelt Improvement Association continued to criticize Greenbelt Consumer Services and call for competition by opening the town to "private enterprise". During 1947 and much of 1948, the struggle between those who wanted the cooperatives in Greenbelt and those who did not want them became bitter and led to several tests of strength.

The awareness that the Federal Government intended to rid itself of the "green towns" low-income housing stirred up in Greenbelt deep anxiety among those who wanted to retain their homes in a cooperative community along the lines laid out originally by Rexford Tugwell in 1937. Leaders among resident families with this kind of vision began moving toward mutual housing as a solution for the day when Greenbelt would be sold.

But there were others, a minority as it turned out, who saw in the sale of the Greenbelt land and houses and shopping center a chance to make money, possibly a lot of money. Some of these lived in the town and there were others who lived elsewhere but hoped to use connections which would enable them to dip their spoons into the honeypot.

Although GCS had signed a lease for 10 more years on store space in the shopping center, its future could be jeopardized if developers interested solely in maximum profits acquired the town. Cooperative-minded leaders in the community feared high rents and an exodus of many families who had shaped the character of the town's institutions. It was understandable, then, that GCS leadership supported and worked closely with the emerging Greenbelt Mutual Housing Association.

At this time, the majority of the five-member Town Council for most of its 2-year term showed a distaste for GCS, the mutual housing proposals, and most other cooperative organizations in the community. As a consequence there were sharply divided opinions in the community about the Town Council. Grievances other than the stand on cooperatives also contributed to controversy about the Town Council.

In May 1947, Mayor George Bauer and Councilman John Cain asked for the resignation of Town Manager James T. Gobbel. Councilman Allen Morrison supported the town manager, claiming that the resignation move was "a pre-election attempt at a show of power." It did not appear that GCS was involved in this dispute, but when 400 residents showed up for the next Town Council meeting a week later, there were spokesmen for the cooperatives as well as for other community organizations. General Manager Ashelman and Benjamin Rosenzweig represented GCS in asking the Council "to forget its differences at this time, and of citizens working with the Council to preserve a united front, in view of the uncertain future facing Greenbelt."

The move to oust the town manager was put on hold until after the approaching election, but those residents who showed concern divided into the same groupings that by then had become a recognizable pattern. It was pro-cooperative and anti-cooperative although other issues and personality differences tended to obscure this underlying contention.

Two weeks before the Town Council election, the GREENBELT COOPERATOR listed four issues:

"1. Sale of Greenbelt. The present council has done next to nothing on this problem which affects the life of every Greenbelter, even though the matter was forced on their attention soon after they took office, Two years of wasted time! To take a stand for Mutual Housing is not enough. Find out what your candidates have done to further the cause.

"2. Opening of the town to outside business interests. The present council almost put over a deal to allow a liquor store to open in the center, but were prevented from doing so by an aroused citizenry. The stand of the present council members at the recent hearings involving Greenbelt Consumer Services was given wide publicity...read what each said and did. Find out what the other candidates have done for or against GCS.

"3. Zoning....

"4. Budget problems...."

From 1,627 families with adults qualified to vote, 1,604 individuals registered. A group of registered voters organized themselves as the Committee for Better Government and after questioning all 20 candidates, picked eight as the best possible choices for the five positions.

In response to key questions, these eight "strongly supported the disposal of Greenbelt to a mutual housing association, the protection of Greenbelt Consumer Services in its plan for expansion of retail services in the center, quick enactment of zoning regulations that would preserve Greenbelt's beauty as it expanded, and adjustment of the budget to permit improvement and enlargement of the services given the residents by the town".

Countering the recommendations of this group, the Greenbelt Improvement Association drew up a slate of five candidates, headed by the incumbent mayor. First point on this slate's platform: "Introduction of private enterprise into the town to offer fair competition to the present exclusive cooperative set-up".

In the 4 weeks of campaigning before the vote, 41 leaflets and circulars were distributed door-to-door. Six of these contained attacks on GCS.

When the votes were counted, the winners were from among those candidates who had expressed support for the Cooperative. The slate of the "Improvement" group which had expressed dissatisfaction with GCS was defeated. Following the election, the Greenbelt Improvement Association met and declared it would continue to be active and "dedicated to furthering the interest of the town as a whole". About 75 residents attended this meeting.

While Greenbelt was voting in an election crucial to the future of the Cooperative, another even more serious threat was unfolding.

The Washington newspapers on August 18, 1947 carried the news that Greenbelt Consumer Services, Inc. was the subject of an investigation by the Small Business Committee of the U.S. House of Representatives.

Chairman of the Committee (actually a subcommittee) was Representative Walter C. Ploesner (R., Mo.). The other members were Representative R. Walter Rielman (R., N.Y.) and Representative Wright Patman (D., Texas). The Committee's press release stated its purpose was "to ascertain whether, and to what extent, tax-exempt privileges of cooperatives are harmful to free competitive enterprise". Although the investigation was reportedly aimed at farm marketing cooperatives, Committee Chairman Ploesner picked Greenbelt Consumer Services, Inc. as first target.

One statement in the Committee's press release contended that the mayor and Town Council in Greenbelt had called on the Federal Public Housing Authority to cancel the GCS lease at the shopping center. This was immediately denied by Councilmen Allen D. Morrison, Paul Dunbar, and Joseph L. Rogers, constituting a majority of the Council. This suggested the probability that Mayor Bauer and Councilman Cain had been in touch with Committee Chairman Ploeser prior to the issuance of the press release.

GCS issued its own press release, pointing out that it enjoyed no tax exemption whatever and that it did not have the exclusive contract for business in Greenbelt.

In an editorial, the GREENBELT COOPERATOR said:

"The committee seems perturbed by the possibility of a "tie-up" between [this newspaper] and Greenbelt Consumer Services....[we are] as you can read on our masthead, an independent newspaper. Greenbelt Cooperative Publishing Association, which publishes it, is a separate and distinct organization, incorporated under the laws of the District of Columbia, with its own by-laws, officers, and membership, having nothing whatever to do with the set-up of GCS. Our sole connection with GCS, therefore, is that of advertiser and publisher."

This declaration was true; but this may be an appropriate point at which to remark that from the first days of the Greenbelt community there was an obvious and considerable overlapping of leadership in the many organizations. An observer recognizing the same names appearing at various times in the masthead of the GREENBELT COOPERATOR and on the boards and committees of the Health Association, GCS, Mutual Housing Association, Credit Union, Cooperative Nursery, and Citizens Association could well assume some connection.

In the hearing before the Congressional subcommittee, the president of the Maryland Economic Council testified that "in every community in Maryland where I have visited...the leading merchants and businessmen express fear and concern over the threatened or existing competition from cooperatives".

A former employee of the old Resettlement Administration testified that there had been complaints from businessmen who wanted to come into Greenbelt that they "were given the runaround".

Mayor Bauer testified that "the people of Greenbelt never had any choice in the matter" of deciding whether the cooperative or "private business" should run the stores. He said he felt the best interests of the town would be served by the introduction of "private business". A letter signed by Councilmen Morrison, Dunbar, and Rogers was introduced a little later which stated that Bauer was not authorized to speak for the Council.

Five other Greenbelt residents spoke in favor of having other businesses in the town. Thomas B. Ricker, former general manager of GCS who had been replaced after disagreement with the Board about time spent on his private business in Cedar Point testified that he would like to see private businesses in Greenbelt. Jack Fruchtman, former manager of the theater, spoke along the same line, saying he would like to operate the theater there. Ricker also complained that the Board interfered while he was general manager.

Allen A. Bryan, a former treasurer on the GCS Board, complained about inability to get information about the Cooperative's finances, and that a letter about this which he wrote to the newspaper was not printed.

Residents who testified for the Cooperative included Town Manager Gobbel,

Councilman Morrison, GCS Secretary Frank Lastner, Greenbelt Mutual Housing Association President Sherrod East, and several others.

General Manager Ashelman was the last witness called to testify. He corrected misinformation and misunderstandings in some of the earlier proceedings, and charged that the Committee's counsel had refused to supply a list of witnesses to be called and to present a bill of complaint.

He explained that GCS:

"...enjoys no tax exemptions, cannot borrow from the bank for (farmer) cooperatives, is not exempt from S.E.C. regulations, has no special privileges under the anti-trust laws, and in general appears not to be involved in any of the things which this Committee states that it is investigating.

"A series of persons, some with personal axes to grind, have been given an opportunity to air their views, to endeavor to discredit the cooperatives, and in some cases to give their explanation for the fact that they no longer hold positions they once held in the Cooperative....When all is said and done, however, it is evident that the Greenbelt Cooperative is itself a small business, struggling to do a good job in the face of problems that face all small businesses today....We think the Committee could undertake no more useful nor more daring project than an attack upon monopoly -- but we must confess that we are amazed to find the Committee's brave sword turned first in our direction."

The article reporting the hearing in the WASHINGTON POST noted that as Ashelman was presenting his answers to Committee witnesses' accusations, the Subcommittee's decision was already typed. The newspaper report also spoke of the applause given Carnie Harper when she described GCS Board meetings and the policy of moving to a larger room if the number of those present crowded the meeting room. This, she pointed out was in contrast to Chairman Ploesner's refusal to move the hearing to a larger room when only a small fraction of those who came as spectators could crowd into the hearing room.

Immediately upon conclusion of the hearing, Chairman Ploesner read a resolution, approved by a 2-1 vote, describing the GCS contract with FPHA as contrary to the purpose and spirit of the anti-trust laws of the United States and urging that the contract be cancelled.

It had been pointed out by an attorney from FPHA during the hearing that the lease's exclusion of competing businesses in the Greenbelt shopping center was no different from countless shopping center lease contract provisions all across the nation. Representative Patman stated that the hearing had not demonstrated that the contract was monopolistic. He said he would oppose the resolution before the full House Small Business Committee, and if it got as far as the Congress he would oppose it there, too. But the resolution never reached Congress. Apparently the investigation simply fizzled out after the Greenbelt hearing. At the end of September, Representative Ploesner is reported to have said to Representative Patman, who had just made a well received speech paying glowing tribute to European co-ops for "keeping the light of free enterprise burning in the face of totalitarianism", "You boys are stealing my thunder. Cooperatives basically are sound, and in a free capitalistic economy they ought to be protected." One wonders if the GCS witnesses at the hearing made a convert? Or what?

The NTEA continued its attacks on cooperatives, but by late fall of 1947 it was under investigation by the Post Office Department for mail fraud. For the Greenbelt Cooperative the tide seemed to have turned. Its severest challengers in Greenbelt had met defeat in the Town Council election. The identity and limited numbers of those who opposed the cooperative idea were now known throughout the town. The threat to GCS (and to the community's other cooperative organizations) at the national level dropped away after the Ploesner hearing. Mutual housing to replace government ownership of the town was well on its way (although many problems lay ahead), and that would seem to assure GCS of a friendly climate in which to develop and offer services.

And, finally, the new store building was underway, at the northeast corner of the shopping center mall.

To raise enough money for escalating building costs, GCS faced a charter change. Because GCS was organized under Maryland's general corporation law, any charter change required approval by two-thirds of all stockholders. This was a near-impossible task with such a large number of members, some of whom had moved out of town. There was no provision for incorporating consumer cooperatives in Maryland until GCS forced the issue in 1979 in the State legislature. Several charter changes were proposed by the Board in 1947. The most pressing would permit GCS to issue up to $1,000,000 in stock, an amount undreamed of when the charter was obtained back in 1937. More than a year was required to gather enough directed proxies for the change. This was eventually approved by the membership. Another change recommended by the Board, to make possible future changes in the charter by a majority vote instead of the two-thirds requirement, failed to win enough votes.

A continuing membership campaign among residents in the war housing at the north end of town achieved gratifying success with John Brown from the GCS staff making personal visits. This campaign was linked to expectations that the new capital raised would make possible a new co-op store that would be located in that part of town. GCS management, with Board approval, negotiated for land. When it became apparent that the new store in the shopping center was the limit of expansion for the immediate future, the Board put its OK on a mobile "Co-op Pantry". This served homemakers profitably for several years, making the rounds in Greenbelt and neighboring Berwyn.

Another innovation that was well received was the sale of prime Christmas trees purchased from a producer cooperative in Nova Scotia. This special feature for the holiday season was continued for many years.

Although a comprehensive price check reported the Cooperative's food store and movie prices lower than those in nearby areas, and despite the auditor's report that GCS financing appeared sound, increasing complaints and problems made life difficult for the Board and management. The complaints came from a small nucleus of stockholders and could be seen as related to the political and personality stresses which dominated community life in Greenbelt during 1947.

The other problems included shoplifting and vandalism which were not limited to the Cooperative's stores. Perhaps these aberrations were no worse in this "model town" than elsewhere, but they were in obvious contrast to the picture of Greenbelt as the model cooperative community which drew praise and visitors from all over the world.

Long-time residents report that the general cooperative spirit of the first years never really returned. Meeting quorums became impossible to achieve. Committees languished as the supply of willing volunteers dwindled. Still, Greenbelt people endured all the controversies and problems. Today this is an unusually beautiful community, with more than the average package of public services and private neighborliness -- and a number of healthy cooperatives.

Returning to the subject of complaints, the most persistent critic was Adelbert C. Long. He began expressing his unhappiness with Boards and management of GCS when he resigned as a director in the summer of 1945. As late as February 1952 he was still writing letters to the editor for publication in the town newspaper:

"In your last issue, [you] suggested, 'It would be interesting to learn Mr. Long's ideas of what constitutes an "honest-to-goodness Co-op".' This, of course, is impossible within the limitations of a letter to the Editor, but I can enlighten briefly on a few points at least.

"An honest-to-goodness Co-op would not risk its members' capital investment by expanding in another community on a basis of a non-quorum vote of only 89 members, mostly employees.

"...would give greater service in Greenbelt and not expand out of town merely to justify the present excessive overhead.

"...would change its By-Laws to keep the employees from outvoting the members -- there are considerably more employees than the number required for a quorum, and we rarely have a quorum at a meeting.

"...would have a decent personnel policy -- not the kind where employees are fired without notice and in such a despicable manner as to eventually bring about a law suit.

"...would not hamper price-checking committees so that the truth can never be published about a comparison of prices.

"...would not attempt to control the newspapers in the community by threatening to withhold paid advertisements when critical items are published in the newspaper. Adelbert C. Long."

"(Ed. Last paragraph deleted due to space limitations.)"

Neither this nor the many earlier charges seriously endangered the survival of the Cooperative, but they did make some people ask, "What the hell is going on in that Co-op?" On the one hand, one could say challenges of this sort kept management and the Board on their toes. On the other hand, they spread suspicion and dissension which no amount of explanation could eliminate.

One of Long's earlier letters gave figures to show how a much larger patronage refund could be paid. When correct audited figures were published the following week by General Manager Ashelman, noting that Long's had no relation to the actual statistics from the auditor's report, the newspaper suggested editorially that Long or anyone else using GCS financial and operating statistics should go to the office and look at the quarterly statements and the auditor's detailed report, for correct figures which were available to any member.

GCS was not the only cooperative organization that had to cope with Long's opinions and actions. In March 1950, Long and four other persons formed a new organization to compete with the Greenbelt Veterans Housing Corporation to purchase Greenbelt. The GVHC was a cooperative-minded outgrowth of the Greenbelt Mutual Housing Association, with a membership comprising more than half of the community's families. This surprise came at a crucial point in the 4-year negotiations which GVHC (and its GMHA forerunner earlier) had conducted with the Public Housing Authority. For a time Long's new enterprise was confusing to PHA and to Greenbelt residents.

The upstart group's effort went nowhere, but threatened the success of mutual housing's claim that it represented Greenbelt.

"Six against 1300" is what the GREENBELT COOPERATOR called the new entry to purchase the town. The paper's editorial called upon Long's group "to consider the interests of Greenbelt ahead of their own", and referred to them as "six malcontents... contending for the role of purchaser."

Other complaints during these years questioned whether GCS was giving enough hiring preference to veterans; advised that local residents should be given preference over "outsiders" for staff positions; called for reducing funds for education and promotion; urged that GCS withdraw from the Potomac Cooperative Federation, the cooperative FM radio station, and Eastern Cooperative Wholesale; advertise less in the GREENBELT COOPERATOR; advertise more in the GREENBELT COOPERATOR; have shorter reports at membership meetings; provide more information to members; reduce prices; change store hours; and remain closed on Sundays.

The Board had to respond to a rumor that the dividend on shares would be reduced when the Government sold Greenbelt.

Net margins were down for 1947, $24,597 representing 1.4 percent of sales amounting to $1,726,666. Ashelman noted in his year-end management report that although this was low as a return on sales it was high in the industry (at 13.6 percent) in relation to invested capital. GCS paid the usual 5 percent dividend on shares, but only a 1 percent patronage refund.

In January 1948, Dayton Hull resigned as president after 4 years on the Board. Frank Lastner replaced him, for a second period of service as president.

At about the same time, proposals which had been under consideration for some time for streamlining Board proceedings were adopted. One improvement was the creation of a three-director Executive Committee to handle routine items, prepare agenda for meetings and proposals for presentation, and put motions in writing. The Executive Committee was also instructed to recommend improvements in the committee structure.

Director Benjamin Rosenzweig subsequently brought in proposals for restructuring the committees; for giving orientation to new directors and seminars on such matters as rules of order, understanding financial reports, and fundamentals of cooperation; and for issuing folders to directors to hold minutes of meetings and reports.

With encouragement from the Board and management, food store employees (but not those in the meat department until later) voted to join the National Groceries Retail Clerks, in June 1948. Announcing this at a membership meeting, General Manager Ashelman said: "Management is very happy to work with the union and believes many benefits will result." This was at a time when the grocery chains in the Washington area were non-union.

The long wait for the new Greenbelt co-op supermarket ended on November 9, 1948 with appropriate ceremony and celebration to open the new facility at the northeast edge of the shopping center.

Construction had started in January, but a ground breaking ceremony had been held the previous August. The construction bid had gone to Geo. H. Martin Co. at $425,000, plus $6,900 for drilling a well. The well was completed by the end of the year, and proved its worth not only in eliminating the GCS monthly water bill but by the very successful air-condition cooling of the building from its low temperature and for making ice.

Despite threatened holdup in materials and equipment due to the war in Korea, the building was completed on schedule. About 9,000 came for the opening to admire the new supermarket. It boasted more than double the floor space of the old food store, five checkout counters, an in-store bakery, and the innovation of a self-service meat department -- the first in the Washington area. General Manager Ashelman explained that:

"Fresh meats will be cut continuously by the butchers working behind the sliding glass wall panels, in sight of the customer. These meats will then be packaged and placed in the cases for instant selection without waiting by the customer....butchers can devote their time to meat cutting rather than waiting on the customer, while a consumer aide will be on hand if needed to help patrons make their selections and suggest good buys. Any special cuts will be taken care of by the butcher on duty as requested by the customer."

The Board intended the large basement to be used as a bowling alley for the community, but GCS lacked the money for that at the time, and war shortages made installation impossible until later anyway. So this space was used for economical wholesale warehouse storage.

A series of stock drives had brought in enough capital to provide a solid base for investment in the new building. A mortgage loan of $150,000 came from the Reconstruction Finance Corporation. Financing was completed by two loans, $10,000 from Prince Georges Bank and Trust and $25,000 from Amalgamated Bank of New York.

In addition to the new supermarket, GCS remodeled its auto service station, providing more space and easier operation as well as improved appearance.

Sales for 1948 totaled $1,881,510, with cost of goods sold at 73.6 percent, salaries at 15.5 percent, and expenses at 8.7 percent. Net margin was $42,332, or 2.2

percent of sales. This made possible a patronage return of 1.8 percent on purchases during the year.

Despite the considerable increase in facilities to serve Greenbelt families and the upturn in financial returns, dissatisfactions, criticism, and apathy about GCS persisted.

Rev. Eric Braund, of the Greenbelt Community Church, protested Sunday sales at the new supermarket, calling this "unwarranted invasion of the day which is holy to large numbers of our citizens here and elsewhere." The Board and management agreed on limited hours and a sign urging that Sunday purchases be limited to "emergency needs", but this did not satisfy those individuals who wanted the day set aside exclusively for their own religious convictions.

Mayor Thomas J. Canning proposed an ordinance to ban "sexy" books sold by GCS in the drug store. This led to community-wide controversy about censorship.

Weekly letters to the editor from Adelbert C. Long continued in the town newspaper, criticizing at length nearly all aspects of GCS operations. These were repetitious and each response to his charges simply provoked further "Long" letters, as they came to be called. The allegations came to the Board and management in the form of letters and as resolutions to go before the membership meetings. The Board and management drafted replies. One director, Richard W. Cooper, summed up his impatience with the charges of "mismanagement and improper management policies" by saying, "Please don't ask GCS to undersell Safeway and then pay 10% rebate." The membership meetings defeated Long's proposals -- when there was a quorum present.

After a failed quarterly meeting which drew an attendance of only 22 members, the weekly newspaper advised in an editorial:

"The members are not really interested in trying to have their own business run as efficiently as possible. If they were, there would be adequate turnout for the quarterly meetings, and even for the Board meetings WHICH ANYONE CAN ATTEND. To try to pack into one evening a whole year's report on how a business the size of GCS is run, and why, is just plain damned silly. But if it has to be done that way, make it a business meeting and not a factional or sales meeting."

In September 1949, the paper criticized in an editorial the GCS Board's failure to provide adequate notification of an upcoming meeting -- only 8 days. "Have the powers-that-be in GCS lost their copy of the bylaws, with its provisions for notice of meetings?" However, this had been an exceptional oversight. For most meetings there were mailed notices at least 10 days in advance, newspaper stories, posters, telephone reminders, and sometimes even a sound truck. Noted speakers, vital decisions, entertainment, refreshments, and door prizes failed to attract the hoped-for large attendance that a healthy cooperative is supposed to have. With a few exceptional intervals, poor attendance continued through the years to be a threat to the survival of the Greenbelt Cooperative as a healthy member-controlled organization. Some members reported that what kept them away was the bickering and controversy which marked most meetings.

Board and management of GCS concentrated attention during 1949 on improving store operations. The variety store was moved into the old food store space. The greater space permitted expansion of merchandise lines, made shopping easier, and permitted better control of shoplifting. The pharmacy was then moved into the front of the space where the variety store had been. This made room for expansion of restaurant space in the drug store.

The Board authorized the general manager to negotiate with the Public Housing Authority for the purchase of the land underneath the new supermarket. This finally was achieved.

At the end of March 1949, GCS in combination with co-op stores in Washington, D.C.; Westminster, Maryland; northern Virginia and Hampton, Virginia, opened a warehouse in Baltimore. It operated under Eastern Cooperatives, Inc. as part of its wholesale structure. The facility had 11,000 square feet for storage and a railroad siding. This immediately reduced shipping costs which had been higher from Philadelphia and New York.

Later in the year Greenbelt joined with other area co-ops in a Potomac Cooperative Purchasing Association, to further reduce wholesale costs.

Another joint venture in which the Greenbelt Cooperative had an interest was station WCFM, the cooperative pioneer FM radio station. It had started with inadequate capitalization, as has been the case with most consumer cooperatives. Securing enough advertising to carry operating expenses was a constant worry, and appeals for financial help came repeatedly to the GCS Board. During 1949 WCFM also faced legal problems because the Federal Communications Commission would not accept the cooperative's bylaws provisions. The station finally closed in 1954.

In an unpublished manuscript, "Reminiscences of a Co-operator", Dr. "Pop" Leroy A. Halbert devotes an entire chapter to the turbulent life of WCFM. He quotes Wallace J. Campbell, four times president of the FM enterprise:

"WCFM was the outstanding success among the independent FM stations.

All the others lived partially or wholly on subsidies or vanished from the scene long before our cooperative WCFM gave up the ghost."

By this time GCS was listed as the fourth largest urban cooperative in the United States. The book value of its $10 shares of stock stood at $12.45. Operating margins improved to the point where the Cooperative fell into the 57 percent federal income tax bracket.

Of all its operations, only the bus line and the north end food store continued to lose money. The bus transportation service had operated at a loss every year from its start in 1945, for a total of $8,500 by end of 1949. The Board supported its continuance simply as a public service -- and partly as compensation for its inability to build a new store in the north end of town as it had planned earlier.

In October 1949, Frank Lastner retired from the presidency of GCS after serving in that capacity for just short of 6 years. Replacing him was Walter J. Bierwagen. Bierwagen later became international head of the Transit Workers Union.

When the auditor, Lou Englander, completed his examination of the 1949 operations, he reported to the Board that "this is the finest internal control I have seen anywhere". Inventories were down but sales were up. Gross margins were down but net margins were up. The current ratio had improved to 2.25:1. Net worth had increased.

The sales figure for the year was $2,199,818. Gross margin was $545,547, or 24.8 percent. Salaries were down to 14.2 percent and expenses also were down -- to 7.5 percent. The net margin worked out at 3.1 percent, and there was a 2 percent patronage refund.

The members, Board, management and staff of Greenbelt Consumer Services, Inc. had come through their worst period successfully.

VI. REACHING OUT (1950-1952)

Occupancy turnover in Greenbelt homes had been high all through the town's first decade. The Government had intended this from the start of its Greentowns experiment in housing for low-income families. A house in Greenbelt was seen as temporary assistance until the family income increased to a level which would permit a move to other housing.

Some of the first families did leave Greenbelt as their economic status improved beyond the limitation specified in their leases. There were fewer of these departures after the Farm Security Administration switched to a graduated rent to match increases in income. The more serious exodus came with the wartime dislocations. Military service and war-related jobs scattered families. When the war ended, the population shift continued as people changed jobs or responded to changes in family size or other needs.

It was rare to find a family which moved in dislike of the community. Despite the frenzy of activities and the clash of personalities in community affairs, daily life in Greenbelt was a rewarding experience well regarded by nearly all who lived there.

Those who had moved to other suburbs of the Nation's capital came back to visit friends still living in Greenbelt and to "shop Co-op". The special attractions were the patronage refund, CO-OP label canned and packaged foods, the comfortable "neighborhood store" atmosphere, and the assurance of honest dealing in the supermarket, pharmacy, and garage/service station which out-of-towners came back to use.

Most former Greenbelters kept their shares of GCS stock. It brought a 5 percent dividend every year, and by 1949 each share had a book value higher than its $10 par value. A share could not be turned back for more than the face value, however, in conformity with the cooperative nonprofit principle precluding a speculative share value.

By 1950 the Board and management of GCS began looking beyond the town of Greenbelt. The Co-op Pantry truck served members and other customers in neighboring Berwyn. A small store had been opened by members in nearby Glenn Dale, with servicing out of Greenbelt. General Manager Ashelman was providing management advisory service under contract for the Westminster co-op and a co-op in Hampton, Virginia. Joint purchasing and some shared management services with co-op stores in Washington, D.C. appeared to be beneficial after several years' experience.

At a Board meeting in April 1949, Director George Davidson raised the possibility of working with former Greenbelters who had moved to the Takoma Park area just northeast of Washington, D.C. to open a co-op store on New Hampshire Avenue. Nothing came of this suggestion until March 1950. This time the idea took hold and planning developed quickly -- amidst concern and controversy about where the Cooperative was headed, and what such a reaching out would do to Greenbelt.

The Board called a special membership meeting for April 19. The announcement, in the form of a letter mailed to each shareholder, said in part:

"The most important item which the Board would like to discuss with you is its belief that it would be wise to open a new supermarket in the New Hampshire Avenue area. Many former residents of Greenbelt have purchased homes in the area and are anxious to secure some of the benefits of shopping locally at a cooperative store.

"We believe that several advantages will accrue to all members through the opening of an additional supermarket. It will enable us to buy merchandise more economically. Additional volume will also decrease the administrative expense percentage."

At the meeting, Board Secretary Paul R. Kasko moved and Carolyn Miller seconded adoption of a resolution:

"WHEREAS, It has been shown that business, especially cooperatives, must expand in self-preservation, and
WHEREAS, It has been shown that in establishing a new supermarket in a nearby area, many advantages and savings will accrue to Greenbelt members, and
WHEREAS, The board and management have shown by report to the membership the lines along which such expansion would follow,
THEREFORE BE IT RESOLVED, That the membership of Greenbelt Consumer Services goes on record as supporting the board's plan for expansion."

After many questions and considerable discussion, and defeat of a tabling motion and of a motion for secret ballot, the resolution was approved by a divided vote.

The resolution had referred to "the board's plan for expansion". Actually there was no thought-out plan at this point. The Board simply acted more promptly than usual on the general manager's proposal. All circumstances seemed to point to the advantages for reaching out beyond Greenbelt at this particular time:

--The impending sale of Greenbelt by the Federal Government raised some question about the Cooperative's security and potential for growth in the town.

--The start-up and growth of other consumer cooperatives in the Maryland-D.C.-Virginia area pointed to an opportunity for an entity like GCS with a decade of successful growth to fill a consumer need.

--Administrative and overhead expense for GCS operations in Greenbelt could be lowered if spread across stores in other locations.

--The new cooperative warehouse in Baltimore could provide lower wholesale prices if volume could be increased by more co-op retail stores.

--A larger organization would attract highly qualified employees by offering opportunity for promotion.

--A favorable cash position and the willingness of banks to provide loans now that the GCS credit rating was solid encouraged investment in a larger operation.

--It was apparent that GCS members who had moved out of Greenbelt could provide a nucleus for a store in another locality, although no survey had been made at this time.

Still, the idea of GCS reaching out beyond Greenbelt had not been anticipated. It was received within the community with some shock and a great deal of opposition. The weekly newspaper, the GREENBELT COOPERATOR, immediately raised questions about how expansion would affect service in Greenbelt. There were complaints that if GCS had money for expansion it should be put to use locally, perhaps for recreation facilities.

While the Board agreed unanimously on the desirability of expansion and on Takoma Park as the preferred location, there were varying views within the Board about two questions.

--At what point should a drive for members and stock sales in the new area get underway and what methods should be used? Organizing Greenbelters into a cooperative had been straightforward. The town was small, compact, and had a precise street and homes layout. This made door-to-door canvassing, distribution of leaflets, and meetings easy. A sympathetic weekly newspaper gave necessary publicity freely. And, from the start, there was little choice in local shopping. Besides all that, the population was rather uniform in age and economic level.

Takoma Park had unknown potential at that time. The geographic area was amorphous, without boundaries, and a hodgepodge of random streets, all kinds of homes and commercial establishments mixed in with vacant spaces. Aside from the families who had moved there from Greenbelt, there would be few households with any cooperative experience or even much information about co-ops. One big plus for GCS Board and management was the observation that there was no modern supermarket in the vicinity of the site they were considering.

--How would a store and members 10 miles distant from Greenbelt fit into the existing organization and control pattern of the Cooperative? To what extent should consumer-members in the Takoma Park area have a say about how the new supermarket in their area would be run? And what would their responsibilities and rights be in respect to the Greenbelt stores? Should they be able to elect a director from their local membership to the GCS Board, or just vote along with the Greenbelt members for election of all nine directors? Should Takoma Park members have separate meetings or join in the Greenbelt meetings? And how would patronage refunds be computed -- separate for Greenbelt and Takoma Park operations or for the combined enterprises?

There were no easy answers to these questions because GCS was pioneering a new field of operations. There was no pattern to offer guidance. Consumer co-ops in the United States at this period were single store or at least single location enterprises.

It was Ashelman's view that some adaptation of the structure used by large consumer cooperatives in Europe, and especially in Sweden, could be developed. The aim would be toward an organizational pattern that would encourage patron interest and participation at the local store level, and at the same time gain the advantages of large volume and centralized management.

The Board decided against launching a membership and stock share drive in the Takoma Park neighborhoods until the store neared completion, to avoid the possibility of such a drive losing steam unless the target of shopping in the new supermarket was clearly in view. However, a small committee of interested members who had moved to the new area from Greenbelt organized and began talking with community leaders about GCS plans.

Management and the Board agreed on a site which Kass Realty Co. was developing on the north side of New Hampshire Avenue just west of Ethan Allen Avenue. This was about half a mile northeast of the District of Columbia line.

The Farm Bureau Insurance Co. [now Nationwide] agreed to a loan of $100,000 toward opening costs. On June 1,1950 the Board approved a lease with Kass Realty Co. for the new supermarket. A dinner for community leaders in Takoma Park, attended also by Wallace Campbell and other outstanding leaders in the cooperative movement, marked the ground breaking September 14. The dinner was held in Greenbelt and was followed by a tour of the Greenbelt supermarket.

Toward the end of the year, the Board appointed Director Robert T. Mitchell to be chairman of the promotional campaign in Takoma Park, in anticipation of the opening of the supermarket, which took place August 29, 1951.

The 17 months between April 23, when first public mention of GCS expansion to Takoma Park appeared in the GREENBELT COOPERATOR, and the opening of the new supermarket bristled with controversy. Most of the criticism targeted the Cooperative's reaching out beyond Greenbelt and much of it reflected a parochial point of view by Greenbelt residents devoted to the town's needs. Beyond that, the complaints and charges dealt with prices, service, overhead expense, Board executive sessions, advertising, operating policies, lack of information to members, and personalities.

There were only a handful of protagonists, but they dominated the editorials, letters to the editor, and headlines of the town newspaper week after week. Much of the argumentation was repetitious. Sample quotations in the paragraphs below will give the flavor of the contentions but cannot convey the extent of the damage to the leadership and employees of the Cooperative and to the community as a whole. No longer was the division in Greenbelt between those who favored cooperatives and those who opposed them. Now it was about how a cooperative should be run -- and who should do the running.

The GREENBELT COOPERATOR for October 12, 1950 carried a long letter to the editor which criticized the Board and management for frequent trips and promotional dinners. This came from Bruce Bowman, who had served as an appointed director to fill a Board vacancy back in 1946-47. There was a response in the following edition by Walter Bierwagen, chairman of the Board, "to set the record straight".

Then another Bowman letter to the editor:

"....I do believe in co-ops and co-op expansion....but let's take another look for ourselves: At a co-op with too much management and high administrative costs -- losing money in four out of fourteen operations; so interested in promoting new stores, we fail to educate in Greenbelt; so ready to help other co-ops -- while our personnel problems mount.

"Perhaps the board, like the membership, just hasn't been informed....A board member, when the committees were being organized, indicated that he wanted to be on the executive committee because so much went on of which he was unaware as a board member....A committee made up of two officers, two board members, and, in effect, the manager...invites the widespread charges of management domination or 'clique control'."

And again, a week later:

"...three major shortcomings of our co-op: top-heavy management, our expansion policy, and the executive committee....How much time (whether paid or unpaid) has Mr. Ashelman been away from the office, out-of-town in fact, during the last few years? Since January 1, 1944 (less than 3 years) he has been to Florida, Cape Cod, Nova Scotia, New York, Chicago, Baltimore, Columbus, and Philadelphia. Does our Greenbelt co-op really have such widespread ramifications? Now that we are importing English bikes -- oh, no -- he wouldn't do that!?

"....our top management is top-heavy! What a reason for out-of-Greenbelt expansion with borrowed capital! But apparently this store [Takoma Park] is considered only a beginning. Did you know that last June (I didn't) that you were voting for the first of a series, for an expansion 'policy' that envisions not two or three more stores but as many as (and I quote) 'twelve or fourteen'?

"Is this our choice? That we build stores with borrowed money (and restrictive management clauses, legally questioned) just to keep our wandering boy busy, or must we resign ourselves to the ever-increasing burden of top-heavy management with their 'automatic' annual increments. Perhaps an expansion policy is what we need -- but I think the membership should decide on it, not board and management...."

In this same period, late October 1950, the editor of the GREENBELT COOPERATOR, Harry M. Zubkoff, printed an editorial on responsibility of the membership:

"When does a co-op stop being a co-op? When its members are too lazy to attend meetings or don't give a tinker's damn what happens, and when management 'forgets' to inform membership or fails to consult it on big decisions....policy problems are in the domain of the members. The co-op becomes what the members make it....The responsibility rests equally with the membership, as well as management, to adhere to the cooperative ideals. The duly elected board of directors are the servants of the members ....it's up to the board to encourage activity on the part of the members and to take them into its confidence.

"The board of directors, at last aware that many people are too frightened to express themselves at a large meeting, has planned to set up small discussion groups, in which individual opinions can be aired with more freedom, at the next general membership meeting on November 1....The first step in sharing this mutual responsibility had been taken by the board and management. Will the membership respond by attending and expressing their views?"

The editorial may have had some effect, because attendance was better at that November 1 meeting, although there was still no quorum. Four discussion groups, each with a reporting leader, searched for understanding and recommendations regarding membership participation, merchandising and loss operations, administrative practices, and the theater. The topic of expansion was not discussed. The meeting format had been proposed by a former Board member, Tom Ritchie. It was used thereafter on numerous occasions, with various adaptations, at general membership meetings and also at training conferences and orientation sessions.

In December the newspaper ran an editorial criticizing GCS for increasing admission to the theater 5 cents.

Then, in the issue of February 1, 1951 came an open break between the GREENBELT COOPERATOR and the GCS Board and general manager. Editor Zubkoff asked that a copy of Ashelman's management report to the Board be given to the paper, on a regular basis. Both Ashelman and the Board turned down his request, citing their reasons -- mainly that this was a report to the Board and not to the public, and that the newspaper's reporting should be based on the Board's actions and not on what the general manager, hired by the Board, reports to the Board.

Under the heading,"An Important Decision", Zubkoff said:

"....The issues here are bigger than the mere refusal to make these reports available to the press.

"When the COOPERATOR requested these reports it had in mind 1.) the extreme difficulty involved in reporting meetings at which discussion revolved upon material included in these reports. Even the Board members, on occasion, have found it impossible to carry on an intelligent discussion without first reading the reports. 2.) The many requests and complaints which the COOPERATOR has received from members of GCS (including Board members themselves) about the incomplete reporting of meetings. Our reports, they say, are factually incorrect, incomplete, quote out of context, and give an entirely false picture to the public of what goes on at Board meetings.

"In a genuine effort to clear up these misunderstandings and to enable us to more accurately report these meetings we requested these [management] reports for use as background material....We went to the Board itself with our problem....They completely rejected this opportunity to improve their position with the membership and retreated behind the statement prepared by their executive committee....

"Their action...is indicative of their attitude toward the membership...a fundamental failure on their parts to recognize their primary responsibility to the membership -- to keep the membership informed!...the fact that Board meetings are open to the membership does not constitute free accessibility to information, nor does it relieve the Board of its responsibility to actively provide the membership with information. For the Board to demonstrate such resistance and such resentment when the membership takes more than a passing interest in their activities is astounding...."

The editor seems to have confused the "membership" with the "public" here, but he was putting his finger on a point which continued to plague the Greenbelt Cooperative, and indeed all cooperatives: how much information about plans and operations should go to the members? how much should go to the public?

In the next weeks, the contentions over GCS expansion beyond Greenbelt and how much information about planning should be released to the membership and to the public and when, stumbled into another crisis.

Paul Ashbrook, a popular and successful agent for Farm Bureau insurance and a member of the Cooperative himself, suggested to General Manager Ashelman that GCS lease the entire shopping center at the New Hampshire Avenue location. The conversation, which took place January 19 at a luncheon meeting GCS sponsored for Farm Bureau agents in the area, touched on possible financing for the addition of a cooperative variety/drug store combination and perhaps other shops.

When Ashelman reported the conversation to the Board at its January 26 meeting, he was asked by unanimous vote of the directors to explore the possibility.

Ashelman reported back to the Board February 9 that he had obtained a sampling consumer survey and traffic count within a half-mile radius of the shopping center under construction and found it favorable. He also reported conversations with other businessmen, banks, and GCS store managers. His conclusion was that opening a combination variety/drug store in the same shopping center with the supermarket "offers a good business opportunity; merchandise and personnel can be obtained, the promotional job would be made easier, and advertising costs could be spread." One serious caveat, however, was the timing. Construction was at a stage where a quick decision would be necessary to avoid expensive changes in plumbing and wiring.

The Board authorized President Bierwagen to send a letter on February 12 to all members:

"An opportunity to consolidate and strengthen our Cooperative further, by leasing a combination drug and variety store, has presented itself. The location is in the same shopping center as our Takoma Park supermarket, now under construction. Prompt action is necessary if we are to take advantage of this opportunity.

"With the freeze on new store construction [this was during the Korean war], it may be a matter of years before another good opportunity for expansion develops.

"Because of the need for a prompt decision, we will not be able to wait for the March 7 membership meeting to discuss this with you. Therefore, we have planned a special Board meeting for this Friday night in the Arts and Crafts Room of the Center School at 8 p.m. to which you are cordially invited.

"Your counsel in helping us reach a wise decision will be appreciated."

Detailed information in the form of a memorandum from the general manager to the Board was given to each member attending the meeting. About 30 members attended and most of them asked questions or made comments.

Several Board members and former Board members spoke in favor of the proposed additional variety/drug store in Takoma Park, including Ben Rosenzweig, Sherrod East, Carnie Harper, Bob Mitchell, and Bob Volckhausen. Speaking in opposition to the proposal were Arthur Wetter, Bruce Bowman, George Nihart, and Mike Salzman, among others.

At a Board meeting February 19 to take action, the directors reviewed for 2 hours the views expressed at the previous meeting. President Bierwagen characterized statements of members as being expressions of fear that the proposed expansion would endanger services in Greenbelt. Mrs. Harper said the Board had been criticized as being business conscious rather than co-op conscious. Mrs. Ritchie concluded that what vocal members were expressing was resentment "that the Board was doing something behind their backs" as a result of having only 2 days notice before the special meeting. Henry Walter advised that "we have a responsibility to do what the articles of incorporation and the bylaws direct us to do. We are faced with an obligation and an opportunity. It is up to us to decide whether we are willing to carry the responsibility. If we are wrong, the membership will replace us." In the end, the Board voted 6-3 in support of a lengthy resolution by Mrs. Harper authorizing and instructing the general manager to proceed with negotiations for the variety/drug store in Takoma Park.

In view of Walter's observation about possible replacement of the Board, the annual membership meeting on March 7 was an affirmation of the Board's action. With a quorum present, the members re-elected all six incumbents who were candidates for another term. One of the other three vacancies was filled by Milton Kramer, a member living in Takoma Park. And the members defeated by better than a two to one vote a motion by Mike Salzman which would have directed the Board to rescind its action on the Takoma Park variety/drug store.

Salzman's resolution is reproduced here because it encapsulated the objections to the watershed decision to expand Greenbelt Consumer Services, Inc. beyond the town where it started.

"WHEREAS, the Board of Directors has authorized the further expansion of G.C.S. outside of Greenbelt without membership approval, and WHEREAS, such authorization must remain in the control of the membership, and WHEREAS, such further expansion of G.C.S. outside of Greenbelt can only result in the breaking down of the Cooperative and democratic process of G.C.S., and WHEREAS, the needs and requirements within Greenbelt must be met first, THEREFORE, Be it resolved that the membership of Greenbelt Consumer Services hereby directs the Board of Directors to rescind the recently authorized further expansion, that is, the variety-drug store, outside of Greenbelt."

Before being defeated, the resolution drew lively debate, but little that had not already been said. President Bierwagen stated for the Board:

"In expanding the horizons of this Cooperative, we have not lost sight of our home base. When practical opportunities have presented themselves for improvement of the situation of the Cooperative locally, we have seized these opportunities. It has been the policy of this Board to give primary consideration to the needs of the consumer-members in Greenbelt, and to this end the Board has authorized the expenditure of $31,750 for improvements in the past year (plus making possible the $35,000 bowling alley installation). Over the past 5 years almost a half-million dollars has been spent for improved facilities in Greenbelt."

Robert Bonham said that he supported the supermarket in Takoma Park, but did not believe the GCS management had demonstrated ability to operate successful variety and drug stores. To this the general manager responded by reading off the margins for these two stores for the previous 5 years.

Wallace Campbell and I, speaking as members who did not live in Greenbelt [I had moved to Montgomery County], both recalled that outside help had made the Cooperative possible in Greenbelt, and now asked that those members still enjoying its benefits in Greenbelt help those outside the town have cooperative goods and services.

Decisions at the membership meeting did not bring an end to the controversy. Salzman went to the GREENBELT COOPERATOR with a letter to the editor nearly a full column in length. He criticized the short notice given to the membership by the Board:

"The short notice and dire urgency for a decision is a sham to steam-roller the expansion through without giving the membership an opportunity to express themselves on the subject. I believe that such a decision rightfully belongs to the membership alone.

"....Expansion by GCS outside of Greenbelt cannot in any way be construed as furthering the cooperative movement. True cooperatives must be owned and operated by the local people that use the facilities, otherwise only the profit motive can be ascribed to it."

The March 15 edition of the town newspaper carried "An Open Letter to the GCS Board of Directors" as a two-column front page editorial. It reminded the directors of their grave responsibilities and expressed sympathy for the "personal sacrifices, headaches, heartaches, hard decisions, broken friendships, many sleepless nights" they would have to endure.

Then: "If we do not see eye to eye on certain issues, it is our prerogative, our duty, to make our respective positions clear, just as it is your duty to consider our point of view. If we believe your actions are contrary to the wishes of the membership, we will criticize, and we ask you to accept our criticism in the constructive spirit in which it is meant. You see, we believe that your first and greatest responsibility is to the membership, and that your decisions should reflect the opinions of those members."

Two weeks later the paper carried another two-column front page editorial which ran over into part of two more columns. This one was by the assistant editor, Isadore J. Parker, and bore the title, "Death of a Co-op?" In it, Parker describes in detail -- from his own point of view -- a GCS Board meeting he attended. Sample paragraph: "The [executive] session was supposed to last 15 minutes. After cooling my heels out in the corridor for a half-hour, I wondered how long this bull session was going to last and if Emily Post would approve a member's ejection from a board meeting. Later I accepted a coke, while assorted cherry milk shakes, cokes, and coffee went inside the meeting room."

Two letters to the editor in the following week's edition probably sum up the quite different viewpoints about the paper's reporting on GCS Board meetings.

ONE: "....the type of reporting regarding the meetings of our local clique, which Mr. Parker presented to the reading public by such an appropriate comparison of 'should be' but 'is it' is to my way of thinking just the sort of unbiased reporting the members and interests of the local co-op should be constantly made aware of....Let's have more of your good reporting, Mr. Parker."

TWO: "I must object to the artistic letter written by Isadore Parker and published on the front page of last week's COOPERATOR ...because some very serious charges were implied in an irresponsible manner:

"1. The board holds executive sessions on matters which should be discussed in public.
"2. Bob Volckhausen has an unjustifiably privileged status within the board.
"3. Board members are contemptuous of 'ordinary members'.
"4. The board of directors are a bunch of nincompoops.
"5. GCS does not give proper consideration to Greenbelt residents for positions that open up.

"If such charges are fully justified, they should be stated and backed up....As a reporter, Mr. Parkers' job should have been to probe fully. Instead he concentrated on real or imaginary slights to his person."

The following week brought more fuel for the heated exchange between the paper's editor and the GCS Board and general manager. The editorial, "Cooperatively Speaking", referred to earlier comments about the Board, and said:

"We are seriously disturbed....we have received an unusual amount of comment...almost all was in favor of the editorial. Almost everyone congratulated us for having printed it. Almost everyone asserted that it was an exact reflection of his thoughts. Almost everyone asked us to keep up the good work, to 'lift the iron curtain behind which the board and management seemed to be operating'. Almost everyone expressed appreciation and stressed the necessity for more such editorials. Almost everyone, that is, except the board members and management....

"Board and management should be aware of their responsibility to the membership. It is not enough to merely conduct business as usual while the members worry about it. They deserve the consideration of being told the truth. They should be told of the reasons which prompt controversial actions....we can only conclude that they are substituting caginess and discretion for honesty and fairness....

"We say this now to make it clear. We are opposed to many GCS actions and policies, and we will do everything possible to change them through the proper channels -- by concerted action on the part of a well-informed membership."

General Manager Ashelman made a point-by-point response which was printed in the next issue of the paper.

But the controversy continued, on an entirely new and different subject. An unsigned letter to the editor quoted an unnamed doctor saying he had been charged 95 cents for 12 sulfa tablets at the Co-op pharmacy, that he could have made the purchase at other pharmacies for a lower price, and accused GCS of "gross mismanagement or abysmal profiteering".

Two registered pharmacists from outside Greenbelt replied, demolishing the claim that had been made. One quoted the wholesale price of sulfonamine tablets, pointed out that the prescription charge must include the container, label, salary and overhead, and that an original container of 100 tablets is broken to dispense such a small quantity, and noted that Maryland's so-called "fair trade" law made a lower retail price unlikely. The other wondered how much cheaper than 95 cents a prescription could have been purchased anywhere; and added that he was familiar with the Co-op pharmacy in Greenbelt and that he knew it to be ethical, honest, and dependable.

Ashelman also responded to the "sulfa" letter, saying that he had checked the prescription price at the two nearest chain store pharmacies and found the price there to be $1.05 and $1.10 respectively. That should have ended that particular dust-up, but the next GREENBELT COOPERATOR devoted another two-column front page editorial under the byline of the assistant editor to refuting Ashelman: "...surely an alert consumer can do better than buy at that chain [where Ashelman had checked]. Why take a relatively poor source as a yardstick?" Parker then mentions he interviewed five Greenbelters who agreed that the GCS pharmacy had high prices. "Does Mr. Ashelman think I invented the interviews?" The editorial then shifted to a complaint about service in the Co-op garage.

Ashelman responded to this in the next week's edition:

"...your paper made a number of statements about the garage....that if the writer's suggestions were followed the garage would stop 'skimming the cream' from the community and begin to operate for the benefit of the members. The writer poses as an expert but his statements show a lack of knowledge of the garage business. Most of what he calls facts reflect impressions or personal grievances, but are not facts.

"....We do want complaints and constructive criticism. However, if the only community paper reverberates repeatedly with personal grievances, real or imagined, which could be better handled through the regular channels of the organization, the friendly working relationship between employees and members will be destroyed. Much of the strength of the organization comes from a sense of teamwork...."

By this time the feuding had escalated to the level where GCS began reducing its advertising in the paper, assuming that the continuing criticism was offsetting the benefits of the advertising. A mid-May meeting of the Board took up the growing acrimony as the main agenda item, and invited the GREENBELT COOPERATOR's editor and any other interested persons to attend. Pharmacist Silas Pearson and the garage manager, Edward Burgoon, were present to receive directly complaints about service or price.

The meeting lasted until midnight, without much being accomplished in the rehash of charges. There was agreement, however, to have representatives of GCS and of the paper meet and try to work out differences.

Such a meeting was called informally by Ben Rosenzweig as a public service, and brought together three former editors of the paper in addition to spokesmen for the present staff and the Co-op. Rosenzweig gave the GCS Board a written report on this meeting for discussion at its next session.

The three former editors had said that if they were on the GCS Board they would refuse to advertise in the paper on the basis of the tone of recent attacks. Nevertheless, there was agreement that the paper was of value to the community and should be a good medium for GCS advertising, that the current controversy should be eliminated from the paper -- that the facts did not warrant the harshly critical attitude of the paper, and that if the paper were to discontinue for lack of revenue, the GCS Board and management likely would be blamed.

At the end of May the editor announced that the paper was about to fold. Sam Schwimer wrote a long letter to the editor criticizing GCS for not placing more advertising in the paper. And Lee Fink wrote a letter to the editor urging lead staff members of the paper to run as candidates for the GCS Board themselves if they thought they could do a better job. And at the 1952 annual meeting they did, as we shall see a little farther along in this story.

Meanwhile, GCS did increase its advertising in the paper, and for a little while the newspaper criticism eased off.

Meanwhile, also, other activities were happening within the Cooperative.

Early in the year, a patronage refund of 2.1 percent went to those who turned in their sales slips. Net savings on sales totaling $2,399,316 in 1950 were $74,044 before income taxes and patronage refunds. Gross margin across the board for all operations was 24.5 percent.

It had been a very good year for the Cooperative's operations despite a divided Board, member apathy, controversy about expansion, and anxiety about the future of Greenbelt.

GCS had leased out the basement floor of the supermarket for a bowling alley, as promised. A year and a half later, by the end of 1951, the operator was behind in his payments, and a new lessee had to be found. Board and management took satisfaction, though, in knowing that the Cooperative had provided additional recreation for Greenbelt residents.

The theater, by the way, had become a loss operation due to continuingly poorer attendance as families turned to television. In 1951, the theater closed two nights a week after various attempts to pull operations out of the red. These included showing foreign and art films, which won praise from a small segment but did not improve receipts noticeably.

One of these films, "Bitter Rice", featuring Sophia Loren, created still another controversy in Greenbelt. Fruchtman canceled the scheduled showing in deference to protests by Philip McGonagle, chairman of the Catholic Action Group, who labeled the film "filthy and unmoral" -- although he had not seen it. His view was supported by Rev. Edwin Pieplow, Lutheran church, and Rev. Charles Strausburg, Methodist church. Fruchtman re-scheduled the film after what the local paper called "a storm of protest of censorship".

At one point, the Board seriously considered purchasing land for a recreational camp for members. Nothing came of this, but Bruce Bowman organized a small group of neighbors into a camping cooperative. The members purchased the old press camp which had been part of the Hoover summer White House at the headwaters of the Rapidan River, in Virginia. This recreation co-op continues today.

GCS closed two experimental operations in 1951 -- the traveling pantry and the bus service, both of which had been losing money. The Town Council picked up the bus service as a municipal responsibility.

With extra space as a result of its own building constructed in the shopping center, GCS provided free office quarters for the Greenbelt Credit Union and rented space to Anthony Madden, agent for Farm Bureau Insurance Co. (which later became Nationwide).

One of the more popular innovations during 1950 was Cornell formula bread, baked for the Cooperative at Taneytown, Maryland. This was a highly nutritive loaf using a recipe developed at Cornell University and sold in the

Washington area exclusively by GCS. For a while the Federal Trade Commission tried to block its sale as bread, saying the formula was too rich for that classification. The product, sold under the CO-OP label, was very popular with consumers in Greenbelt and later in the other co-op marketing areas.

During much of 1950 through 1952 food prices were of special concern because price controls by the Office of Price Administration created a squeeze between wholesale and retail prices for many retail food distributors. GCS pledged to hold the line on prices and also took measures to discourage hoarding of goods in short supply. [This was during the Korean war.]

Morris Solomon became active in price checking in 1951 and 1952, publishing the reports of his committee in the town newspaper. GCS management and the Board exhibited mixed feelings about Solomon's activity -- appreciation for his assistance in keeping the Cooperative's prices in line, but distrust of his methodology. Efforts toward cooperation were made from time to time to assure fair and useful results, but there were also differences of opinion about the findings and the way they were reported.

Minutes of Board meetings during the spring of 1951 show some weaknesses. Committees appear to have disintegrated -- there is no indication of an Education Committee reporting over a period of many months. At the Board reorganization meeting following the election at the annual membership meeting, minutes relate at length the explanation of individual directors why they cannot accept the various committee chairman assignments.

A reading of the minutes makes it clear that much of the uncertainty and wavering in discussions and voting resulted from lack of background and knowledge about Greenbelt Consumer Services as an organization and about its operations. The need for orientation of newly elected directors was acknowledged by the Board. Plans were made for tours of the stores, study of each of the operations, and training sessions on what directors need to know.

Some of this had been tried in the past, and orientation for leaders became much more important in the following years as GCS grew in size and complexity. But although leadership development was recognized as a top priority, planning and accomplishment were somewhat sporadic over the years.

Besides orientation provided within GCS itself for employees and for leaders, there was the Cooperative Institute Association. This organization will be referred to later, but it was already functioning in these early years. Supported and controlled by the consumer co-ops in the New England and Mid-Atlantic states, this was a nonprofit, amateur, and loosely organized group of cooperative leaders who offered a week of classes each summer in one of the land-grant colleges.

In April 1951, the GCS Board designated Ben Rosenzweig as this Cooperative's representative on the CIA board.

It had been apparent for some time that GCS needed a promotional and educational employee on the staff. There was division of opinion among the directors as to whether such a position should be created, what the employee's role should be, whether this should be a full-time or part-time job, and whether GCS could afford such an addition to the staff. The Cooperative had such a staff position in earlier years, filled by various individuals, sometimes on the payroll of the Potomac Cooperative Federation and at other times on the GCS payroll. Assistant General Manager Bassett Ferguson, Jr., emphasized to the Board in April 1951:

"We get to the point where we save our money and lose our Cooperative. I think it is a fairly serious situation. GCS is entering a period of expansion, and throughout the country other cooperatives are very much interested and impressed with what Greenbelt is doing, but here in Greenbelt we have very few really active members, so few in fact that we have trouble finding people to serve on a committee. If we don't have interested members we don't have a cooperative. To a certain extent, expenditure for securing member participation is a necessary business expense. I don't think the present trend can be reversed through volunteer efforts alone."

After much discussion and wavering by directors, the Board authorized the position. Shortly after that, Edith Christianson came on the staff and was placed in charge of consumer education at the Takoma Park supermarket when it opened. This was the beginning of her long, warm, and memorable attachment to the Cooperative over many years.

GCS opened its cooperative supermarket on New Hampshire Avenue on August 29, 1951. The opening followed several months of intensive and very successful co-op educational efforts and stock sales to build a membership base in Takoma Park.

The new store offered a 90- by 75-foot selling area, a 93-foot meat counter, automatic photo-electric doors, powered checkout counters, self-service bakery section, murals, and a play area for small children while their mothers shopped.

The Greenbelt paper reported the store opening:

"The grand opening of the brand new co-op in Takoma Park had all the gala earmarks of a Broadway premier, from the well-rehearsed cast of managers and assistants to the eager, expectant crowds.

"On hand were such prominent figures as Representative Fred Marshall of Minnesota, Federal Trade Commissioner John Carson and Mayor Ross Beville of Takoma Park to address the great numbers who had gathered bright and early to witness the show.

"Behind the scenes, Basset Ferguson, assistant general manager of Greenbelt Consumer Services had toiled all night readying the store for the 9 a.m. opening. Harley Mimura, produce manager, started at 6 a.m. stocking the sparkling new counters with dew- fresh vegetables and fruits. George Spillman, manager, and all his assistants, from the checkers to the stock men, were ready to carry through their roles...."

Customer response to the new Co-op supermarket was enthusiastic. The local newspaper called it "the addition of an important community asset". On November 9, the Co-op variety/drug store in the new shopping center at Ethan Allen and New Hampshire Avenues opened.

By year's end, the new pair of facilities were contributing income for GCS. Changes in the Cooperative's operating statement and balance sheet were dramatic. Sales increased almost 30 percent, even though the Takoma Park additions counted for but a short period. Net savings were down, as expected in opening new stores. Here are the comparative figures for 1950 and 1951:

Condensed Income Statement

	1951		1950	
Sales	$3,064,408	100.0%	$2,399,316	100.0%
Gross margin	688,766	77.5	588,725	75.5
Salaries	421,648	13.8	329,338	13.7
Net operating margin	68,173	2.2	73,347	3.1
Store opening expenses	21,359	0.7	-	-
Net savings*	46,814	1.5	74,044	3.1

*(before income tax and patronage refund)

Balance Sheet as of December 31

	1951	1950
Assets		
Current assets	$429,732	$232,709
Cash on hand		
and in banks	$110,927	$ 59,743
Accounts receivable	12,807	12,024
Merchandise inventories	265,646	144,025
Prepaid expenses	15,182	9,464
Investments	17,650	5,598
Fixed assets	506,985	338,386
Equipment (net)	209,281	157,379
Greenbelt market (net)	222,135	228,166
Leasehold improvements (net)	75,569	15,860
Total assets	$945,367	$576,693
Liabilities and Capital		
Current liabilities	$286,791	$102,481
Vouchers payable	$214,778	$ 58,648
Expenses accrued payable	32,331	23,367
Mortgage payable	19,992	19,992
Long term debt	212,740	73,549
Net worth	445,836	400,663
Stock outstanding	329,861	272,435
Reserves	69,341	54,184
Net margin	46,814	74,044
Total liabilities and capital	$945,367	$576,693

The above figures are taken from an attractive 16-page 1951 annual report published by GCS in place of the usual mimeographed year-end report. In addition to the conventional income statement and balance sheet, a page near the front stated in plain wording "What we own", "What we owe", what the expenses were, and the distribution of net savings.

In the report of the general manager, Ashelman wrote:

"Advantages hoped for to the Greenbelt stores as a result of additional volume from the new stores in Takoma Park are now being realized. One of these was the immediate strengthening of our buying position. Suppliers are now willing to grant us more favorable prices on many items we regularly purchase. Another is the reduction of our costs in handling groceries in the Baltimore warehouse of Potomac Cooperators, Inc, of which we are the largest stockholder....expenses dropped 2% below those of a year ago. The savings that resulted were passed on to us.

"In business generally, margins of profit have been reduced, largely by the

Office of Price Stabilization regulations, while at the same time operating expenses have been increasing. Our operating expenses, however, dropped from 21.4% to 20.3%. Total administrative expenses instead of being 3% of total sales as in 1950, dropped to 2.6% in 1951....

"Ten years ago we had only a handful of employees. Today several of these have risen through the ranks to very responsible positions, and in a growing organization there is always room for promotion. Where there is opportunity, your organization can keep and attract better people."

Thus the case for reaching out beyond Greenbelt was justified. The explanation did not satisfy all of the Greenbelters, however. Although Bierwagen, in his "From Your President" section of the annual report, stated that "The Cooperative ended the year 1951 on a high point of success," and talked about "working together", the minutes show that he worked with a badly divided Board and continuing criticism from a vocal segment of the membership.

Dissension and divisiveness increased during 1952.

The several individuals who had been using the weekly newspaper, GREENBELT COOPERATOR, to attack the way the GCS Board and general manager ran the Co-op, decided they could do a better job than the incumbents. Editor Zubkoff ran a long and reasoned editorial in the January 24 edition setting forth a minimum program any candidate for the GCS Board should offer. The next week's paper carried lengthy excerpts from the GCS bylaws regarding responsibilities of directors and the details of election procedures. The February 14 paper gave a nearly full page chart showing how each director voted on selected issues during the previous year, along with absences from Board meetings. The paper also announced the candidacy of Morris Soloman, staff member who headed the price checking committee and published the results regularly in the paper. Sam Schwimer, who had written several letters to the editor critical of the way GCS was operating, announced in a long letter to the editor that he would run for the Board.

At the annual meeting March 5, 1952, there were 14 nominees for the nine Board positions. Editor Zubkoff also ran as a write-in candidate. Three incumbents, including President Bierwagen were returned to the Board, but six positions went to newcomers, including Soloman, Schwimer, and Zubkoff. This was the first time a majority of the Board was changed at a single election, and the result guaranteed another sharply divided Board for the coming year.

This annual meeting, held in the theater and using a format based on results of a lengthy questionnaire earlier in the year, was an improvement over the previous three quarterly membership meetings. Two items of importance were voted: amendments to the bylaws which raised the capital stock limit to $550,000, and changing the beginning of the fiscal year to February 1. David Reznikoff introduced a detailed resolution to have GCS "immediately dispose of all business enterprises which are not located within...Greenbelt...by sale of said business enterprises to a corporation which shall be cooperative in nature and which shall be owned and controlled by residents of the community in which said business enterprises are located...."

Pretty much the same members spoke against raising the limit on sale of capital stock and in favor of restricting GCS to Greenbelt. Reaching out was a "no-no" to some members who simply had no interest beyond their local community. There were others -- and this is important -- who sincerely believed that democracy and effective member control of a cooperative would be lost if the enterprise became too large or spread-out.

Looking back from nearly 40 years later, it seems clear that there were two options for GCS when the members defeated the Reznikoff resolution. One was a federation of locally owned and locally controlled cooperatives, with centralized services for purchasing, accounting, training, promotion, etc. The overall servicing entity could be owned and controlled by the individual retail cooperatives. The other choice was one big cooperative. This was the path taken by GCS.

Each of the two directions offered its own advantages and posed its own dangers. I personally supported the idea of one big Co-op, along with a majority of voting members. Well, Greenbelt Consumer Services, Inc. (later Greenbelt Cooperative, Inc.) grew and lasted for 50 years -- most of them successful years. At this writing in 1990, it is a paper organization with a handful of loyal members in their senior years, and no facilities remaining. And two separate local co-ops, once part of GCS/GCI, are serving members and returning an annual patronage refund.

Westminster, Maryland, has a supermarket and 3,700 members. In its 1990 fiscal year, it had $859,807 in assets, registered $$5,289,571 in sales, and ended up with a net income of $51,620 after paying $21,000 income taxes.

Greenbelt, Maryland, has a supermarket, pharmacy, and service station, with 3,400 members. James Cassels, chairman of the board of Greenbelt Consumers Cooperative, Inc. which replaced the original co-op in that community, reports sales of $6,970,888 for its most recent year, with a net margin of $117,000. Member patrons realized a return of 1.69 percent on their purchases. Assets of this co-op total $1,177,760, with $991,894 in members' equity.

This would appear to be an appropriate point at which to conclude this chapter on "Reaching Out" beyond Greenbelt, but additional incidents of significance need mention before we can take a look at "Wheaton and the Co-op Congress".

Following the March 5, 1952 election, the reconstituted Board reelected Bierwagen president by unanimous vote, but that note of harmony did not last very long. The issue of expansion which seemed to be settled by membership vote at the annual meeting surfaced again when the general manager reported to the Board a possible opportunity to operate a co-op grocery on 14th Street NW in Washington, D.C., and a month later when he recommended that GCS take over a Sunoco service station at the corner of Ethan Allen and New Hampshire Avenues. By the end of May, votes of 5-4 and 6-3 recorded in the minute book the evidence of another split Board.

The June 6 Board meeting saw an open break between Bierwagen and the minority directors who had won election in March. The minutes open with this entry:

"Mr. Zubkoff inquired whether or not Mr. Bierwagen and Mr. Walter expected to leave the meeting to attend a housing committee meeting....(and) said that he wanted to go on record as very violently objecting to a board member accepting an appointment for any meeting on a board meeting night, particularly on such short notice."

Bierwagen explained that Mayor Lastner had asked him to appoint two representatives for GCS to meet with representatives of the Greenbelt Veterans Housing Corporation and the Town Council in connection with preparations for the sale of Greenbelt, and that he was notified of the meeting on the afternoon before the GCS Board meeting. He asked what was the seriousness of the two of them missing part of the meeting.

Zubkoff then asked, "if you are going as a representative of GCS and if so by what authority? Did the Board appoint you or did you appoint yourself?"

In the exchanges which followed, reference was made to the bylaws, Board procedures, and Robert's Rules of Order, to establish the right of the president to appoint committees. Then Schwimer said, "You will report back to the Board -- you will not make any commitments?" Bierwagen responded, "I object to this questioning of my integrity."

After Bierwagen and Walther had excused themselves and left for the mayor's meeting, Solomon pointed out that Charles Bicking was automatically dropped from the Board because of excess absences, and that a replacement should be made. Ben Rosenzweig and Carnie Harper, former directors attending the meeting as members of the audit committee, advised that it was customary to fill Board vacancies by putting the selection on the agenda for the following meeting and then to consider runners-up from the previous election.

After some discussion, Zubkoff moved and Schwimer seconded a motion to "proceed tonight" to fill the vacancy, even though Rosenzweig pointed out that only five directors were present, and that Bierwagen and Walter might return later in the evening.

The minutes read:

"Mr. Zubkoff said a qualified candidate was present, Mrs. Ritchie, and asked if she were not available. Mrs. Ritchie replied that she was available and would be happy to accept the appointment to the board."

Davidson stated, "that in all fairness, consideration should be given to a candidate representing the Takoma Park area." Mrs. Harper asked, "Has there ever been at any time in the history of this cooperative that a member of the board had been declared out of office and at the same meeting an appointment made without giving the full board a chance to consider the qualifications of candidates?"

Mrs. Ritchie was approved by a 4-1 vote, Davidson voting "no".

Two directors called a special meeting a week later ostensibly to determine what should be done about buying or not buying the Greenbelt shopping center properties GCS was leasing, in view of the impending sale of Greenbelt by the Government. All directors were present, as well as two dozen other members. Discussion immediately turned to the previous week's action in declaring a Board vacancy and then filling it when only five directors were present.

President Bierwagen reviewed the circumstances requiring Walter and himself to leave the Board meeting early. He then charged:

"...the vehement protest of the president's absence was merely stage setting...and those responsible for the action taken had their intentions clear in their own minds when they adopted the agenda without noting a possible election....In the interest of good public relations, in the interest of maintaining the dignity and integrity of this Board, I ask that those that participated in this highly unethical act reconsider their action. I further ask the appointed member to reconsider her acceptance, in view of the cloud under which she would serve."

After a long and heated discussion, Winegarden summed up the position of the four who had declared the vacancy and installed Mrs. Ritchie, that they "would under no circumstances reconsider the action". Since the minority of four directors on the Board was now a majority of five, with the addition of

101

Mrs. Ritchie, the subject was dropped "at this time".

The controversy did not stay dropped very long. In a community as closely knit as Greenbelt, word spread quickly and residents began taking sides. The Auditing Committee, headed by Mrs. Harper, took action at this point and notified President Bierwagen that unless the Board called a special membership meeting to consider the dispute, the Auditing Committee would do so.

Three days after the Board dropped the subject "at this time", it met again and after more heated discussion adopted the Auditing Committee agenda for a special meeting of the membership on June 27. These were the items for the agenda:

    1. Action on the Board's recommendation on the purchase of commercial facilities in Greenbelt.
    2. Report of the Auditing Committee.
    3. Consideration of the method by which a vacancy on the Board of Directors was filled at the Board meeting on June 6, 1952.
    4. Consideration of a recommendation that vacancies on the Board shall not be filled until all Board members have had an opportunity to propose candidates.

Item 1 was required because PHA had set a June 30 deadline on response regarding purchase of Greenbelt's commercial area. Having it on the agenda made it easier for the minority (now a majority with the addition of Mrs. Ritchie) of the Board to accept with some grace the other three items.

The Board met again on June 19 and June 26 to review GCS options regarding government sale of commercial areas in the town. During this period, the general manager and the Cooperative's attorney learned that PHA would require purchase of all the commercial property as a unit and not just any part of it, and that the price would come out at $629,000. It was agreed that this price was higher than GCS could manage, and would amount to as much as $17,000 more annually than the current rental cost. It was noted that the Cooperative's leases had 4 1/2 years to run, no matter who owned the property.

On Ashelman's recommendation, the Board agreed to recommend to the membership against purchase at this price, but keep open to possible further negotiation either through GVHC or directly with PHA, and to inform the GVHC board that GCS wants to avoid any action that would impair the housing mutual in its negotiation with the Government.

The special membership meeting on June 27 attracted a quorum, unusual when so many special and quarterly meetings had failed to achieve a quorum.

Members present approved the Board/management recommendation to not purchase the commercial property at the price asked by PHA. They then turned their attention to the controversy around the filling of the Board vacancy.

The Auditing Committee distributed a 4-page report which reviewed the sequence of events from the determination that Bicking, under the bylaws, had vacated the directorship by excessive absences to the selection of Mrs. Ritchie by four directors: Schwimer, Solomon, Winegarden, and Zubkoff. The report cited two basic reasons for finding the procedure improper and explained them in detail. In summary, they were:

"1. Not all the board members were advised in advance that a vacancy existed and an election would take place. A careful check of the 27 times that the board has filled vacancies since the Co-op was organized in 1940 shows that the board never filled a vacancy without advance notice to board members of the existence of the vacancy....The agenda as accepted at the beginning of the board meeting did not include the election, and two directors left the meeting on GCS business without knowing that an election was impending. Even the president of the Co-op did not know that an election was being held; and he was not asked whether he could suggest any possible candidates. Holding an election under such circumstances is completely unprecedented in GCS history....

"...in filling a vacant directorship, the board is taking over a function which normally is the prerogative only of the membership; and that in making the decision to elect a given person the board is affecting all future board decisions of any kind — since the new director will participate in such decisions. Inasmuch as the decisions to be made by the board in the next few months are of a most basic nature and could unalterably change the course of the Cooperative for years to come, the significance of the board's action should be apparent.

"2. In filling the post vacated by a director from the Takoma area, no consideration was given to seeking qualified candidates from that area. The remaining Takoma area director was not present, nor were any residents from that area. Although a candidate from the Takoma area received more votes at the annual meeting than the new director selected by the board, his name was not considered...."

The report pointed to three consequences of the action by the board's minority:

"1. Alienation of a considerable number of members in the Takoma area....at a time when sales in Takoma have been advancing steadily and there is every evidence that the Co-op is winning strong consumer support in the area.

"2. Lessened confidence in the board at a time of important decisions....

"3. ...If the action should stand unchallenged, a most unfortunate precedent should be established for future elections.

....We do not believe that the members should view lightly a departure from democratic tradition."

Members at the meeting adopted the Auditing Committee's report and resolutions which called for corrective action by the Board, by a vote of close to two to one.

At the Board's regular meeting July 11, the first agenda item was action to implement the vote at the membership meeting. After discussing an opinion by the Cooperative's legal counsel, the Board heard a three-page statement by Director Walter which pointed out that no Board member's personal interest was more important than the good name of the Cooperative, and offered four legal options to offset some of the damage done. The simplest of these was a letter of resignation by Mrs. Ritchie. She asked for more time to talk with her friends before responding, so a special meeting on July 18 was agreed to for further consideration of the matter.

Finally, at that meeting, her letter of resignation came. In it she maintained that she had been legally selected to fill the Board vacancy, pointed out that "it has not been pleasant to be at the center of controversy", and concluded that "as of now it seems that the best service I can perform for the organization is to offer my resignation."

At a meeting on July 31, 1952, the Board split 4-4 on two candidates from Takoma Park. A meeting August 8 could not resolve the impasse. It was not until a special meeting on August 14, that the Board agreed unanimously on Frank W. Lewis, who lived in the Takoma Park area.

It had taken more than 2 months to resolve a question of Board control. There still was a split Board, but several determinations had been made:

--A quorum of members could be counted on to respond in a crisis.

--The filling of Board vacancies between annual meetings would be fair and democratic.

--The policy of reaching out beyond Greenbelt -- of expansion -- would continue; but attention would have to be given to some kind of geographical representation for the membership.

VII. A POLICY OF EXPANSION: BITS AND PIECES (1953)

By the end of 1952, Greenbelt Consumer Services, Inc. was committed to the path of expansion. There was no turning back, but Board and members were still divided about the extent and timing of expansion.

General Manager Ashelman was saying repeatedly and with increasing emphasis that the future for GCS and for all consumer cooperatives must depend on growth, on reaching out both geographically and in types of merchandising and services, and in consolidating small organizations.

In his annual report to the membership for 1952, he said:

"We have seen how the Takoma stores have strengthened our operating picture. Another store would help immensely...another $3 million volume would save us about .5% in our present stores. Additional stores would give us still greater efficiency, and would soon put us in the position where we could take real leadership in bringing better values and services to consumers."

The Board was pretty much persuaded in principle. Meeting minutes for December 5, 1952 state:

"It was moved by Mr. Lewis, seconded by Mr. Walter, and unanimously voted that the Board approve in principle the general manager's exploratory action in expansion possibilities, and in area management problems, and that he continue to report to the Board as to developments...."

"It was agreed to ask the Potomac Cooperative Federation to arrange for a joint meeting of the boards of GCS, Rochdale of D.C & Virginia, and the expansion committee to discuss area expansion and related subjects.

"...the planning committee of the Federation is arranging a meeting to be held sometime in the spring of Co-op leaders in the Washington area. Mr. Jerry Voorhis is to be the speaker and the topic for discussion will be area management, expansion and related subjects....possibly 200 cooperators may attend."

The December issue of the GCS house organ for its members, "Co-op Newsletter", carried a lead article citing how chain supermarkets make their profits by increasing the number of retail outlets, to buy in larger quantities and to spread overhead costs. It discussed in some detail the possible "formation of an area management corporation" for cooperatives:

"The major retail cooperatives in the area (including the one at Westminster,

Maryland) would take the lead. On a contract basis each individual society would be serviced by the new central management (for) bookkeeping, advertising, personnel training... skilled buyers.

"Were such a plan to shape up, the question of control arises. Can locally owned co-ops be centrally managed, yet retain local democratic control over their own facilities....Each society would retain full ownership and control of its store and would continue to elect its own local board. Questions of a purely local nature such as price policy, store budgets, distribution of patronage refunds...and membership activities...would be left to the local boards. Local boards in turn elect representatives to the central governing board. No single society, however, would be permitted to hold a majority on this board...."

The house organ article even speculated that such an umbrella cooperative "might purchase an outright chain, turning it into a co-op". GCS actually did that in 1967, when it purchased the entire Washington division of Kroger supermarkets. How that worked out is described in Chapter XIV.

Meanwhile the policy of expansion still had its critics. Board member Solomon wrote in a GREENBELT COOPERATOR article that there were two methods of expansion: "One way is to get members and open stores, as most co-ops have done, and the other is to open stores and then get members from the area, as GCS did in Takoma Park." President Bierwagen responded in a subsequent edition: "On the question of whether a co-op...can be built from the top down and still be democratic, I think it can."

Schwimer, another new director on the 1952 Board, said in a long letter to the editor in the weekly newspaper on the subject of "GCS Expansion Policy":

"I favor the principle of expansion of cooperatives generally, however....We must first be sure that we are on a sound financial basis, not by borrowing and getting deeper into debt, but in accordance with sound cooperative principles, by raising a large proportion of the necessary capital from the prospective members of the new project before leaping into any new enterprise....(no) new undertakings until our Takoma Park members and prospective members have assumed the full burden of financing the stores in their area.

"....growth should come from the needs of the consumer, with members and employees sharing together in the economic advantages which sound operation of a growing organization can bring. Cooperative stores and services should be controlled by their members. When new stores or services are opened, they should be in response to the needs and desires of consumers in the area they are to serve and be financed by those who want them.

"....decentralization of control is the essence of democracy, which is one of the major tenets of the cooperative movement and a guarantee against control by the few."

After the winter quarterly meeting attracted only 31 members, the paper charged in an editorial that "A board responsible to the membership presents tangible issues rather than academic questions -- issues such as management's preoccupation with expansion."

Dividends from GCS early expansion into Takoma Park showed in the fiscal 1952 year-end operating reports. During the year, the membership approved changing the end of the fiscal year to January 31, so the condensed income statement figures for 1952 are for 13 months:

Sales	$4,834,350	100.0%
Gross margin	1,036,677	21.4
Salaries	615,771	12.7
Expenses	341,430	7.1
Net savings	75,410	1.6

Net working capital increased to $172,291 from $127,137 in the previous year. The current ratio improved to 1.64 from 1.47. A patronage refund of 1.2 percent was declared on 1952 purchases. All operations except the convenience store in the north end of Greenbelt operated in the black. Sales in the Takoma Park supermarket exceeded those in the Greenbelt supermarket, and continued to show sizable increases despite a temporary setback when a new Safeway opened nearby.

GCS used the Takoma Park variety/drug store space for three innovations. A shoe department and a department for men's clothing operated for a considerable time, but ultimately discontinued.

Lasting longer was a community meeting room which proved very popular for neighborhood affairs of all sorts. This met a community need and brought into the store people who were newcomers to the cooperative idea but who became customers and members. It also served for occasional Board meetings and other Co-op activities such as the well attended consumer advisory groups. So well received was the meeting room as a member relations and public relation feature, that future GCS stores included a meeting room if at all possible.

Several other happenings in 1952 deserve mention. An area-wide annual get-together brought cooperators to Greenbelt Lake in October for food and fun. Greenbelt cooperator James Smith barbecued three pigs over hardwood coals in an open pit. Carnie Harper supervised the chopping of 125 pounds of cabbage for cole slaw; and into a cast-iron kettle went 18 chickens and 36 pounds of prime beef for the Kentucky burgoo. In the evening, many of the one thousand cooperators attending enjoyed square dancing. The Potomac Cooperative Federation, sponsoring the affair, proved again that cooperation can be fun.

Meat cutters in the GCS supermarkets joined the Amalgamated Meat Cutters and Butchers Union during the year.

And most important, the Federal Government agreed to the sale of most of the Greenbelt housing, including the shopping center, to the mutual housing group, Greenbelt Veterans Housing Corporation. GCS agreed to lease from GVHC the space it needed.

By the end of March 1953, negotiations with PHA for purchase of the land underneath the Greenbelt supermarket and adjoining parking lot reached a satisfactory agreement, and the sale was finalized. GCS obtained financing for the purchase from the Farm Bureau Insurance Companies.

Murray Lincoln and Richard Carlson of the Farm Bureau organization maintained a close and continuing association with the Greenbelt Cooperative over a period of many years, but 1953 may have revealed the first full scope of the expansion program which held the attention of both groups. At one meeting where Carlson emphasized "the Farm Bureau's sincere interest in the development of consumer cooperatives," he urged that "as early as possible there should be a pilot operation of seven to ten stores centered around a warehouse, and the Co-op here in Greenbelt is their white hope."

Several possible projects for cooperative expansion came up for attention in 1953. Some fell by the wayside for various reasons. In January, the board of directors for Rochdale Cooperative of D.C. met with the Greenbelt board to consider a supermarket location in McLean Gardens on Wisconsin Avenue, in Washington. The two boards had different ideas on management responsibility and ownership of this proposed cooperative venture, but Farm Bureau did not want to finance it, so the project was dropped.

In Shirlington, Virginia, just across the Potomac River from Washington, a group of cooperators had opened a department store in 1948 with financing from CDC. By spring of 1953, this consumer cooperative venture was in financial trouble and its board made the hard decision to dispose of it. A number of cooperative leaders, both national and local, urged GCS to take over the Shirlington department store, as its closing would hurt the business reputation of the consumer cooperative movement. The GCS Board voted to make an offer to CDC, with financing assured by the Farm Bureau investment division. A better offer, however, came from a commercial department store corporation, so the GCS interest was turned aside.

A third unsuccessful attempt at expansion was the bid GCS put in for purchase of 6.5 acres of land at the intersection of Edmonston and Branchville Roads, about half a mile west of Greenbelt. The PHA sold it to a higher bidder. The Board vote on this proposal was 4-3, another indication of disagreement on the expansion program.

When Prince Georges County re-zoned Shrom's airport, immediately south of Greenbelt, for commercial development, the GCS Board was interested in its potential but the price was far above the Cooperative's financial resources.

In Takoma Park, however, there were two additional steps in the advance down the expansion road. GCS signed a lease for the lower level of the building which housed the variety/drug store, just about doubling the floor space. And on May 15, GCS opened an auto service station on the northwest corner of Ethan Allen and New Hampshire Avenues.

This had been a Sunoco station, and GCS converted it to a Co-op station by taking over the lease. Weekly gasoline sales before the changeover were $2,500; under the Greenbelt Co-op weekly gasoline sales jumped to $4,350. Weekly sales of automotive supplies went from $700 to $1,600. Grease jobs moved from one per day to between three and eight per day. Tying together sales of a supermarket, drug store, variety store, and auto service station at one location proved to be a strong marketing strategy. It became the preferred pattern in future expansion projects -- one-stop Co-op shopping.

And the success at Takoma Park was being accomplished in a competitive situation, putting at rest the nagging question in Greenbelt about whether success there was due solely to absence of competition within the community.

Quoting the treasurer's report for 1953:

"The year ending January 31, 1954 was one of your Cooperative's best. Sales increased 4.1% over the comparable period a year ago and net savings increased 50%. All-time records were established during this year for sales, net savings, net worth, net working capital, capital stock outstanding, number of members, and patronage refunds declared. Our current ratio (is) 1.95. A year ago it was 1.64. In 1951 it was 1.47....GCS now has the enviable record of having paid 5 percent dividends (on stock shares) for 13 consecutive years."

The income statement for the fiscal year 1953 included the following key figures:

Sales	$4,629,114	100.0%
Gross margin	1,038,086	22.4
Salaries	587,044	12.7
Expenses	341,375	7.3
Net savings	99,726	2.2

The patronage refund was 1.9 percent on the year's purchases for consumers who turned in their shopping receipts -- and most of them did. As in previous years, there was a choice of taking cash or applying the refund toward additional shares of stock. A majority opted for stock.

At the beginning of 1953, General Manager Ashelman brought to the Board an employee retirement plan which included profit-sharing and a number of other provisions that provoked extended discussion. The Board approved the plan by unanimous vote and agreed to submit it to the annual membership meeting, as there was some thinking that the adoption might require a change in the bylaws. Legal counsel, however, gave an opinion that no amendment to the bylaws was needed. The general manager therefore dropped the item from the proposed agenda in mailing out the notice of the annual meeting, notifying the Board of his action, by memorandum.

At the next Board meeting, Directors Zubkoff and Schwimer took exception to what the general manager had done, with a motion "that management take no action in the future to contravene any action taken by the board without first obtaining the board's approval." The motion was defeated 5-2, whereupon Schwimer stated for the record, "This vote indicates this board is completely ineffective and subject to what management wants to do. The manager can revoke board action and they give in to him."

When the matter came up for discussion (but not for action) at the membership meeting, there was a vote of approval for the Board's adoption of the retirement plan. Some months elapsed before the program could be implemented, as several changes in wording were necessary to meet Federal Government requirements.

The 1953 annual membership meeting defeated amendments to the bylaws which had been proposed by the Board: limiting time in office for directors and members of the Auditing Committee to two 1-year terms; making quarterly meetings optional; and permitting ballots for directors to be cast all day on the date of the annual meeting, at a designated polling place.

The general manager's report at this annual meeting noted that Greenbelt Consumer Services, Inc. was at this point the largest consumer cooperative in the country in terms of membership and volume of business.

The 1953 election of directors enlarged the representation from Takoma Park and reduced the minority faction on the Board from three to two directors. But there remained a sharp difference of opinion within the Board and among members on how the Cooperative should be governed.

During the year, discussion of expansion continued, and Board and management agreed on objectives, methods of financing, and a rough timetable, which were put into writing for future guidance. Carlson, speaking for Farm Bureau Insurance Companies, advised "a policy of owning just as few fixed assets as possible and of renting facilities rather than owning them".

Ashelman told the Board that as general manager he believed "that co-ops should move in the direction of handling general merchandise in the supermarkets...as none of the chains in the Washington area have done this." In line with this thinking, GCS arranged for shoppers to order CO-OP brand refrigerators (and later some other big-ticket appliances) direct from the factory at considerable savings. Samples were displayed in the stores.

Three directors' comments on expansion help summarize the various views at this time. Rosenzweig: "If we don't expand and do it effectively, then Greenbelt will ultimately fold. We can't expand without cooperative education and participation of membership, but cooperatives should be looked upon fundamentally as a tool." Solomon: "If the Co-op can't do a better job than competitors, there is really no reason for expanding." Zubkoff: "No matter how many benefits could be derived from expansion, unless the membership approves it would be folly to attempt it. We can do more to help expansion of cooperatives by developing new stores that retain their identity and are not part of a GCS empire."

There was by now widespread general agreement on cooperative expansion. Emphasis was shifting to the problems of organization and control. Director Frank Lewis reported in the fall of 1953: "Takoma Park members are very much concerned with the organizational structure (of GCS) and how to achieve membership participation in an expanding organization." The Board was holding some of its meetings in Takoma Park by this time, and a membership meeting as well. But talk about GCS stores in other locations brought to the surface concerns about the geography of meeting places and communication with members, and the question of area representation on the Board and committees. One big cooperative spread across several locations? Or several small cooperatives under some sort of a protective umbrella?

VIII. WHEATON AND THE CO-OP CONGRESS (1954-1955)

The basic character of the Greenbelt Cooperative changed in 1954, with the opening of its most successful shopping center and adoption of a new organizational structure to fit its growth.

General Manager Ashelman had been continuing his search for promising store locations, and on January 23 he took the Board to the Wheaton triangle in Montgomery County, Maryland. Here, on a main traffic artery feeding into Washington, was an undeveloped tract of a little more than four acres on which Ashelman proposed a one-stop Co-op shopping center. It would have a large supermarket, drug store, and auto service station, with a number of small shops which GCS could lease out for services that would round out an attractive center for shoppers. The Wheaton triangle was a relatively new commercial area where three major streets intersected and it had an obvious potential growth for a large middle-class residential area. Some Co-op members had already moved into the neighborhood from Greenbelt and could be counted on to provide local leadership.

The Board liked the location, and 3 weeks later gave Ashelman the go-ahead signal by unanimous vote. By the middle of February, the Farm Bureau's investment people had examined the project and said they would provide financing.

At this point, no one had raised the question of getting membership approval -- quite a departure from the earlier years when the price for a cup of coffee at the drug store lunch counter provoked enough controversy for a membership meeting. Some details about this new expansion appeared in the town newspaper in April and in the April issue of the GCS CO-OP NEWSLETTER. When the annual meeting convened April 14, there was no call for a vote following the report on the Wheaton development. The lease had been signed April 1.

Even before the end of 1953, the board had faced up to the need for changes in the Cooperative's organizational structure to assure fair representation and democratic control by the members in the geographic expansion. Director Frank Lewis was appointed chairman of a planning committee assigned the task of drafting proposals to cope with future growth. By the time of the annual meeting in April, more than 50 members had provided input to a number of studies, meetings, and reports on what would work best for the expanding organization.

The planning committee and management had looked at the responsibility and control structure of large consumer cooperatives in Europe and at the

113

districting pattern of American farm cooperatives. From experience, the Greenbelt leaders knew that member participation is strongest at a local level. And they recognized the advantages of training and hands-on experience in developing competent directors for the board.

Any new pattern for a larger organization would have to include ways to assure both of these results.

The concept agreed upon by Board and management called for area organization of members around the cooperative store or shopping center they supported. Members in each area would elect representatives to a local council which should be attentive to needs of the members of that area, work closely with management of the area store or stores, and plan and carry through local membership activities.

The elected representatives from each area would comprise the GCS Co-op Congress. This body would meet periodically as specified in revised bylaws to bring together the ideas and concerns of the members in the several areas. It also would report back through the area delegations to the membership.

Its most important task, however, would be to develop and select candidates for the Cooperative's Board of Directors. In a compact community like Greenbelt, members could be acquainted with candidates for the Board. With the Cooperative membership growing and spreading across many miles of the suburbs, however, there was little opportunity to know the best candidates among the whole membership. Members could be expected to know some of their own neighborhood leaders or other members shopping at the local Co-op store well enough to trust their judgment in picking Board candidates. The area representatives working together in the Congress could be in a position to evaluate qualifications of their peers for service on the Board of Directors. The Congress could require that the Board candidates they select have the benefit of training sessions -- in cooperative principles and background, the responsibilities of a director, how to read a balance sheet and operating statement, etc.

There would still be an annual meeting for all members, with directed proxy voting for members who could not attend in person. Provision was made for additional nominations for the Board by petition.

Replacing the Auditing Committee would be a Supervisory Committee elected by the Congress. It would have both Congress and non- Congress members. As a sort of "watchdog", the Supervisory Committee would monitor Board actions against "any matters within the organization which hint of impropriety, willful neglect, or illegality".

Bylaws amendments for all of this were presented as a package to the membership at the April 14 annual meeting. After some discussion, the changes were adopted by the members present (well over a quorum) with only two dissenting votes.

The new structure would go into effect when a third store area (Wheaton) achieved at least 200 new GCS members.

In addition to the Congress structure, the 1954 package of bylaws amendments contained some other significant changes. One was a switch from the Hare system of proportional representation voting to majority voting. What brought this about after 14 years of wrangling in Greenbelt about proportional representation voting was a ruling by Maryland's attorney general that the State's corporation law did not permit voting by proportional representation. Following the April election of directors by majority ballot, the Board took the precaution of back-validating all actions of previous Boards elected by the older method.

Another change was staggered terms of office for directors. Instead of electing all nine at one time for 1-year terms, the revised bylaws provided for members to elect directors to 2-year terms: four one year and five the next. The intent was twofold. The longer term recognized that the Board responsibilities for an organization that had become large and complex required some learning time. Two years gave a director more time in service to use what he had learned in the first few months on the Board. Staggered terms provided better continuity, more stability.

There were changes in neighboring areas, too. In northern Virginia, Rochdale Cooperative opened a new supermarket in Falls Church. In Washington, D.C., the Potomac Cooperative Federation was suffering from a cutback in funding from the Farm Bureau Insurance Companies, and was trying to adjust staff and program to the changing needs of Greenbelt and other member cooperatives. GCS was still supporting the Federation and using its services in 1954, although there was increasing criticism of its structure, the cost to the Greenbelt Cooperative, and some elements of the Federation's program. Its weekly publication, "Co-op News Flashes", and its Monday luncheon round tables for cooperative leaders were much-appreciated standbys, but its role in tying together the area's cooperatives was edging into GCS' own area expansion plans.

The Federation's autumn barbecues continued to be popular attractions. A feature of the program for the get-together in 1954 was awards in recognition of outstanding service to consumer cooperatives in the metropolitan Washington area. Greenbelt's nominees were: Walter Volckhausen, Leroy Halbert, Ed Behre, Sam Ashelman, Wallace Campbell, Carnie Harper, Walter Bierwagen, Dayton Hull, and Florence Parker. Five of these were currently Greenbelters. The cooperative FM radio station was still begging for financial help as it neared shutdown. GCS was sympathetic but unable to supply the amount of continuing funding required. The station made its last broadcast in October 1954 and then closed down after 6 years of listener ownership and control.

Closer to home, Greenbelt's cooperative weekly newspaper switched from free home delivery to paid subscriptions and changed its name from the GREENBELT COOPERATOR to the NEWS REVIEW. From this point on, although the paper was still the product of the Greenbelt Cooperative Publishing Association, its staff devoted less space to GCS and to cooperatives in general. This could have been due partly to a greater preoccupation with the town's growth and interaction with the surrounding county and State of Maryland, now that Greenbelt was no longer a Government housing project.

Questions about communism and loyalty came up again in Greenbelt during the spring of 1954. There were rumors, some of them the outgrowth of Government security investigations involving interviews with people living in the community, mail watch at the post office, and garbage checks. Then there were newspaper articles, some of them naming Greenbelters who were leaders in the town's cooperatives and other activities. This was at the height of the much-publicized charges by Senator Joseph McCarthy (Wisc.) about communists in the Government. Three incidents merit comment here.

Volckhausen, at this time head of Potomac Cooperative Federation, was so plagued by accusations that he sought to place a paid advertisement of disavowal in the weekly Greenbelt newspaper. The advertisement was not accepted -- which led to charges of censorship on the part of the paper's editor. Volckhausen was a candidate for president of the Greenbelt Citizens Association at the time. At the May 1 meeting he was elected 50-6.

More complex were two other cases. During 1953, Abraham Chasanow was the subject of a security investigation based on reports from unidentified sources which THE EVENING STAR of Washington, D.C. later dubbed "the secret six". Chasanow was cleared by the security board at the Department of the Navy, but then later was fired from his job. Unlike many who, during this period, suffered in silence for lack of any means to fight anonymous accusations, Chasanow had the courage to go public. In April 1954 he was cleared, reinstated, and given a public apology by Assistant Secretary of the Navy J. R. Smith. Washington newspapers followed the story with editorials and near-full-page articles. Among the names of other Government employees accused of being part of Chasanow's alleged "radical group in Greenbelt" were several former GCS directors. THE WASHINGTON POST AND TIMES-HERALD, April 16, 1954 said in part:

"His case is more than just another security case. Woven inextricably through it is the history of the Greenbelt controversy which has surrounded the 'model community' since it was built as a New Deal depression-born experiment in living." The news story noted "loose charges such as 'radical' that are freely tossed around by disgruntled persons in Greenbelt. These include accusations by those who don't like cooperatives against those who do."

The Chasanow story was subsequently made into a movie, "3 Brave Men", starring Ray Milland and Ernest Borgnine and produced by 20th Century-Fox.

Some of the same Greenbelt names, including "Mr. X" who was on the original GCS Board of Directors in 1940, were hauled out during the McCarthy-Army dispute in May 1954. After Joseph Welch exposed the McCarthy excesses, after Co-op leaders in Greenbelt listed as security risks had been cleared, and after the "red scare" had passed, the trauma of those fearsome days persisted in the memories of those who had been falsely accused. The charges, despite subsequent clearance, remain in the Government's security files. Individuals who had made the accusations were never publicly identified nor held accountable for their damaging actions.

In Greenbelt, GCS still had a divided Board but managed a successful roundtable in June which clarified and updated functions of the Board, its Executive Committee, the general manager and his top staff. Management launched a formal training program for employees. For members, an insurance-savings program was offered, to encourage sale of capital stock. This was dropped when it failed to measure up to expectations.

By the end of October, Potomac Cooperatives, Inc., wholesale supplier for GCS, other mid-Atlantic co-op stores, and co-ops in Puerto Rico, opened a new 40,000 square foot warehouse in Baltimore. Greenbelt's operations accounted for the largest part of the warehouse sales, and GCS was a principal owner of the wholesale. Within a year the warehouse had doubled its sales volume as GCS expanded.

In this same month, the GCS Board authorized creation of Consumer Realty and Equipment Corporation as a wholly owned subsidiary. First use of the new entity was for submitting the Cooperative's bid to purchase the Greenbelt Shopping Center. The bid was not high enough, so the existing lease was continued.

Opening the Wheaton Co-op Shopping Center was front page news in the Washington, D.C. newspapers. More than 20,000 visitors crowded into the preview opening on Sunday afternoon, December 12, 1954.

Twenty community leaders, the heads of all of the Wheaton area's business and civic associations, lined up to cut an 85-foot silk ribbon with a 20-foot-long pair of scissors on signal from GCS President Bierwagen. Short congratulatory speeches were made by the Farm Bureau Insurance Company's Murray D. Lincoln, by the president of CARE and the head of the Cooperative League of the U.S.A.; Gottlieb Duttweiler, founder and president of Migros, the giant Swiss cooperative; GCS general manager Ashelman; and a representative for Maryland Governor McKeldin.

Radio station WGAY's Chuck Dulane said, "I have attended in the past several years hundreds of store openings, and I have never seen anything come close to this in crowds and enthusiasm. It's a store opening you just wouldn't believe if you didn't see it." Charlie Wilson, business agent for the Retail Clerks International Association called it "a stupendous opening. It's the greatest merchandising mart that's opened in Washington in many years." A photo of the opening day crowd made the front page in the Washington papers.

Lloyd Lovass, manager of the Wheaton Co-op General Store, pointed out that Wheaton was a pioneer in "one-stop shopping", with a food market, general merchandise sales, pharmacy, auto service station, and seven independent specialty shops all in one place, with parking space for 350 cars. Special features, some of them new to Washington area supermarkets, included: an entire wall of canned and packaged groceries stocked automatically behind the wall from specially designed conveyor belts that fed items into slanted slots -- a "Food-O-Mat", restrooms for customers, a community meeting room, and a snack bar under a hanging canopy in the center of the store -- with a 5 cent cup of CO-OP label coffee. The store had 25,000 square feet of open shopping space.

The Co-op pharmacy with a separate entrance onto the parking lot offered a 24-hour prescription service for the first time in Montgomery County.

A 75-foot trilon at the Georgia Avenue entrance to the parking lot announced "CO-OP" in 6-foot neon letters. For close to 30 years, this was an area landmark, visible for miles and used in giving directions for drivers unfamiliar with the street pattern in and around Wheaton.

GCS took a long-term lease on the land for the shopping center, and had it built by George C. Martin Co. McGaughan and Johnson were the architects.

During opening week, sales in the General Store (supermarket) exceeded $100,000, and for the first 5 weeks sales were over $350,000. This was at that time a record in Washington food marketing. Sales in the Co-op service station were more than 55,000 gallons of gasoline in that period, one of the largest opening volumes for any station in the Washington area.

Although this third Co-op shopping center was in operation only 6 weeks before the close of the fiscal year, it substantially improved the GCS operating statement and balance sheet. Current assets doubled the figure for 1953. Net worth gained $115,000.

Income Statement for 1954

Sales	$5,450,131	100.0%
Gross margin	1,209,771	22.2
Salaries	668,748	12.3
Expenses	418,742	7.7
Net operating income	122,551	2.2
Net savings	116,000	2.1

The current ratio for the year was 1.7, compared to 1.9 for 1953. The above figures were after writing off all of the Wheaton opening expenses. A patronage refund of 2.1 percent was declared for purchases in 1954.

Within a month of the Wheaton opening, membership in that area passed the 200 goal, and the total membership of GCS exceeded 5,000. In compliance with the vote at the April 1953 annual membership meeting, the Board declared the new organizational structure operational, and determined that the first area meetings for the new Co-op Congress would be held in April 1955. Each area delegation would be entitled to elect one Congressman for each 200 members in its area.

Wheaton members met April 14 and from eight candidates nominated, picked the following as their first delegation to the Congress: Robert T. Bonham, Jack T. Jennings, John S. Kenestrick, and Henry Redkey.

Takoma Park members met April 20 and elected the following nine delegates from 14 candidates: William C. Arntz, Herbert M. Avram, Joseph Horn, Eugene Johnson, Frank W. Lewis, Larry A. Oosterhous, Jack Resnicoff, Norman E. Tubiash, and Clifford J. Waldron.

Members in Greenbelt met April 22. They had 15 candidates and elected the following 11 to represent them in the Congress: Walter J. Bierwagen, T. George Davidson, George Eshbaugh, Albert K. Herling, Robert C. Hull, Hans Jorgensen, Carolyn R. Miller, Ben Rosenzweig, Sam Schwimer, Jane Volckhausen, and Henry R. Walter.

At each area membership meeting Sam Ashelman gave a report from management, the movie "Where People Count" was shown, and amendments to the bylaws were discussed and approved.

The first meeting of the GCS Co-op Congress convened in the Takoma Park meeting room April 27. George Eshbaugh was picked to be secretary, with President Bierwagen presiding as chairman.

The assembled delegates selected Arntz, Davidson, Herling, and Miller as the Congress slate to stand for membership vote on directors to fill the four Board vacancies. These four were elected to the Board by the membership of the Cooperative when the ballots were counted at the annual meeting May 26. Two petition candidates failed to gather enough votes for election. The required two-thirds vote given at this meeting ratified the changes in the bylaws which were needed to complete the new organizational structure.

And in this way representative democracy became the pattern for Greenbelt Consumer Services, Inc. There was criticism that individual members no longer had direct input on Board and management with the insertion of the area delegations and the Congress between membership and the Board. But there was general recognition that the large membership and the geographic spread of the Cooperative precluded the "town meeting" democracy which Greenbelt residents enjoyed in those first years.

"Exploratory" describes the first year of the Congress. There were no examples among other American consumer cooperatives to provide guidance. The Board and management arranged to have Richard Carlson, management advisor for the Cooperative League of the U.S.A., look at the Cooperative's structure and recommend the role for the Congress. Out of this came the following objectives and responsibilities:

Congress objectives:
   1. To maintain and promote channels of communication between the Board and the membership.
   2. To increase member participation and interest in Co-op activities.
   3. To develop the best possible candidates for the Board.
   4. To give the Board advice and counsel on matters referred to it.

Congress responsibilities:
   1. To select candidates for the Board.
   2. To appoint a Supervisory Committee.
   3. To call special membership meetings when necessary.
   4. To encourage development of consumer advisory committees.

To flesh these ideas into workable procedures, President Bierwagen with Board approval appointed a Committee on Congress Functions and Procedures. William Arntz was chairman and represented the board. Other committee members were Dayton Hull, Henry Redkey, Norman Tubiash, and myself, with Kay Hildeen as staff advisor. Hildeen was in charge of personnel for GCS and had been with the organization since 1951.

The Committee's first report defined the role of the Congress and then the purposes and functions of the body itself and its committees and the area delegations. In a special meeting of the Congress in the Hamilton Hotel (gone now) in Washington, the recommendations were discussed and given general approval. The Committee was asked by the Congress to draw up detailed procedures for a weekend seminar in May 1956 at Hilltop House, Harpers Ferry, West Virginia. The Co-op get-together was the first scheduled at this historic old hostelry after its new owners began refurbishing it and opened it as a conference center. And this was the first of a long series of annual weekend organizational and review workshops for the GCS Co-op Congress. These retreats did double duty, also serving as annual meetings for the Congress to elect its officers and standing committees and select its slate of candidates to stand for election to Board vacancies by the membership.

The Committee headed by Arntz was continued for most of 1956 and its work resulted in a detailed manual which served for more than a decade without major change. Some of the features were significant in assuring maximum useful information in two-way communication between members and their Board, in protecting membership control of the Cooperative in a democratic way, and in promoting member interest and participation at the local store level. Here are a few in summary:

--A specified period from half an hour to an hour of each quarterly Congress meeting is set aside as a forum for the area representatives to question individual directors about GCS operations, their opinions, their votes at Board meetings. The directors sit apart from the Congress participants, at the front of the meeting room. This "Committee of the Whole" is conducted by a specially elected chairman for this particular function. Dayton W. Hull was the first to fill this sensitive position, and he set a precedent for impartiality and for effective control of the questioning period, as an experienced chairman.

It was made clear from the beginning that strict rules govern the session. No speeches or opinions by the questioning representatives. Time limit on each question. No second question until all have had a turn at a first question. No insults or innuendos in questions. The purpose is to enable members of the Congress to obtain information about how the business of the Cooperative is being run and how well the individual directors are doing their jobs. Discussion and any action by the Congress is held until after the question and answer period closes.

Both Board and Congress were fortunate in the special chairmen chosen for this question and answer forum, and in my opinion these sessions were a most useful device for informing representatives of the members in their store areas who could not attend Board meetings, and also for keeping directors on their toes. This inquiry period fell into disuse around 1970. Continuing the guidelines:

--The Congress elects its own officers – speaker, deputy speaker, secretary,

121

and treasurer -- who may not be directors.

--Congress meetings are open to all members of the Cooperative (as are Board meetings).

--Congress representatives elect two very important standing committees, with selection and functions set forth in the bylaws.

One of these, the Elections Committee, has three Congress members and two non-Congress members from the general membership of the Cooperative. They have complete responsibility for all details for holding honest elections at area, Congress, and Cooperative- wide levels, using written rules. In most years, the chairmen and members of this Committee took their responsibilities seriously and ran elections that were above reproach -- even though the election results often failed to please all the members of the Cooperative.

The other standing committee is the Supervisory Committee, also with three Congress and two non-Congress members. In practice these often were former directors on the Board, for their experience tipped them off as to where trouble might arise. Attendance by at least one Committee member is required at every Board meeting, including executive sessions. The Supervisory Committee member can ask questions but not otherwise take part in Board meetings. The Committee chairman or deputy may examine any records, contract, or correspondence at reasonable times. The Committee is not to "second guess" the Board on matters of judgment, but is to report to the Board in writing any findings which hint of impropriety, willful neglect, or illegality. If the Board fails to take remedial action, the Committee reports in writing to the Congress, and may call a special meeting of the Congress if it thinks the situation calls for that.

Over the years, alert Supervisory Committees occasionally found situations that merited scrutiny, and remedial action was taken.

In some years, ineffective Supervisory Committees or lack of follow-up by the Congress allowed actions or lack of action to harm the Cooperative.

The very first Supervisory Committee elected by the Congress took exception to a Board vote to withdraw GCS from the Potomac Cooperative Federation in 1955. The Congress sustained the Committee's finding, and the Board agreed to postpone the withdrawal. Prominent Washington attorney William C. Wise, who was an effective supporter of cooperatives, warned that "GCS withdrawal from the Federation will kill it."

What followed, however, were 7 years of inconclusive negotiations which had nothing to do with the Supervisory Committee except to prove that it had put its finger on an area of contention that ultimately did kill the Federation and ended cooperation among the big three -- Greenbelt Consumer Services, Nationwide (formerly Farm Bureau Insurance Companies), and Group Health Association -- on the one hand, and the District of Columbia's many very small co-ops on the other.

So unfortunate was this irreconcilable confrontation, that it deserves some explanation. It touches on a problem which has always troubled the cooperative movement: how do you get cooperatives to cooperate with one another?

In the early years when GCS was still a one-community cooperative, there was a close working relationship with the Federation (PCF). There followed a period when both GCS and PCF explored and experimented with programs of shared services and joint merchandising among the consumer cooperatives operating stores in the Washington area. As the GCS growth began to overshadow the other cooperatives, some of the newer GCS leaders wanted PCF to concentrate its efforts on public relations for cooperatives rather than providing direct services for the miscellaneous smaller organizations. There was a stalemate because GCS, along with Nationwide and Group Health were financing PCF while the small co-ops controlled the board of directors because of their considerable number, and therefore controlled activities and program.

Management consultant Richard Carlson made a study of PCF problems and organization in early 1955 which resulted in PCF committee recommendations for changes. A majority of the GCS Board and some management input, "after much wrangling" came back with a different proposal. A major point was that representation on the PCF board should be in proportion to dues paid, and further that management should be represented on the board. An explanation in the GCS newsletter for members pointed out that "...the controlling majority on the PCF board represent societies which contributed less that $1,000 out of a total budget of $27,000 and which have less than 20 percent of the total area cooperative membership".

A report entitled "Facts on GCS-PCF Relations" prepared by C. Edward Behre, PCF board representatives for "small societies" quoted John Mellon, regional manager for Nationwide as saying:

"The GCS position gives the impression that it would be satisfied only with complete domination of PCF and with that domination expressed by the few people on GCS Board rather than by GCS members or their Congress."

After 3 years during which GCS made a sustaining payment but held no regular membership in PCF, it rejoined in 1959 at the time of its merger with

Rochdale Cooperative of Virginia. Early in 1961, the PCF board brought Albert Marble, formerly executive secretary of the Michigan Credit Union League, to Washington to analyze the situation and make recommendations, including the possibility of an area-wide credit union which GCS General Manager Ashelman had proposed. Following this, nothing happened.

A year later, W. W. Falk, speaking for Nationwide, wrote to the member organizations of PCF:

"I see no need to rehash the problems...except to say we are fast approaching the time when some definite decisions must be made if there is to be a central organization for cooperatives in the District of Columbia area....Greenbelt has indicated it intends to again withdraw from the Federation....Nationwide has sent official notice that unless a satisfactory program and budget can be developed for the balance of 1962, it will be necessary to terminate its contract with the Federation...."

Falck and Calvin Kytle for Nationwide and Jerry Voorhis for the Cooperative League of the United States arranged for management consultant Robert C. Sampson to make one final effort to find a solution to the dilemma. His 14-page report in July 1962 contained the following summary of findings:

"1. The potential for cooperatives (in the D.C. area) has not been touched. About this there is unanimous agreement by cooperative leaders.

"2. The cooperatives, except for a few, are muddling along and missing a great opportunity individually.

"3. After some 15 years of the PCF trade association experience there is (a) no real common bond among the co-ops; (b) no recognition of a mutuality of interest for their own selfish purposes; (c) no substantial association program for the co-ops.

"4. There are over 75,000 co-op families with less than 10% overlapping memberships. Yet there has been no concerted effort by the cooperatives or PCF to capitalize on this.

"5. ...there is no coordinated planning.

"....We see the Potomac Cooperative Federation suffering badly from a power struggle....It tried to be all things to all people.

"....cooperatives appear to be scrambling to make more and more out of their few differences....Some of the present and past cooperative management and elected leaders appear to use the cooperative movement as cloak for their own personal needs to dominate or stamp out opposition, personal frustrations and hostilities or as a vicarious outlet for other crusades.

"(Personal note.) No assignment has been as stimulating, personally satisfying, and as full of exciting discoveries as this one. The people with whom I have been working are superior to those in many other organizations."

In response to this, a letter from Robert E. Morrow, at that time acting resident general manager for GCS, indicated general agreement with much of Sampson's findings and recommendations, but warned:

"...over the matter of finances, I am not merely reluctant, but am strongly opposed to anything which would materially increase expenses during this critical period for GCS. I would be guilty of gross negligence if I did not take this position at this time."

And that was the end of the Potomac Cooperative Federation. My own assessment -- and I worked closely with the organization for some years -- is more charitable. I believe that in its early years it filled a critical need for linking big and little cooperatives and serving as a forum for exchanging ideas and mutual encouragement.

George Eshbaugh served as secretary for the first 2 years of the GCS Co-op Congress, and Bierwagen as GCS president chaired the meetings. At the organizational meeting of the 3rd Congress, Henry Redkey was elected speaker and took over the executive officer responsibilities.

Organization of the Congress on a firm basis was completed just in time for a burst of further expansion and additional activities by GCS. For the next years, all resources of the Cooperative were severely tested to keep abreast of growth in store locations and services, staffing, membership, and financial requirements. Rapid growth demanded increased attention by management, board, Congress, and the area delegations to problems of communication, training, and policy.

The financial position of GCS offered a sound base for the continuing expansion. This is the balance sheet as of January 28, 1956:

Assets

Current assets	$ 945,855
Cash on hand and in banks	426,584
Accounts receivable	33,806
Merchandise inventory	440,520
Prepaid expenses	34,189
Investments in cooperatives	52,021
Fixed assets	654,759
Greenbelt market land	51,515
Greenbelt market bldg. (net)	197,484
Leasehold improvements (net)	117,034
Equipment (net)	288,726
Total assets	$1,652,635

Liabilities and Capital

Current liabilities	$ 487,619
Vouchers payable	254,286
Notes payable	40,391
Reserve for income taxes*	45,114
Expenses accrued payable	86,515
Reserve for dividend and patronage refund*	53,540
Long term debt	316,046
Notes payable, stockholders	48,546
Notes payable, other	267,500
Net worth	848,970
Capital stock outstanding	644,348
General & permanent reserve	124,312
Reserve for dividend and patronage refund*	80,310
Total liabilities and capital	$1,652,635

*These entries are part of a new format; net margin no longer listed. In the annual report for 1955, the 1954 figures in the comparative balance sheet were changed to fit the new format. Net working capital at end of fiscal year 1954 was changed from $342,192 in the 1954 report to $284,656 in the 1955 report, and the current ratio was changed from 1.7 to 1.5.

It should be noted that year-end figures were sometimes modified slightly when appearing for comparison in the following year's annual report.

Income Statement for 1955

Sales	$8,909,200	100.0%
Gross margin	1,873,582	21.0
Salaries	954,565	10.7
Expenses	706,557	8.0
Net operating savings	212,460	2.3
Net savings	198,129	2.2
Federal income tax paid	40,988	
Total taxes paid	95,097	

There was a 1.8 percent patronage refund, and the usual expected 5 percent dividend on shares of stock.

IX. EXCITING YEARS (1956-1957)

In mid-1955, Ashelman brought to the Board a proposal to build a fourth Co-op shopping center. This one would be on Piney Branch Road, just off Flower Avenue, in an older section of Takoma Park, Maryland, about 2 miles north of the shopping center GCS opened on New Hampshire Avenue in 1951.

The Board voted its approval, and management negotiated the purchase of about 2.5 acres through the Cooperative's wholly owned subsidiary, Consumers Realty and Equipment Corporation. The price of the land was $150,000. Although the site was adjacent to existing shops, it was zoned residential. Securing a zoning change to commercial held up the project for some months, so that by the time financing was obtained, construction completed, and the shopping center opened for business, it was not the fourth but the sixth Co-op supermarket for GCS.

Meanwhile, management and the Board undertook a schedule of projects and activities undreamed of by the earlier Greenbelt pioneers. This frenetic period saw GCS's Maryland charter amended to permit up to $50 million in stock sales, with removal of the $1,000 limit on individual stock holdings. Membership doubled and tripled. General Manager Ashelman and the Board took the Cooperative into the real estate market and financing arrangements at a fairly high level.

Within a period of 3 years GCS:
   --built two additional Co-op shopping centers and had two more on the drawing board;
   --expanded and remodeled two existing supermarkets;
   --built a new auto service center for Greenbelt;
   --built and leased to Nationwide Insurance Company a building for its auto claims office;
   --arranged mergers with two other consumer cooperatives, which would add three more stores;
   --explored the possibility of buying a controlling interest in a bakery;
   --provided a team to launch a network of cooperative supermarkets in Puerto Rico on request from the Commonwealth Government.

It was also in this period that a number of operations were closed down because they had been losing money or because leases could not be renewed.

Another distinction of this period of growth was a stable Board of Directors. This probably was the result of three factors: (1) selection of a slate of candidates by and from the GCS Co-op Congress, (2) departure from the Hare system of proportional representation in voting, and (3) the increased work load for directors which would scare off all but the most serious candidates.

Bierwagen had served on the Board and as president from 1948 through several turbulent years and then through this period of fast growth, retiring in June 1958.

There were fewer Board meetings in the late 50s, less than two a month; and the executive sessions which in earlier years provoked loud protests in Greenbelt rarely occurred except for discussion of personnel or contract negotiations. With 23 meetings in 1956 there were five executive sessions. Meetings normally ran from 8 p.m. until between 11 and midnight. To keep in touch with the scattered membership, Board meetings were rotated among the areas, on a schedule planned and announced a year in advance.

In 1956 the Board arranged with the general manager to have each department of management present a written and oral report in depth annually (supermarkets every 6 months). Directors found this gave them a better overall view of operations, provided an opportunity to hear from the department heads, and avoided surprise emergency decisions because planning could be done on a longer time frame. The Board required that management reports be mailed ahead of the meeting along with the meeting notice and minutes of the previous meeting, in order for directors to come to the meetings informed and prepared to discuss and take action.
The Board also saw to it that the monthly financial summaries were mailed to all area delegates to the Congress.

Operating and financial figures again showed satisfying improvement in fiscal year 1956. Net worth topped the $1 million mark at $1,099,173.

Income Statement for 1956		
Sales	$9,324,452	100.0%
Gross margin	1,916,114	20.5
Salaries	1,036,756	11.1
Net operating savings	152,720	1.6
Net savings	155,938	1.7
Patronage refund		1.4
Net working capital	751,631	
Current ratio		2.6

In the 17th Annual Report for the Cooperative, featuring the twin pines on the cover, Treasurer Robert T. Bonham noted the strong financial position: "Our auditors stated that we could borrow a half million dollars on short notice from a strong bank without collateral if such a sum were needed". He explained that net savings for the year were down because GCS had the expense of opening two new stores so close to the end of the year that they could not show profitability on the 1956 income statement. Bonham forecast continuing rapid growth "toward achieving a basic size essential to longer term stability -- a minimum of $30 million in annual sales". And by the end of 1964 GCS reached that level.

The Washington newspapers were beginning to report GCS growth in their financial section. President Bierwagen quoted in his message to the 1957 membership meeting from an editorial in THE WASHINGTON POST:

"The cooperative movement has made, we think, an exceedingly valuable contribution to American democracy. It has not only given many people a stake in the economy which they would not have had otherwise, but it has demonstrated the feasibility of applying democratic controls to economic as well as to political affairs."

This was the credo not only of Bierwagen but of just about the entire leadership of the Greenbelt Cooperative during the fifties and sixties. Membership numbered more than 11,000 by 1956, and the Congress was taking seriously its mandate to be the link between these member/owners in the store areas and the Board and management.

One evidence of this awareness showed in the attention given to a study and report by the Congress-elected Supervisory Committee to the Cooperative's information and educational program. In response to a complaint that the Board was ignoring its responsibility for cooperative education and keeping members adequately informed, the Committee of five made a formal written report to the Board with a finding that considerable information reached the members, but that it came from the GCS office with no apparent Board responsibility for it. The report acknowledged 12 significant informational and training activities, but "seven are management items, and of the remaining five one is just getting underway and two are still projections for the future".

The report cited the bylaws requirement for a Board "membership relations committee" and then stated, "Other than a chairman, there are no members of this committee. There has been no meeting in more than a year, and no reports in more than a year, and no budget."

The report concluded with the warning that:

"The greatest potential strength of a cooperative business is its membership, but the only way to assure wholehearted support of the membership is to make sure that the members know what a cooperative is and understand their rights and responsibilities as member-owner-customers. To build such understanding is the responsibility of the Board of Directors. Experience of co-ops of all types has shown that, next to inefficient management, an uninformed and therefore indifferent membership has been the chief cause of failure in cooperative business."

Response was positive. The Board appointed a committee, with instructions to meet and report. And the Supervisory Committee informed the Congress of the Board's cooperation. As time went on the member relations and information program had its ups and downs, but it was never far from center stage. The Board assumed responsibility for policy and adequate budget, management did the implementing, although in some years only in response to considerable prodding. Planning programs for membership and furnishing the volunteers to carry out the programs became more and more a principal function of the Congress and the area councils.

While construction of the Co-op shopping center at Piney Branch was pending, other expansion opportunities drew attention. A potential location in the southeast sector of Washington, D.C. was hopefully explored as an entry to service in a low-income neighborhood, almost entirely blacks. This was dropped for lack of parking space and the little interest shown by area residents. Earlier, the Frederick Douglass Co-op food store had been organized by local residents in Anacostia and operated for a time before closing as a result of insufficient patronage, as well as lack of working capital and other factors. (See Chapter I.)

Still looking for additional sites, Ashelman found a new shopping center under construction on the main street in Rockville, county seat of Montgomery County, in Maryland. Rockville is located northwest of Washington, just off the main highways to Frederick and points west. Now it is part of the suburban sprawl around the Nation's capital, but in 1956 it was a model American community with a notable historic past.

The decision to open a Co-op supermarket here was made hurriedly, without consideration by membership or the Congress. Curiously, I can find no record of Board approval in the official minutes of Board meetings, but this must have been oversight. All the directors favored the project, and the Supervisory Committee found no flaw or complaint in the decision. The "Congress Newsletter", October 4, 1956 says:

"We have now signed a store lease with the owner of 'Rockville Center' which is literally within a stone's throw of the old county court house. We are sorry as heck that we had to be so mysterious at the last Congress meeting but the lease had not then been signed....Bassett Ferguson and his facilities division moved in on this deal just in time to prevent...any major alterations in plans even though construction was already under way."

With May 1 set as the opening date, GCS staff and volunteer committees undertook a "get-acquainted" campaign and membership drive in the community by March 1. There were already some members of the Wheaton

Area Council, including three representatives in the Congress who lived in Rockville. This aided acceptance of the new store and quick organization of a Rockville area delegation in the Congress.

The new supermarket contained 17,000 square feet, plus 5,500 in the basement for grocery stocking and a community meeting room. The market opened with six checkout stands, a co-op information booth, and a "kiddie corner" to make shopping easier. Leasehold improvements were estimated at $160,000. The shopping center had parking for 1,100 cars. There were plans originally for a Co-op drug store and Co-op service station across the street, but acquiring the location proved impossible.

Several other projects shared attention with Rockville during this time frame.

Ashelman, with Board approval, had been providing management services to the consumer cooperative at Westminster, Maryland, for several years, and that store did most of its buying from the Potomac Cooperators, Inc. warehouse in Baltimore.

Westminster was a farm marketing center about 35 miles north of the Capital Beltway which encircles Washington. About 800 members made up the Westminster Cooperative, Inc. Many were also members of farm marketing cooperatives. Some background on this cooperative is related in Chapter I.

As early as September 1955, the Westminster board approached GCS about the possibility of merging operations. Members in Westminster wanted a new and larger store, but could not manage that with the resources at hand. At a meeting in November, the GCS directors agreed unanimously to a merger providing Westminster members would subscribe to $50,000 worth of GCS stock, agree to have their board continue in an advisory capacity, and also provide that a lease for a new supermarket and service station could be obtained in a projected shopping center on the main highway to Baltimore, at the edge of Westminster.

By March 1956 the lease was approved, and a month later the Westminster members had fulfilled their membership requirement. The merger became effective October 1, when GCS purchased all the assets and assumed the liabilities of the Westminster Cooperative. At the ceremony, President Bierwagen and Treasurer George T. Davidsen signed for Greenbelt, and President Solomon L. Hoke and Treasurer Ruth Rinehart signed for Westminster. Four members from the Westminster board represented that area in the GCS Co-op Congress until an election could be held. Westminster store manager John R. Brown stayed with the GCS staff for another 20 years.

In the City of Greenbelt (no longer just a town), the long- promised improvements and expansion to the Co-op supermarket became reality. The monthly "Co-op Newsletter" house organ announced in its February 1956 issue:

"The plan is to build an addition to the present supermarket building now owned by G.C.S. It will then be remodeled to include a big food store, a large variety store and a drug facility, patterned after the phenomenally successful 'general store' in Wheaton." Improvements nearly doubled the floor space, added an automatic electric sensor door and a covered loading area at the southeast corner, a Food-O-Mat along the west wall to keep restocking operations out of the aisles, new lighting, full air conditioning, and a much larger parking area. On the lower level the bowling alley remained open, and much needed office space was added for the growing staff. The remodeling package totaled $200,000.

"Why wasn't the debt of Greenbelt's Co-op loyalty repaid long before this with the finest consumer-owned facility GCS could provide?" the newsletter asked. The article then explained that it had proved impossible to upgrade the store buildings while they were leased from the Government. When Greenbelt was sold, a business man from Philadelphia made the highest bid for the commercial facilities. Now that the Cooperative's leases were expiring, the best choice appeared to be to move the most important consumer services into a new improved building and to close out the marginal activities which could be provided by individual owners.

Finally, after years of operating the makeshift Northend Store at a loss for the convenience of the local neighborhood, the Board closed it down. The Greenbelt Theater, America's only cooperatively owned cinema so far as can be determined, was sold to Jack Fruchtman. The barber shop, beauty parlor, news/tobacco store, valet shop and shoe repair were turned over to their respective managers practically free of charge when the leases ran out, with the proviso that current employees be kept so far as possible.

The Co-op service station posed special problems. More space was needed but the location made enlargement impossible. So with the expiration of the lease, GCS built a new station on Southway, at the entrance to Greenbelt from the Baltimore-Washington Parkway and from the Greenbelt Road to NASA and to Berwyn on Route 1.

The Board approved the lease for the new service station by unanimous vote in May 1956. It opened October 20 after two delays. One was for the time needed to obtain consent from families living in nearby homes and to secure re-zoning of the property. The other occurred during construction when the State Highway Commission unexpectedly decided to change the grade level of the intersection in front of the new station.

Marcel Brot, president of the International Cooperative Alliance, was visiting Washington from France at the time of the station's completion, and he cut the ribbon at the opening ceremony. Other dignitaries included City Manager Charles T. McDonald and representatives from Southern States Cooperative which provided financing for the $100,000 facility. The new station had eight gasoline pumps and six bays for auto servicing and repairs.

On the occasion of the opening, the "Co-op Newsletter" paid tribute to Ed Burgoon, who "worried the station into existence". Burgoon had come to GCS in 1946 as a filling station attendant and by the end of 1956 was head of the Cooperative's petroleum division, employing 47 men and taking in almost $1 million a year.

While all these projects were reaching completion, the Co-op shopping center at Piney Branch referred to at the beginning of this chapter began to take shape. This was another Co-op center in the one-stop shopping concept that GCS initiated: supermarket, drug store, service station, and community room, along with four small shops leased out to individual proprietors.

This supermarket, too, offered a Food-O-Mat along one wall, which dropped another can into the slot when the customer removed one. It had a kiddie corner where mothers could park small children while shopping, a snack bar with Co-op coffee at 5 cents a cup, glassed-in meat cutting area, co-op information desk, and especially wide aisles. The community room was equipped with a demonstration kitchen where weekly activities involving local homemakers could be held.

One special feature at Piney Branch was the preservation of two fine old white oaks in the middle of the parking area. But alas, they did not long survive the paving over of the area above their widespread roots. For the open house on September 22, 1957, the Cooperative published a 12-page supplement enclosure to THE WASHINGTON POST. Besides advertising for merchandise on sale, there were two full pages of photographs of the center's features -- paid for by the equipment suppliers and construction subcontractors. The front page carried a large photo of Dayton Hull, "one of the pioneers of Greenbelt Consumer Services, Inc.", carving the Thanksgiving turkey for his family -- Anne, Deborah, "Chip", "Chuck", and John Tucker -- gathered at the table. Articles by Murray Lincoln, Ashelman, and Bierwagen explained what a consumer cooperative is and told the story of the growth of GCS.

Also for this occasion, Ashelman published and distributed an 8-page brochure to merchandise suppliers, urging their participation in the "week-long gala promotion" for the opening of this "$1 million ultra-modern Co-op shopping center". Nationwide's Murray Lincoln was the special guest for the ribbon cutting. This had special significance because Nationwide was providing the financing for the center. Before Piney Branch opened, GCS had arranged for Nationwide to buy the entire shopping center at a price of $705,000 for the building and $200,000 for the equipment, and then lease it back at $59,000 a year for 20 years. This lease like others had a renewal option, on the assumption, presumedly, that the neighborhood would not change and that the Co-op supermarket business would go on for decades at that location.

"Sale and lease back" was management's new pattern for financing and it was used from 1956 on for all its facilities wherever possible. The rationale was that the Cooperative's cash would yield a higher return if invested in merchandise inventory than in real estate. It also released cash that could be used in negotiating for new store sites. Sale and lease back was becoming the preferred method for all the grocery chains and for many other lines of retail business. The renovated and enlarged Greenbelt supermarket and headquarters building was sold and leased back in this same year, 1956.

Greenbelt Consumer Services was becoming such a cooperative success story that a steady stream of VIPs from other parts of the United States and of the world came for tours of the stores and to participate in meetings and other activities. During 1956 alone, GCS staff, Board, and members played host to several hundred foreign visitors. These included government officials, labor leaders, journalists, officials of cooperatives, and students. They came from Ethiopia, Turkey, Switzerland, Ceylon (Sri Lanka), Israel, Indonesia, Thailand, Pakistan, Viet Nam, Japan, Denmark, India, Finland, South Africa, France, New Zealand, Austria, Cambodia, Sweden, West Germany, Philippines, and included "a group of 40 labor leaders from Central and South America".

During this year and over a period of many years, the Greenbelt Co-op participated in an exchange program for training employees in cooperative-owned stores in several countries. In response to a request from the Cooperative League of the U.S.A., General Manager Ashelman with Board approval set up a training program in the GCS supermarkets for several employees of consumer cooperative stores in Puerto Rico. That was introduced in 1955 with appropriate fanfare. The experiment proved so satisfactory that the Governor of Puerto Rico proposed a contract which would have GCS allow Ashelman and other personnel from Greenbelt Co-op to invest time in developing a comprehensive program of cooperative stores and supermarkets for the Island. The contract took Ashelman, Comptroller Robert Morrow, and others to Puerto Rico for short periods during 1955-57. Board member Robert Bonham spent some days there, using his legal background and GCS experience to help draft suitable bylaws. President Bierwagen helped with definition of Board responsibilities. A big market at Dos Pinos, and a smaller one at Mayaguez opened in Puerto Rico by the end of 1956. John Brown, manager at Westminster, was assigned to be a store manager in Puerto Rico for 2 years, and saw the buildup of the consumer cooperatives there that lasted for many years.

Long-time Personnel Director Kay Hildeen recalls that "our international involvements really enriched staff at all levels. It raised the sights of our store employees to learn that GCS had big and interesting cousins across the sea."

By the end of 1957, customer growth at Takoma Park made the Co-op's facilities at that location obsolete. Parking space was totally inadequate, the supermarket needed upgrading, and the corner service station was too small. Management had the Board's approval to build a much larger Co-op shopping center across the street on the southeastern side of New Hampshire Avenue.

Other plans called for building the new supermarket and service station in Westminster, constructing additional auto repair bays at the Wheaton service station, merging with Rochdale Cooperative, Inc. in northern Virginia, and for still another Co-op shopping center south of Alexandria, Virginia.

Sales had taken a great jump in fiscal year 1957. Net income in dollars increased, but income as a percentage of sales showed no gain. Net worth improved by more than $100,000. Here are some key financial data.

Income Statement for 1957		
Sales	$11,082,256	100.0%
Gross margin	2,308,374	20.8
Net savings	188,271	1.7
Patronage refund		1.2
Working capital	549,633	
Current ratio		2.1

In his last year as president of the Cooperative, Bierwagen stated in his annual report message:

"The basic role of our Cooperative is to create a system, owned and democratically controlled by the people it serves, for the distribution of goods and services. GCS is the only business owned, not by unknown, absentee investors whose sole interest is their dividend, but by 13,000 local customers -- you and I and our neighbors -- whose primary aim is to guarantee quality products at fair prices with a type of personal service and integrity we wish other stores had.

"To develop this efficient distribution system we obviously need the economy of mass buying and selling....One of our most important duties, therefore, is to broaden the understanding of the cooperative concept.

"In the Washington area we reached agreement in principle to combine resources. As a first step, Greenbelt Consumer Services, Inc. in October (1957) entered into a management contract with Rochdale Cooperative, Inc., thereby eliminating duplication in staff and offices and resulting in economies for members of both organizations. This paves the way for a united cooperative movement in this area and will make possible faster and stronger growth."

This was a clear map for moving away from the idea of a little store-front co-op on a back street, staffed by volunteers, and featuring natural foods and lots of social philosophy. There were still some members dedicated to "small is beautiful", and the leadership still took time to offer help to start-up cooperatives in other areas, but GCS was headed for the big time.

General Manager Ashelman already had advised the Board that the goal was to "make an impact on the Washington market area". At this time, the supermarket industry in and around Washington was dominated by Safeway, Giant, and A.& P., with several very small chains of less than a dozen stores. The smaller chains did not appear to offer much potential competition or long-term stability.

X. AIMING FOR THE SKY (1958-1961)

As GCS entered 1958, additional new expansion projects were in the planning stage or already underway: merger with the Rochdale Cooperative in northern Virginia; a wholly new shopping center across New Hampshire Avenue from the original Takoma Park location; a Co-op shopping center at Penn Daw on Route 1 south of Alexandria, Virginia; and a controlling interest in a bakery.

There was more to come -- much more. Management's appetite for growth increased as the decade of the 1950s moved into the 1960s. An article in the trade magazine FOOD TOPICS for November 1960 titled "Co-op Campaigns To Outdo Chains", stated:

"General Manager S. F. Ashelman, Jr., ventures the guess that his is the fastest-growing retail business in the Metropolitan Washington Area. Currently, Co-op is scrambling as fast as it can to achieve a sales volume that will put it on an even basis with the competition it worries most about -- Giant, Safeway, and A&P.

"....The Greenbelt Co-op became the first Washington area store to put many services under one roof...with extensive stocks of non-food items....(New) stores are unique in design in the Washington area, and carry infrequently purchased but large expenditure items such as furniture and major appliances...a complete pharmacy that is set off from the main part of the store and a luncheonette. Customers entering the store are greeted by a hostess...and finally, a community bulletin board and a convenient hospitality room."

Of the expansion projects laid before the Board at the beginning of 1958, the most significant probably was the Rochdale merger. It signaled the outreach of GCS beyond the borders of the State of Maryland for the first time, and it brought into the organization experienced, dedicated employees and leaders whose influence helped shape the consumer cooperative movement in the Washington area for the next three decades.

The beginnings of Rochdale Cooperative, Inc. were explored in Chapter I. In 1958, when the merger was agreed to, Rochdale had a small, walk-in neighborhood market on Quaker Lane, in Fairlington; a supermarket on Broad Street, in Falls Church; and a service station adjacent the Falls Church store. These were just across the Potomac River from Washington, D.C., in Virginia. There also was a service station on Virginia Avenue NW, in a part of Washington known as "Foggy Bottom". William Petri was manager.

President of Rochdale was W. Gifford Hoag, who later served the Greenbelt Cooperative in many capacities. Hoag remembers that prior to the merger some members of Rochdale had apprehensions about GCS, regarding it as more commercial oriented and less cooperative minded than Rochdale. He credits Murray Lincoln of Nationwide, Kenneth Stern of the American Institute for Cooperation, and Jerry Voorhis of the Cooperative League for bringing GCS and Rochdale together.

Rochdale Cooperative listed assets amounting to about $600,000, against liabilities of about $390,000, and a net worth around $210,000. Sales had been dropping in all the facilities, and sale of the service station on Virginia Avenue had already been decided.

From October 1, 1957, the Rochdale and Greenbelt Cooperatives had a management contract which consolidated bookkeeping, auditing, some buying arrangements, and supervisory services. When the Rochdale board of directors went to the membership in a special meeting June 17, 1958, the recommendation for affiliation with Greenbelt listed these advantages:

"(1) Improvement of our chances for a more consistent patronage refund on your cash register slips. GCS refunded $82,259 last year at the rate of 1.2 percent of sales. It has paid patronage refunds and 5% dividends on stock every year since 1940.

"(2) Improvement of our chances for maintenance and expansion of modern facilities. We will have a combined net worth of nearly $1.2 million. This will put us in a favorable position for securing leases and financing future development.

"(3) Larger organization which can employ more specialists, wield greater bargaining power with suppliers, and more rapidly engage in production of items where better quality can thus be secured or costs reduced."

Rochdale members at the special meeting voted 74-1 to merge with GCS by exchanging stock shares on a one-for-one basis. The book value of Rochdale shares at that time was $10.91, and for GCS shares $12.00. A volunteer committee helped bring in the Rochdale shares for exchange.

Management began putting the two organizations together. Some immediate improvements went into the Fairlington and Falls Church stores and the Falls Church service station. Planning started for expansion of the Falls Church shopping center. Rochdale held its last annual meeting December 3 and made preparations for area representation in the Co-op Congress. Falls Church and Fairlington became separate areas to represent the former Rochdale membership.

Directors of both GCS and Rochdale met with Wallace Campbell who headed CARE; Jerry Voorhis of the Cooperative League, and O.E. Zacharias, manager of Southern States Cooperative, for dinner at the National Press Club to celebrate the merger which went into effect February 1, 1959. Zacharias announced on this occasion that GCS was the largest single member-purchaser of gasoline from Southern States, in the amount of 3 million gallons the previous year.

The merger with Rochdale Cooperative, which was incorporated in Virginia and had its operations and membership in Virginia and the District of Columbia, required GCS to file with the Securities and Exchange Commission (SEC). Until now, membership shares (Class A) and non-member shares (Class B), had been sold only in Maryland, where GCS was incorporated.

The offering circular dated September 25, 1958 noted that "These securities are offered pursuant to an exemption from registration with the Securities and Exchange Commission." This initial circular was an offering of 30,000 shares at $10 par value.

"Both the A and B stock are common stock. They are identical except that A stock carries the right to vote. One person can hold only one share of A stock (a husband and wife can hold two jointly). No one person can hold more than $5,000.00 of stock in the corporation. No other type of stock has ever been issued by Greenbelt Consumer Services, Inc. The first share of stock issued to any person is A (Voting) stock. All subsequent shares of stock purchased are issued as B (Non-Voting) stock. A and B shares would share equally in the event of dissolution. Dividends are non-cumulative. The rate is established in the   bylaws at 5% per annum on the par value of the shares. Shareholders desiring to dispose of their shares must first offer them to the issuer which has a three month first option to purchase them. The Board of Directors is authorized to cancel shares issued to shareholders whose whereabouts have been unknown for seven years. The Board of Directors has the authority to repurchase outstanding capital shares when deemed in the best interests of the issuer."

The following year GCS moved to full registration, and from then down through the years until 1980, re-registration with SEC and publication of disclosure circulars was a regular and increasingly expensive requirement in order to secure members and increase equity capital.

While the merger with Rochdale took shape, GCS's Board and management also moved ahead on planning the layout and financing of the large new Takoma Park shopping center across New Hampshire Avenue from the original facilities. The site comprised 14 acres of undeveloped land on a deep fill. The property had a little over 700 feet of frontage on the 4-lane thoroughfare which led directly into downtown Washington. A newly erected Hot Shoppe restaurant occupied the corner lot adjoining the proposed shopping center.

At a Board meeting November 9, 1956, General Manager Ashelman obtained unanimous approval to invest $50,000 in a new corporation, Takoma Park Shopping Center, Inc. This gave GCS a 50 percent ownership of this tract of land, with the original owner retaining the other 50 percent. By agreement, GCS assumed majority control of the proposed development, with two board members plus Ashelman and Morrow from staff holding four positions on the corporation's board of seven directors.

In mid-1957, GCS secured $70,000 in financing from Southern States Cooperative toward construction of a 6-bay service station which opened for business on this new site October 18, 1957. Sales immediately doubled what the earlier Takoma Park service station took in. GCS also constructed a small office building for about $145,000 on a part of this land and leased it to Nationwide Insurance Company for a claims center and other business. This was completed in mid-1958.

And it was mid-1958 that marked a change in the Cooperative's top leadership. Bierwagen retired from the Board after 10 years as a director and 9 years as president. Robert T. Bonham moved up from the post of treasurer to president by unanimous vote of the Board and held that position until April 1962. It was at this time, in June 1958, that I came back to the Board and served as vice president again and then from July 1959 as secretary until I left the Board in 1967.

Now, we turn again to development of the new Takoma Park project. William Bateman, facilities specialist on the GCS staff, and the architects retained by Takoma Park Shopping Center, Inc. designed a Co-op supermarket of 40,000 square feet plus 20,000 square feet of rental space for 12 small shops. The layout for the supermarket was radically new and different, with aisles radiating out in a fan pattern from the checkout counters. The plan called for space for in-store bakery, drugstore, and variety items sections. All the latest supermarket innovations were included, such as the glassed-in meat-cutting room and self- service displays, large community meeting room with kitchen on partial second floor, customer rest rooms, snack bar, and Co-op information booth.

Since the building was on a gentle slope, it was easy to provide basement space for a bowling alley. Parking space was almost unlimited.

Potential annual sales volume was estimated at $3 million, based on a commercial survey which showed a daily average traffic count of 47,000 cars, and a stable population of 26,000 white collar workers and skilled artisans within a half-mile radius and more than 78,000 within a 2-mile radius.

This "Super Co-op", which had been proposed to the Board in late- 1956, opened September 20, 1960. It was an impressive step ahead for consumer-owned marketing in the Washington metropolitan area. It did not, however, live up to its rather glowing expectations. Construction had not moved as fast as anticipated. There were substantial cost overruns. The extent cannot now be determined, as early records of GCS were disposed of long ago during one of several headquarters moves. Rosenzweig, who was re-elected to the Board in 1960, remembers the cost overrun at close to half a million dollars.

Initial satisfactory sales began falling off as competing supermarkets followed the Co-op into the New Hampshire Avenue strip beyond the D.C. line.

It is worth noting here that Giant and Safeway provided aggressive competition throughout the years of Co-op growth. Safeway opened a huge supermarket on Georgia Avenue two blocks from the Wheaton Co-op shopping center within 6 months of the latter's opening. When GCS planned the regional shopping center at Penn Daw in northern Virginia there were only one small grocery market and two service stations within a half mile. A year after the Co-op supermarket, drugstore, and service station were in place, there were two other new supermarkets and six service stations.

While the new package of Co-op facilities for Takoma Park was being assembled, the old ones had to be closed out. The shoe store in one of the small shop spaces was the first to go. It had not proved to be a profitable operation and filled no vital community need. It was sold for the price of inventory. The corner service station closed at the end of 1957, replaced by the new one across New Hampshire Avenue.

An interesting deal was worked out for the variety/drug store premises. With approval of the landlord GCS subleased it to the Transit Workers Health Fund and several other union groups as a Labor-Management Health Center managed by Group Health (the large and successful Washington, D.C. medical care cooperative). It was remodeled and dedicated April 6, 1959, with George Meany, president of the AFL-CIO, and O. Roy Chalk, president of the D.C. Transit System, Inc. as featured speakers. GCS continued to operate the pharmacy, which then served the new health center patrons as well as Co-op members and other customers. Much later, the supermarket space was subleased to another business when the new and larger Co-op supermarket opened across the street.

This may be an appropriate place for observation of another significant change. When the Board considered the first expansion, in 1950, it went to a membership meeting to seek approval. By the late 1950s, members learned about planned openings of new stores when the newsletter came in the mail. As GCS expanded its operations and increased membership, area representatives in the Co-op Congress were kept informed of plans and progress, but no approval was needed nor sought for new projects. Suggestions from members were encouraged. While the big Takoma Park shopping center was under construction, more than 200 members attended a walk-through and meeting to express their ideas about what the new supermarket should look like, what it should sell, and how it should operate to best serve members.

Although many cooperators in the leadership were reluctant to admit it, Greenbelt Consumer Services was beginning to be run from the top down instead of from the bottom up. Members, or at least those members elected as area representatives, were active and had some influence at the local store level. However, the big decisions were proposed by Ashelman and the management team and then approved -- sometimes with modifications -- or infrequently, rejected by the Board. The only ultimate control by the membership lay in election of local representatives who then picked Board candidates for the members to ratify. With the member/stockholders now climbing above 15,000, spread across two states, there appeared to be no other way to run the business.

The shift did not come all at once. At any given point in time, it was easy to point to policies and procedures and activities which maintained some evidence of genuine member participation. And down through the years until the Chapter 11 bankruptcy proceedings, it was true that any member could be heard and someone in the leadership and/or management would listen and perhaps be influenced. And at all times the road to leadership was wide open for anyone willing to devote some time and energy to the Cooperative. There was a continuing plea for volunteers to work on the many committees and to stand as candidates to serve on the area councils and be representatives to the Co-op Congress. Almost any ambitious member with some intelligence and personality and enough drive could win election to the Board. A few mediocre people and a few with personal agenda did reach the Board, but in the main the Greenbelt Cooperative was blessed with high caliber directors who believed in cooperatives, took their responsibilities seriously, and made significant contributions.

Under revised bylaws adopted by the membership in May 1958, directors received compensation of $125 per quarter. Those who served as officers could receive additional amounts, but the total paid to all the officers was not to exceed the total paid to all the directors. The president was allocated $500 per year, the other officers $100, and each of the three on the executive committee $350. These payments were to cover expenses for transportation, postage, meals, etc. However, travel costs away from the Washington area could be billed separately. This schedule held for many years.

During late 1958, the Board reviewed and expanded its manual of procedures and its policies book, putting these on a continuing update basis. One interesting change assured more democratic election of officers by doing away with nominations. For each office, each director wrote his choice on a slip of paper, considering all directors to be nominees. Balloting continued until one secured a majority of the votes.

From 1958 onward the Board improved its operations in many ways, not all at once but continually across the years. All reports were required to be in writing and included in the packet mailed to each director and the chairman of the supervisory committee well in advance of the meeting. Motions, except for those in emergency situations, were written in advance with the purpose explained and pro and con information if controversial. The packet mailed prior to meetings was color coded for quick reference. The Board instructed the general manager as to what information it needed.

One particularly valuable innovation was a quarterly report on 10 basic financial ratios and several operating ratios which needed to be watched for trend changes. Comptroller Morrow gave training sessions periodically for new directors and any representatives to the Congress who wanted to understand the normal ranges of key ratios and what they signified. These sessions also covered balance sheet and operating reports.

An effective Executive Committee saved time at Board meetings by screening proposals to eliminate duplication and overlapping and to assure adequate research ahead of any action. The Executive Committee also disposed of many routine matters, always reporting to the full Board. At one point, with a divided Board, there was a power play to expand the Executive Committee to five, which would have been a majority of the Board and could have simply disregarded input from the Board minority. This was defeated but caused bad feeling at the time. Some years later, there was again a five-member Executive Committee for a while.

During the period when the new Takoma Park shopping center was moving toward completion, other projects went into operation.

On November 15, 1958, there was a ground breaking ceremony at the new Westminster shopping center on Route 140 at Englar Road. On completion a Safeway supermarket anchored one end of the shopping center, and the Co-op supermarket and service station stood near the other, corner end. At the open house preview and ceremony, August 30, 1959, Edmund Carr, president of Carroll County's Board of Commissioners, praised the appearance of this newest GCS supermarket as the largest in the County. More than 4,000 members and their neighbors from Westminster and surrounding farms inspected the store. Next day and all the next week, they came back to shop. Sales so far exceeded expectations that both the store and the wholesale staffs worked overtime to keep the shelves stocked.

John Brown was brought back from his assignment in Puerto Rico to be store manager again in Westminster. A special characteristic of this Co-op supermarket and service station from the start was the loyalty and support of members. After GCS ran into bad times and gave up its supermarkets and service stations, the Westminster members bought back their facilities and still operate them successfully. This makes the Westminster cooperators the longest continuous owners and operators of a co-op food store in the region around Washington, D.C.

After contracting with Smith's Bakery in Ladiesburg, Maryland for several years to supply Cornell formula bread, GCS bought a controlling interest in the bakery in 1958. The bakery at this time improved and enlarged its plant to accommodate the demand for CO-OP label breads and other baked goods. GCS Board and management then went ahead with a program to install baking equipment in its supermarkets. Most of the production was prepared in the Ladiesburg bakery, frozen there, and then transported to the various stores for "bake-off". This innovation was most successful at the Wheaton supermarket. Along with the installation of baking equipment, that store was enlarged in 1958 to the tune of $200,000.

In January 1958, GCS signed an option for 10+ acres at Penn Daw, south of Alexandria, Virginia. Development of this shopping center marked a departure from earlier projects. There was no cluster of families who already were cooperative members in the area, and any serious campaign to build membership before building the store was pretty much neglected.

The prospectus presented to the Board and passed on to the Congress appeared favorable:

"The proposed shopping center will be located in a heavily populated residential section with a 'long reach'. The tract has over 1,300 feet of frontage on Kings Highway, U.S. 1, and Poag Street....The recently completed intersection at this point provides the utmost in accessibility to the proposed center....

"The market analysis of this site indicates that there is a definite need for a shopping center at this point. Over 30,000 cars pass the intersection daily. The primary trading area lies within a two-mile radius of the proposed center in which over 26,000 people live....There are no large markets south of the site for a distance of 45 miles so that it should attract large numbers of rural shoppers....We hope to do an initial volume of something in excess of three million [dollars].

"We expect to purchase the land at a cost of $315,000 and then sell it to a syndicate which will raise $600,000. Weaver Brothers is presently seeking to obtain a mortgage for about $800,000 for us....We will guarantee the rent on the entire center to the syndicate. In turn, we will sublease all the stores we do not operate."

There followed detailed cost and revenue estimates for a supermarket building to include drugs, variety, and bakery departments (40,000 square feet); bowling alley (48 lanes) under the supermarket; service station (6 bays and Virginia State inspection station); rental stores; and parking lot for 500 autos. Total project cost was estimated at $1,390,000.

This appeared to be a golden opportunity for expanding the Cooperative, but several flaws came to the surface later:

--The entrance was not exactly on U.S. 1, but on Kings Highway which at that point made a bend in what proved to be a very difficult intersection to negotiate. What looked simple on paper turned out to be a traffic problem which discouraged drivers trying to enter the shopping center.

--Actual costs exceeded estimates (here again, records were long ago disposed of).

--The necessary membership base never developed. The top count of stockholders later barely exceeded one thousand, and only a select few of these had much understanding of what a consumer cooperative could be. One negative factor seemed to be lack of a sense of "neighborhood" which had encouraged organization in previous store locations.

--Unexpected rapid growth of competition developed along U.S. 1. Today (1990), there is a solid strip development extending some 5 miles south from the Capital Beltway. The Huntington station terminal of Washington's Metro system is a half-mile north of this Penn Daw shopping center, on Kings Highway. The difficult intersection which made an awkward entrance to the shopping center has been redesigned. The former Co-op shopping center is now a prime location, but there is no longer a co-op to benefit from it.

GCS picked up the option on the Penn Daw site in January 1958, construction got underway in March 1959, and the supermarket opened for business May 17, 1960. In addition to the usual grocery, variety, drug, bakery departments, and community meeting room, there was a watch repair service and the first SCAN furniture section (more about SCAN later).

Two months before Penn Daw opened, GCS added still another supermarket to its collection. This one was in the Pennmar shopping center, in a relatively low-income area northeast of the District of Columbia, called Forestville, Maryland.

This was a hurried decision. Food Town, Inc., with eight stores in the Washington area, went into voluntary bankruptcy in the summer of 1959. Although the management staff and the Board of GCS was already heavily involved with expansion projects, they decided to explore acquisition of this small chain. GCS made a bid but lost out to the Kroger Co. However, Food Town had a supermarket under construction in the new Pennmar shopping center, and the lease for this facility was offered to GCS.

General Manager Ashelman reported to the Board an opinion from a staff member of the Park and Planning Commission that "the center is going to be a good, healthy one". It contained 80 acres, although only half would be developed in the first stage comprising 33 stores including Peoples Drug, Kresge, J. C. Penney, and a Grand Union supermarket at the other end from the location the Cooperative was examining. There was direct access from Pennsylvania Avenue S.E. and from the Marlboro Pike. Ashelman estimated the break-even point for the market would be $30,000 a week, but that sales of $40,000 a week could be expected.

The Board approved the leasing, at a minimum rent of $41,500 against 1 1/4 percent of sales, and plans were rushed to fit the 25,000 square feet as near as possible to the Greenbelt Co-op pattern. A hoped-for Co-op drugstore and service station could not be secured, so Pennmar did not fit the "one-stop Co-op shopping" concept. There was a community meeting room, though.

The supermarket opened March 8, 1960. The records show that at this time there were only two members of GCS living in the area. The membership relations department of the Cooperative was holding meetings at the store and about 200 persons attended in the month prior to the opening. Within a few months enough customers had signed up to create a Pennmar area Council with representatives to the Congress.

Sales at Pennmar for its first full year showed a weekly average of $22,990, far below the $30,000 break-even point and just over half of the predicted $40,000. Results at the much larger Penn Daw supermarket located within a Co-op shopping center did not look much better.

In other store areas, the Cooperative's member relations and customer relations programs had proven satisfactory and for some activities even spectacularly successful. Over the years these efforts had their ups and downs, depending on whether there was an effective person from staff or membership in charge. At some times a dedicated, skilled professional hired by management together with a strong volunteer heading an educational committee or a member relations committee made an impressive team.

From the experience of early years, the Board agreed on a policy statement in 1959 which became Policy No. 4, "Member Relations". Revised slightly in

1962 and 1967, it read as follows:

"The Cooperative will maintain a member relations program with the following principles, objectives, and implementation.
1. Principles:
    a. Development of trained leadership is essential to the continuity of democratic control by the members.
    b. Cooperative techniques will be promoted to inform members and consumers of the economic and social advantages to be gained from consumer cooperation.
    c. Member relations activities shall be based on present social and economic conditions, and an understanding of the attitudes and values of members.
2. Objectives:
    a. To provide a continuity of trained consumer leadership;
    b. To maintain channels of communication so that members will be
        (a) Aware of their rights and responsibilities as owners,
        (b) Informed about activities and operations of the Cooperative,
        (c) Stimulated to make recommendations for improving the Cooperative.
    c. To secure greater member participation in the activities of the Cooperative.
    d. To obtain better consumer understanding of cooperatives.
3. Implementation:
    a. The Board shall be responsible for the development of policies governing the general direction and scope of the member relations program and for its evaluation.
    b. The General Manager shall be responsible for carrying out the member relations program through the use of a professional staff.
    c. The program shall utilize to the maximum extent practicable the Congress organization, area delegations, and volunteers from the membership, working in coordination with the professional staff.

In the main, this policy was followed and worked well. There was a wide range of emphasis, of course, on techniques used to achieve desired results in member relations. This came in part from shifts in the importance placed, for instance, on cooperative education, on consumer information, on member sign-up, on leadership development, on participation in activities, or on increase in sales. Another variable was the availability of competent staff and volunteers, and on funding for member and consumer relations.

The semi-annual report of management to the Board on the GCS membership relations department in August 1959, for example, showed Wayne G. Smith as head of the department's staff, with two assistants working out of the office, and customer advisers in most of the supermarkets. Reported program activities included:

--In-store suggestion cards. In previous 4 months, 772 cards, totaled by stores, by months, and by subject (69% re products, 7% re operations, 3.4% compliments, 2.2% re out-of stock items, etc.); all responded to if signed; some of suggestions complied with noted in newsletter.

--Newsletter. Changed from monthly to bi-weekly; CO-OP tire ad brought good response; planning increase in size.

--New member nights. Continuing on regular schedule; attendance from 5 to 70; good help from Board and Congress volunteers in conducting meetings or presenting topics to new members.

--Outside customer promotion. Discarding individual calls as too time-consuming. Now having Co-op member serve as hostess in own home for neighbors or nearby non-members; GCS furnishes refreshments; average attendance is eight; also talks to organizations in store area...(including) Penn Daw Chamber of Commerce. "General opinion of staff and members that there really is no good substitute for personal contact."

--Library of CONSUMER REPORTS. Back issues have been ordered in order to set up reference library at Co-op information booths in each store. Also using info from CONSUMER REPORTS in GCS newsletter.

--Employee training. Under leadership of Ed Burgoon, employees in all stores participate in program of co-op orientation, using carefully prepared course outline, with visuals. "Enthusiastically received by employees and store managers....many requests for copies of course outline from other co-ops....presented in program of (Cooperative) League's public relations conference in May".

--Committee activities. "Helped to a great extent by an active Congress organization and assisted by staff, the last few months have shown a marked increase in member interest and participation. The impetus for most of the committee activity has come from the members." The report cited the following special committee activities:

Wheaton meat survey. Study completed by members of Wheaton area delegation, suggestions adopted by management for improving meat department sales in all stores.

Falls Church consumer survey. Studied shopping habits of 508 customers to help management plan merchandise selection.

Piney Branch "Homemakers Open House". Weekly morning sessions in community meeting room for shoppers, various topics with knowledgeable leader.

Products testing committee. Member volunteers using facilities at new warehouse to make taste and use tests of CO-OP label products, reporting back to their areas.

Takoma Park home meeting committee. Members of the area delegation invite shoppers into their homes to discuss the Cooperative and urge membership in preparation for the new shopping center.

Non-profit membership benefits study group. Congress committee to develop group buying techniques GCS can offer members.

Not mentioned in this particular report but in a later one, were the very popular in-store demonstrations, and the cooking schools and homemaking and shopping skills classes in the community meeting rooms which Louise Gibson, Edith Christianson, and other staff home economists and store hostesses presented. These reached more than 3,000 shoppers in 1959. In some supermarkets these sessions were held weekly, with topics announced in the newsletter and on the bulletin boards at the Co-op information booths. Some of the topics: The CO-OP label, meat grades, taste testing, low budget meals, candle making, Christmas decorations.

Other features of the Greenbelt Cooperative's consumer education program in the stores included recipes tied in with shopping specials, organically raised fruits and vegetables, "best buys" indicators on the shelves, nutrition leaflets, and tours of Co-op supermarkets and of suppliers' facilities such as the bakery at Ladiesburg, frozen food plants on the Delmarva peninsula, fruit orchards, cooperative poultry farms, etc. A few years later when reduced operating margins forced staff economies, the information programs for shoppers could not be maintained. While they lasted, however, they were an attraction that no other supermarket offered. Later, Giant supermarkets, which along with Safeway dominated the retail food trade, adopted many of the benefits for shoppers that GCS had experimented with.

A number of former GCS leaders wistfully recalled in later years that the Cooperative never really capitalized on most of its innovations. Giant, picking up and then maintaining shopper benefits such as unit pricing, understandable freshness codes, see-through meat packaging, and leaflets on health and nutrition, accepted credit for introducing them.

A corollary of the efforts to help shoppers become smarter consumers was the growth of interest in product standards and informative labeling and in protective legislation for consumers. As early as February 1960, a Board resolution proposed formation of a national consumer organization. This was a forerunner of a continuing effort which, in company with the support of other organizations, created the Consumer Federation of America a few years later.

The GCS Co-op Congress carried the leading role in the Cooperative's field of consumer information and protective legislation. Most of the area councils maintained customer advisory committees which worked closely with the local supermarket managers. The Congress structure provided an especially active Legislative Action Committee during 1960 and 1961. Richard Abell and, later, Robert Dressel chaired this Committee. In May 1961 it was responsible for a highly successful Maryland Consumers Interest Workshop in Rockville which drew in representatives from several farm, labor, and other groups in the State. Out of this came permanent consumer advisory councils in both Maryland and Virginia. Leadership and funding for both organizations came from GCS until they won broad enough support to stand on their own. A similar group formed in D.C. but was less successful.

The Legislative Action Committee of the GCS Co-op Congress organized resolutions, testimony, and witnesses to appear before committees of the Maryland Assembly and the U.S. Senate and House of Representatives as well as hearings by the U.S. Department of Agriculture and the Food and Drug Administration. They testified on behalf of such legislation and regulations as Senator Hart's bill on packaging and labeling, water content of hams, the "truth in lending" bill, repeal of the so-called "fair trade" law, and removal of the regulation barring pharmacies from being under the same roof with food stores. Co-op members provided strong support for the content labeling which is now required on most canned and packaged food.

Another product of the various membership relations committees, staff efforts, and Board resolutions, was the continuing introduction of new services and products. Some were for members only. Such benefits were expected, of course, to encourage some non-member shoppers to join GCS. Other innovations were open to everyone.

Many proposals failed to reach actuality. In this period from the late '50s into the '60s, the general manager brought to the Board such ideas as a site for recreation and vacations for Co-op members, an arrangement for nonprofit funerals, a mutual investment club for Co-op members, made-to-measure men's suits, car leasing, cooperative housing in the D.C. area, low-cost eyeglasses, books on a discount basis, cooperative child care, and a plan to convert the Embassy Dairy to a cooperative milk supply for GCS stores.

Other management ideas won Board approval and became part of the GCS operations with varying degree of success. Some continued for years; others had a short life. Here is a sampling.

Danish furniture. This was an idea that Ashelman brought to the attention of the Board in August 1958. It grew until it supported GCS when other operations went sour. As SCAN, it was the only remaining asset when the Greenbelt Cooperative went into the Chapter 11 bankruptcy settlement in December 1989. Chapters XII through XIX deal with these later years. Here, though, is how GCS got into the Scandinavian furniture business.

At that Board meeting on August 8, the general manager reported on his trip to Brussels for the meeting of the International Cooperative Alliance, and added that he had brought back samples of furniture made in cooperative workshops and factories in Denmark. His opinion was that the careful workmanship and simple design would sell well in the Washington area, and that the margin in furniture sales was so high that GCS could pass significant savings on to consumers.

He arranged a preview showing of samples to the Board and the GCS Co-op Congress in November, and the Board authorized the necessary import arrangements. Temporary displays of Danish furniture attracted attention in the hospitality rooms at the Falls Church and Piney Branch stores. Orders were accepted for delivery when the shipment arrived from overseas.

So well received was the furniture, that display sections were a part of the Penn Daw and the new Takoma Park supermarkets when they opened. For FY 1960, furniture sales were $92,000, with a net operating loss of $6,400. Sales in 1961 jumped to $237,000, with a net operating profit of $26,000. It should be noted that the Co-op was selling furniture at a gross margin of 32 percent at a time when furniture store gross margins in the area were believed to be at least three times that figure.

The next step for GCS was separate furniture stores under a separate department, and that was headed by Robert Gowell, who had come to Greenbelt Consumer Services from Rochdale Cooperative in the 1958 merger.

Charter flights. Another innovation which became a successful hallmark of GCS was its co-op charter flights. These, too, were an Ashelman proposal. It came to the Board at a November 1958 meeting as an idea for consumer cooperatives in Denmark, Sweden, Switzerland, and Germany to exchange round trip charter flights with American cooperatives. Development of this idea, however, came within the Board. The exchange concept was dropped as too cumbersome. Information on charter to Europe was developed during the next 3 years by President Bonham and Director William C. Arntz, with the assistance of Wayne Smith, staff member in charge of the GCS member relations program. Restrictions on group travel charters imposed by IATA had to be resolved, but there seemed to be a genuine demand for lower-priced air fares to Europe.

Even before reservations opened for the first two GCS charter flights, scheduled for June and September 1961, more than 200 inquiries had been registered. When the planes took off there was a standby waiting list. Co-op members who made the first charter flight saved $250 against the lowest scheduled air fare. Mr. and Mrs. Bonham were the flight leaders for the first trip. Leaders for the second flight were Richard Barrett and his wife.

"Shop Co-op" bumper stickers. Co-op shoppers who paid cash for their gasoline and agreed to have a red and white "Shop Co-op" sticker affixed to their car bumper earned a one cent per gallon advertising discount. It was one of the most effective promotion devises management ever thought up. Members travelling as far away as the Pacific Coast reported the joy of spotting a fellow cooperator and feeling enough kinship to stop and get acquainted. How much improvement this had in gas sales is difficult to prove, but the idea did get publicity. The WASHINGTON POST printed an observation that a "Shop Co-op" sticker on the bumper of a Volkswagon was a sure sign of a Democrat owner.

Credit Union. Residents of the town of Greenbelt had formed a credit union in the community's first year. While most members of GCS who lived in Greenbelt belonged to this credit union, the thousands of families who joined the Co-op after the expansion into other areas around Washington, D.C. either had a credit union available at their work place or had no credit union within reach.

Some members in the large Wheaton area delegation organized a Wheaton Co-op Credit Union in late 1958. By April 1959, Area Chairman Louis R. Stolcis could announce that it was serving a substantial number of Co-op members and store employees. He credited Phil Ritz, one of the Wheaton area representatives to the GCS Co-op Congress, for much of the project's leadership. Thomas L. Landers was the first president.

The GCS board from time to time talked about credit union services for all employees and members. It was not until many years later, however, that arrangements were made to have the Greenbelt Federal Credit Union expand its charter from the local community to accommodate the Cooperative's employees and members -- merging with the Wheaton Credit Union which had a different name by that time.

Heating oil. For a couple of years at the turn of the decade, management arranged with Southern States Cooperative to give a discount on heating oil delivered to GCS members.

Auto club. Ashelman pushed the concept of a Co-op auto club for GCS members as a way to boost service station sales. The Board approved the plan by divided vote to get underway January 1, 1961. The general manager estimated a membership of 5,000, with a net operating cost to GCS of $8,250 which would be more than offset by an increase of $12,500 in gasoline margins alone.

A year later the auto club had 1,000 members and the net loss on the operation was troubling the Board. The project was dropped a little later, because it simply did not live up to expectations.

While management and the Board experimented with new services, they continued to open additional stores. Before the Co-op shopping center at Penn Daw and the supermarket at Pennmar opened, management and the Board had agreed already on picking up a lease for a new supermarket at Capital Plaza. This was another hurried decision. Again, it was in an area lacking a cooperative membership base.

The location was in Bladensburg, Prince Georges County, Maryland, at the northeast intersection of the Washington-Baltimore Parkway and Route 450. This new development was a large regional shopping center, with a Grand Union supermarket at the other end from where GCS leased a 25,000 square foot location.

The presentation to the Board set the estimated break-even point at $40,000 to $50,000 but estimated gross sales at $50,000 to $60,000 per week. When the Capital Plaza supermarket finally opened in May 1966, weekly sales averaged $39,000 for that year and the next.

This was the first store area for which no membership council or representatives to the GCS Co-op Congress developed.

At the end of September 1959, the Greenbelt Cooperative moved its headquarters from Greenbelt to a new warehouse and administration building in Beltsville, Maryland, a few miles west of where the consumer-owned enterprise began and had its offices for two decades. The new facility, at 10501 Rhode Island Avenue, had been conceived by General Manager Ashelman back in 1958 as another Co-op shopping center to serve an area where some shoppers at the Greenbelt stores lived, in addition to centralized warehousing and headquarters. However, the crowded schedule of construction projects in the expansion of GCS at this time was beginning to curb its sources of financing. The shopping center was never built.

The new building offered double the space that GCS had in its old Baltimore warehouse. Located on an 11.3 acre site, the half- million dollar building had its own railroad siding and specially designed loading platform. The location was just a few hundred feet from U.S. 1. The warehouse featured four chilling and cooling rooms, zoned for dry cold and moist cold, for storage of vegetables, fruits, dairy products, and candy. Flexible doors provided uninterrupted entry and exit for fast product transfer. Translucent plastic siding around the warehouse admitted maximum light. The modern labor-saving equipment for handling merchandise included invoice and inventory control.

The offices included a testing kitchen, conference room, and an "IBM" room with special heat and humidity controls.

Some of those members of the Cooperative living in Greenbelt were understandably unhappy about the move of the headquarters from its long-time location.

GCS went into the Baltimore area for its next supermarket. In the summer of 1960, Ashelman obtained Board approval for purchase of the N&W Supermarket, 2825 Old North Point Road, in Dundalk, Maryland. This was a stable working class neighborhood, with most families owning their homes. It was an established store with a solid customer base built by the owner. Failing health was forcing him to retire and he declared himself unwilling to have a chain take over the business. GCS purchased this store for $200,000, and for a time retained the original name and advisory services of the former owner. He became the Cooperative's first member there and encouraged what became a heavy investment in GCS stock. In less than a year, Dundalk had enough members to become an area council within the GCS Co-op Congress structure. This became one of the strong groups in the Cooperative's family and provided significant leadership.

Estimated weekly sales would be "between $60,000 and $75,000" according to the proposal given to the board. Actual sales averaged $41,799 for 1961 and fell to $35,066 for 1962.

The Board had become accustomed to performance falling short of forecast budget, but after 1959 the shortfalls seemed to getting worse. Looking back over the operating reports, 1959 is obviously a peak year followed by a slump. Total annual sales for GCS increased in 1960 and 1961. With new store openings and some general inflation in the economy affecting prices, this was to be expected, but the sales totals at individual stores fell.

There was a gain in sales for 1960 but it was the result in part from a strike in February which closed 257 of the largest grocery stores in the Washington metropolitan area. The GCS contract with the meat cutters and grocery clerks unions expired a few months later than the contracts which Giant, Safeway, and the other chains did. The Cooperative, therefore, was in a position to benefit from a volume of sales nearly three times what it did normally. The real gain was largely in the favorable publicity for the way it coped with the emergency and for not raising prices. As a result, many new shoppers became steady Co-op customers and some became members. Little profit was realized from the strike bonanza, because of overtime pay rates and premium prices which had to be paid for emergency transportation re-routing of merchandise.

Looking at net margins (before deducting allocation of central office expenses), six supermarkets registered a gain from 1959 to 1960, and in the following year only two showed any gain while eight had a worse showing. Service stations showed some improvement during this period. Drug stores did not register much change. Neither of these two divisions accounted for any large percentage of total operating results.

Substantial increases in facilities, staff, and inventory in the late '50s and into the '60s in the face of declining operating margins posed a cash flow problem that became apparent to management and the Board in 1960 and grew critical in 1961. This required some tightening of expenditures and some careful shifts in debt financing.

In December 1960, Ashelman surprised the Board by an offer to lend money to GCS to alleviate the tight cash flow. Another offer was for purchase of the warehouse at Beltsville by himself and his wife, with possible resale back to GCS when the cash position was more comfortable. Both propositions were dropped when the question of conflict of interest was examined.

Here are key figures from the operating reports for fiscal years 1958, 1959, 1960, and 1961, presented close together so that comparisons can be made.

Income Statement for 1958

Sales	$13,158,965	100.0%
Gross margin	2,722,448	20.7
Net savings	192,038	1.5
Patronage refund		1.0
Working capital	646,195	
Current ratio		2.4

Income Statement for 1959

Sales	$15,634,833	100.0%
Gross margin	3,243,102	20.7
Net savings	251,127	1.6
Patronage refund		1.1
Working capital	688,249	
Current ratio		1.6

Income Statement for 1960

Sales	$21,860,112	100.0%
Gross margin	5,002,719	22.89
Net income	212,000	.97
Patronage refund	none	
Working capital	860,866	
Current ratio		1.57

Income Statement for 1961

Sales	$22,842,971	100.0%
Gross margin	5,078,351	22.23
Net income	34,586	.15
Patronage refund	none	
Working capital	872,201	
Current ratio		1.59

Continuing the main balance sheet items at 5-year periods for comparative purposes, here are figures as of January 28, 1961:

Assets

Current assets	$2,362,566
Cash	$ 487,546
Accounts receivable	73,473
Merchandise inventories	1,651,620
Accounts receivable from affiliates	19,910
Sundry receivables	26,846
Prepaid expenses	89,174
Investments (affiliates, others)	550,065
Net fixed assets	2,429,027
Deferred charges, other assets	53,783
Total assets	$5,395,441

Liabilities and Capital

Current liabilities	$1,501,700
Vouchers payable	$ 544,588
Notes payable	554,811
Accrued expenses	202,745
Reserve for income taxes	71,587
Reserve for dividend and patronage refund	34,268
Long term debt payable	93,701
Deferred income	25,886
Long term debt	,525,909
Net worth	2,289,702
Capital stock outstanding	1,941,172

Reserve for Rochdale contingent certificates of indebtedness	43,020
Reserve for dividend and patronage return	51,402
Surplus (reserve?)	254,108
Total liabilities and capital	$5,395,441

The Board watched the monthly financial and operating reports with increasing apprehension as loans were adjusted to get extensions and better terms, as sales failed to meet budget projections, and as net savings dwindled. The directors also took alarm at the trends in the quarterly charts of 10 basic financial and operating ratios. In January 1956 and January 1957, all but two of the key indicators had been in the satisfactory range. By January 1961, seven of the ten were unsatisfactory, and this was still the situation in January 1962.

The comparisons and the danger points can be seen in the chart below:

Basic Ratios	Norm	Jan.1958 OK	Not OK	Jan.1961 OK	Not OK	Jan.1962 OK	Not OK
Net worth -:- total assets	over 50	63			42		47
Current assets -:- current liabilities	2 or over	2.1			1.57		1.58
Fixed assets -:- net worth	under 75	51			106		83
Long term debt -:- net working capital	under 100	41			177		121
Wages -:- sales	10-12	11.1		11.87		11.96	
Sales -:- inventory (inventory turnover)	14-21	14.5			13.2		12.7
Net savings -:- sales	2-4		1.7		.98		.25
Gross margin -:- sales	20-23	20.8		22.89		22.22	
Other expenses -:- sales	7-8.5	8			10.03		9.84
Sales -:- net worth	10-20		9.8	10		10	

The GCS Co-op Congress also became increasingly concerned as the 104 delegates from the 11 store areas read the operating and financial reports which were provided. During this period, the Congress, first under the leadership of Henry Redkey and then Jack Besansky, was a strong institution with active committees and a record of accomplishments that benefited consumers and strengthened the Cooperative. Written reports displayed a level of professionalism equal to the best being produced in government agencies or the area's universities. This volunteer work reflected the educational and professional backgrounds of the GCS leadership during these years.

The Board made sure that detailed quarterly reports kept the Congress delegates current on the operations and financial affairs of GCS and its wholly owned subsidiaries. Annually, in the late spring, Board and key management personnel met with the new Congress after each membership election for a 2- or 3-day orientation which included discussion of operations. In June 1960, for instance, President Bonham presented a four-page report, "Development of Greenbelt Consumer Services and Plans for Future Growth". In it he said:

"The first 11 years...you can be sure there was a good deal of hard work, disappointment, frustration, mistakes large and small, but there was an eye on the future....In 1951 the opening of the Takoma Park supermarket represented a whole new concept in the expansion of a co-op. (Instead of) the laborious method of recruiting members in a given area and when the number of members reached a certain size, the facilities to serve them were provided -- the new concept involved moving the Co-op to the people in a new area and showing them what it has to offer, how it can serve them better, and let this fact itself bring in the new members.

"The next step was as revolutionary....Wheaton...put the whole of Main street under one roof -- grocery, hardware, dry goods, drug store. Other chains soon began to copy the pattern, but your Co-op was the leader on the East Coast.

"...an even newer concept in Penn Daw...we have dropped the old rectangular store and built a spacious semi-circle, low shelves, color blended, wide aisles. To be sure we stay ahead we have retained one of the world's leading designers, Victor Gruen....

"We feel (we) must be a big business whose aim and interest is to serve not some absent owners but our ever present customer- owners....You are now a partner in America's largest and fastest growing co-op....I believe we have chosen only the sky as our limit."

Nevertheless, some Congress members had misgivings. In September 1960, Congress staged a discussion and debate with prepared position papers on the question of how much expansion, how fast, and by what methods. In the selection of Board candidates by the Congress in both the spring of 1960 and 1961, questionnaires requested detailed explanation of nominees' views on expansion, their grasp of financing, how the Co-op's stores should differ from other stores, and how management should be evaluated. Written responses from each candidate ran into several pages of well thought out views. It can be seen, then, that both Congress and the Board took their responsibilities seriously.

As operating conditions worsened, Treasurer William C. Arntz reported to the Congress in December 1960:

"The balance sheet as a whole is not satisfactory. I call your attention to three of the most important relationships. Current assets divided by current liabilities or the current ratio indicates the number of times we could pay off our current liabilities with our current assets. The norm for a business of our type and size is two times. Our October ratio is only 1.1 times. Secondly, net worth divided by total assets. This shows the percentage of total assets which are financed by members as opposed to the percentage financed by creditors. The norm is about 50% or more. Our current balance sheet shows only 37%. Finally, long term debt divided by net working capital. This measures the liquidity of our long term debt -- how much of a cushion for protection we have for the debt. The norm is under 100, while our balance sheet shows nearly 400. Simply stated, our major problem is that we have too much investment in fixed assets such as real estate."

Arntz went on to enumerate other problem areas such as high inventory, due to low turnover, and he explained in detail the significance of each item in the financial report. The Congress as well as the Board had an appreciation of the dangers ahead for GCS. The Sixth Co-op Congress appointed an ad hoc committee under Louis Stolcis, then chairman of the Wheaton delegation, to examine in detail and report on the financial condition of the Cooperative in relation to its expansion program.

The committee met with top management and the Executive Committee of the Board. On March 10, 1961, it reported in writing:

"....Our expansion has been so rapid that management, the Board, Congress, and the members may not yet have fully caught up with it....The Penn Daw store has not come up to expectation for several reasons. The population within a 2-mile radius seemed adequate to supply the necessary sales volume (but) the census tract study did not show how the people got from one place to another to shop....The steel strike and building delays made the opening one year late at a cost that was $180,000 over budget. The area now has more stores than are needed to serve its population. At the present time the Penn Daw earnings are not enough to pay anything toward its share of such indirect expenses as the warehouse, central office, etc....

"The Board's attitude toward new store offers has changed. The possibility of stores in Thurmont and at the intersection of U.S. 29 and Maryland route 32 will be considered only if the developer builds and equips the stores. GCS will pay a fixed minimum rent plus a percentage of gross sales. This would allow a minimum overhead operation....The Board is searching for effective techniques for better evaluation of information supplied by management (and) techniques for supervision of management."

In September 1961, Comptroller Robert Morrow warned the general manager and the Board against any further projects which would require capital.

For some time during spring and into the summer of that year, cutbacks on store maintenance and in personnel resulted in increasing complaints by member and non-member shoppers.

Individual directors began complaining that management did not seem to be keeping on top of projects. On one director's operating report from the general manager during this period is scribbled " Same old problems -- we have gone over this with Sam for years." A notation on the margin of another director's copy of a report reads "if we can't possibly break even, why are we in the real estate business? Another: "Petroleum sales above budget and loss goes up? Something very wrong here!" And still one more sample: "Fuzzy report -- not responsive to question." As one director commented to the general manager during a Board meeting, "You keep telling us the reasons last month was so bad and saying things will be better next month, but supermarket sales are still under budget and getting worse."

The Supervisory Committee proposed to the Board that a management survey be made to straighten out some of the problems. The head of Nationwide's investment department also suggested an outside management consultant might be helpful. Nationwide had been for many years both a principal source of funding and a strong advocate of expansion.

Board policy called for the presence of the general manager at meetings of the Board, but the Board met in Arntz's home in June just after the annual corporation meeting to discuss concerns about management. The Executive Committee -- President Bonham, Treasurer Arntz, and Director Edward Weinberg -- announced that "Ashelman has to go". With some reluctance a majority of the Board agreed. Then the Executive Committee proposed that Bonham become the general manager. That was not agreeable. Richard Barrett joined with the Executive Committee members in supporting Bonham's bid. Ben Rosenzweig, George Weber, and Donald Cooper together with the two new directors, Aileen Newman and Henry Redkey, made it a 5-4 vote against Bonham.

We cited the conflict of interest clause in the bylaws:

"No Director and no member of the immediate family of a Director shall be accepted for employment or other positions receiving remuneration from the co-operative within a period of one year after his term of office shall have expired except with the express approval of the membership at a regular annual membership meeting or a special corporation meeting."

Then, to the Board's surprise, we found that this provision somehow had been dropped in the last previous bylaws revision. Nevertheless, the majority opposition to Bonham as general manager held firm. After June 1961, there were other informal meetings of the Board and portions of the Board, with no minutes nor public revelations. Regular Board meetings, however, continued as usual and Ashelman continued to wrestle with GCS operations.

There were two caveats of importance in appearing to carry on as usual. It was agreed that Ashelman was chiefly responsible for the growth and success of GCS in the years after 1944, and no director held personal animosity nor did anyone want him hurt by a separation from the position of general manager. The second caution was to avoid public action that would damage the image of the Cooperative. We did not want creditors alarmed.

Nationwide had to be informed, as it had the largest financial investment in GCS and one that had extended over many years. Consent from Nationwide's investment department was necessary for a change in general manager. Nationwide's Murray Lincoln was a strong backer of expansion for GCS. Lincoln, along with Ken Stern of the American Institute of Cooperation and Jerry Voorhis of the Cooperative League were in touch with officers of GCS off and on during the autumn months. At this particular time, Nationwide had some contract arrangements with Checchi and Company, a Washington based management consulting firm with a good reputation and a growing list of clients

An oral agreement was reached, whereby the firm of Checchi and Company would offer Ashelman an attractive position on their staff. Vincent Checchi, president of the management firm, recognized Ashelman's talents and could use him to advantage in his own growing enterprises. The Board then would sign a contract with Checchi for management services.

And so it was worked out, with no adverse publicity. The minutes of the executive session of the regular GCS Board meeting of December 2, 1961 read:

"Ashelman announced his contemplated affiliation with Checchi and Company in a capacity not associated with GCS, as a result of inquiries and negotiations not related to the Board's interest in a contract with Checchi and Company. He suggested February 1, 1962 as a termination date for his services as general manager on the payroll of GCS, and said that he would so inform his key employees."

A draft proposal for a contract for management analysis and management services was discused at length, with particular reference being made to the period of the contract in view of bylaws restrictions on the maximum term of any contract which the Board may sign for management, and with particular reference being made to a question raised about possible conflict of interest involved in a contract which Checchi has with Nationwide as a GCS creditor. It was agreed that these points as well as others which might arise would be referred to legal counsel in the drafting of the contract.

Following the discussion, the Board took action, still within the executive session:

"ON MOTION, Weinberg/Barrett, to retain Checchi and Company along the general lines of the draft proposal presented to the Board for management analysis and management services, after checking with the Corporation's attorney, and within any limitations imposed by the bylaws of GCS, and that appropriate officers of the Corporation be authorized to sign the contract and other necessary papers, CARRIED UNANIMOUSLY."

XI. CHANGING TO CHECCHI (1962-1963)

Officers of Greenbelt Consumer Services, Inc. signed the contract with Checchi and Company on February 9, 1962. By that time the change in management and the new contract had been examined and approved by the attorney for GCS and by J. C. Beall and Forest Lombaer for Nationwide Insurance Company. The initial agreement was retroactive to December 2 and extended only until the Cooperative's annual meeting and election in June. At that time the new Board could renew the contract. The bylaws limited the Board to management contracts of not more than 1 year.

The contract provided for management analysis and management services. The firm specialized in studies for entering new markets, building new facilities, and financing. There were at that time about 45 employees on Vincent Checchi's staff, and he described his organization as "employee-owned". Among the firm's clients were cooperatives in Sweden and Italy.

Before the end of January, Checchi installed Comptroller Morrow as acting resident general manager. The changeover was announced first to the Executive Committee of the GCS Co-op Congress. Then on January 19, the full Congress heard the news and gave retiring General Manager Ashelman a rising vote of thanks for his past services of 17 years to the organization. Notification went to the membership January 31 in the weekly CO-OP NEWSLETTER.

Morrow had been on the GCS staff since 1946 and served as comptroller for the previous 6 years. He had frequently served as acting general manager when Ashelman was away from the office. Morrow was a graduate of the University of Michigan with a BS degree cum laude and a Phi Beta Kappa key. Before coming to GCS he was selected as one of four outstanding students nationally by General Motors for its summer training program. By the time of the Cooperative's changeover in management, Morrow was vice president of the Montgomery County Board of Education as well as comptroller for the Cooperative. Like Ashelman, who preceded him, Morrow was a Quaker by conviction. Morrow remained resident general manager until the spring of 1970, under the successive management contracts with Checchi which were continued until the end of 1970.

The directors of the Greenbelt Cooperative were aware of the experimental nature of a contract with a management firm in place of hiring an individual person to be general manager. It was another one of the innovations which highlighted so many of the Cooperative's years.

Among the benefits anticipated by the Board were these:

--A management firm offered a large staff of specialists which the Co-op as a small business could not afford to hire and anyway needed only occasionally or on a part-time basis. These specialized services included talent search for middle-management personnel, commercial surveys for site selection, advertising effectiveness surveys, sources of financing, legal services, analysis of economic trends, and recommendations for effective management procedures and communication techniques.

--A contract with a firm reduced the precariousness of depending upon a single individual in the top slot and the difficulties of making a replacement when that became necessary. At least this was the hope of some of the directors after the trauma of closing out Ashelman's management and avoiding Bonham's bid as his replacement.

--Some wider commercial contacts and access to operating information of other business enterprises.

By the end of March, the new management clipped some $200,000 from annual operating expenses. Morrow was known to be a proponent of holding overhead to a declining percentage of sales as the operations grew. Some of the savings was a thinning out of what was seen as over staffing, part was from reduced advertising in the Washington daily newspapers, but another economy came from elimination of the store hostesses. This last move was sorely felt by members and other shoppers. Food and homemaker demonstrations had been attracting as many as 125 women at a session.

In line with the economy measures, Checchi reduced his management fee for the initial contract period, and the directors voted themselves a 10 percent cut in compensation. These were only symbolic economies but were intended as acknowledgement that changes were necessary at all levels -- 1962 would be the second year without a patronage refund. The 5 percent dividend on shares of stock was still being paid, however, so purchase of additional shares continued to bring in much needed capital.

Before the change in management had time to really make a difference in operating results, a night-time fire gutted the Greenbelt supermarket and pharmacy building April 11, 1963. A defective lighting fixture apparently ignited the fire which smoldered for several hours before heat burst the windows and brought the fire-fighting trucks. Hero of the hour was Eddie O. Wolfe, the Co-op's pharmacy director, who entered the flaming building in company with one of the fire fighters and recovered the 100,000 prescription records.

Management, staff, Board, and members of the Greenbelt area delegation responded immediately to restore Co-op service to the community's residents. A free shuttle bus carried shoppers to the Takoma Park Co-op shopping center on Thursday evenings and all day Fridays and Saturdays. For those needing groceries or prescriptions home delivered, orders totaling $5 or more could be left at the Twin Pines Savings and Loan Association office for same-day or next-day delivery. Customers wishing to carpool for shopping at either the Piney Branch or Takoma Park Co-op supermarkets could get one gallon of gasoline free for each passenger.

By April 20, management opened a small temporary grocery in the basement of the old store building. Twin Pines Savings and Loan gave some of its office space for a temporary pharmacy. Insurance offset losses in the fire, including some "loss of business" coverage. Planning began immediately for a replacement which would improve on the original building. Knowing the cost would exceed proceeds from the insurance, a call went out from the Board asking each member to buy an additional share of stock. The response was good. Members who bought 10 shares ($100) were named on a bronze plaque mounted on the wall in the replacement building.

With surprising speed a new structure was completed and equipped, so that the Greenbelt supermarket and pharmacy was opened for business again on November 12, 1962 -- only 7 months later.

Aside from the setback in operations resulting from the Greenbelt fire, sales and net margins for 1962 showed some improvement over 1961. Central office overhead which had been 7.17 percent of sales in the first quarter of 1962 dropped to 6.26 percent in the second quarter and to 5.93 percent in the third quarter.

An "everyday low price" sales strategy in the supermarkets which was launched in December 1961 was dropped by Checchi because of the heavy advertising costs it would require for effectiveness.

At the same time GCS tried another innovation to give consumers savings in their purchases. A vacant shop space in the Takoma Park Co-op shopping center was used for case-lot and half-case sales from stacks on the floor. This economy sales technique featured CO-OP label merchandise which carried margins which could be cut to an attractive price for shoppers. This was a forerunner of the popular "wholesale" or "warehouse" no-frills supermarkets that gained acceptance two decades later. The idea at this time did not catch on, however, and the case-lot experiment was dropped after a few months.

Another and more important "forerunner" in the spring of 1962 was the first separate furniture store for GCS. It was in the Takoma Park Co-op shopping center and named SCAN because it offered products almost entirely from the Scandinavian countries and also suggested that the Co-op scanned the market on behalf of the furniture shoppers. The suppliers had not been happy about their products being sold alongside groceries, so the move to a separate store was largely in response to the overseas suppliers. It was also in line with the vision of Robert P. Gowell, long- time staff member from Rochdale Cooperative and then GCS after the merger and now in charge of the Cooperative's furniture division. From opening day, April 18, 1962, SCAN's low-price concept for high-quality furniture was a winner.

An innovation which promised to be a boon to members was buying at a discount by ordering from catalogs in the supermarkets. This was for merchandise not carried in the GCS stores. Unfortunately no way could be found to guarantee quality of goods ordered. The Board closed down the project in less than a year.

Off and on for many months, GCS had been in conference with Southern States Cooperative about price protection on gasoline at the service stations, the way patronage refunds were computed, and a credit card for patrons. When satisfactory arrangements could not be worked out, the Board reluctantly accepted a contract with Sinclair Oil Company.

This shift in suppliers brought strong criticism from members who viewed the removal of "CO-OP" gasoline as a serious setback. Despite the unhappiness, sales figures at the service stations climbed as additional drivers responded to the credit card availability and the familiar dinosaur emblem. This episode in GCS operations was an illuminating demonstration of the overall problem faced by consumer cooperatives as they grow beyond service exclusively to members and begin depending upon non-member shoppers to support enlarged facilities and increased overhead.

We need to turn back here to examine changes that took place in the Cooperative's political structure at the opening of 1962.

Although the nine directors continued to work together on Board matters which had to be taken care of, following the unpleasant split over President Bonham's bid for the general manager job, there was an underlying difference in attitude that was a little hard to define. It showed in votes on how much information should go to the members, control of the educational program, whether GCS should stay in the Potomac Cooperative Federation, and the intensity with which expansion should be followed.

One could have said in 1961 that the Board was rather evenly split with Redkey as the swing vote in the summer and autumn, but the president no longer could be sure of majority control as he was earlier. At the close of the year there was a proposal to increase the size of the Board to 11 directors. On January 6, 1962 a written committee report recommended that the amendment to the bylaws for this purpose not be adopted, explaining:

"Among the arguments considered against the amendment were: (a) A special committee of the Congress studying the matter of equitable representation on the Board concluded and recommended that election be entirely on ability of the candidate and discouraged the use of the geographical factor except as a secondary consideration; (b) any increase in Board membership would tend to make it unwieldy, prolong debate and otherwise slow up action; (c) adoption would invite pressure to increase the size of the Board each time a new store was added."

On a motion not to have the Board recommend approval of the bylaws amendment, only Bonham and Weinberg voted "no", i.e. favoring enlargement of the Board to 11 directors. The issue was dropped.

At the same January 6 meeting, another controversial proposal came up for consideration. This also was a written report and read in part:

"ASSIGNMENT. Recommendation by Supervisory Committee, December 4, 1961, that the Board initiate a bylaw amendment to prohibit a member of the Board from becoming an employee of the Cooperative for one year following termination of his service as a director.

"DISCUSSION. Among the arguments considered for the amendment were: (a) Such a provision is not uncommon as a check upon a body exercising great power; (b) because the Board is, to a very considerable degree, the final authority in the expenditure of corporation funds it needs at all times to be not only proper but above suspicion of impropriety;...

"There is testimony to the effect that the similar provision in the bylaws prior to 1958 was not left out inadvertently..."

"RECOMMENDATION. That the amendment be adopted by the Board and submitted to the Congress for comment and to the membership for action at the 1962 annual meeting."

This was voted into Board policy, with Arntz and Weber opposed and Bonham not voting. However, it was not possible at the time to write this restriction into the bylaws. It was included, though, by membership vote in the 1964 bylaws revisions.

The Supervisory Committee noted by letter to the Board, January 26, that excessive absences automatically dropped Richard Barrett from the Board. With nominations for directors scheduled for the middle of March, the directors decided by a split vote not to fill the vacancy by Board appointment.

Nothing had been said in public nor published in the CO-OP NEWSLETTER about the differences of opinion between President Bonham and his supporters and the other directors on the Board. As the date for Congress consideration of candidates neared, however, the Supervisory Committee prepared for distribution to area delegates to the Congress a record of all Board votes and attendance in the previous year. Because at least one member of the Supervisory Committee had attended every meeting of the Board, views about how each director stood on the issues even in executive sessions became part of the candidate selection process.

At the March 16 Congress meeting, representatives from the 11 areas selected eight nominees for the six vacancies. Two more were nominated by petition signed by 10 members of the Cooperative. Some input for judging the qualifications of nominees was provided by the written responses of those seeking election to questions prepared by the Executive Committee of the Congress. In addition, nominees appeared at area meetings of members to present their views. Petition candidates also published statements in the weekly GCS house organ which was mailed to all members.

Issues in this election which could determine control were: makeup and role of the Board's Executive Committee, dissemination of information from meetings of the Executive Committee, responsibility for the previous year's operational problems and financial losses (no patronage refund), weakening control of the Cooperative by the members as a result of growth and expansion.

When area representatives in the Congress voted in the April 6 meeting, Bonham and Weinberg failed to win positions on the Congress slate. They resigned and walked out of the Board meeting next day with angry words. The minutes of the April Board meeting, however, read:

"Bonham and Weinberg addressed the Board, submitting their resignations, effective immediately,in view of the results of the Congress nominating election the previous evening. They wished success to operations and pledged their continued interest and cooperation. They said they were resigning at this time in order that the newly designated nominees might assume their new responsibilities as soon as possible. Bonham also read a letter of resignation submitted by Arntz (who had not been a candidate for reelection), to become effective the day after the annual corporation meeting in June."

The Board accepted the resignations "with profound regret". The Board then appointed the designated Congress nominees to fill the vacancies until the June elections. Rosenzweig was elected president by unanimous vote. GCS then had a Board of compatible directors and a management firm under contract as general manager. Robert J. Dressel replaced Besansky as speaker of the GCS Co-op Congress.

Despite the changes in management and the Board, employees carried on the day-to-day operations and activities of the Cooperative without showing the strain under which they had been working:

--Second quarter figures showed the stores moving into the black but not enough to offset losses in the first quarter of the year.
--In the month of October 1962 alone, six new chain supermarkets opened in the neighborhood of GCS stores, posing more competition to erode sales levels.

--At the end of June, sales of stock shares just about equaled requests for repurchase, and the backlog of those requests amounted to $54,000. By November the backlog of requests to have GCS repurchase shares was down only a little, but sale of new shares was nearly double the requests for repurchase.

--The long search for a relocation of the Fairlington store (the lease was running out) proved successful although more expensive than had been hoped.

--Replacement of the burned-out supermarket in Greenbelt was on schedule and the new facility opened November 12 with a great celebration planned and executed mainly by local members through the Greenbelt area delegation under the leadership of its chairman, George Adams. Murray Lincoln, president of Nationwide Insurance Company, cut the ribbon in the presence of several hundred members and visitors. Jerry Voorhis, Howard Cowden, Arthur Smaby, Wallace Campbell, and other cooperative leaders in Washington for the 23rd Biennial Congress of the Cooperative League participated in the opening. The Greenbelt Band, a buffet supper, and square dancing added to the festival.

--Two more charter flights took members to Europe. The price for the September round trip, New York to Brussels, was $245, but then after returning home each traveler received a refund -- standard co-op nonprofit procedure. So successful were the two years of charter flights that the Board put together a policy statement and procedures for future flights based on the experience of the first flight leaders.

The Board assumed responsibility for determining the number of flights, general time of year, contract signing, and for selecting flight leaders using pre-established criteria. The GCS office took care of publicity (mainly through the weekly house organ), handling the payments for fares, accounting, and insurance. The flight-leader couple put the flight package together, receiving inquiries, giving flight information, organizing get-acquainted meetings, and taking care of participants' needs during the trip. For this work, the leaders earned free tickets. A written report was required from flight leaders after return from the trip.

Charter flights and other travel proved to be one of the Cooperative's most successful member benefits over a period of 30 years.

--The Board approved auto insurance with Nationwide at a special discount rate as a member benefit.

--Another small victory for consumers was won when the U.S. Department of Agriculture ruled that processed hams containing water be so labeled. Richard Abel, a Wheaton area representative to the GCS Co-op Congress, and others from GCS had testified effectively at hearings on this complaint. Other consumer affairs rulings and legislation kept Greenbelt Cooperative members busy all through these years. Dorothy Wheeler and Don Lefever were especially effective in testimony for better packaging and labeling.

--In an attempt to clarify the image of GCS as a consumer cooperative, a joint committee from the Board and the Congress with Henry Redkey as chairman prepared a report. The study, entitled "Operation Compass", was reviewed by the Congress and then a final draft was forwarded to the Board. The nine-page report laid out two directions for the Cooperative to explore in presenting a clearer image of itself.

"(1) Our store operations should reflect, in radically new ways if necessary, the concept that the Cooperative is a **purchasing agent** for our members (and incidentally for our non- member patrons). Merchandising should always be conducted as a service in such a manner as to warrant the faith and trust of members. Information on goods and services should be adequate, accurate, and not misleading...with a view of assisting the buyer to make the best possible choices in terms of his own needs.

"(2) We should encourage members to pursue special interests and meet special needs through specific cooperation with other members having the same interests and needs....Special projects, unless selected for wide promotion purposes, would be self-sustaining but entitled to the services of a coordinator, the newsletter, and use of the meeting rooms. Such projects [should] contribute insofar as possible to the support of overhead costs."

These aims were not too far different from what GCS was already purportedly doing. The "Operation Compass" report went into some detail on what steps could be taken to clarify the image and then match reality to that image.

During the latter part of 1962, the Congress representatives from the 11 store areas also held a formal debate about the importance of the patronage refund in comparison with other cooperative benefits. Another useful project was a comprehensive survey and recommendations on expansion, urging caution and more careful advance planning. At the urging of several leaders there was an examination of whether in future elections the Congress slate should include more nominations than the number of vacancies on the Board. No change was made, relying on the proposition that additional candidates could run by petition, but the idea became a perennial issue.

In October 1962, Checchi presented the comprehensive report on the Cooperative's operations as specified in the management contract. Much of the content was put together by Morrow. This was undoubtedly the most discerning and helpful analysis of GCS ever made. The study was "Confidential -- For Board Information Only", 37 pages in length, with 14 exhibits. It clearly set forth why operations had run into trouble, and it proposed remedial actions for management and for the Board.

Because this analysis explains why GCS was facing a crisis after two decades of heady success, much of it will be reproduced on the following pages. It should be noted that Checchi's team spotted weaknesses that continued to haunt the Greenbelt Cooperative through the next three decades until the bankruptcy in December 1989. It may be observed also that many of Checchi's findings and recommendations can apply today to other cooperatives that have large plans.

These were the analyses covered:

--Financial analysis of the various operations and the profitability of each.
--Organizational structure.
--Functioning of the Board of Directors.
--Relationship of the Board of Directors to the management.
--Personnel policies and personnel evaluations of the staff.
--Procurement, advertising, sales and price policies.
--Greenbelt member relations program.
--Location and site analysis of present and proposed operations.
--Proposals relating to establishment of a management development and training program.
--Definition of objectives and standards to assist the Board of Directors in short-term and long-term planning for operation and expansion of the business.
--Proposals relating to development of data collection and reporting procedures designed to provide a regular flow of information to enable the Board to measure progress and performance in terms of the defined objectives and standards.

"Last January when Checchi assumed management responsibility GCS was in very serious difficulty. The organization had lost $35,000 before capital gains in the preceding year. Patronage refunds could not be paid for the second year in a row. Sales were declining and losses were accumulating at a rapid rate. In the first quarter of the year there was a loss of $127,000. Cash was extremely low.

"Six principal reasons stand out why GCS got into difficulty:

"1. <u>Too rapid expansion.</u> In a short period of time GCS expanded too much and too fast. Within a period of 8 months in 1960 the organization added four stores to the chain -- [new] Takoma Park, Penn Daw, N&W and Pennmar. The cash resources of Co-op were seriously depleted by the opening of these stores in such rapid succession. In addition management spent so much of its time on the four stores that regular operations were neglected. Unfortunately the sites did not turn out to be favorable. None of the four stores has achieved anywhere near their forecasted sales level thus causing a continuous cash drain from operating losses....

"2. <u>Failure to stay within budget on new store construction.</u>
...construction costs at Takoma Park and Penn Daw exceeded budget by $400,000. This sum is approximately equal to 20% of the value of GCS shares outstanding....

"3. <u>Involvement in unprofitable real estate transactions.</u> GCS first entered the real estate field at Wheaton, where it was spectacularly successful. This success encouraged the organization to enter into other transactions, where unfortunately GCS was an amateur in a highly professional field. In the first 6 months of this year there was a loss from real estate operations of $23,856. Furthermore, GCS has $861,000 of badly needed cash tied up in real estate....almost $500,000 has been invested in the Takoma Park Shopping Center and will be unrecoverable for a number of years.

"4. <u>Insufficient caliber of management staff.</u> As a concern grows...there is needed a larger amount of expertise in store operations, merchandising, advertising...it is more necessary than before that there be competent store managers who are thoroughly trained. The staff did grow in number but management resources at the various levels did not grow sufficiently to match the requirements.

"5. <u>Failure to keep costs in line.</u> Overhead expenses had been allowed to get completely out of hand. A large warehouse was built though there was not nearly sufficient volume to support it on a cost basis. Advertising expense as a percent of sales was significantly higher than the national average. There was too large a staff in almost every department. Annual central overhead costs had risen by more than half a million dollars and as a percent of sales from 5.97% to 7.17% in a little over 2 years....

"6. <u>Over-saturation of supermarkets in Washington area.</u> Co-op sales have declined sharply in a number of stores because new markets have opened in the locality. The most recent example is Piney Branch [Safeway and Food Fair stores within a 2-month period]. Within a little over a year new competition has caused major declines in sales in Falls Church, N&W, and Greenbelt...."

The report identifies improvements which have been made and are underway: expense reduction ("every $1,000 cut in expenses has approximately the same effect as if sales rise by $10,000"); cash preservation; supermarket improvements ("cleanliness, reduction of out-of-stock items, more courteous service"); improvements in other divisions (petroleum showing 20% increase in sales with Sinclair as supplier and will show profit for year, pharmacy division in black for first time in several years but return on capital still very low).

The furniture division, in contrast to other operations, had a big 42.2% sales increase and $6,098 in earnings for the first 6 months of 1962 compared with the year-ago figure. This division "produced a handsome 71.2% return on investment".

"Other areas of management concern" were discussed. These included:

--"Develop a solid overall **merchandising** program....displays have been poor and sparse...signs need to be improved...programs have not gotten across to customers....

--"**Personnel**....there is no training program to develop employees for senior positions....this deficiency puts too great a burden on the general manager....

--"There is no spark to the **member relations** program and very little in the way of benefits. The very great majority of members are inactive in Co-op activities. The lack of young members is especially noticeable....responsibility properly lies with the Board and Congress but management will provide all possible assistance....The member relations program cannot be effective if it depends solely on resources of men and money provided from the income of the Co-op....Promote activities initiated by members....which may be financed by the members themselves.

--"**Capital structure**....the 5% dividend is in effect a true cost of over 11% since dividends are paid after taxes [plus] cost of maintaining stock records, processing redemptions. Co-op stock is treated as demand money...GCS cannot count on permanent use of the proceeds.

--"**Price policy.** The aim of last year's every-day low price policy was to lower prices on 125 of the fastest-selling items to a level below the competition. The lower price was to be made up through higher volume. This program never got off the ground. Massive additional advertising [needed] to support the program was out of the question in light of the acute cash position....In any event it did not create enough volume and when Kroger instituted discount food prices, it definitely had to be abandoned."

--"**Site Analysis.** Poor site selection is one of the significant factors in the unsatisfactory performance of some GCS stores which have never met expectations and have never made a profit. ...Last year GCS had to absorb a $91,000 operating loss at **Penn Daw**. It would be cheaper to move out entirely and just pay rent on the property [but] the terms of the lease stipulate that a supermarket must be operated on the premises. Every effort will be made to find a tenant. The **Piney Branch** store was built perpendicular to the road rather than parallel. The service station was then built in a way to completely obstruct the entrance and the front of the store. The store is largely hidden from view and many potential customers pass by without realizing a Co-op store is there. Three major chains -- Kroger, Giant and Food Fair -- opened in the immediate area. For the first 6 months of this year the store had a loss of $22,000....Management is looking for means to dispose of the store. **Takoma Park** was built too far back from the road. However, apartments going up directly behind the store may help the [losses] there.... **N&W** is the only Co-op store in the Baltimore area...uneconomical. It was a mistake to enter a different market on a single store basis
without plans to expand in Baltimore.

"There has been in the past a mistaken policy in regard to loss operations. Substantial amounts of money and management time were spent on unprofitable parts of the organization at the expense of the profitable parts. This will not be done in the future....To pour money blindly into losing operations is to weaken the Cooperative. GCS should be flexible, closing stores when necessary...."

--"**Organizational structure.** Two major changes have been put into effect this year. One removed a level of management...producing swifter communications...and sizable savings....The other reflects the increasing importance of furniture to GCS operations. The furniture director now reports to the General Manager rather than to the Supermarket Division....This [new] division has its own budget, is a profit center by itself and is better prepared to continue its expansion into the future."

--"The **Board of Directors.** Few corporations in American industry can claim as high a standard of integrity, devotion or sense of purpose as this Board. **But** -- the Board should be able to distinguish what is important and to approach major decisions and assess the performance of management with competence and assurance, whereas in fact the Board does frequently spend too much time on trifles....the Board must have at its fingertips the fullest statistical and analytical data it is possible for management to provide. In order to meet this need, management has introduced the 'Green Book' [for] operations information. Whenever management now presents to the Board a recommendation for action, the data in support of the action as well as data counter to the recommendation are presented...[so as] to make decisions on the basis of all the relevant data.

"GCS has a dual character; it is (1) the largest consumer cooperative in the country, and (2) a business operating in the context of the American economic system. By the nature of the co-op movement and because of the method of election the GCS Board tends to be slanted wholly to the Co-op side of its dual character. The difficulty of the Board's work is aggravated by the lack of a balanced expertise such as is present on a well selected private corporation board....

"The Board must become more involved in business analysis and long-term planning....There is still an unfortunate tendency for some Board members to see themselves as representatives of their respective areas on decisions concerning operations in the neighborhood where they live. This is obviously not the intent of the bylaws....

"An even more disturbing tendency is that of Board members presenting a disorganized view to the membership. There must be genuine differences of opinion on such important matters as the Board discusses and such differences must be forcefully presented for the Board's deliberations. However, once such differences have been resolved, or in the absence of unanimous resolution a majority vote has decided the Board's position, it is irresponsible of Board members whose opposing views have not prevailed to take their views back to the membership for airing. There are obvious risks that a majority decision may not be the correct one, that a faction may be strong enough to control the Board in a consistently arbitrary fashion. Clearly, on matters of principle a member must reserve the right to disassociate himself from the Board's position by resigning or by getting Board's permission to present his views in another forum.

"The Board also devalues its role by spending far too much time on relatively unimportant matters and not enough time on the major problems....It is much too touchy about fine points, wordings, definitions and procedures when debating general policies....It is recommended that when the Executive Committee goes over the agenda prior to Board meetings it should provide a provisional timetable for the items on the agenda...would serve as a guide to the chairman in running the meeting."

--"**Future planning.** No expansion of any magnitude must be undertaken until the financial position is satisfactory. This means not only that GCS should be operating in the black, but also that the cash position, reserves, and credit standing must once again be restored to realistic levels. These have been seriously depleted by past ill-judged expansion and the payment of poorly advised patronage returns. In addition, management staff must be built up, in ability and strength, to where it can handle the existing operation before it undertakes any substantially enlarged responsibilities....

"Protection of the assets of the Co-op is a greater service to the members and the consumers than risky investments. The Board should satisfy itself that, if the investment proved to be a mistake, GCS could take the losses without sinking the Co-op....

Another factor to be considered, no matter how promising the opportunity, is whether GCS has the money to carry the investment through....Just as cash and credit are limited resources, management talent is a limited resource. Its allocation requires thought as to alternative advantages.

"Of particular concern to a co-op is whether the proposed expansion would fill existing consumer needs....If adequate shopping facilities are now provided, it would be unwarranted for GCS to use resources to enter into head-on competition with the others....Where an activity has proved, after reasonable test, to be uneconomic, or to provide less than an optimum return on investment, or to fail to meet members' needs, it should be discontinued.

"GCS experience in real estate operations reflects an amateurism that gives little hope of future success...try to divest itself of this type of business....A policy that merits further investigation, is that we should plan smaller, expandable supermarkets in the future. They might revert to being primarily food stores...soft goods buying and merchandising calls for different talents than those required for groceries....Reduced size will require a smaller investment of men and money, with a commensurate smaller risk....Some consumer needs may be provided now, but at prices which GCS could reduce significantly while still satisfying its investment criteria: home repairs, lawn and garden shops, do-it-yourself shops, etc....For the time being, expansion plans will be developed only as and if the financial and administrative capabilities warrant and only in accordance with sound planning."

After directors read the report they met with Checchi in a day-long discussion of the many details and possible remedial steps to be taken. Various directors took exception to some findings and conclusions, especially some points relating to overall observations about consumer cooperatives and the Board. A host of questions were asked. Follow up conferences explored various facets of the reports and discussed management recommendations and Board actions to reduce real estate holdings, put together a better advertising program, lower wholesaling costs, and to decide when and how to expand or limit facilities for the good health of the Cooperative.

The Board was unanimous in agreeing that this was the only thorough and detailed analysis of Greenbelt Consumer Services, Inc. ever made up to this time. There was a feeling that after 2 years of escalating problems and discouraging operations, the Cooperative was pointed in the right direction and could expect better performance for its 24,000 member-owners. One hopeful sign was the tapering off of requests for GCS to purchase back shares from stockholders. By May 1963, the backlog of requests had been liquidated and there still remained several thousand dollars in the reserve fund for repurchases.

However, despite many improvements in operations and despite phenomenal sales and net margins for the new SCAN furniture division, there were disappointing slippage in sales and continuing operating losses in supermarkets, service stations, and pharmacies.

Retiring director Henry Redkey left with the Board on June 7, 1963 a five-page memo in which he said:

"I had hoped to find encouragement, but I must sadly confess that I found none. Throughout these [financial and operating] reports there is the same dreary, dismal tale. Here are some direct quotes, out of context to be sure, but they throw a spotlight on the road ahead:

"'For the 3 months ending April 27, the company (note that we call it a company now, not a co-op) operated at a loss of $57,000, attributable to retail operations....Assets declined and also liabilities and stockholders equity....Our first objective has been to improve sales. Here, progress has been slow....As the year progressed our sales picture became continuously more unsatisfactory....We are attempting in our ads to create a more aggressive price image and remove the feeling that many people have that we are high priced....The competition situation continues to get more severe....This is an older store and one that is on our priority list for renovating. Our competition would close a store of this vintage and replace it with a new one in that area or further out....Sales promotion is the major current problem in the supermarket division....Advertising has been increased....In our market all major chains except Safeway and A&P use stamps....In retailing a sales problem is usually met with a more aggressive advertising and pricing program....We are penalized with a number of stores that are much too large for the volume of business done....We need to reach non-shoppers in our immediate trading area....Reactions of competitors to aggressive price and advertising programs are very important in determining their success....[etc.]'" Redkey's memo went on to criticize management's cuts in the member relations program and proposal to change the CO-OP NEWSLETTER from weekly to once-a-month publication.

Although the Board renewed the Checchi contract in June, and the Morrow/Checchi management team and the Board continued to work well together, the rosy glow had faded by the middle of 1963. Ahead some very tough decisions had to be made.

The Board scheduled a regular Board meeting once a month, taking a full Saturday. These were rotated around the 11 store areas, to encourage attendance by members. Meeting dates and places were planned a year in advance and published in the CO-OP NEWSLETTER. As the heavy workload for the Board continued there were frequent special meetings.

The directors took time out for fun on occasion. In August, Director Solomon Hoke invited the entire Board and key management staff and other Co-op leaders to his farm north of Westminster, Maryland for a barbecue. This was a fine old family farm with a home built around the original house from the early 1880s. Hoke was well known in Carroll County as a leader in farm cooperative and rural community activities. He was valued on the GCS Board for his sound judgment and unassuming role as a balance man.

During these critical years, Greenbelt Cooperative was blessed with directors who brought skills to the Board as well as mature judgment and devotion to their responsibilities. George Weber, for instance, from Fairlington, was one of the most knowledgeable treasurers we had. Bob Bonham, earlier also had proved especially qualified in that position.

Aileen Newman, from Wheaton, was an effective and untiring advocate of consumer issues -- one of a proud list of women on the Board over the years who made a difference in county, state, and Federal legislation and regulation of the market place on behalf of consumers. There were many others: Bertha Maryn, Carnie Harper, Doris Behre, Dorothy Wheeler.

Gif Hoag, who was vice president in 1963, came from Falls Church and brought to the Board a wealth of knowledge about cooperatives gained in his position with the Farm Credit system. Hoag was active in one leadership position or another through all the years even through the bankruptcy year of 1989. He was the one who could be called upon to find a compromise in disputes or point a way out of a dilemma.

And for expertise on how a Board of Directors should perform or how to run a meeting, Ben Rosenzweig (Greenbelt) went on to teach courses at the Cooperative Institute Association summer sessions. Years later, Paul O. Mohn (Wheaton) brought professional skills in leadership to the Board.

Checchi, in a talk one time, commented that the GCS Board during the mid-60s was the hardest working and best performing that he had observed among all the corporations with which his firm had worked.

The GCS Co-op Congress, too, carried a heavy agenda and had outstanding leadership during these years. In 1963, this 104 delegate body from the 11 Co-op areas elected John F. Staehle to be Speaker.

Despite the moratorium on expansion for GCS, there were two additions in 1963. After a long search, management negotiated a new location for Fairlington when the lease expired on the original store building. The floor space was 25 percent larger in the new location, and there was more parking capacity. The rent was higher than management or the Board wanted to pay, but sales justified the decision. This continued to be the smallest of the Cooperative's stores.

The other expansion project was a SCAN furniture store on West Broad Street in Falls Church, about a block from the supermarket and service station.

XII. THE CHECCHI/MORROW EXPERIENCE (1964-1965)

After the summer of 1963, operations began to improve, slowly and haltingly. The bottom had been reached and GCS was still in business. What made that difference? Four actions mainly:

      1. Deep cuts in staffing and controllable expenses (and some of these hurt!).

      2. A wide range of improvements in operations, including attention to store maintenance, shifts in merchandising, better training of personnel, and more efficient use of resources.

      3. Sale of real estate, which had been tying up capital (this relieved the cash crunch).

      4. Conversion of the supermarkets to a new marketing strategy identified as Consumers Discount Supermarkets, with a new logo.

We will want to have a closer look at all four of these moves, but the most drastic and controversial -- as well as the most successful -- was the changed identification of the stores to fit the discount merchandising fight for higher sales volume against the flood of competing new supermarkets.

Management's report on the supermarket division for the June 8, 1963 Board meeting showed Penn Daw making the poorest showing of the Cooperative's 11 supermarkets. Its 1962 fiscal year registered an operating loss of $76,867. The store's average weekly sales for May 1963 had fallen to $20,772, less than a third of what had been forecast when the store was opened. Average weekly sales per square foot were a miserably low 99 cents compared, for instance, with Wheaton's $4.05. Inventory turned over 11.02 times per year compared with an industry-wide figure of more than 14 times.

As an experiment, the Board approved management's proposal to convert Penn Daw to a lower retail price format in the expectation of higher sales. Senator Maurine Neuberger (D., Ore.) cut the ribbon at a ceremony on July 24, 1963. First week sales jumped to $57,135. Average weekly sales for December 1963 were $54,310. Weekly sales per square foot went up to $1.60, and inventory turnover improved to 16.69! In the first 3 months as a Consumer Discount Supermarket, Penn Daw registered an operating profit of $10,627, as against a loss of $13,516 for the 9 months prior to the conversion.

Encouraged by results at Penn Daw, the Checchi/Morrow management team recommended to the Board that the aggressive, low-gross-margin program be introduced at the N&W market in Dundalk and in the Pennmar supermarket. These stores, like Penn Daw, had gained only a few hundred members each, were somewhat isolated, and faced declining sales that were far below the forecast.

Here, too, conversion to Consumers Discount Supermarkets improved sales, though not as much as at Penn Daw. Westminster was next on the list, although it had a large membership of dedicated cooperators and was not in such bad financial shape as the first three that were converted. Morrow reported to the Board in a confidential memo on November 19 that there had been a 70 percent gain in sales at the four stores since the changeover.

Operations had improved by this time to a level where all the GCS facilities except two supermarkets and two service stations were making some contribution to central office overhead costs.

The Board voted on November 20 to let management convert the remaining supermarkets to the Consumers Discount format. Sales improved only modestly, because by this time competing chains were aware of the GCS marketing plans and fought back with discounting schemes and sales promotions of their own.

But for some members and leaders of the Greenbelt Cooperative there was a down side to the switch to Consumers Discount -- not to the merchandising technique but to the loss of "CO-OP" identity. These feelings expressed in letters, telephone calls, and comments and questions in meetings were summarized in a four- page memo Director Donald Cooper wrote to each of the other directors on February 5, 1964, together with a lengthy motion for consideration. Here are excerpts:

"....Conversion to discount pricing and merchandising...was approved after questions were raised about signs on the stores and about preservation of 'CO-OP' identity. This was especially important at Westminster, which has a long and honorable experience with cooperatives.

"It was not really until after the conversion of the remaining supermarkets that the extent of 'Consumers Discount' replacement of 'CO-OP' became apparent. Then over a period of some weeks, the following developments gradually came to our attention:

(a) 'Consumers Discount Supermarket' or similar signs went up on the remaining store fronts, and the familiar local store identification which thousands of members and other shoppers had known for many years came down.
(b) Newspaper advertising was increased and changed 'CO-OP' to 'co-op CONSUMERS DISCOUNT'. Then the word 'co-op' was dropped entirely.
(c) 'Consumers Discount' shopping circulars have been distributed door-to-door on a wide scale -- with no addresses for the stores.
(d) Inside the stores, signs calling attention to 'CO-OP' and to member

ownership were removed.

(e) The well known 'CO-OP' identification on shopping bags was replaced by 'Consumers Discount'.

(f) 'Consumer' and 'Discount' signs appeared in the pharmacies.

(g) In the CO-OP NEWSLETTER, which goes to members, advertising dropped 'CO-OP' and substituted 'Consumers Discount' not only for the supermarkets but for pharmacies and for service stations. This action is contrary to Management assurances that 'Consumers Discount' would be used to bring non-shoppers into the stores, where they could then be exposed to 'CO-OP' and become participating members. Dropping 'CO-OP' in the newsletter seems singularly ill-advised. Referring to service stations as 'Consumers Discount' clearly goes beyond authorization of the Board, and indeed carries with it a bit of merchandising fraud inasmuch as no change had been made in pricing or merchandising.

(h) Telephone calls to the GCS office at Beltsville were greeted with 'Consumers Discount'....

"The net effects....The sales picture has improved, in some cases beyond expectations....[but] has caused confusion, uncertainty, and loss of identity for some members....Combined with failure to earn a patronage refund, restrictions on repurchase of stock, and sale of assets, the move to get rid of the name 'CO-OP' has given the impression that we went out of business or reorganized or changed ownership. This Director has had more inquiries about 'What happened to our Co-op?' than about any other single event in the entire history of GCS...."

The accompanying resolution was discussed at length at the Board meeting, but a shorter and less specific motion was substituted and passed on a divided vote. Management was thereby alerted to the confusion and displeasure of some members, but was given approval for a change that obviously was reviving the business.

For legal and accounting purposes, the Board created an additional corporation as a wholly owned subsidiary -- Consumers Discount Supermarket, Inc. Other wholly owned subsidiaries at this time were:

Rochdale Cooperative, Inc. -- to permit operations in Virginia.

Potomac Petroleum Distributors, Inc. -- for contracts and purchases for the service stations.

Consumers Realty and Equipment Corporation -- to handle real estate transactions.

Potomac Export-Import Corporation -- for overseas buying and selling transactions.

N&W Consumers, Inc. -- to afford legal and financial protection for the supermarket at Dundalk.

The GCS Board served as the board for these wholly owned subsidiaries. Also, the Board elected the allocated number of directors to boards of the following partially owned corporations:

Potomac Cooperators, Inc. -- to handle warehouse real estate and financing.
Takoma Park Shopping Center, Inc. -- real estate partnership for this development.
Smiths Bakery.

During the shortage of cash in 1963, $60,000 in dividends from profits in these subsidiaries was declared by the Board, payable to GCS. Such inter-company dividends were not subject to Federal income tax and made no change in the Cooperative's consolidated financial statement. Having these funds in the parent company was a help in financial planning since they were not needed at this time in the subsidiaries.

More cash came from the sale of real estate and equipment, which could then be leased back and the rent charged off as an expense of doing business. This was more economical than borrowing cash for operations and was preferable when the debt ratio was already high.

By the end of 1963, all but a small parcel of the GCS holdings in Greenbelt had been sold. At the end of that year, the Board, on recommendation of management, sold the Beltsville warehouse and land options for $557,133.82 to Parkwood, Inc. One hundred thousand dollars of this was in cash, which was a real boost for the Cooperative's operations. This sale gave GCS a net gain of $94,977.

Much later, Parkwood ran into financial troubles that caused legal problems for GCS involving a long and costly lawsuit. But in 1964 the warehouse sale supplied needed cash. GCS continued to use space in the Beltsville warehouse on a rental basis, and then later contracted for warehouse and wholesale operation elsewhere. Offices of the Cooperative were maintained at the Beltsville location until 1969 and then moved to the Piney Branch store.

GCS continued to lose money on its real estate operations. It had over $500,000 tied up in the Takoma Park Shopping Center, Inc. partnership. Because this real estate corporation operated at a loss, GCS had to supply cash for interest payments on a bank loan to the Takoma Park corporation. There was no early prospect
of unloading this albatross.

The GCS management was able during the latter part of 1963 and into 1964 to rent out shop spaces which had been standing vacant in Takoma Park, Penn Daw, Piney Branch, and Wheaton. This improved the income picture a little.

The bowling alley under the Greenbelt store stood empty for many months after the operator was evicted for not paying his rent.

Garage space at the Wheaton, Takoma Park, and Piney Branch service stations was rented to independent auto mechanics when figures showed that GCS was operating repair service at a considerable loss. This service continued at the Greenbelt station though, which had built a reputation for dependable work and where the financial returns were satisfactory.

Improved performance in Co-op facilities came also from better merchandising. Managers paid more attention to keeping the stores and service stations clean, and the maintenance schedules were kept current.

As money became available, the older supermarkets were renovated, one by one. Remodeling Wheaton took $40,000 in leasehold improvements and $185,000 in the leasing of new equipment. But on completion, sales rose 39 percent over the same period a year earlier.

The percentage of out-of-stock items was reduced to acceptable industry levels. Some slow moving goods were removed from the shelves. The number of brands of a particular product were reduced in some instances, in order to lower inventory. CO-OP label products carried on the shelves actually increased to 364 by mid-1964. Sales of CO-OP label items supplied through the warehouse increased 55 percent to 76,642 cases for a 13-week period. This did not include CO-OP label frozen foods, bread, potato chips, etc. packed and delivered directly on GCS contract.

Recipes and homemaker suggestions accompanied shopping specials in the stores. The CO-OP NEWSLETTER devoted space to articles for consumers on how to select and prepare various cuts of meat, seasonal good buys in fruits and vegetables, product packaging and labeling, auto care and maintenance, and other concerns. By the end of 1964, homemaker sessions were again attracting shoppers in the stores.

Management's 19-page report on supermarket operations for the Board's meeting on April 11, 1964 noted, in part:

"...so as to better reflect the objective of serving as a purchasing agent...each of the major departments was given a program in which the areas needing improvement were identified

....assigning to each member of the staff specific responsibilities and authority to more effectively use the managerial and merchandising skills available.

"...improvement of buying procedures and re-negotiation of present buying arrangements....adapting the in-store merchandising to dominant race, religious, nationality, and income concentrations in the trading area....correct allocation of shelf space to product groups....Standards are intended to give the store manager a guide of what is expected of him and his personnel in the performance of listed specific tasks related to the effective operation of the supermarket....

"Programs being developed...job descriptions for each position, shrinkage control [theft, breakage], improved operational forecasts, inventory control...."

On product diversification, for example: "We now carry 29 varieties of cheese, a larger selection of this type of product than any of our major competitors...in response to customer suggestions. This program is being copied by a major chain...."

A "Handbook for Checkers" was developed as a revision of an earlier guide, and training sessions for all levels of the staff improved employee performance. In a personnel report in November 1964, a listing of training experience for improvement in job performance filled six pages.

By mid-1964, sales per man-hour in the GCS supermarkets averaged 34.1 against the Supermarket Institute figure of 27.4 for the industry. Average hourly salary rate for store personnel (excluding the manager and department heads) was $2.48 for GCS, compared with $2.00 as the SMI industry average.

All of these factors helped build sales volume and net margins -- and reduced customer complaints.

In response to insistence by the Board and Congress which had continued over the years, management prepared for all new employees an orientation into consumer cooperatives and some background of Greenbelt Consumer Services. This had been done in some of the earlier years. Unfortunately, in the years following the Checchi/Morrow management this orientation was offered only sporadically.

Management maintained a schedule of training and development for top staff and middle management. This included supervisory skills, marketing, and the range of specialized information needed for grocery, auto service, drug store, and furniture operations. Seminars, workshops, conferences, and classroom courses provided by trade associations, universities, the American Management Association, and cooperatives were used as appropriate. This program filled a long-felt need.

While money went into employee training and staff development, economies were realized from reduced travel and conferences during the critical period of operating losses. From the beginning of 1962 well into 1964 there was a conscious policy of pinching pennies.

One measure of economies could be seen in the reduction of administrative staff in relation to total staff. In a period of two and a half years, while the total number of employees increased by 65, and with more facilities and much larger gross sales, the number of administrative and supervisory personnel was reduced by 40, a drop of nearly 50 percent.

By the end of 1964, it was clear that GCS had emerged from its sales decline and financial threat. Supermarket sales for the calendar year were above the projected budget and 44 percent above the previous year. Every store was above its 1963 sales level. All four divisions showed net operating savings, and the net income total for GCS was $304,183.

All of the 10 basic operating and financial ratios at the end of December had improved over the figures at end of calendar 1963, and all but three were acceptable.

For the previous year the dividend on shares was 4 percent, paid largely from reserves. The 1964 dividend was back to 5 percent, but still no patronage refund. Morrow advised, in a management report to the Board, that members actually were getting a patronage refund up front through the discount prices. As a matter of policy, the Board determined that if net savings continued they should be used to rebuild reserves before consideration of patronage refunds.

GCS used its improved financial position to bring up to date all requests for repurchase of stock. By end of 1964, enough confidence was restored so that purchases of new shares exceeded by a little margin the repurchase by the Cooperative of old shares. The directors and general manager felt justified in rescinding the 10 percent cut in compensation they had adopted earlier when things looked bleak.

Better sales, improved operations, and favorable margins also allowed some selected expansion. First on the list was a new SCAN furniture store. This third "Co-op Contemporary Furniture" store was on T street NW just off Connecticut Avenue, in Washington, D.C. It was a good location, and after an elegant opening it added sales and profits as well as prestige to the Greenbelt Cooperative.

Looking ahead, the Board added another wholly owned subsidiary corporation, SCAN, Inc., to its structure. This new corporate entity was organized under the District of Columbia model consumer cooperative law and was advantageous to GCS in computing state income taxes.

Sales and net margins from the three SCAN furniture stores were so far ahead of expectations that Morrow/Checchi recommended a furniture warehouse. GCS was importing direct from Denmark and the other Scandinavian countries through the port of Baltimore, so it was imperative to have warehousing northeast of Washington, preferably near I-95 and the Capital Beltway.

In a 9-page presentation to the Board, Morrow and Checci said:

"Leasing this warehouse space increases our fixed commitments in the furniture division and thus increases our risk. However, it is vital that we lease the space if we are to continue to grow and if we wish to handle furniture efficiently....There is the possibility that consumer preference may shift to other styles, but there is no evidence of this thus far. Our pricing structure [less than 50 percent markup] has significantly increased the market for this furniture and middle and upper middle class income families can afford it.

"The risk always exists that supplies may be cut off....import restrictions...higher duties...our government's balance of payments...international monetary changes affecting the dollar...strikes. It is management's judgment that despite these risks, we should continue to expand the furniture business as fast as we can secure personnel to handle the additional responsibilities. It is expected that sales of furniture will exceed $2,000,000 next year...."

A new warehouse in the industrial area of Beltsville, Maryland provided 25,000 square feet at 85 cents per square foot, with room for expansion. This was a 15-year lease, with good possibility of subleasing out part of the space without loss, in case SCAN needs did not develop as forecast. The equipment budget was $45,000 with two-thirds of it leased, so that minimum cash investment was required.

One other expansion project in the fall of 1964 added a twelfth supermarket to the GCS chain. This was for a former Safeway market that had closed during an extended strike in the Baltimore area. The building offered 32,000 square feet with plenty of parking, located in Glen Burnie, Maryland. The site was on the Baltimore-Annapolis Boulevard, about half way between the two cities.

A detailed market survey showed that this was a blue-collar community with population growth. The area was already saturated with stores, but the leasing terms were attractive and only for an initial 2-year period. After study of management's 10-page information packet and considerable questioning, the Board approved the project by a 4-1 vote in hopes that this might be a companion co-op venture to the store in Dundalk.

Approval of any expansion project by less than a majority of the full nine-director board was unusual. In this case no question about the decision was raised later by the remaining directors. It can be noted here that this store did not do well and no real customer interest in the Cooperative was developed.

New ventures were required to be in accord with and within the limitations of the Board's written policy on expansion and contraction of facilities. They also had to be in compliance with the Cooperative's One Year and Five Year Plans.

As a direct result of the earlier crisis, the Board in 1962 had adopted a written policy statement on long-range planning. It called for the Board and the general manager to agree on a plan for each of the coming 5 years, in general form to cover:

--Types of services and location of facilities.
--Amounts and sources of financing.
--Membership and stock outstanding.
--Adequate staff, training programs, and executive development.

Planning to be based on:
--The Cooperative's objectives and policies.
--Stated assumptions regarding the Cooperative's ability to serve its consumers, improve its competitive position, and maintain a sound financial position.
--Sound economic and financial analysis and thorough marketing research.

The first year's planning would be detailed. Annually during the first quarter of each new fiscal year, performance in the previous year would be reviewed and the plan revised to advance one year.

During all of the Checchi years as general manager, this long-range planning was a foundation for the Cooperative's operations. It was especially valuable in scheduling the financing program so that borrowings and repayments could mesh without causing cash flow problems.

Another strong support for the success of GCS operations was the management contract itself, into which the Board built incentives for meeting specified goals. The contract was for one year at a time, in line with a bylaws provision. There was a flat annual fee to be paid in equal monthly instalments to retain Checchi and Co. as "managing agents" for Greenbelt Consumer Services, Inc. This included the salary for a resident general manager who would manage the day-to-day operations and report directly to the Board as well as to Checchi. Morrow was the resident general manager -- the "acting" designation had been dropped after the first year. For 1964 the management contract figure was $30,000. It was raised to $42,500 for 1965, of which $12,000 went to Morrow. Anything above that amount for Morrow was Checchi's responsibility.

As incentive, the Board agreed to a bonus of 5 percent of net savings before taxes in excess of $200,000, payable upon completion of the annual audit. This was designed to encourage margins for GCS which would assure the 5 percent dividend on shares of stock and hopefully patronage refunds at some point.

The Board had additional concerns. It wanted from the new management something beyond good operating margins. An attachment to the contract stated in part:

"The Board is interested in a well balanced operation and will require at least satisfactory performance in all important areas as set forth in objectives and certain priorities selected by the Board and agreed to by the General Manager....

"Objectives will be those set forth in the bylaws, the policies and directives of the Board, and the minutes of the Cooperative, with special reference to points listed in Policy No. 17, 'Duties and Responsibilities of the General Manager'.

"Priorities will include the following:
    1. Improved member relations....To accomplish these aims, there must be an increase in the number of members who recognize their rights and responsibilities as joint owners of GCS and understand the Cooperative's organization, goals, policies, and problems. [Seven specific programs were spelled out here.]
    2. A revised capital structure program in keeping with the needs of the Cooperative for the years immediately ahead -- as related to stock, debentures, dividends, reserves, patronage refunds, and capital investment.
    3. Improved consumer-orientation as evidenced through employee attitudes and through in-store signs, displays, and activities."

For achievement in objectives and priorities listed in each year's attachment to the contract, the general manager could receive an additional bonus, from 0 to 10 percent of any net margin before income tax above $200,000. The percent was determined at the end of the year in the board's annual review of the performance of the general manager.

This annual evaluation was taken seriously by both the Board and the general manager. Quarterly checkups against points in the contract and in board policy no. 17 were made but these were brief and served mostly as reminders. The annual review and evaluation in 1964 involved 11 meetings or mailings spread over 3 weeks, with one director elected to prepare the final draft using input drafts from each director.

During 1964, improvements in operations and good working relations between management and the Board and the GCS Co-op Congress with its store area delegations encouraged more activities to benefit and involve members.

The 25th annual GCS membership meeting included a chicken barbecue at Greenbelt, in a wooded area a few hundred feet behind the supermarket building. Some 70 volunteers fed 600 members, who paid for their dinner. At the meeting in the Youth Center, 2,178 votes were cast for directors and bylaws amendments. Displays, literature tables, and a speaker on consumer affairs were added attractions.

John S. Staehle was Congress Speaker, and the representatives from the store areas produced several significant contributions to the Cooperative in this period. One with great promise never quite reached fulfillment. The Wheaton delegation tried to establish a constituency for each representative. This attempt to make democracy work better was great in theory and looked good on paper, but required more effort than most of the elected representatives could afford. Realizing that a representative could not keep in touch with 200 members, which was the election quota specified in the bylaws, some obtained from the office the names, addresses and telephone numbers of from 10 to 25 nearby members. The intent was to have them bring suggestions, questions, and complaints in person or by telephone for response. It worked for awhile in some areas, and there were enough neighborhood meetings to give hope for a network. A few additional potential leaders were discovered, and from time to time in subsequent years the idea was again tried but without much lasting success.

Some other projects turned out better. One of these was the Congress committee study on what the GCS Co-op image should be. The committee's ideas were passed to the Board, and management input also went into policy statement no. 37. This ended up as a four-page listing of 21 qualities that should be perceived in appraising GCS. The last of these points read: "We seek the support and participation of all in making GCS at one and the same time a successful competitive economic enterprise and an organization concerned for individual human values." This pretty well summed up the dichotomy that produced contention all through the 50 years of the Greenbelt Cooperative's growth and decline.

One small victory for those pledged to the Rochdale tradition was management's agreement to post a uniform green, gold, and black decal on the glass doors of all GCS facilities, showing the twin pine trees and the words: "Another consumer-owned store".

Congress and area delegation committees conducted customer surveys and price checks in the stores which assisted management in upgrading operations. Other rewarding activities involved proposals for additional member benefits, continuing testimony before Congressional committees, and work with state legislators on legislation for consumer protection.

A major change in 1964 was the hiring, again, of a full-time staff member in charge of a member relations department. There was a lot of catching up to be done from the cutbacks 2 years earlier. The expanding travel program which had been a direct responsibility of the Board was turned over to the member relations staff. Besides the charter flights, the Co-op offered its members eight money-saving charter bus trips to the New York World's Fair in 1964. The first 4 years of charter flights saved participating members $291,300 cash-in-the-pocket in contrast to fares for the same accommodations on regularly scheduled flights. Many new members came into GCS to take advantage of its travel program.

When the Cooperative Institute Association held its 35th summer training courses at Hobart College, 17 from GCS joined more than 125 other leaders and potential leaders from other cooperatives. Several were young people on scholarships provided by GCS's member relations program. This was the beginning of a Co-op Youth Group which would produce, it was hoped, future leaders and an influx of younger people into the aging membership. After a brief flurry of activity which included Board participation, the well intentioned project faded away.

The Greenbelt Co-op was a major supporter of the Cooperative Institute Association during the '60s, both in its financing and its staffing. Victor Smith, the staff member who now headed up the member relations program, Rosenzweig, Hoag, and Cooper from the Board, and others from GCS led classes and served on the Institute board.

With improved net margins from the stores, there was more leeway for working with other cooperative entities like the Institute, and the International Cooperative Development Association, which GCS joined as a charter member to assist cooperatives overseas. This was a link for GCS with farmer production and marketing cooperatives. The Board also authorized a donation of $2,500 to the Cooperative League for its Worldwide Extension Service.

There was money, too, for some public relations promotion. GCS took part in the International Food Show when it opened at the Armory in Washington. The booth was manned by 45 member and staff volunteers, taking turns.

Some other public exposure was free. Scandinavian Airlines featured SCAN furniture in a downtown window display. Pepsi-Cola sponsored a nationwide "shopping spree" contest which was won by a refugee Cuban family in the Washington area -- a family with 14 children who happened to be a strong supporter of the Co-op and regular shoppers at the Takoma Park supermarket. In a 15-minute race through the aisles, they carried $11,002.49 in meats and groceries to the checkout counter to the cheers of hundreds of onlookers. Pepsi-Cola picked up the tab plus damage and cleanup. The newspaper and radio publicity was a priceless boost for Co-op.

The Greenbelt Cooperative also picked up public relations kudos for being the first merchandisers in the Washington market area to sell biodegradable detergent. At the end of the first year, this CO-OP label product had out-sold all other detergents on the shelves, and helped the GCS reputation as an innovator.

Tours of the Co-op's facilities by school and kindergarten classes and neighborhood groups were encouraged. And there was a constant stream of visitors from other cooperatives and from government and industry people in many foreign countries.

By the time 1965 was ushered in, management had completed its streamlined reorganization of staff and had its training program in place. Operating standards were proving their worth. Catherine Hildeen, head of the personnel division, noted in her 31-page annual report on GCS personnel that employee turnover was decreasing and stood at a better level than the industry average. She stated that "our union relations continue to be good". Hildeen, by the way, continued in charge of personnel until 1978, completing 27 years with the Cooperative.

The Board had moved past the frantic pace and workload of the earlier '60s. Meetings were back to a once-a-month schedule. There still was plenty of homework for directors, with a packet of reports, motions, back-up information, industry magazine and newspaper clips, and minutes which measured from a quarter- to a half-inch thick. The packet used color-coded paper for easy reference.

Minutes of Board meetings were posted on supermarket bulletin boards, and a summary published in the NEWSLETTER. Written minutes of Executive Committee meetings were distributed to all directors and actions taken by the Executive Committee required verification by the Board. Confidential minutes of the Board's executive sessions were kept in a separate "green book" and turned over by retiring directors to their successors. From time to time confidential minutes were proposed by the secretary for declassification.

The president, secretary, and treasurer, making up the Executive Committee, checked several times during 1963 and 1964 on time devoted to the Cooperative. The totals came to between 18 and 41 hours a week. They had occasion to wonder how they found time for family life and for earning a living.

Board turnover in the '60s averaged about one or two directors per year, which was quite a contrast to high turnover in some earlier years.

In 1965, the Board voted to invite former directors to serve as an advisory panel to the current Board. This move was not followed up after the first year, however, so no further use was made of this reservoir of valuable experience and resource skills.

One of the Cooperative's best innovations may have been a few years ahead of its time. The National Council of Senior Citizens, which had been a major supporter of Medicare and had strong union ties, inquired whether GCS would be interested in a joint venture to provide a prescription-by-mail service for senior citizens and Co-op members who did not have easy access to a drug store.

After some exploration of the idea, the NCSC found that it lacked the necessary capital for such a project. GCS management and Board thought so well of the concept that they talked with other groups and found that the National Farmers Union was interested. It was agreed that GCS would manage the service with NFU sharing the start-up capital. Both NFU and NCSC would do the promotional work to maintain the business. Older members of all three organizations would be eligible to buy prescription drugs, vitamins, and health accessories by mail at discount prices.

In the spring of 1965, Senior Citizens Direct Drug Service, Inc. began operations from a pharmacy located near a post office, at 823 Upshur Street NW in Washington, D.C. The Co-op's pharmacy division director, Norman Stein, supervised the new endeavor. He pointed out in the announcement of the service that:

"Registered pharmacists will make up the staff, and all local and national pharmacy and health regulations will be strictly observed. We feature our own CO-OP label top-quality drugs and vitamins. We will also feature generic drugs which can be used to fill your prescriptions, if specified by your doctor, at a big saving."

This enterprise should have been a spectacular success. There was an obvious need, and the three sponsoring organizations had enough membership to support it. The American Association of Retired Persons ran a similar mail order prescription program that was not in competition with the one GCS was operating. The GCS-NFU-NCSC enterprise was moderately successful, and lasted until 1974. The investment had not been large, so the loss was negligible. Best estimate would be that the idea of mail order pharmacy service was too new for widespread acceptance and the promotion was inadequate. Increased postage rates and packaging costs were the factors cited for closing.

Another service which should have been a great member benefit was a credit union for members of Greenbelt Cooperative who did not already have access through their work place. Those Co-op members who lived in the City of Greenbelt had their own Greenbelt Credit Union. GCS members in the Wheaton area had organized a credit union which all GCS employees could use.

Joseph Comproni, manager of the Greenbelt Credit Union, was able to get a charter change so that GCS members could join. After much haggling, a branch office was opened in the Takoma Park supermarket for a time, but there were continuing problems about the size of the space, the service provided, and provision for covering costs of the branch office. The GCS Board sought a merger of the Greenbelt and the Wheaton Credit Unions. This was finally achieved in 1975. By then the Wheaton group had reorganized and had a different name. Later, a branch office was installed at the Aspen Hill SCAN store on Georgia Avenue in Montgomery County, Maryland for a short time. Really satisfactory credit union service for GCS members never was achieved.

Car leasing was another member benefit that was tried but was not very successful. About 1,500 inquiries came to the member relations office following the announcement in the NEWSLETTER. This was another of those projects that just sort of drifted off and disappeared.

Other, smaller ventures won endorsement from members and became part of the Greenbelt Co-op legend. The annual Christmas tree sale was one of these. In its best years, an entire boxcar load of prime trees would be ordered from Canada, usually from a forestry or Christmas tree cooperative. Sales were directly from the railroad siding, with member volunteers unloading and handling the sales. Proceeds after covering the costs generally went to some goodwill fund like the Cooperative Worldwide Extension Service.

Discount tickets for performances of various sorts proved popular. These were handled through the restored member relations program. Folk dancing, group camping, and art classes were other activities sponsored as part of the member benefits program. Within the growing membership there were many hobbies and special interests. The Board adopted a policy which provided a meeting place and publicity for these groups of members. The main stipulation was that activities would have to pay their own way after an initial start-up period.

Demonstrating that the Co-op was more than merchandising, SCAN stores arranged art shows. The supermarkets sponsored contests for window drawings on Halloween. Bake sales by non-profit neighborhood organizations were encouraged. "Edie" Christianson taught hundreds of members how to make glo-candles. Information about cooperatives was placed in local libraries by GCS area councils. The Greenbelt area delegation sponsored a concert for the community.

The Morrow/Checchi management and the Board continually came up with innovations that benefitted all shoppers. One of these was a new type of plastic milk carton with stiffened sides not so likely to collapse as the type in general use. Other chains adopted it shortly thereafter. Bulk sales from covered containers, at prices lower than packaged goods -- such as beans, rice, dried fruits, nuts, coffee beans, some candies -- was another idea that was copied.

In early 1965, GCS obtained a dairy contract which permitted vitamin D homogenized milk to be sold at 5 cents less than the going market rate. This time the arrangement was found acceptable by the unions. An earlier attempt -- also with a unionized dairy -- was put aside by threats of a boycott due to a jurisdictional dispute. Another earlier boycott, over the bread and other baked goods from the partly GCS-owned bakery at Ladiesburg, was avoided by unionizing the bakery. GCS also had difficulties on occasion about union rules on the proportion of part-time employees, and on seniority rules, but these were always ironed out. Strikes were avoided because the GCS contract dates followed those of the larger chains, and GCS acquiesced to whatever terms the others wrote into their contracts. Sometimes the union negotiator could make concessions because of the great difference in number of stores and number of employes.

There was additional expansion in 1965.

GCS's eighth pharmacy opened about a mile south of the Falls Church supermarket and service station. It was the largest drug store and the only one at a separate location from other Co-op facilities -- except the pharmacy in the Takoma Park clinic and the mail order pharmacy in Washington, D.C. The new drug store had 3,000 square feet of floor space. It was located at the corner of Arlington Boulevard and Annandale Road, in northern Virginia. September 8 was the opening date. Identified as "Consumers Discount", it had little "Co-op" identification. Sales and margins turned out to be below expectations. It was later closed.

At almost the same time, the Falls Church supermarket got a major face lift which was much needed.

The biggest and most important expansion project in 1964 was a fourth SCAN furniture store. This one was located, after an exhaustive study of options, in the western suburbs of Baltimore. The building, at 404-406 Reistertown Road in Pikesville, had been built for a savings and loan that failed to move in, so it was a handsome facility for SCAN. It was new, and the price was acceptable because it had been standing empty. The cost was $157,000 for about 6,200 square feet of floor space. Purchase was contrary to the Co-op's policy of leasing facilities to avoid tieing up capital, but in this case, the Checchi/Morrow recommendation concluded that returns could be 22.5 percent over renting.

The Pikesville SCAN opened September 1964, and sales were up to expectations. News came from Denmark that the GCS SCAN operation had become the largest customer of the export agency for Scandinavian cooperatives.

As fiscal year 1965 came to a close, members and shoppers in the Fairlington neighborhood had their long-cherished hope for an auto service station realized. This eighth station was located at the intersection of Quaker Lane and King's Highway, about two blocks from the small Fairlington market.

XIII. THE TAKEOVER ATTEMPT (1966)

At 11:15 on the night of April 25, 1966, Secretary Cooper answered his door at home to five strangers.

"Are you Don Cooper?"

"Yes."

"You are the secretary of Greenbelt Consumer Services?"

"Yes. What can I do for you?"

"We have some petitions for candidates for the Board of Directors. It's not midnight yet, so they are valid."

I assured them that petitions for candidates could be accepted up to midnight, and explained that the petitions would be valid as long as the candidates and at least 10 of those who signed the petitions were members of the Cooperative. Before giving me the petitions, the spokesman for the group gave me a prepared receipt for me to sign "as proof that you have received the petitions".

That's how 7 weeks of a bizarre attempt to take over GCS began. What followed seemed quite threatening at the time, though in retrospect there were some comical aspects.

By 1966, GCS' success under the Checchi contract was well established, and the Washington newspapers had carried articles on the increased sales and "profits".

As provided in the bylaws, the 11th GCS Co-op Congress meeting in early April selected five candidates from those nominated to run as the Congress slate in the June 12 election by the members of the Cooperative. These five would constitute a majority of the nine-director board.

News of the petition candidates hit the front pages of the Washington newspapers the next day, one with a banner headline. Two spokesmen for the group were quoted at length about their intentions to use the Co-op to help the poor.

In the CO-OP NEWSLETTER to members, Congress Speaker Irving Rotkin stated the viewpoint of GCS leadership:

"As in the past, the Congress members have had the opportunity of observing for at least the past year the nominees they select. During this time, the behavior, sincerity, and capability of each was continuously on display at Congress meetings, committee meetings and other Cooperative activities. Thus, a basis for the selection, part of the fundamental rationale for having a Congress, was established.

"This year 20 individuals have filed as petition candidates. None of these 20 are or have been active in the Congress, or for that matter in the local area delegations or other units of the Co-op....Only 32 names (including those of the 20 candidates) appeared as signatures for all the petitions. This is legal under the bylaws but betrays a rather woeful lack of membership support.

"In the absence of any information, I assume that the candidates are honest and sincere, that their intentions and ideals are of the highest. I am even willing to grant, sight unseen, that they may be capable and successful in their respective fields of endeavor.

"However, I must challenge whether their knowledge of Greenbelt Consumer Services, its policies and objectives, or their previous involvement in the Co-op's activities is sufficient to enjoy even being candidates for the Board of Directors. I must also question the propriety -- regardless of the nobility of their professed aims -- of attempting to start from the top....

"I would urge the 20 petition candidates to become active members. Get to know the people and ideals that motivate the Cooperative. Give GCS the benefit of any ideas or proposals they may have. Only on a basis of mutual respect and understanding coupled with demonstrated activity and concern for the Cooperative should they really expect any measure of membership support."

The next edition of the NEWSLETTER carried a special report which was a factual chronology:

"**Editor's Note.** During the past week, several newspaper accounts have appeared in Washington and Baltimore, reporting the attempted takeover of Greenbelt Consumer Services, Inc. The following is a chronological summary of the events:

"A group of people identifying themselves with the civil rights movement are attempting to take over control of GCS by electing five of their members to the nine-person Board of Directors in the annual election June 12.

"L. D. Pratt, identified by the press as an active member of the Free D.C. Movement, is reported to claim credit for the takeover attempt. In interviews, candidates seem divided in their willingness to acknowledge Pratt as a member of their group. However, Pratt's signature appears on 18 of the petitions filed by the candidates.

"L. D. Pratt first came into the GCS picture...in a series of meetings beginning in November 1965. Pratt and a local worker for SNCC, Ralph Featherstone, presented a proposal for ultimately taking over your Piney Branch store by the Washington-Baltimore Freedom Partnership (WBFP) which Pratt proposed to organize. WBFP was to solicit funds to purchase a fleet of Volkswagon buses to be driven by high school dropouts. They would transport shoppers from D.C. to the Piney Branch store. WBFP was to designate the new assistant store manager (orally identified as Pratt). The shoppers were to refund to WBFP from 50 to 100 percent of their savings resulting from shopping at the Piney Branch store.

"GCS questioned the merit of some of these proposals, pointing out that operating a fleet of buses might necessitate complying with Transit Commission regulations; that the WBFP proposal to collect fees from its own members might involve the sale of securities and require compliance with the Securities and Exchange Commission regulations; and that the proposal which ultimately entailed operating a non-union store and specifically required that the usual union regulations not be enforced with respect to Mr. Pratt would violate GCS' contract with the union.

"They replied that they would "love to take on" the Transit Commission and D.C. Transit; would be glad to picket the SEC; and they had people just as big as the union.

"At this point Pratt suggested that WBFP could use persuasion on GCS by picketing the stores, blocking aisles, picketing officials' homes. [Following this conversation] GCS retained Philip Hirschkop of Lainhof, Cohen & Cohen, a firm actively representing civil rights causes. Mr. Hirschkop advised that any threats against GCS in order to secure financial gain for the threatening individual could be treated as criminal. On December 21, 1965, a final meeting was held with Mr. Pratt. He was accompanied by counsel who opened the conversation by saying that he understood some threats were attributed to his clients and he wished to eliminate any inferences of threat making it clear that in the event GCS rejected the WBFP proposal as a business proposition the matter would be closed.

"Mr. Pratt was then informed that the Piney Branch landlord, Nationwide Insurance, had stated through counsel that under Ohio insurance law they could not approve such a group as WBFP as a tenant.

"GCS [management] offered to recommend to the Board the opening of a store in the low income area of D.C. if a suitable site could be found. WBFP was asked to suggest feasible locations. This they declined.

"...then offered to extend the Co-op's discount program to community organizations, donating to WBFP 1 percent of their members' purchases at the Piney Branch store. They declined.

"Next was an offer to assist WBFP in establishing their own cooperative in the District, including surveying a location they might come up with, suggesting a layout of the store, assisting WBFP in purchasing equipment, assisting them in organizing the store, and in approaching GCS suppliers to see if GCS buying arrangements could be extended to them. Once again, they declined.

"On April 25, Mr. Pratt filed papers for 12 petition candidates. That evening, 11 more were delivered to the home of the Secretary, Donald H. Cooper. Some were duplicates. All told, 20 persons had filed as petition candidates, 18 bearing Pratt's signature and 17 Featherstone's. Because the candidates had co- signed each other's petition, only a total of 32 signatures were represented. [All 20 had the requisite 10 signatures.]

"Eight of the 20 joined the Co-op by buying one $10 share April 25, the day they filed as candidates for the Board. Seven others had joined April 23. Only two have been members for more than a year. None of the candidates have previously served [in any capacity] or known to have attended any Co-op meeting.

"When the Board and other Co-op leaders met with five of the candidates May 17, the petition candidates talked in generalities about civil rights and poverty and the 'Dynamics of Power Change'. Their statements did not disclose any previous co-op experience. They seemed unaware -- and uninterested -- that in the Co-op we have been concerned with the plight of the less privileged groups for more than a quarter of a century.

"At this meeting, a spokesman for the petition candidates requested a copy of the GCS membership list. The Board pointed out that it is the Cooperative's policy not to make the list available to any group. However, [the Board] offered to address and mail to the membership, for the actual cost of the mailing, any material which the petition candidates presented for mailing, provided it meets the requirements of the SEC. The group has not accepted the offer."

The petition candidates were invited to address any or all of the area membership meetings along with the Congress slate of candidates, and were given the schedule of meetings. Several did attend and speak at one or more meetings. They were courteously received but not much enthusiasm was observed.

Directors, Congress leaders, and management staff were deeply concerned, not so much about the possibility of petition candidates winning -- obviously 20 candidates vying for 5 positions were going to split their own votes -- but the impression a high vote for the newcomers would make on the membership and on the public. It seemed that an effort was being made to cast the Cooperative in the light of the "bad guys" of the establishment ignoring the poor and the defenders of civil rights.

Victor Smith, head of the Member Relations Department, and a committee made up of directors and Congress leaders organized and launched a campaign to inform members what was at stake in the election and to get out a record vote. Area leaders who carried out the campaign were:

Dorothy Wheeler for Fairlington; Eben Smith, Falls Church; Benjamin Rosenzweig, Greenbelt; Henry Saltzgiver, Dundalk; Jim Westby, Penn Daw; Bob Dressel, Pennmar; Louis Granados, Piney Branch; Ed Bushong, Rockville; Carl Twining, Takoma Park; Paul Fritz, Westminster; and Darwin Bremer, Wheaton.

More than 400 member volunteers visited other members door-to- door or by telephone, persuading them to read information being provided and to vote. Car pools and baby sitters were provided on the day of the annual meeting, which was again held in the Greenbelt Youth Center.

There was a record turnout on June 12. Some but not all of the petition candidates came to the meeting. Candidates were invited to make short presentations if they wished. Ralph Featherstone said from the platform that he would like to stay for the entire meeting, but that he had to leave because his group was picketing the White House.

When the votes were counted, 8,940 valid ballots had been cast. Votes for the Congress-nominated slate ranged from 8,855 to 8,868. Four of the petition candidates had 18 votes each; one had 15, two received 4, two received 2, and the others received a single vote each.

Never again did any organization, company, or individual attempt to take over the Greenbelt Co-op. One lesson I had learned while assigned to defending rural electric cooperatives from hostile takeovers by power companies (when working for the Rural Electrification Administration and later for the National Rural Electric Cooperative Association): A cooperative is most likely to be a target for takeover or "sellout" when (a) it has accumulated capital, especially cash, or profit potential, and (b) at the same time there is a vulnerable board or a membership which does not understand its strength or advantages as owners. The Greenbelt Cooperative fitted criteria (a), but not (b).

Shortly after this demonstration of member loyalty, the new Board, still under the leadership of Ben Rosenzweig as president, sat down with their management team and planned defense measures which would protect the corporate integrity of the Cooperative in future years. One step adopted by the membership was a change in the Board from 2-year terms which elected a majority of directors every other year to 3-year terms, with three directors up for election at one time. Another bylaws change required 100 signatures for a petition candidate instead of only 10. Still a third safeguard called for a Board candidate to have served in some participatory role in leadership or committee work within the previous 5 years.

It is ironic that the ill-conceived idea of taking control of the Greenbelt Co-op for the asserted purpose of helping the poor came at a time when groups in GCS already were at work doing just that. The Penn Daw area delegation had its own "War on Poverty" project under the leadership of Eleanor Thompson and Edna Wiggins. Coordinating with a representative of the Gum Springs Community Action Group, they attempted to start a credit union and set up home tutoring for young people in this impoverished black community just off of U.S. 1, south of Alexandria, Virginia. Other volunteers were trying to start neighborhood or church-oriented buying clubs in Washington's Shaw area.

For some months from 1965 into 1966, GCS had a committee working on establishment of a housing cooperative for low-income senior citizens. This was at first a committee of the GCS Co-op

Congress, with Ernest J. Wolfe as chairman. In June 1966, the Board unanimously voted to explore "the feasibility of GCS sponsorship of a cooperative housing project for the elderly in this area through the use of financing under Section 202 of the National Housing Act." I was designated as the Board representative on a joint committee that then made a detailed study of what would be involved and how such a project could benefit older members of GCS. We consulted at length with Fred Thornthwaite, manager of Consumer Services, Inc. in Detroit which was developing the very successful senior citizens' cooperative apartment housing in that city.

Wolfe devoted hundreds of hours interviewing officials in the U.S. housing agency and county officials, as well as banking and legal consultants. By the end of the year, he had located a suitable site on Carroll Avenue in Takoma Park, Maryland. It took a year to complete all the steps necessary for the loan application to HUD: zoning approval, option on the site, HUD agreement on feasibility, incorporation papers for the nonprofit entity to apply for the Government loan and to own and operate the project, preparation of the loan application, selection of an architect, attorney, and appraiser. The volunteer committee did all of this without cost to GCS.

The architect prepared preliminary drawings that called for 187 units in three sizes in a high-rise apartment on the 6,800 square foot site at the edge of the business district. He did this for free, in expectation of reimbursement if the project would be approved. It appeared that Twin Pines Senior Citizens was ready for launch.

The remaining requirement was a sponsor, willing to put up about $8,000 and assume responsibility for implementing the preparations which had been made. At this point the GCS Board was divided on assuming the advance of funds and the assumption of responsibility. By a one-vote margin, sponsorship was rejected.

With so much time and money invested, and the need for senior citizen low-cost housing so evident, Wolfe then went to the Montgomery County Revenue Authority, which had already expressed interest in the project. The County agreed to be the financial and legal sponsor if GCS would be sort of an unofficial hand holder. GCS management and Board agreed to this arrangement, and Wolfe with some of his committee stayed with the development until it was built and occupied. The result was not a cooperative, but nevertheless a valuable addition to low-cost housing for the elderly. It exists and is successful now as a result of the Greenbelt Cooperative's volunteer initiative and hard work.

During the year, efforts of membership groups within GCS to help families suffering from poverty and discrimination were put on a more organized basis. The 12th Co-op Congress, under the leadership of Speaker Irving Rotkin, adopted unanimously a resolution officially involving the Cooperative in "Inner-City Anti-Poverty Activity", emphasizing the techniques of cooperation and self-help. The area delegations were encouraged to find and carry forth local projects, while the main thrust for Board and management concentrated on establishing one or more cooperative stores in the poorer sections of Washington.

Many chain markets as well as "mom and pop" stores closed in the "inner city" following the 1968 riots sparked by the assassination of the Rev. Martin Luther King, Jr. In those first days, the Greenbelt Cooperative immediately arranged for quantities of food to be donated for distribution in the burned-out neighborhoods. Later, GCS leaders attempted to reopen one or more supermarkets as locally owned cooperatives. When that effort failed and Greenbelt Cooperative's own supermarkets began closing, the work continued with buying clubs.

For several years, GCS provided full scholarships and transportation for individuals from Washington's "inner city", selected locally, to attend the summer courses of the Cooperative Institute Association.

207

GCS staff people and directors met with OEO and UPO officials in Washington and tried to establish relationships through local churches and neighborhood leaders. Pauline Meyers, who lived in Washington, tried for several years to organize a temporary D.C. area delegation which could sponsor local interest in a store. GCS offered to either open a cooperative supermarket and operate it as part of the Greenbelt Cooperative, or provide advice, staff training, buying and merchandising assistance, and the GCS wholesaling arrangements for an independent cooperative store.

Several buying clubs and two small stores did develop and survive briefly. One of these buying clubs, operating out of St. Marks Church, established five auxiliary clubs with a total membership of 200 families after the first year. Its first president said in a letter: "We have been a great success in showing people CO-OP products and saving money for them....We are sold on the cooperative idea and thank Greenbelt for getting us started."

The stores called themselves "co-ops", but appeared to be under complete control of the managers. Some time later the "co-op" sign disappeared.

One success stemming from the efforts of Meyers and other GCS leaders was the establishment of an Office of Consumer Protection in D.C. In 1967, Evelyn Adkins, GCS non-foods merchandiser, was cited by the Washington Urban League for volunteer service in connection with the War on Poverty.

Cooperative endeavors beyond the Baltimore-Washington also engaged the interest and won assistance from GCS. In the supermarkets, fruit cake from the Southern Consumer Cooperative and watermelons and other produce from small farm cooperatives in southern states were promoted. Funds for Southern Consumer Cooperative's legal fight against in-state harassment were raised by GCS, in response to an appeal from Rev. A. J. McKnight.

The annual sale of UNICEF Christmas cards in SCAN stores brought in a profit of $1,473 in 1966, all of which was donated to Childrens' hospital in Washington and to child medical care in Baltimore. By 1977, these annual sales had run up a total of $425,000 which was turned over to UNICEF, with the profit margin going to local children's hospitals.

Altogether, 1966 was a most challenging year for the Greenbelt Cooperative, and one of the most successful. The annual report differed from the usual prosaic recitation of stockholder appeal. It bore the title, "A Report to Cindy" and featured a 7-year-old girl, a share holder in a member family. Inside the cover, President Rosenzweig wrote as his message:

"Dear Cindy: If you are surprised that this report for grownups is written this year for you, one of our youngest owners, let me tell you why.

"Our Co-op exists to help mother and dad build a good today for themselves and you. But we all want to build a better tomorrow, especially for you and all the other children....As more and more people learn what Co-ops do, they join and make our "family" bigger. We are now big enough and efficient enough to save thousands of dollars for shoppers who use our stores. Besides, we provide hundreds of good jobs which put millions of payroll dollars into the places where we have stores. More hundreds of thousands of dollars have been paid in taxes to support county, state and nation. Your Co-op has tried to be a good citizen....

"Co-op is part of a much bigger national movement owned and supported by millions of American families. It is also part of a still bigger international effort of hundreds of millions of families in Co-ops around the world. Hundreds of visitors from many lands came to see our Co-op last year and carried back helpful ideas they learned. Some younger people from across the sea came to stay and work with us for several months to learn skills to take home to help their own Co-ops. We sent some of our teenagers to tour Scandinavia for a month last summer and learn about their Co-ops....[In this report] we want to explain what we did with your money last year, Cindy, and tell how it helped mother, dad and you and all our other shoppers and members as well....The good results for the year are a tribute to each of our 750 employees...."

A new simplified balance sheet, in addition to the formal statement required by the SEC, said:

"We received during 1966--
from our customers for products and services	$32,757,522
from interest earned on investments	9,408
Total we received	$32,766,930

What we did with the funds received--
We bought materials and supplies and paid for services provided for our members and customers	$28,329,924
Co-op employees earned wages and salaries of	3,442,451
The Co-op provided additional employee benefits and paid payroll taxes in the amount of	428,213
We contributed to our communities through State and Federal income taxes	153,000
We paid interest of	42,570
We allowed for depreciation	210,106
We provided for a minority interest in our operations and paid dividends on the preferred stock of a subsidiary	1,258
The total we paid out or provided was	$32,607,522

We had left as net income	$ 159,408
We used this net income	
to pay dividends to our member-owners	$ 86,715
to reinvest in the Cooperative	$ 72,693

Following this were four pages of photos and text describing the pharmacies, service stations, SCAN furniture stores, supermarkets, co-op information centers, homemakers demonstrations, Consumer Education Committee, Christmas tree sale which offered members a saving and raised $2,500 for a Worldwide Co-op Partners project in Latin America, and work with buying clubs in D.C.

The next section pointed out the 5 percent dividend on shares and mentioned member benefits including:

--Travel program with five charter flights to Europe; tours to Scandinavia, the Mediterranean, and Hawaii; domestic trips and entertainment; saving $280,000 for 900 members as a result of special group rates.

--Term life insurance in the amount of $5 million at reduced rates with Nationwide, as well as auto insurance.

--CONSUMER REPORTS at reduced rates for 800 members, as well as reduced rates on other periodicals.

A page on how members control their Co-op featured a statement by Irving J. Rotkin, Speaker of the 12th Co-op Congress:

"....The several workshops for this year should provide the basis for a better understanding of how member participation can be made more meaningful....We need new faces, new ideas, and fresh enthusiasm...from members, local delegations, the Congress, and the Board. Participation and involvement will assure continued control by the membership and consumer orientation for our Co-op."

The operations summary by Resident General Manager Morrow noted:

"....This has been a year of rising prices. We have fought this trend all year, even to the extent of taking significantly lower margins....Yet our sales for the third consecutive year set an all-time record....Our net savings were the second highest ever."

Net working capital at the end of fiscal year 1966 was $822,488, and the current ratio of assets to liabilities stood at 1.58, better than previous years but still not as high as it should be.

Vincent Checchi had set the sights for GCS and for all cooperatives earlier in the year when he addressed the annual conference of the Association for Cooperative Educators, at the University of Maryland:

"We don't want to create great, soulless co-ops like big corporations, but we don't have to be small....[Remember] these three steps in attaining growth: Set high standards at all levels for members, board of directors and management; do a few things well -- budget your financial, management and technical resources; and look ahead to target social and economic goals for 10, 20 years from now and plan for them."

XIV. KROGER BUYOUT AND SHIFT TO SCAN (1967-1969)

During 1966 the only expansion in supermarkets had been a $130,000 remodeling of the Rockville store. However, by the end of the year the Board was considering a management recommendation to lease a supermarket operated by Acme in Arlandria. This was a low-to-medium income neighborhood not far from U.S. 1 and the National Airport in northern Virginia. The site was less than 2 miles from the Co-op store on Quaker Lane in Fairlington, but the street pattern kept them separate and distinct.

This was a free-standing supermarket, although several shopping centers were nearby, with competing supermarkets. GCS leased the building and parking lot for $36,000 a year and purchased the equipment already in the store for $50,000. The building, at 107 Old Glebe Road, offered 11,500 square feet of selling floor space, with ample storage and work space. Street access was good. Management estimated $25,000 a week in sales as the break-even point.

The Arlandria supermarket opened March 21, 1967. For its first two months, sales were a disappointing $20,000 under budget. Average weekly sales for the 1967 fiscal year stood at $17,706. The store never did measure up to expectations, and after a disastrous flood from Four Mile Run in June 1972 it was closed. The flooding was a tragic disappointment for the store employees. Management had put substantial money into a remodeling. The staff had worked long hours for a reopening on Thursday. Hurricane Agnes hit Wednesday. The devastation was so complete that a bulldozer was required to clean out the mess of foodstuffs and equipment from the floor. Some of the loss was covered by insurance.

Now GCS was about to take the biggest plunge in its history.

On April 19, 1967, Greenbelt Consumer Services, Inc. bought out the entire Washington Division of Kroger Company. Reviewing the action, CO-OP REPORT, published by the Cooperative League of the USA, wrote in its June issue:

"This purchase represents the largest single, one-shot expansion ever made by a consumer-goods cooperative in the United States. The WASHINGTON POST, under a four-column headline, said in a byline article:

"The Kroger Co., third largest grocery chain in the Nation, has sold its nine supermarkets in the Washington area to Greenbelt Consumer Services, Inc. of nearby Maryland. The price was not disclosed but was believed to be in excess of $3 million for [leases], inventory, fixtures and leasehold

213

improvements. Land and buildings were not owned by Kroger....

"Explaining the sale, the Kroger president said: 'acquisition of new store sites in this area was difficult and expensive...we will be better able to realize company assets in expansion plans elsewhere'."

Eight of the supermarkets reopened May 1 as GCS' Discount Supermarkets, with no initial change in managers or employees. The first four stores were in Maryland; the second four in northern Virginia:

Aspen Hill, 13701 Georgia Avenue, Montgomery County, north of Washington.

Kensington, 3715 University Boulevard, Montgomery County, north of Washington.

Eastover, 4881 Indian Head Road, Prince Georges County, just southeast of Washington.

Capital Plaza, 6200 Annapolis Road, Prince Georges County, northeast of Washington.

Pimmit Hills, Route 7, Falls Church, west of Washington.

7235 Arlington Boulevard, Falls Church, west of Washington.

2425 No. Harrison Street, Arlington, west of Washington.

10364 Lee Highway, Fairfax, west of Washington.

The ninth supermarket in the deal was under construction and would not open until August. It was another Virginia location, at Route 236 and Backlick Road, in Annandale, southwest of Washington.

All of the directors, including me, voted to take over these additional stores after 2 1/2 hours of discussion in executive session on April 8. Checchi and Morrow urged the purchase and presented projections which seemed attainable. President Rosenzweig announced to the Congress and membership that the expansion could "be carried within our present resources". A year later I think we all realized we had been over-optimistic.

The store on Harrison Street, in Arlington, had to be closed and was lost after the first month by court order over a legal problem beyond the control of GCS. That left the Cooperative with eight supermarkets from Kroger for a total of 21.

At the end of the first fiscal year, these were the average weekly sales:

Capital Plaza	$38,903
Kensington	33,357
Arlington	28,837
Aspen Hill	23,893
Eastover	22,197
Annandale	18,829
Pimmit Hills	15,138
Fairfax	10,163

All eight were below projected budget. Of more significance, the trend was discouraging. The weekly average for sales in March 1968 for each store was below the 1967 average and it was below the previous month for all except Kensington and Aspen Hill. Four had made some contribution toward administrative overhead during the fiscal year; four showed a loss even before considering central office expenses:

Kensington	$47,181
Capital Plaza	21,008
Arlington	14,056
Pimmit Hills	4,005
Eastover	(5,177)
Fairfax	(36,306)
Annandale	(37,877)
Aspen Hill	(45,879)

The disappointing results from the Kroger acquisition were felt all through the Cooperative's operations and structure. Management's annual in-depth report to the Board on the supermarket division at its meeting in May 1968 acknowledged:

"Operating results for this division were unsatisfactory during 1967 and thus far in 1968....This was the first year in the past four that we failed to achieve an increase in sales and net margins in the first quarter (13 weeks).

Year	Sales	Net Margin
1964	$6,142,028	$43,263
1965	6,745,004	48,228
1966	7,021,353	78,732
1967	6,791,660	22,584

"....This [Kroger] acquisition was quite an undertaking for a company of our size. We realized the transition period would not be an easy one....

"We underestimated the cost and the length of time necessary to effect the transition of the Kroger management, personnel and stores into our organization. It was difficult to change Kroger managers from policies and procedures which they had worked under for up to 10 years to our own....We also found it difficult to liquidate the Kroger label merchandise at an acceptable margin

....This acquisition pointed out very clearly the great need for management development and training. We are spread very thin in several areas....New stores and conversion of existing stores to discount operations continue to cause sales problems....Major road construction at Pimmit Hills, Aspen Hill and Capital Plaza further complicate the sales picture....Acquisition of the Kroger stores placed an added burden on maintenance."

Looking back it was easy to see that GCS had swallowed more than it could digest. The Greenbelt Cooperative had a giant stomach ache. The report from Morrow and Checchi covered only part of the problem. There was not enough money on hand to remodel, rearrange, and redecorate the acquired stores to meet GCS patterns and standards. There was not enough staffing in the member relations department and there were not enough volunteers from the Congress organization leadership to convert shoppers to knowledgeable cooperative members in eight new areas all at one time.

The Kensington store was only a mile from the Wheaton Co-op shopping center, so membership recruitment and in-store co-op information was successful there. The Wheaton and Rockville area delegations both tried to work the Aspen Hill store. The Falls Church delegation was overwhelmed with four additional supermarkets on the fringes of their area. Fairlington area delegates assumed responsibility for recruiting at the new Arlandria store (not a Kroger acquisition). No new area councils of members were developed around any of the nine supermarkets picked up in 1967, except for a brief period when one Fairlington delegate represented the members around the Annandale-Fairfax store. Except for Kensington there were very little consumer information or homemaker activities.

The Fairfax store was closed in 1968. Another Virginia acquisition, the store in Annandale, was closed in 1971.

Something else occurred in 1968 that foreshadowed what was to come. The year-end report which came to the Board for fiscal year 1967 showed that, for the first time in 28 years of operation, the supermarkets were not the main support of the Cooperative. For the 52 weeks ended January 27, 1968, the SCAN furniture division rang up net operating savings of $298,921. All other divisions ended up in the red: supermarkets ($91,039), petroleum ($4,887), pharmacy ($2,083). From here on until the bankruptcy court order in December 1989, SCAN furniture carried Greenbelt Cooperative.

This was a major shift. The Co-op was built on savings and high quality in groceries, as a store to which members and potential- member shopper came once or twice or more every week. Here they became familiar with the CO-OP label, knew the clerks, talked with neighbors and friends, could participate in homemaker activities, and pick up information about their Greenbelt Cooperative.

After 1968, as sales diminished, operating margins disappeared, and supermarkets closed one after another -- and then the auto service stations and pharmacies also closed in the competition for sales and margins -- the Cooperative became essentially a furniture business. Families shopped for furniture perhaps as much as once a year. They came from greater distances and from more scattered locations than grocery shoppers. And to some extent, people who became enchanted with the style and quality of SCAN furniture were not necessarily the same ones that looked for weekly grocery bargains.

From any viewpoint SCAN was a tremendous success.

And the man largely responsible for that success was Bob Gowell. As mentioned in an earlier chapter, Gowell came to GCS from the Rochdale Cooperative at the time of its merger. Ashelman had brought him to Washington back in 1942 to work in the small co-op stores there. That was before Ashelman was hired by GCS. Gowell next managed the Fairlington store and then the Falls Church supermarket when it opened in 1954. How Gowell and Danish contemporary furniture evolved into SCAN makes an unusual story.

In 1956 the small consumer cooperative stores in Denmark were converting to supermarkets, and sought help from both GCS and Rochdale to train employees. A series of trainees came to Rochdale's Falls Church supermarket on invitation. One suggested to Gowell, "Why don't you sell some of our furniture made in Danish cooperatives?" He gave price lists to Gowell, who showed them to Ashelman. Ashelman checked local prices and found that the few examples which were available in the Washington area were 3 1/2 to 4 times the Danish prices.

When Ashelman went to a cooperative conference in Copenhagen, he brought back about 30 sample pieces of furniture and had them placed in the meeting rooms at Piney Branch and Falls Church. Gowell took orders for $10,000 worth in the first month. He related later that most of the GCS staff thought selling Danish furniture in a supermarket was "a nutty idea", but it worked. That early growth has been touched on in earlier chapters.

As head of SCAN for more than 20 years, Gowell's central idea was "high quality, contemporary furniture at low prices ordinary people can afford".

The low prices were based on buying directly from the manufacturers instead of through importers and wholesale houses, shared overhead with other departments, minimum advertising -- and markups about half what furniture stores and department stores were charging. There were very few price increases in the 1960s, made possible in part by stable exchange rates.

In 1966, Gowell appointed Nordisk Andels-Eksport as the buying agent for SCAN, paying 3 percent and enjoying a business relationship that remained above suspicion in a segment of industry fraught with kickbacks. Close personal ties which developed in these years served the Greenbelt Cooperative well, Gowell has said. These ties made it easy in 1971 to set up a new buying corporation, Nordiscan, owned 50 percent by Danish manufacturers and 50 percent by GCS' SCAN. According to Gowell, this arrangement between sellers and buyers would appear to risk some conflict of interest, but in practice this was recognized and the partnership worked very successfully for the years that followed.

The SCAN logo was designed by Frits Moltke-Hoff, for which he was paid $250. That was in 1962, and the logo was still modern and attractive at the end of the 1980s.

In 1966, SCAN shifted deliveries to its own trucks and drivers, a move that was more expensive but a great improvement in customer satisfaction and reduced damage. By a year later, deliveries had speeded up noticeably.

Another improvement came in the shift to shipping by container. This cut costs of shipping and of crating individual pieces, and it reduced damage. A lack of sophisticated inventory control was solved by installing a Dennison inventory control system. By the middle 1960s, training programs were underway for the design staff and the sales staff and for improving middle management. Manuals helped establish high standards in performance. On a planned, routine schedule, SCAN employees were sent to Denmark for two or more weeks to observe how the furniture was made. It was Gowell's belief that sales people could sell with more assurance if they knew the materials and crafting techniques which went into the furniture SCAN was selling.

A SCAN store was opened in 1966 for Penninsula Cooperative at Newport News, Virginia. A short time later, one was planned and opened for Chicago's Hyde Park Cooperative.

Then, on March 20, 1968, "a new member of the SCAN family made its bow in the elegant new Van Ness Center on Connecticut Avenue, NW. -- lovely to look at and delightful to visit". That is how the GCS CO-OP CONSUMER announced it. The reception for the opening was a gala occasion, with a prize list of invited guests, catered buffet refreshments, free garage parking, and a busy photographer. About 2,000 members and guests enjoyed the event. This was the largest SCAN store, and was cited in the newspapers as having "the largest collection of Scandinavian contemporary furnishings in America."

At about the same time, the Wheaton pharmacy was closed. Two others were also closed in 1968 -- Piney Branch and the one in Oxon Hill which was just opened the previous year. The Board voted to terminate the Co-op Auto Club, as it had never achieved its projected membership and by this time was losing members. As the year ended, GCS moved from the Beltsville offices it had occupied ever since building the warehouse there. The Co-op's lease was expiring on the office space it had retained in the warehouse building following the sale of that property. The new location was in half of the Piney Branch supermarket which had been losing sales and operating in the red. Management estimated an annual saving of $20,000 from the move.

Along with this move, the Board announced that beginning in 1969, all its meetings and those of the Co-op Congress would be held in the Piney Branch meeting room. The Board would no longer make the circuit of its area supermarkets from month to month.

There were other changes, too, in 1968. Some were obviously good news; others were not. Look at those on the positive side first. With 42 retail outlets, GCS sales hit $1 million a week by the end of the year. Someone on the staff did a little research and publicized the finding that GCS had more stockholders than any other business firm in the Washington area. This was cited as democracy in the market place.

Several women shoppers in the Wheaton area council brought into the supermarket an innovation which changed grocery merchandising in the Washington area. Weary of looking at cans and packages of varying sizes, weights, and prices, and trying to figure which was the best buy, they proposed that shelf markers show the price per ounce. At first, staff said this would be too expensive to implement, but agreed to let the volunteer committee place markers on some items as an experiment. The idea was so popular, that in June management announced the work of the Wheaton volunteers would be taken over by employees. Unit pricing was tried first in the Wheaton store, extended to five Co-op supermarkets the following week, then to all the others. Within a few weeks, Giant and Safeway followed, and now unit pricing for shopping comparisons is universal.

Another innovation for shopping introduced to the Washington area by the Greenbelt Co-op was "see-thru" meat packaging. Tiring of complaints from shoppers who suspected their roasts, steaks, and chops were placed in the plastic trays with the best side up, GCS supermarkets introduced use of a clear plastic tray which gave shoppers a view of both sides. This consumer benefit, too, was picked up immediately by other supermarket chains.

Expansion of GCS took another leap in 1968 when the Peninsula Cooperative Association members voted to merge with Greenbelt Cooperative Services, Inc. Peninsula at this time had about 4,000 members in Hampton, Newport News and Norfolk, Virginia, about 200 miles from the GCS office. The Peninsula cooperators operated two markets (Southampton and Sherwood Park), a bookstore, and a Scandia furniture store opened in 1966. A third food store, Newmarket, was closed in 1967 to stem losses. All the stores were losing money until a management contract with Checchi and Company found economies that put them in the black.

It was agreed that GCS would exchange shares of stock on a one- for-one basis. Peninsula members voted approval in June and the Board of GCS approved in August. It took time, however, to recover the required number of shares to finalize the merger. This took place in February 1969, but by then activities of the two cooperatives already were being put together. A Peninsula delegation to the GCS Co-op Congress was elected and participated in nominations for directors in the 1969 election.

One of management's first steps was to close the book shop.

Here are some random notations to round out the year 1968:

--The Board voted to have membership cards prepared and sent to all holders of A shares of stock, for the first time.

--The SEC approved a new securities prospectus for GCS, so it could again sell shares of stock and debentures. This had been held up due to completing the Peninsula merger.

--The Maryland Assembly passed into law a meat inspection bill which had been drafted by a director on the GCS Board to bring the State's inspections up to Federal standards and to cover intrastate slaughtering.

--Largely as the result of pressure from the Cooperative's Legislative Action Committee over several years, the Maryland Assembly established a State office for consumer protection. A good friend of GCS, Norman Polovoy, was appointed to head the office. The Maryland Consumers Association formed by members of the Cooperative were especially active in this accomplishment.

--GCS put money and leadership into forming the Consumer Federation of America. First executive director of the CFA was Erma Angevine, active member of the GCS Penn Daw delegation. Her husband David was secretary of the GCS Co-op Congress and was appointed administrator of Farmer Cooperative Services in the U.S. Department of Agriculture.

--The Board voted $2,500 additional investment in the American Travel Association, $100 to the University of Wisconsin International Cooperative Training Center, $1,000 to aid D.C. families in need following the riots, $150 to the Maryland Consumers Association, $225 to the Consumer Federation of America.

--In response to the grape boycott, to which some members took opposing sides: "GCS was asked by a local union not to advertise the California grapes. We complied with this request, although we continue to carry the grapes in our supermarkets. We feel that the decision with respect to the grapes should not be made [by board or management] but by you, the consumer. We plan to continue to carry but not promote the grapes, not endorsing either side of the issue, but leave it up to you." A statement on both sides of the controversy was placed in the produce section of each supermarket.

This did not satisfy those members of the Cooperative who felt social consciousness of GCS should be demonstrated on its store shelves. A similar controversy within the Berkeley Co-op in California was being watched by GCS leaders. As there were other arguments about products from time to time -- lobster tails from South Africa, lettuce picked by non-union labor, the use of pesticides on produce for instance -- the Board adopted a written policy on controversial products. It said, in effect, that barring all items that some group within the membership of 25,000 families wanted to boycott was unworkable. There were also the non-member shoppers to consider. Posting information in the stores about product controversies was the practice followed.

--The Wheaton Co-op Credit Union celebrated its tenth anniversary 1968, but there still was no credit union for all GCS members.

--Robert J. Dressel replaced Rosenzweig as president of Greenbelt Consumer Services, Inc. Paul O. Mohn was elected the new speaker of the Congress.

--There was an 18 percent return on the investments of the Employees' Benefit Trust Fund.

--The new union contract called for a 9 percent increase for supermarket clerks.

--The Board late in the year agreed to increase the compensation for officers. A few months later, the amounts were again adjusted, so that in addition to $1,200 per year for each director, officers would get: $1,600 for the president, $750 for vice president, $900 for secretary, and $750 for treasurer. Compensation for speaker of the Congress was set at $1,200, with $650 for the vice speaker, $600 for secretary, and $300 for treasurer.

221

--In another change, the Board decided that all four officers should comprise the Executive Committee, and that other directors should rotate in attending and having a vote at meetings of the Executive Committee. The result was that the Executive Committee, which had the power of the Board between Board meetings, now made up a majority of the Board. Anything decided in Executive Committee sessions probably could not be undone at a subsequent Board meeting.

--Then, at the end of the year, the Board decided to change some titles. The president became chairman of the Board. Instead of a general manager, there would be an executive vice president. Designated staff in top positions could be given a vice president title. The following year saw a further change to president and chief executive officer for the top management position hired by the Board.

--CO-OP CONSUMER, the house organ, published less and less information about the Cooperative's activities as the year progressed. Space was filled with what newspaper people call boiler plate and filler. The December issue of the newsletter was 8 pages with less than one column for GCS news. One entire page was an article copied from a cooperative periodical. Much of the remaining space was given to household hints and general consumer information available in any of the women's magazines.

Sales and both operating and net income for GCS improved in 1968 in contrast to the discouraging results of the previous year.
Operations in 1969 were still better. Here are some of the key figures:

	FY1969	FY1968
Sales	$50,122,294	$ 42,755,021
Operating income	500,843	263,768
Other income	69,346	29,352
Net income	206,402	92,709
Total assets	7,310,013	6,354,642
Shareholders' equity	2,621,204	2,143,242
Current ratio	1.45	1.36
No. of shareholders	33,357	27,907
No. of employees	1,070	923

Two of the above figures are benchmarks in the history of Greenbelt Consumer Services, Inc. Sales topped $50 million for the year. The number of employees passed the one thousand level. Also worth noting: the current ratio of assets to liabilities continued to indicate under capitalization. The Board obtained SEC clearance for a new issue of debentures in 1969. These carried 7 percent interest for the 5-year series and 7 1/2 percent for the 10-year ones. A total of $124,000 were sold in the two months of November and December.

Ben Rosenzweig retired from the Board in May 1969 after serving on that body in three separate periods which added up to 16 years, the longest service in the Cooperative's history. Following a reception in his honor, the CO-OP CONSUMER carried a full page of pictures and review of Rosenzweig's accomplishments. The Greenbelt NEWS REVIEW also published a long article. Senator Millard Tydings (D., Md.) inserted into the CONGRESSIONAL RECORD of October 20, 1969 a two-column account of Rosenzweig's service in the Cooperative:

"The rise of the consumer cooperative has been an exciting and productive development in our society. I am proud to have one of the most progressive, successful consumer cooperatives in my State in Greenbelt, Md. The Greenbelt Consumer Cooperative has not only provided quality service to the consumer in many areas, but has served as a valuable information resource to those of us in public life who are concerned with the welfare of the consumer.

"Ben Rosenzweig, who has just retired from the governing board of Greenbelt Consumer Service, deserves special recognition for the contribution he has made to the cooperative movement. His life has been devoted to this worthwhile cause....he began his association with GCS thirty years ago when he rang doorbells to solicit memberships....was one of the principal founders of the Cooperative Institute Association. For the past twelve years, at CIA's summer rally, he has conducted a course on the responsibilities of a co-op director....active in Group Health Association and credit unions....vice president of GCS for five years, president for six years...."

The tribute included a sketch of his family and professional life and then quoted from his statements in GCS annual reports on the health of the Cooperative. Further, let it be recorded here that he was still deeply involved with the Greenbelt Cooperative at the end of fifty years, serving on the Review and Evaluation Committee.

By 1969 the membership had grown to such a size that representation on the Congress was changed to one for 400 members instead of 200. The Supervisory Committee elected each year by the Congress was changed in the bylaws to the Review and Evaluation Committee, with six members instead of five and terms of 3 years instead of one. Its scope of scrutiny was broadened to the entire organization instead of Board and management.

Another bylaws change permitted the Board to sign management contracts for periods of 18 months in place of 12. This was because election of directors and reorganization of the Board took place in May or June, while the fiscal year and management contracts were based on the first of February.

It may have not been significant, but the minute book of Board meetings by this time was referring to the "Company" instead of the "Cooperative".

Five leaders from GCS attended the meetings of the International Cooperative Alliance in Hamburg, Germany, in September 1969. Doris Behre, deputy speaker of the Congress, represented GCS at the annual meeting of the Consumer Federation of America, in Denver. She was elected to a 3-year term on the CFA board. Behre was also head of the Virginia Citizens Consumer Committee.

This was a year marked by more introspection as leaders tried to get a fix on what GCS really represented and where it was headed.
Several committee studies were underway.

One was on possible alternatives to a patronage refund, inasmuch as the prospects for enjoying that hallmark of consumer cooperatives appeared remote after paying a 5 percent dividend on shares, building adequate reserves, and paying State and Federal income taxes.

A more important one was on image and communications. This was a lengthy study by a committee headed by John Staehle. The task force met with the Board and other leaders August 8 and 9 in Fredericksburg, Virginia to consider the report. Here are some excerpts from the discussion of the report.

John Staehle: "I can recall similar efforts in the past....This task force was free-wheeling. We were groping for some key concepts that would enable us to understand what we were trying to deal with. Opportunities have slipped by and there is a vague feeling that we should be doing more than we are. We have not been precise as to what we are talking about."

Oscar Meier: "It doesn't do any good to raise expectations if they are not filled by some activity which demonstrates reality....Is consumer ownership worth doing anything about?....How do our members and customers in each store feel that they are a vital part of our operation? This is where we have missed the boat. I have a feeling that there is a tendency to feel that papa knows best and we are reluctant to decentralize the control and operation of the enterprise. In the early days every member of the co-op thought he could run the business -- management says now that we are trying to play store....If we are going to expand, we have to develop the technique of giving groups in each area a larger voice in the operation of those units. Unless we can achieve that, we are going to be just another business."

Ben Rosenzweig: "There is an image which we can consciously try to project. We have been successful in bringing down the price level of the whole area through our discount program. We should let the membership know this. Our largest fault is that we have conceded to management the image-making. The newspaper ads are strictly commercial. Our stores should project the clear-cut image that this is a consumer-owned store. I charge management with complete dereliction in this area. People are confused."

Bob Norton: "There really is no one on the management team who is competent in the area of press relations to get out the news at minimum cost. This is important to the whole operation, not just to making an image."

Gif Hoag: "You have to show people what this co-op ownership gives them that they want and is different from what they get elsewhere....We have done that in SCAN but we haven't been able to do it in the supermarket business except to keep our noses above water. I don't think this board knows what we want to do. We decide what it would be nice for people to have."

John Staehle: "We have adopted a 'holier than thou' attitude without developing a program to demonstrate it."

Sol Hoke: "We have accomplished many things -- like the meat inspections law."

Jim Westby: "Some years ago we had a poll in the Congress that there would not be any expanding until there was a nucleus of people in those areas [who were interested in a co-op]. Lately we have been doing the opposite, choosing stores only from a business standpoint. As a board are you agreed on this later approach and have you left the other one behind?"

Bob Dressel: "The one we left behind was voted off the policy statement some years ago. We agreed with management's concepts on this."

Vince Checchi: "Every time we get into public relations we get conflicting guidance. You give us too many views. I find no perspective in any remark today that the management is doing anything right. Seven years ago when we took over you would soon have been out of business. Now you are one of the top 5 percent retail businesses in terms of growth....You voted 5-4 on Consumer Discount, and would not have done it if management had not pushed it. We are trying to build a co-op bringing honest prices....
When we took over, member relations budget was $30,000; now it is $170,000. Larger growth than any other expenditure. Keep the thing in perspective. We have a good image. Our job primarily is to be good at what we do. We can't do everything. Image will follow good performance."

Bob Norton: "The board has been negligent in not giving guidance.

Management knows the board is floundering. Good PR is an amalgam of many things. Lack of comprehension of this is part of the problem we are running into between board and management."

Vince Checchi: "Management could benefit by reasoned judgement by the board. Is a large membership desirable and at what cost? Get all the members we can at $10 and end up with an expensive capital structure. Stress quality of membership -- we can spend too much money on getting members involved."

Dorothy Wheeler: "Homemakers program per capita cost is the most expensive program we have."

Vince Checchi: "The board clearly may request management for any program. But better give careful thought to what it will cost....The implication here is that there is no plan. That tripling of GCS sales has taken place by happenstance. If you mean (by a motion to make a marketing study) that what you want is a complete redo of the marketing plan we have, this might cost you $100,000. Cut your cloth down to what your organization can afford."

Board and management clearly were not working together as a harmonious team. A little over a year later the Board decided not to renew the management contract with Checchi and Company.

Some additional expansion took place before that happened. On April 1, 1969, GCS acquired Skinker Tires, Inc. This was a family business established in Washington in 1919. The acquisition included a retail Sinclair gasoline service station and Goodyear tire distribution franchise at 4444 Connecticut Avenue NW, about two blocks north of the Van Ness SCAN, and a fleet truck tire business and warehouse on Butler Road in Bethesda, Maryland. The business specialized in tires and tire servicing for heavy construction equipment.

The CO-OP CONSUMER, reporting the purchase in its April 23 issue, said:

"The Skinker staff will remain as is and all 25 employees will continue in their same capacities, according to Pat Moreland, GCS Vice President, Petroleum Division. Although Skinker Tires is now a part of GCS, no immediate changes will be made and the business will continue to run as it has for fifty years."

No "Co-op", "Consumer Discount", or "Greenbelt Consumer Services" sign appeared on the premises. I can find no mention of the purchase in the official minutes of Board meetings. The business was closed late in 1973 and the Connecticut Avenue building was   subleased.

The emphasis in 1969 was SCAN and the travel program, both of which were highly successful.

XV. SLIPPING (1970-1972)

The business operations of GCS in 1969 had been successful, with a new record in sales and a new record in savings or income. Sales for 1970 were a little higher due largely to the opening of two new SCAN stores, but the end of the year showed a serious loss instead of earnings. The end of 1970 also marked the end of the GCS contract with Checchi and Company for management services.

A service station was opened in the spring of 1970 at 4625 Silver Hill Road, in Suitland, Maryland. Again, I can find no reference to this in the official Board meeting minutes nor in the house organ, CO-OP CONSUMER, which went to members. This station was closed in June 1973. There is no record of Co-op members in the neighborhood where the station was located, nor was any effort made to secure members around the station.

GCS's sixth SCAN store opened with the usual reception and guest list on March 25. It was a departure from the others in two respects. The location was a pricey one in Washington's Georgetown, at 1034 Thirty-first Street NW, overlooking the historic C&O Canal. The building was an old warehouse which was converted to the Canal Square complex of fine shops. The other feature which distinguished this Georgetown SCAN was in its line of merchandise. This was not so much a furniture store as a home accessories and gift store. Here were imported fabrics, dresses from Finland, Rya rugs, lamps, kitchenware, and handicrafts.

Another SCAN, the largest of them all, had been scheduled for an autumn opening in the new Loehmann's Plaza at 7311 Arlington Boulevard, but the builder ran into problems which postponed deadline after deadline. Finally, on January 10, 1971 the doors opened for 1,500 Co-op members and invited guests to prevue the room settings of furniture and enjoy the buffet refreshments. This SCAN, boasting 20,000 square feet of floor space and a corner location, replaced the smaller Falls Church SCAN on Broad Street.

Another new thrust was a retail "outlet" store open every Saturday at the Beltsville warehouse. The booming sales in the SCAN stores demanded more wholesaling capacity. The warehouse space was doubled from its original size and there were now 11 trucks for deliveries.

SCAN's best advertising was by word of mouth, and the six stores became the "in" place to buy.

In an effort to maintain sales levels in the supermarkets amid increasing competition, two were extensively remodeled: Kensington and Westminster.

About $110,000 was needed for the face-lifting at Westminster, so the area delegation launched a capital contribution drive. Within a very short time, enough shares of stock and debentures were bought to provide the refurbishing. GCS debentures were so popular, that the Board had to go to SEC for approval of another issue of $100,000. The 7 percent series was sold out in 10 weeks.

The only other expansion project during 1970 was at the Direct Drug Service, which GCS owned together with the National Farmers Union. In October, it moved to a much larger space at 6905 Fourth Street NW, in Washington. Here, the mail order prescription and medical supplies service was able to fill one thousand prescriptions a day and mail them at the nearby post office. The original three sponsors of the discount operation by this time had a dozen more labor groups and other organizations using the non-profit service.

Unable to organize a consumer-owned cooperative store in the poverty areas of Washington, GCS contented itself in 1970 with helping the Martin Luther King Food Stores. Checchi and Company had by this time started an Inner-City Project, headed by a former store manager from the Greenbelt Co-op. GCS helped with equipment and wholesaling service for CO-OP label products. The aim was to "train and develop employable people for the labor market and to save low-income residents considerable money on their food budgets compared to the convenience-type stores in which they previously were forced to shop."

Members of the Piney Branch and Takoma Park area delegations worked with a local community organization in a program to help the disadvantaged in those neighborhoods, and the Board authorized a cash contribution. In Tidewater Virginia, members of the Peninsula area delegation of the Co-op were working on a similar project.

Other efforts to be useful to consumers showed in the work of the Co-op's legislative and consumer protection committees. Doris Behre, vice speaker of the Congress, was especially active at this time. She also served as head of the Virginia Citizens Consumer Committee and was on the board of the Consumer Federation of America as the representative of GCS. Her testimony before the Congressional committee considering packaging and labeling legislation was reported in the newspapers. GCS Secretary Dorothy Wheeler also made effective contributions in this work.

The experiment in unit pricing (posted prices of canned and packaged products by the ounce, pound, quart, etc.) which a committee of members had made in the Wheaton supermarket in 1968 received increasing attention in 1970. It had been extended to other GCS supermarkets on a limited number of items. The Commissioner of Consumer Affairs in New York City pushed for introduction of unit pricing markers on grocery shelves but was forestalled in legal opposition brought by the supermarkets there. Legislative inquiries into the matter in several states stirred the chains to examine the advantages and the costs of unit pricing. Of course, the Berkeley and Hyde Park cooperatives had been doing it for years. A new Consumer Advisory Committee under the direction of Phyllis Falcao and with support from Evelyn Adkins, newly appointed consumer programs manager on the GCS staff, recommended full application of the program in GCS stores. This was done. It was publicized as the Cooperative's "Best Buy Pricing". The newspapers picked it up, and the local chains quickly followed and claimed it as their own idea.

In another area of services for consumers, the Wheaton Co-op Credit Union announced that it had at last won approval to serve all members and employees of GCS in all store areas except the town of Greenbelt which had its own credit union.

The benefits of membership in GCS had become considerable. The travel program now included local trips as well as charter flights and was largely in the hands of a Board-appointed travel committee. Doys Shorb and his wife were the leaders at this time, but the chairman position changed periodically.

GCS charter flights were endangered in 1970 by very restrictive regulations proposed by the Civil Aeronautics Board in favor of regularly scheduled airline flights. GCS lobbied for public hearings on the matter, pointing out how unreasonable the proposals were. The outcome of this effort protected the non-profit charter flights of the Cooperative.

There appears to have been an increase in travel during 1970, aside from the official travel and recreational program. The GCS youth group raised money and selected Paul Thompson for a visit to cooperatives in India.

The entire Board went to New York City for one of its meetings and to Fredericksburg, Virginia for another. Doris Behre's trip to Europe for the Biennial World Conference of International Organizations of Consumers' Unions was paid for by GCS. Behre and Norton represented the Co-op at a Consumer Federation of America meeting in Madison, Wisconsin. Two representatives were sent to a travel association conference in Columbus, Ohio. There were, of course, the usual scholarships for the CIA's summer institute but it was held this year at the University of Maryland and GCS served as host, so there was almost no travel expense. Management continued with its training program schedule, which involved considerable travel.

There were several serious committee studies, as in other years. One of these was the Ad Hoc Committee To Review the Congress Structure. This was the follow-up to a complaint by Greenbelt Delegate Seymour Kaplan that newly adopted bylaws changes to the Congress, in 1969, would impair democracy and effective membership control of the Cooperative. Kaplan and others had stressed the point that the pattern of organization left the individual member with no effective voice.

Congress Speaker Paul Mohn had appointed Jim Westby to chair a select committee which then made a 6-month study, including many interviews and a review of how the Berkeley (California) Cooperative organizational structure was working. The committee's report contained five findings plus twelve appendices. The identification of some of the appendices give a good indication of the report's coverage:

> "Reflecting Democracy" (John Heckman).
> "Indirect Voting as a Principle" (Dwight Townsend).
> "A Resume of Democracy and Control by Membership in GCS over Three Decades" (Don Cooper).
> "Problems Encountered in Recruiting Competent Co-op Leadership" (Olman Hee).
> "Democratic Control of Co-ops in Sweden" (Ben Rosenzweig).
> "Remarks (on membership responsibilities in cooperatives)" (Ken Naden).
> "Memorandum to Area Council Chairmen (on communicating with their members)" (Joe Brown).
> Notes from interviews with Harold Ostroff, executive vice president, United Housing Foundation; Howard Cowden, retired president of Consumers Cooperative Association (now Farmland Industries); Desmond Hopwood, former staff member of the British Cooperative Wholesale Society visiting here to make a comparative study of democracy in American and British cooperatives.

Committee members also examined techniques for democratic control in credit unions, rural electrics, farm marketing association, and cooperatives in Puerto Rico.

The Committee's findings clearly identified a basic problem in the GCS structure, and could serve as a warning for any large cooperative. Here are salient extracts:

"**Finding No. 1.** Records from the period when the Congress was created make it clear that the purpose was (1) to recognize the value of member loyalty to a particular co-op store or co-op shopping center and (2) to provide representation to every member in a growth situation where geographic spread and increasing membership made direct nominations and balloting in a 'town meeting' atmosphere impractical. Now a second layer of representation has been created between the membership and the

Board....Indirect election of Congressmen in the 1969 Bylaws amendments make the Congress a representative body of the Councils, not of the membership. The Congress is a link between the Councils and the Board, not between the membership and the Board."

"**Finding No. 2.** The new unit of political control in the Cooperative is supposed to be the Area Council...[but] the Area Council in 1970 is quite a different creature from the Area Delegation of 15 years ago. When the Congress structure was first assembled, an Area was automatically determined by the members who patronized a given Co-op store or shopping center....
The new Bylaws provide...Areas whose number and boundaries shall be determined from time to time by the Board after consultation with the Congress. Note that both Board and Congress are elected bodies, not the members themselves....An Area can be anything a Board and Congress want it to be....A less dedicated Board majority than the one GCS now has could gradually create 30 Area Councils or combine the existing ones to 3....the key result is a general lack of member identification with specific stores.

"**Finding No. 3.** Nearly all cooperatives...guarantee direct voting by members rather than the representative system now used by GCS....although the practice is common for federations or associations of cooperatives. Berkeley recently rejected a proposal to change to indirect voting similar to what GCS now has.

"**Finding No. 4.** ....either direct voting or indirect representation on the Congress will work if (1) competent local leadership is developed, (2) members are informed and encouraged to participate, and (3) existing voting procedures, whatever they may be, are effectively used in the interest of the member- owners....problems of democracy arise not so much from apparatus as from implementation.

"**Finding No. 5.** There is evidence that neither the Bylaws nor Congress Procedures are being observed to the extent desirable for workable democracy and adequate protection of members' interests as owners and consumers....In at least some of the supermarkets, as well as service stations, pharmacies, and SCAN stores there was no evidence in this spring of 1970 that an election was being held for local representatives...."

About a dozen examples of the above findings and then a summary concluded this report which targeted so accurately the malaise which was beginning to show in GCS.

The Board continued to have differences of opinion among themselves and with Morrow and Checchi about the image of GCS and about the ratio of attention and funding that should be devoted to "co-op" identification and to stress on member ownership and information for members. Dressel remembers that during this time when he was president, Checchi strongly emphasized the business side of GCS.

For the first quarter of 1970, net margins held up well. When they began to slip away, some of the directors expressed dissatisfaction with operations. To delve more deeply into the business side of the Cooperative, the Board agreed to have each director assigned to one division's annual reports: pharmacies, real estate, personnel department, etc. The director would study the report in detail before the Board meeting where it would be considered. He would take up questions with management and be prepared to analyze for the other directors important and significant aspects of the report from the standpoint of the Board in the same meeting at which management orally explained the written report.

In August, as pressure on cash flow developed, the Board approved a notable assembly of additional lines of credit: Suburban Trust $250,000, Union Trust $200,000, National Bank of Maryland $180,000, Security National Bank $80,000. Individual drawdowns required Board approval.

The 1970 annual review of the "general manager" by the Board took place April 15.

Checchi announced to the Board in mid-May that his company required Morrow's services for some of its contract work with cooperatives overseas. Paul Nelson replaced him as executive vice president of GCS, with Board approval. Nelson had been for 5 years the assistant general manager and then administrative vice president.

In June the Board after some soul-searching decided the time had come for a return to a single individual as chief executive officer instead of a management firm. Checchi was notified that the management contract would not be renewed upon termination at the end of the fiscal year.

The Board thereupon authorized $12,000 plus costs for an executive search by the firm of Joseph L. Rodgers & Co. It also called for a management audit; an outside evaluation of the GCS organization, operations, objectives, and key personnel; and proposals for a study of supermarkets in the Washington marketing area.

The CO-OP CONSUMER for January 6, 1971 announced "GCS has a new president and chief executive officer, Eric Waldbaum, 32 years of age, dynamic business executive from New York City." Board Chairman Dressel emphasized Waldbaum's extensive experience in food marketing -- a factor the Board had told the management search firm was a "must" -- as well as his record on consumer issues and a stated commitment to cooperation.

"Gif" Hoag, then vice chairman of the Board, paid tribute in the CO-OP CONSUMER to the Checchi era:

"For 9 years the GCS Board of Directors contracted with Checchi and Company to supply management under the policies established by the Board. This was a unique arrangement among domestic cooperatives and had few parallels elsewhere....It was a relationship that produced many giant steps forward for the Cooperative under the direct leadership of Robert Morrow.... GCS was restored to healthy financial condition by cutting expenses and increasing volume with Washington's first true discount program....The relationship has been a fruitful and friendly one with high respect on both sides."

Sales in fiscal 1970 totaled $50,974,463. The operating loss was $227,420, and the net income loss was $169,049. This figured out at a loss of $.81 per share of capital stock, compared with $1.17 income per share in 1969. Members' investment had slipped slightly, from $2,226,597 to $2,170,680.

The early months of 1971 were given over to adjustment of the Board and the staff of GCS to Waldbaum as the new president and chief executive officer. And everyone was preoccupied with stemming the losses.

In July of 1971, Waldbaum and his key executives held a briefing for the Board in the meeting room in the Penn Daw supermarket. The subject was leases in which GCS was involved. He identified each lease, with cost and renewal options. With the discussion he presented slides showing the state of depreciation for each supermarket. He explained that the industry standard was never to let a supermarket depreciate more than 20 percent and that the better operations kept maintenance of equipment, fixtures, and exterior at no more than 10 percent. Most of the GCS supermarkets were obviously far below the industry standard. The Board went away from that briefing quite shaken about future prospects.

Looking back, this was a year of mixed successes and problems that did not get solved. Part of the difficulty may have stemmed from divided viewpoints among the directors. Paul Mohn, who was a director on the Board at this time, reported as an example that "the balance of power shifted from a Board which usually supported management's position of maintaining a high degree of confidentiality to a Board which felt more information should be passed on to the area councils about facilities in which they had a concern".

Waldbaum and GCS scored a benefit for consumers and a public relations bonanza by unlocking the Freshness Code Book that all supermarket chains used but kept carefully hidden from the shopping public. In a news conference on March 8, the new president and CEO announced that beginning immediately the guide to coded dates on some 2,000 items on the supermarket shelves of all GCS stores would be available to shoppers, along with explanation on how to use the books.

Attending the meeting were not only representatives of the press and radio/TV but Rep. Benjamin Rosenthal (D, N.Y.), and representatives of Maryland and Federal offices concerned with consumer affairs, as well as "Nader's Raiders". After Chairman of the Board Bob Dressel introduced him, Waldbaum acknowledged the help from more than 100 firms in the food industry who had supplied information on their date coding systems and from GCS employees who prepared the guides for display in the Consumer Discount supermarkets.

For this innovation GCS reaped deserved credit from all who were interested in consumer affairs. Some merchandising leaders made their displeasure known, but knowledge about freshness was, like family and the flag, something you could not very well oppose. At the press conference, Seymour Seleznow, executive vice president for supermarkets and pharmacies, announced that Consumer Discount supermarkets would also introduce several more "freshness" programs. These included a new 90-hour time limit for sale of milk (current practice was 7 to 10 days), 1-day limit on CO-OP label bread (current practice was 3 to 5 days), and 3 days for fresh red meat and poultry with the pull date plainly marked and obvious.

Immediately following this, the long controversy about what physical symbol should be used to help unify the Cooperative's image was settled by adopting the unity look of the new logo developed by National Cooperatives. Just prior to that, GCS had briefly used a five-section pictograph in place of the twin pines in a circle. The experiment was set aside as "too busy". The newsletter went back to the twin pines symbol, but before the end of 1973, the National Cooperatives' logo was being used. This identification with the letters of "CO-OP" in Lydian style and the hyphen replaced by a symbolic man with outstretched arms was used by GCS thereafter for everything except SCAN.

After the introduction of unit pricing by GCS, followed by the big chains, the Maryland Assembly put this consumer protection device into law -- the second state to do this.

After Consumers Union published their findings about "A Close Look at Hamburger", meat specialist Pete Caruso and his staff at GCS did a study of their own and found that the ground beef in Consumer Discount supermarkets exceeded the norms cited by Consumers Union and that the fat content was less than the allowance set by the U.S. Department of Agriculture by five percentage points for hamburger, and much less than that for ground chuck and ground round. This was announced in the markets and in

Consumer Discount advertising, and fat content was indicated in the labeling.

Later in the year, in response to requests from members and other shoppers, natural and organic foods centers were set up in Consumer Discount supermarkets. Vice President Seleznow announced that prices would be lower than those charged in the specialty health foods stores. These proved popular and brought in new shoppers.

The Cooperative's travel program had grown so big and so popular by the 1970s that management assigned a staff member to work with the Co-op Travel Committee which involved more than 100 volunteers from the membership. In 1971 alone, more than 1,800 members went on trips. Besides enjoying charter flights at fares far below those charged for scheduled flights, funds left over after each trip was paid for were divided up and returned to the participants as an immediate patronage refund. These returns added up to $15,000 for that one year.

A critical letter from a member in October served as an opportunity for the CO-OP CONSUMER to enumerate a long list of activities the Greenbelt Cooperative was carrying on to help preserve the environment. Ecology concerns involved: products from recycled paper, returnable bottles, baling of cartons for salvage instead of burning them.

A controversial spot in the Cooperative's member relations program was the change in the newsletter, CO-OP CONSUMER. In February 1971, its publication schedule was shifted from twice a month to once a month. This brought some protests from members. But the size was doubled to eight pages, and most importantly it began carrying much more news about GCS. New features were quarterly reports on overall financial figures,lots of photos, and informed articles on SCAN furniture that helped build the SCAN image.

In May, member volunteers with Board Secretary Dorothy Wheeler as promoter staged a fashion show in the SCAN store in Loehmann Plaza. It featured the bright-pattern dresses from Finland which were very popular in the SCAN furniture and gift stores.

Another high-style SCAN store opened August 2 in "the magnificently designed Mall located in the new city of Columbia, Maryland in the Washington-Baltimore corridor off State Route 29". With 1,200 square feet of selling space, this SCAN offered imported jewelry, dresses, fabrics, gifts, and household accessories, as well as furniture.

SCAN's heady success suffered a series of setbacks in the latter part of 1971:

--President Nixon unexpectedly announced a 10 percent import surcharge on foreign goods.

--The U.S. dollar was cut loose from the gold standard, leaving it to float on international exchanges.

--The Government imposed a wage-price freeze.

--There was a 56-day strike by dock workers followed by a 90-day cooling off period.

The first two actions by the Government immediately raised the cost of furniture to SCAN stores. To maintain faith with customers who had already ordered furniture, SCAN honored all orders placed prior to the Government action at pre-surcharge prices, even though the Co-op had to pay the difference when the furniture was delivered. Although the surcharge was lifted after an interval, devaluation of the dollar in relation to Scandinavian currencies made imported furniture substantially more expensive.

The situation for all businesses was complicated by the period of confusion over the issuing of new rules and guidelines which followed the Government actions. This was especially true for the wage-price freeze. Some employees of the Cooperative, including those in the SCAN stores, had been promised increases which were then barred by Government action. Pricing, too, was thrown into disarray for all businesses by the freeze on prices. In pharmaceuticals, for instance, the freeze order came into conflict with existing State law in Maryland.

While the dock strike delayed deliveries, Vice President Gowell placed extensive orders so that deliveries could be resumed immediately following the strike.

Despite setbacks, SCAN finished the year with substantial increases in sales and net margins.

GCS as a whole did not fare so well. Although total sales were up by about $4 million to a total of $55,139,097, the net loss for the year amounted to $813,267. This was a loss of $3.79 per share of stock. The board voted a 5 percent dividend, but it had to be paid out of dwindling reserves. A large chunk of the net loss, about $375,000, was attributable to closing supermarkets which had been operating at a loss. This included Annandale on November 1, and anticipated the closing of eight supermarkets in 1972. High labor costs and intense competition were taking their toll.

The number of employees had been reduced slightly, but total labor costs increased by more than $850,000.

The balance sheet for fiscal 1971 showed cash on hand down to less than half what it had been at the end of the previous year. Total assets were down by $1.25 million.

The sale of shares and debentures was brisk during the first quarter of the year, but in June sales were halted, and repurchase of shares was stopped. This was due to the rising level of operating losses.

The Aspen Hill supermarket was remodeled in March 1971, and first week sales were $100,000, but this sales level did not hold. This was the last of the supermarket remodeling. By the end of the summer, Board and management were negotiating with Checchi and Company to divest the Skinker Tires acquisition from GCS. Waldbaum had reported to the Board that this operation was losing money and had no membership constituency.

Although Waldbaum had come to head GCS management at the first of the year, his contract was not completed by the Board until August. At the annual corporation meeting on May 26, the Board had introduced a bylaws amendment which would allow the Board to sign a management contract for up to 5 years.

Bernard Easterson was elected speaker of the Congress, after several years of service along with his wife Evelyn on the Travel Committee. "Bernie" had visited more countries than any other member on the Committee. He was also an amateur photographer of professional quality who had to his credit several pictures used in Pan Am Airlines calendars. He brought to GCS leadership not only an interest in cooperatives but also a successful business career.

When he died in an auto accident in June 1972 in the U.S.S.R., Fred Schmidt became the next Congress speaker.

One major success brightened the GCS picture in 1972, but by the end of the year it was evident that operations were slipping badly. It is not possible to report this year with much assurance. Much of what the Board of Directors considered was in executive session. If there were minutes of these secret sessions, they were long ago destroyed. What voting records are available in open sessions reveal a badly split Board. Reportedly each of the factions met from time to time ad hoc, which further polarized Board decisions. The differences of opinion also show up in tape recordings made of recollections.

The bright spot of the year came in May. Beef prices had been high, squeezing supermarket margins and outraging shoppers. It may have been coincidence, but at the point when wholesale prices for beef started to drop, Giant and Safeway in the Washington area kept retail prices up. GCS Chief Executive Officer Waldbaum had a full-page advertisement prepared for the

WASHINGTON POST and the STAR to challenge the claim of the big chains that beef's wholesale prices were still too high for reduction in retail prices. The Consumers Supermarkets ad featured a photo of a beef animal with the caption: "While the giants of the food industry were feeding you bull we were feeding you beef."

The two Washington dailies refused to print the advertisement. They claimed it was in poor taste and affronted the competition. The result was a PR bonus for GCS. The suburban MONTGOMERY COUNTY JOURNAL published the ad, along with an editorial headlined "Freedom of Information". The hubbub had to be reported in the daily papers after radio stations picked up the censorship aspect. Secretary of Agriculture Earl Butz, two U.S. Congressmen, and spokesmen for the farm lobby took up the issue and all sided with the Cooperative. Finally Secretary of the Treasury John Connally called a conference of representatives of the Nation's 12 largest supermarket chains. And with that, beef prices in supermarkets came down. Consumer-owned GCS had scored a valid point about profit margins.

The public pat-on-the-back did not save the Consumer Discount supermarkets, however. Sales, after some fluctuation, again decreased, and losses kept climbing. Management made another change in the wholesaler for the stores after failing to resolve an accounts payable dispute dating back to 1970. This change was also an effort to secure better service, fewer out-of-stocks, and better prices.

After Hurricane Agnes flooded Four-mile Run in northern Virginia and ruined the inventory and equipment in the just-remodeled Arlandria supermarket, that store had to be closed. In June both supermarkets in Baltimore -- Dundalk and Glen Burnie -- were closed as hopeless loss operations. Another long-time loser, the Piney Branch supermarket, closed its doors July 9. The next casualty was Penn Daw in October. The Penn Daw pharmacy shut down the following month.

In several areas, members of the local councils made efforts to step up sales, but these were ineffectual and not consistent. There were no longer funds for store hostesses, coffee at co-op information booths, or homemaker activities. At one point the Board talked about bringing Esther Peterson, the Co-op's good friend, onto the staff but nothing came of it and she eventually joined the Giant supermarket staff in the Washington area.

In the face of these failures, SCAN furniture operations continued to prosper. On February 17, 1972, the National Association for Danish Enterprise presented their "Oskar" award to SCAN Manager and GCS Vice President Bob Gowell. The presentation was made by the Danish Royal Consul General, at the Danish Embassy during a reception for officers of Greenbelt Consumer Services and officials from Denmark's export trade and furniture industry.

This was also a good year for the two credit unions serving GCS employees and members. Both set new records for number of members, money in shares, and loans. There still was no progress on unification sought by some GCS leaders. Discussion about adequate space and outreach for members not being served continued without solutions.

Doris Behre was elected chairman of the Board following the annual meeting, replacing Dressel. The shift in leadership came in the midst of what can only be described as turmoil. The cooperative's annual meeting had been held up from its usual late May or early June date to September 8. There had been ongoing questions regarding the annual report and audit. At one point the auditing firm reported "poor internal control". Securities and Exchange Commission requirements for certified audit figures had to be met before it would permit an annual meeting election of directors to be held.

One director had resigned in March 1972. Resignations of key staff people included:

> Head of the petroleum division, October 18, 1971.
> Comptroller, February 9, 1972.
> Head of the pharmacy division, May 8, 1972.
> Head of member relations division, October 20, 1972.

By the year's end, visitors to Board meetings were required to sign a confidentially form in order to be permitted to sit in on executive sessions. The Board was discussing the closing of remaining pharmacies. Management reported they were too small to be profitable. And the five-year projections apparently were abandoned.

Notes attached to the annual report on operations in fiscal year 1972 are essential for interpreting the financial figures:

"Restatement of Previous Financial Statements. Pursuant to an agreement which was executed in July 1972, Takoma Park Shopping Center, Inc. became a wholly owned subsidiary of the Company and was merged into the parent on January 25, 1973. Under that agreement, Takoma repurchased the stock (50%) not owned by the Company.

"For comparative purposes, the consolidated financial statements as of January 29, 1972 have been restated to include Takoma as a consolidated subsidiary. Previously Takoma was carried on the equity method of accounting; and, therefore, the restatement does not change the net loss previously reported by the Company for the year ended January 29, 1972.

"Discontinued Operations. Beginning in November 1971, the Company has been proceeding with plans to close certain unprofitable operations. The loss from discontinued operations shown in the accompanying consolidated statements of loss includes the operating loss through the date the operations were discontinued, losses on disposition of equipment and abandonment of leasehold improvements, settlement of lease liabilities, losses on liquidation of inventory and moving expenses.

"The accompanying consolidated statement of loss for 1972 reflects reclassification of the results of operations of the discontinued operations as a net amount, whereas such results previously have been included in the various income and expense classifications. Sales of these closed operations were $7,786,405 in 1973 and $12,712,688 in 1972."

For the 52 weeks ended January 27, 1973, sales had amounted to $43,122,933, a little more than in the previous year, due largely to SCAN sales increases. There was a net loss for the year of $507,429, resulting in a deficit at the end of the year amounting to $1,519,306. From the sale of assets during the year, working capital had been increased by $83,721. Total current assets stood at $5,356,275, but current liabilities were $4,818,113 at the close of the fiscal year. This showed a very poor current ratio of 1.11.

The membership total stood at 38,411, although how many could be considered "active" would be hard to prove. Employees had dropped to 875.

XVI. DECLINE -- AND SOME RECOVERY (1973-1975)

The slippage which became so evident by 1972 worsened in 1973. Losses and supermarket closings continued, and the nation-wide gasoline shortage threatened to close down the auto service stations. Beyond that, there appeared a disintegration in nearly all aspects of operation and communication within GCS.

First, the Board itself. The directors differed in their basic concepts of the Board's role in the Cooperative's performance and its future. Former Chairman of the Board Dressel had to comment, in a September 24 meeting, that he "would like to see the Board develop as a nine-man team". Director Staehle, responding to complaints that inquiries to the Board from area councils received no answer, commented that "the Board must communicate promptly to the Congress and members". He observed, too, that directors "must anticipate problems, competition, the market place, must be more future-minded". After taking notice of area council resolutions which had gone 4 months without acknowledgement, the Board passed a motion to have the secretary "write a letter to each council chairman with appropriate apology that the Board has, in some cases, failed to follow through in replying to resolutions...."

The Board minutes show committees not functioning or late with their reports, Board indecisiveness -- with some directors abstaining from votes and many postponements of agenda items. There were more special meetings and changes in scheduled meetings than in the previous years.

Several directors recall a flurry of ad hoc meetings toward the end of the year. These were held in homes of the directors with no one present from management or from the Congress or its Review and Evaluation Committee. No minutes were kept. One director has reported that "the primary purpose was to discuss the Cooperative's finances, potential of survival, and most importantly the extent to which we trusted management. To some of us management appeared top-heavy and second-line executives were coming and going with little apparent improvement in operations".

Doris Behre was still chairman of the Board. Director Mohn has said that "meetings on December 29, 1973 and January 12, 1974 indicated a new resolve by the Board as a more cohesive body and a key turning point to have the Board become the initiator of direction for the Cooperative".

Moving back to March 10, it was noted that renewal of Waldbaum's employment contract as CEO of GCS had taken place automatically because the Board had not taken action. The Board already had decided by a divided

243

vote not to attempt an evaluation of the Chief Executive Officer at this time.

As another indication of looseness, Director Leonard Lineberry complained that action taken in an executive session had leaked to members in his area and had caused him embarrassment. In another incident, the Board tightened its security after it found a non-member of the Cooperative sitting in an executive session. At every Board meeting during the year, there was at least one executive session. More and more considerations seemed to require secrecy, and this drew criticism from some members.

It had long been recognized that any forewarning of a store closing led to serious "shrinkage" (theft and failure to charge fully at the checkout counter for friends) and to lower productivity as employees turned their attention to replacement jobs. Matched against a need for secrecy in planning for closings was the anger of employees and members at not being informed well in advance. While employees were at least aware of operations problems in advance of the closing of a facility, members and shoppers for the most part failed to understand the economic imperative and responded with resentment.

L. Glen Whipple, speaking for the Wheaton Area Council, told the Board in a memorandum:

"Closing a store of the size and in a prime location as Wheaton is an indication of mismanagement over an extended period of time. Perhaps management has become too large and remote to become adequately involved in operation of the Wheaton store.

"The Wheaton Council requests a one-year period with a manager with authority to act and a willingness to cooperate and work with the Wheaton Council. Closing now will be over the opposition of the Wheaton Council and contrary to the apparent mood of Congress as expressed in its March 24 meeting."

Because of the tension with the area councils, some directors were reluctant to close facilities and most times delayed the decision while measures were tried to breathe life into the sales volume through various schemes.

For a period of time, notices, agenda, and reports of Board meetings were not posted in the stores or published in the newsletter for members, but in October of 1973, Rozensweig as secretary prepared a resume of Board actions for the house organ. Waldbaum prepared a summary report on operations for the quarter and this was published.

In 1973 the CO-OP CONSUMER, now issued once a month, offered 12 and 16 pages, but it was reverting to extensive display advertisements for the travel program and long articles on the economy, safety, health, auto care, consumer legislation, and what other cooperatives were doing in other places. Certain special events involving GCS staff or leaders were publicized, but little news appeared about what was happening to the Cooperative.

What was happening to the Co-op would have made dismal reading in the newsletter. As nearly as can be determined from Board minutes, the newsletter, the annual report, and recollection of directors who were serving at the time, four supermarkets, three service stations, and a pharmacy were closed during the year:

--Takoma Park pharmacy sometime early in the year.
--Wheaton supermarket April 7.
--Pennmar supermarket and Suitland service station in June.
--Falls Church supermarket in July.
--Service stations in Fairlington and on Connecticut Avenue in August.
--Arlington Boulevard supermarket in September.

Two service stations were reclaimed by the gasoline distributor, BP Oil Corporation (British Petroleum which had replaced Sinclair). The supermarket locations were subleased -- although the Wheaton building still stood empty in December. Net loss from discontinued operations was listed in the annual report for fiscal year 1973 at $93,441 (including a credit of $87,000 for earlier income taxes), far below the previous year's losses of $491,570 for the same facilities.

One thing that most members and even some directors did not understand was that even the closing of loss operations involved some additional costs, such as lease obligations, employees' severance, legal fees, inventory disposal, and cleanup.

Total deficit at the end of the 1973 fiscal year was $1,293,795. The consolidated statement of income and deficit took a different format from what had been used in previous years in order to show income from continuing operations and loss from discontinued operations separately. Income from continuing operations was shown at $216,952. Capital shares at $10 par value appeared on the balance sheet as $2,182,900. However, shareholders' equity had dropped to $4.15 per share.

Takoma Park Shopping Center, Inc. was merged with GCS and liquidated as a subsidiary corporation in January 1974. Vice President for Finance Donald O'Keefe explained to the Board that this would enable GCS to take advantage of tax benefits in the event of possible future sale of the shopping center.

The strained financial position of GCS may have become known to the two brothers who owned the controlling interest in Smiths Bakery at Ladiesburg,

Maryland. They offered to buy back the GCS shares. The Board declined at the price offered but indicated GCS would be open to a more reasonable offer.

GCS operations had been hit by some events beyond its control in this year of decline. Added to competition which had been especially hurtful to the supermarkets, there had been rapid inflation which ran up the costs of doing business and resulted in higher prices, angering bargain shoppers. Of course, this had worked a hardship on all retail businesses. In Maryland, the supermarkets were hurt by an appeals court ruling that the "blue laws" from many years ago were still valid. Stores with more than six employees had to close on Sundays.

This was also the year the OPEC oil crisis hit. BP Oil Corporation, which supplied the GCS stations, favored its own company-held stations and cut the allocation to leased stations. The company even attempted to cut off GCS entirely, informing management that there would be no more deliveries after July 9. Chief Executive Officer Waldbaum fought the order and threatened to go public with the question of whether BP was trying to force up the price of gasoline through monopoly manipulation. After a difficult negotiation, BP agreed to provide gasoline to GCS for a limited period, but terminated the franchise identification. GCS management came up with an "EXVAL" identification and logo (note: not CO-OP, Consumer Discount, or GCS).

The only expansion for GCS this year was a doubling of warehouse space for SCAN. Price inflation in the U.S. and in the Scandinavian countries plus the decline in the value of the dollar in European markets was cutting into SCAN's profitability. Nevertheless, this division of the GCS operations had found a product that households in the Washington area wanted. It had begun to appear that Contemporary Scandinavian furniture held more promise for the future than supermarkets, pharmacies, and service stations.

One crisis after another confronted management and the Board all year long. Over and above their opposition to store closings, members were disillusioned and upset about the disappearance of patronage refunds and dividends on their shares. In an effort to compensate, management began putting discount coupons in the   CO-OP CONSUMER for members only. Occasional checks on coupons used suggested this was no big deal compared with promotions competing chains were offering shoppers.

Because shares could not be sold until SEC sanctioned a new prospectus, the Board approved an amendment to the bylaws to allow "associate" members at a flat fee of $8. This was a benefit to people who wanted to sign up as members for the Cooperative's charter flight bargains. After a year there were 700 associate members. At that point the idea was dropped due to a restriction by the National Credit Union Administration which would bar associate members from using either of the credit unions available to GCS members.

Delegates to the Congress fretted about lack of financial reports that would explain what was happening. The question and answer periods with all directors facing the area leaders who had elected them had been dropped by the wayside.

There were complaints about poor morale among employees and about maintenance in the stores -- although not the SCAN stores. From leaders among the membership there were repeated demands for more orientation that would help employees to realize they were working within a consumer cooperative, and that this was different from other supermarkets and service stations.

The closing out of loss operations put a special burden on the accounting staff and involved the need for outside legal counsel. Reports were required to the Internal Revenue Service and the Securities and Exchange Commission. The December monthly operating report was not available to the Board until March 16, not really timely enough for the Board to use it for any decision making. Donald L. O'Keefe, vice president for finance, explained the delay as "inability to obtain qualified employees".

The year-end operating report and financial data normally were ready for the Board at its February meeting or early March at the latest. In 1973, however, Waldbaum reported on May 12 that the auditors would not have a certified statement until after June 30. This meant postponing the 1973 corporate annual meeting which the byaws required be held before the end of June.

The annual meeting was rescheduled for September 6, postponed again and finally held on October 11. Behre was reelected chairman of the Board. Differences of viewpoint among the directors about many issues continued.

When Fred Schmidt resigned as speaker of the Congress in May, he was succeeded briefly by Wilbur Wright until Wright was elected to the Board of Directors. Thomas J. Martin became the tenth speaker of the Congress.

Other problems of Board and management at that point in 1973 included: (1) a delayed budget forecast which normally received approval at the start of the new fiscal year, (2) inability to tackle a long-range plan for GCS, and (3) multiple lawsuits. Some of the suits were against GCS, others were filed by GCS against other entities. Most of the legal actions concerned leases. The following are most but possibly not all the legal actions in which GCS was involved in 1973:

--Sothoron/Parkwood, involving settlement for the Beltsville warehouse, finding for GCS.
--Acme, re Arlandria lease, finding for Acme.

--Fox Grocery Co. re payments, settled early in the year.
--Harriet R. Jones litigation re former Wheaton service station property, settled November 9.
--B. Green, Greenway Distributors, Inc., payables dispute, settled November 1.
--Loeb litigation re 1969 accounts payable, settled for $125,000 to Loeb.
--BP Oil Corp. re price of purchased gasoline.
--Louis A. Klenkel lawsuit for breach of contract re car wash at Takoma Park service station, finding for GCS.
--Lyon, Roache & Horan, by GCS, re negligence in title settlement of Beltsville warehouse sale, favorable judgment in November or GCS.
--Checchi and Company, by GCS.

At an executive session on March 26, the Board voted unanimously "that legal counsel...institute legal action against Checchi and Company for damages incurred by the company arising out of Checchi's negligence in regard to the sale of the Beltsville property to Parkwood, Inc.; in not obtaining compensation for property leased to Center Hardware, Inc. at Takoma Park Shopping Center; and in not obtaining consent of the landlord with regard to certain actions at the Wheaton Shopping Center". On May 28 a charge regarding "an offer to purchase the property behind the Falls Church Supermarket" was added to the claim.

Chief Executive Officer Waldbaum and Stephen A. Brown of Kirkland, Ellis & Rowe, special counsel to investigate the Checchi matter, met with the Board in executive session December 22. The allegations now included: "...payment of excessive fees to real estate agents, handling of short-term loans, and the use of Greenbelt bank balances as compensating balances for Checchi & Company loans."

Reading from the confidential minutes of December 22, 1973:

"Counsel advised that Checchi and Company had threatened a suit against each member of the Board if this suit is filed....Each... was asked to satisfy himself of the accuracy of the statement in the complaint and advise the President or counsel of any inaccuracy....Counsel advised that if litigation is necessary, it could be a lengthy, time-consuming, and costly matter...."

The Board met in a special executive session December 25 (Christmas Day!) with five directors present and voted unanimously to authorize filing of the suit. Three other directors later signified their concurrence. The suit finally was settled in February 1976 by a $20,000 payment to GCS.

Meanwhile, the Board tried to strengthen its own capabilities. There had been a 3-day conference on the Board's role in planning and the objectives of the Cooperative, in Fredericksburg, Virginia in April 1973. The Board then planned a 2-day training workshop in August with Leon Garoyan directing the session. Owen Hallberg, president of the American Institute for Cooperatives, was brought in for a workshop in January 1974 on "Director Responsibilities and Qualifications in a Cooperative".

The Board repeatedly during the year requested from Waldbaum data on key financial and operating ratios. At the end of August, Directors Bob Dressel and Wilbur Wright submitted to the Board their own two-page listing of key information the Board should have from management in order to evaluate the operation of the supermarkets. A response from management within 60 days was requested. A discussion was held on this but the key information requested was never specifically received and the issue died, according to one director.

At the end of December, the Board listed delayed annual division reports and asked Waldbaum to have them for consideration in January: furniture, insurance and bonding, pharmacy, petroleum, real estate and leases, member relations, and management priorities. He responded that some would have to be presented at a later date because of time pressure "to make reports useful to frame issues and invite responsible decision making".

The need for development of middle management was also picked up again for emphasis. Having a possible replacement for the top management position in the event of any emergency was always a Board objective never realized.

The Board at this time also considered a number of other matters needing attention: improving the CO-OP CONSUMER, a fairer allocation of the limited supply of gasoline to members, use of the logo and co-op image in the stores (again), information to members on auto repair service in the stations, listing of GCS affiliate organizations with financial obligations entailed and identity of the designated represenatives, role of the Board and its committees, security of corporate records, approval of minutes of Board meetings as far back as September 24, and other housekeeping items.

One action taken after a great deal of controversy was a divided vote in which it was determined not to carry grapes in the supermarkets. This did not end the controversy, however, and it was recognized as a reversal of an earlier Board policy on the sale of controversial goods.

Leaders in both the Board and the Congress realized how precarious the GCS position was in the face of problems which had accumulated. The Congress held a workshop in November for answers to the question: "What Kind of a Co-op" do we want? Many suggestions were listed; most of them would have to carry a substantial price tag.

Probably the most significant findings were the acknowledged realizations that:

(1) Among the Cooperative's 38,000 members, there was a tremendous reservoir of untapped leadership -- several new faces showed up for the discussion roundtables. It was acknowledged, though, that new volunteers seemed to lose interest quickly.

(2) The current leadership was made up of familiar faces that had been in the leadership positions for a long time and were beginning to show their age. These two verities were going to show up over and over again in the years ahead.

As the year closed, the Board resolved by unanimous vote: "That the Management Committee bring a plan of survival to the Board and continue to examine plans for further improving profitability, for growth, for cutting costs and for using the human resources of members and employees, as a priority."

S. L. Seleznow, vice president for supermarkets, resigned at the end of 1973. Charles Heft was employed to replace him.

GCS entered 1974 slimmer but healthier and with some optimism for the future. Earlier losses were being reversed, and sales for the continuing operations were $4 million higher. SCAN continued to win public acclaim and was contributing net margins despite the unfavorable currency exchange rates that forced increased prices. In the spring of 1974, this situation became even worse. The U.S. dollar vis-a-vis the Danish kroner declined 10 percent in one month, resulting in an overall 6 percent increase in SCAN prices.

In spite of increases, SCAN prices remained lower than prices for identical furniture in other cities. The April issue of the   CO-OP CONSUMER listed the retail price of 48 pieces in SCAN and the identical pieces in 10 other cities. Only one item in one city was lower than at SCAN. Over the years this price differential prevailed, because of SCAN's reduced import and marketing costs and lower markup.

The sense of value and integrity in SCAN's merchandising and advertising was recognized by the Federal Trade Commission which cited SCAN advertisements as a model for the furniture industry. A year after this, the Advertising Club of Metropolitan Washington awarded SCAN a certificate of merit for advertising excellence. Vice President Gowell repeatedly stated the Cooperative's basic philosophy for SCAN:

"Good design should be for everyone, that families with moderate incomes can afford good furniture if it is bought in volume from manufacturers and if it is marketed efficiently and priced as low as possible." This general observation was backed up with ads and articles describing the origins of Scandinavian contemporary furniture, how it is made, information on woods, fabrics, styling, and how to recognize quality fabrication and materials when shopping for furniture. Art shows and receptions in SCAN stores along with well informed sales people who were not "pushy" added to SCAN prestige over the years.

The only serious problem with the SCAN operation was high inventory, about half a million dollars above what management judged it should be. The problem was linked to the tendency to buy larger quantities in anticipation of continuing price escalation. This was a sensible precaution, but it kept GCS short of cash for other operating needs.

The pressure for operating cash became especially acute at mid- year when a large issue of debentures had to be repaid. This required an additional bank loan. Fortunately the SEC cleared the way for a new prospectus, so GCS could issue up to $750,000 in 10-year subordinated debentures at 9 percent interest and 3- year debentures at 7 1/2 percent.

The need for cash was great during the year as management scheduled remodeling for most of the 12 supermarkets still operated by GCS. Takoma Park was completed in April, Capital Plaza in September, and Rockville in November. All showed immediate increases in sales. Sales at Takoma Park jumped by $15,000 per week. Capital Plaza was reported as "doing great". Management selected Richmond Foods as produce supplier for the stores, in a shift during the year.

For an innovation in food marketing, GCS opened a fresh produce store in the space vacated at Penn Daw by the closing of the Consumer Discount pharmacy there. The proposal from management's six-man operating committee had in mind a "farmers market" image and estimated weekly sales at between $22,000 and $38,000, with a gross margin of 23-26 percent. This was a self-service store, identified as "Straight from the Crate", with three checkout registers. The doors opened November 12. In operation, the atmosphere was informal and friendly; there was some problem with neatness, produce from bushel baskets spilled onto the floor.

In September there was an 8-day strike against the large unionized supermarket chains. The contracts all expired at the same time, but the contract which GCS had with the union expired a bit later. GCS supermarkets in the Washington area picked up about an extra $1 million in sales. Extra costs for overtime pay, emergency deliveries, and some higher wholesale prices consumed any additional net margin, but GCS won some goodwill and retained some of the new customers. Shoppers and leaders of the Co-op praised employees for their cooperation and cheerfulness in meeting the emergency.

But GCS had its own strike when furniture warehouse employees walked out June 4-10. It appears that the GCS personnel office thought it had an agreement worked out with the president of the union, but ratification did not follow. From checking all records of the Cooperative, this appears to be its first labor strike. It is worth noting that a strike against SCAN and the Cooperative in 1988 lasted longer and was considered by some members of the Board to have been a factor in forcing bankruptcy. While the furniture stores and supermarkets were producing satisfactory results in 1974, the auto service stations surmounted the gasoline shortage crisis and began to move into the black. Sales at the Penn Daw service station were $20,000 ahead of 1973. However, there were customer complaints that the Wheaton station was untidy and giving poor service.

Shortly after management had put "EXVAL" signs on the service stations, EXXON Corporation threatened suit as an infringement on their own identity. GCS management found it could not register its EXVAL trademark, so it offered to sell all rights to the identification to EXXON. There was no response to this. At the end of 1974, management announced it was once again buying some of its gasoline from Southern States Cooperative.

"The pharmacies are a real problem," Waldbaum told the Board when he made a report on operations in September. The Takoma Park pharmacy had been closed at the beginning of the year. In the early part of 1975, two more pharmacies were closed, leaving only the one adjoining the Co-op supermarket in Greenbelt. Today, this still serves the people of Greenbelt, although now it is operated and owned locally by the Greenbelt Consumers Cooperative, Inc. which purchased the facilities from GCS in 1984.

Of greater significance was the liquidation of the Senior Citizens Direct Drug Service, Inc. which GCS had been operating in conjunction with the National Farmers Union and a number of other organizations. Opened in March 1965, the non-profit mail-order service had reached thousands of elderly and low-income people beyond the Co-op members in its supermarket areas. Now it was losing money with no prospect for improving.

A management memorandum pointed out that: "Postage and packaging costs have escalated substantially with no relief in sight and the sum of all these factors is more bad news in view for this operation." By April 1974, the mail order drug services had a retained deficit of $60,000. The Board approved management's recommendatdion to terminate this operation, together with the schedule of steps to be taken to notify participating organizations of the action to be taken, and to advise customers as to possible options for having prescriptions filled.

Another landmark closing was the GCS participation in Smiths Bakery in

Ladiesburg, Maryland. Although the bakery partnership had provided Cornell formula bread, other CO-OP label bread, and a wide variety of baked goods beginning in 1958, the financial returns in most years had been marginal. For 1973 there was an operating loss of $17,000.

Waldbaum reported to the Board at a meeting on March 29, 1974 that the family stockholders, with voting control on the Bakery's board of directors, had: (1) voted themselves a 39 percent salary increase and a 14 percent bonus increase; and (2) proposed a pension plan that would pay officers at age 63 (one of the Smith brothers was 65 and the other 63) an amount greater than 50 percent of the firm's equity and more than 90 percent of the earned surplus.

As one of the two GCS representatives on the board of Smiths Bakery, Waldbaum voted against the salary increase and threatened legal action against the directors voting for the pension proposal in order to preserve the GCS equity. GCS Director Joseph L. Brown was the other director on the board of Smiths Bakery, and he voted for the salary increase. Some days later when an attorney for GCS warned directors of Smiths Bakery of possible legal action by GCS, Brown replied to him:

"As a member of the Greenbelt Consumer Services Board of Directors, I wish to advise you that you do not represent me in this action. Accordingly please also be advised that the views you express in your letter do not represent my views."

During the summer Waldbaum explored other possible suppliers for bread and other baked goods. He recommended at the September 9 meeting of the Board that GCS sell back its shares of stock in Smiths Bakery, for $64,000. The Board voted to do this, with Brown opposed. The sale of stock was consumated September 20. Smiths Bakery continued to supply the GCS supermarkets for a while.

Then Brown announced to the Board that the officers of Smiths Bakery were asking him to continue on their board of directors. Discussion about conflict of interest followed. A motion was made and seconded to allow Brown to accept the Smiths Bakery appointment "if he agrees to abstain from action affecting GCS". At this juncture, Waldbaum "expressed dismay that no one at the meeting was speaking for the membership and suggested that not only conflicts of interest but even the appearance of conflicts of interest should be avoided". He read from the bylaws and responded to a director's remark that the Board had the power to approve Mr. Brown's serving as a director of a supplier to the Co-op by pointing out that "the Board also has the responsibility to represent and protect the membership."

The motion to allow Brown to serve on the board of Smiths Bakery was postponed indefinitely, with Brown not voting.

The above extract from the Board's confidential minutes is just one indication of a growing tension between several directors and Waldbaum and members of his staff. Questions about the management contract with Waldbaum had surfaced in February 1974. The existing management contract, for which both Waldbaum and the Board had been represented by separate legal advisors, had been the subject of study by a committee of two directors and a new attorney, Stephen M. Katz. At an executive session of the Board February 11, Katz discussed problem areas which were set forth in five pages of confidential minutes. Included were the following:

--Under article 23 of the Maryland Code, "The president shall be elected from among the directors." Waldbaum's title therefore should be "chief executive officer", not "president".

--The provision for a bonus of 7 percent of profits over $200,000 is too rigid.

--It is possible to manipulate figures, still keeping within "generally accepted accounting principles". Who controls the accountants? The contract's "final and binding" clause makes litigation the Board's only protection.

--The contract provides for an "unlimited expense account" and "all the prerequisites of the office of chief executive". "He has a blank check to do almost anything he wants to do."

--There is no mention of sick leave, and "reasonable vacations" is not sufficiently specific.

--He should be bonded in case he commits a fraudulent act. There should be some kind of indemnification as a protection for the CEO if he is sued by third parties. There should be a clause that says he cannot sign a contract over a basic dollar amount. The Board should have the right to fire him for certain things -- under the existing contract he still has to be paid his salary even if fired.

There was more, but the advice was summed up by this:

"A Board of Directors has a duty not just to oversee what the officers are doing; it has a responsibility to supervise what is going on. If this corporation doesn't write a contract that lets its Board supervise, it could be in trouble because it will not have the right to protect its members."

The Board voted unanimously to retain the firm of Katz & Frome "to draft, negotiate and carry through to conclusion a contract with the Chief Executive Officer suitable to the Board". When the attorney's bill came in May, the amount was $1,735. Director Leonard Lineberry observed that "this year's experience should put the Board on guard in the future to be more specific in seeking an estimate of attorney's fee".

The contract apparently was approved by the Board in an executive session on August 13, 1974 although the minutes mention only action on amendments. Waldbaum had been managing GCS for 3 1/2 years before this latest and more carefully drafted version of the employment contract was signed.

Board functioning during these months appears from notes in the minutes to have lacked organization. The budget for 1974 was not adopted until the May 11 meeting. At the March 18 meeting scheduled evaluation of Waldbaum as chief executive officer was postponed "as the directors felt they lacked criteria". This still had not been done as of May 11. Selection of a date for the annual corporation meeting as provided in the bylaws was recorded only in the confidential minutes of an executive session on April 13 -- no explanaftion of why this could not be done in open session. An item in the April issue of the newsletter mentions that "the Board adjourned after a long session with many agenda items tabled."

Anyone looking through the minute book of Board meetings in 1974 must wonder why so many were rewritten at a later date or have been assembled from cut-and-paste sections. Of this, Waldbaum said, "I drafted most minutes for Board consideration. I had a word processor and was quite attentive to how minutes looked. There was no cut and paste when I was CEO."

Director Rosenzweig stated at an executive session on September 21 that as a director he "views with dismay the failure of the officers to perform the duties of the Board: the absence of corporate minutes since July, the failure on the part of the treasurer to make any analysis, the failure...to report on the activities of each phase of GCS...to present to this Board the auditors' commitment letter and report. As a result, the operation is drifting without any direction on the part of the Board. The Board is taking its responsibiliy too lightly. If the individuals involved are not able to do their job, they should relinquish the position."

Dorothy Wheeler, on retiring as director earlier in the year, described the malaise in broader terms:

"...any Board member who wants to serve a second term must eschew all independent judgment and vote the 'party line'. The result is an emasculated Board which too often postpones decisions, side-steps its responsibilities and, in its insecurity, sets up an adversary relationship with management.

"Surely I am no more qualified than anyone else to have served... [but] we need to look even more carefully at the selection of Directors -- those nine persons who are legally and morally responsible to operate the Co-op in the best interests of all members....candidates must be nominated by their peers. This gives the "social club" veto power over who can and who cannot be on the ballot....The growing parochialism often restricts operations....Each spring it becomes necessary to 'beat the bushes' to find enough candidates to fill area delegations. Friends prevail upon friends and the result is a self- perpetuating Congress that is more of a 'social club' than a deliberative or representative body of the membership....Busy, effective people seldom have the desire or the patience to sit through endless meetings on unimportant subjects that have nothing to do with operating the business. Good people, when elected, are too often lost upon exposure.

"We've come a long way from Toad Lane and the Great Depression, and perhaps even the idealism that made cooperatives grow. We're going to have to learn to compete. It's a tough new world... either we will find a more professional way to supply our own needs or someone else will be supplying them for us."

This was one articulate view, reflecting the opinion of many members. Other leaders on the Board, in the Congress, and working with committees supported the original ideas which prompted the creation of the Cooperative: people working together in harmony and cooperation to build better neighborhoods and a more equitable society. In every year which made up the 50-year history of the Greenbelt Cooperative, there were workshops and seminars and conferences trying to find an amalgam which would pull together the best ideas and the most effective leaders for an efficient business with a heart and a soul.

The range of matters to which Congress, Board, and management devoted time in this particular year can perhaps be illustrated by two samples at opposite ends of the spectrum.

One was the marketing of 60 tons of watermelons raised by very poor small-farm families belonging to the Federation of Southern Cooperatives. Countless hours went into the arrangements and promotion for selling these watermelons in the GCS supermarkets. It was one link in a program of assistance to self-help programs that the Rev. A. J. McKnight and other poverty fighters were putting together. Nobody calculated what those watermelons cost. This was the sort of project a co-op would undertake, but in those years no profit-oriented supermarket chain was interested.

A contrasting project might be the sophisticated level for understanding business requirements in SCAN's switch from FIFO (first-in, first-out) method of valuing furniture inventories to LIFO (last-in, first-out). The 1974 annual report explains to GCS members:

Both are "generally accepted accounting methods available to value inventories. The LIFO method of valuing inventories eliminates substantial amounts of inflationary cost increases from ending inventories. Its use has a substantial downward effect on recorded earnings; however, the economics of the business are not affected by the accounting method used...."

The explanation, which takes two-thirds of a page, shows how FIFO "maximizes reported profits during an inflationary period by attributing the widest possible profit margin to sales, since the oldest and lowest amount paid is used to determine the cost of an item sold during the year. It also places the highest possible valuation on year-end inventories, since the most recent and highest acquisition cost is used in that calculation....the same process has the effect of reducing the amount of cash for operating purposes...the more reported profits, the more income taxes to pay...."

This project to change the entire furniture inventory, like the watermelon project, took countless hours of time by management and staff to accomplish and time for directors and other lay leaders of GCS to understand and approve. Its sole purpose was to run the business more efficiently towards reducing taxes and maximizing profits. The watermelon project's primary purpose was to extend a helping hand to a struggling new cooperative made up of poor, black, farmers.

This was the kind of contrast and dichotomy which characterized GCS through the years.

Paul O. Mohn became chairman of the Board in June 1974. Behre remained on the Board. In the District of Columbia an area council was formed for the first time and elected delegates to the Congress. In some other areas activity and interest had fallen off. Store closings were responsible for some of this, but aging and impatience with bickering and tinkering with organization and procedures also took a toll.

By year's end, the Board was taking steps to fill the gap created when its committees -- executive, management, member relations, and others -- became inactive. Director Wilbur Wright was assigned to produce a membership program by March 1975. Director Rosenzweig agreed to restructure the Executive Committee. Mohn arranged for the preparation of a manual of essential information for each director. The Board agreed that reports should be prepared and mailed to each director ahead of the Board meetings. There was also agreement that the chairman of the Board would assign each director an area of operations for special study and detailed report. Director Gordon Steele undertook the updating of Board policies and Board procedures.

There was a demand, too, that the Review and Evaluation Committee of the Congress be reactivated. Some of this revival may have been in response to criticism from leaders in the area councils and former directors.

Seymour Kaplan, a frequent critic of apparent shortcomings, at one point called attention to a problem he saw with one of the affiliated organizations of GCS. He suggested:

"That the Board review the direction that the Cooperative Institute [Association] seems to be taking....presently engaged in furthering the aims of its officers to the detriment of the recommendations of the members during the last summer session. As one of the major underwriters of the organization, GCS should look into it to see if the present direction is in accordance with those of GCS." In the several years after this alert, the purposes and structure of the Cooperative Institute Association were completely changed. It became the Consumer Cooperative Association. Institutes were continued but these were more concerned with lobbying and political affairs than training leaders, middle management, and employees. The CCA gave the "new wave" co-ops a nation-wide forum where they could exchange ideas. This was just one of a great many concerns facing the Board.

Kaplan and others also took exception to the major revision of bylaws which took place in 1974, especially as they changed election procedures. Paul Mohn and Eleanor Thompson were heavily involved in this project.

There was to some extent an awakening in 1975. Local area leaders offered suggestions. Committees were functioning better and coming up with meaningful reports. Workshops and seminars attracted large attendance. The Board showed signs of improved organization. And management paid more attention to the membership potential of the Cooperative. In the January issue of the CO-OP CONSUMER, Chief Executive Officer Waldbaum wrote:

"....A return to 'CO-OP' represents an affirmation of our belief in cooperation as a way of life, a conviction that the name 'Co-op' on our supermarkets will appeal to shoppers in this time of renewed interest in consumerism and cooperation, and a confidence that we can promote our cooperative ownership to benefit SCAN and EXVAL as well as Co-op Supermarkets.

"When your Board charged us to develop a common identity, we decided to utilize a trademark or logo for our Co-op which would reaffirm our bond with other cooperatives. The logo we selected had been developed by Universal Cooperatives, Inc. through whom we get our fine CO-OP label products. The cooperative unity symbol represents a person with outstretched arms -- indicating the close ties in the family of cooperatives and our working together in friendship....We will be striving for increasing recognition by the public that our facilities are owned by concerned cooperators."

It began to look as though the struggle to unite sound business practices with the "Co-op" identity had succeeded. Reports from management and the Board at the 1975 annual membership meeting gave a fair appraisal of GCS operations and the problems from inflation and the shortage of gasoline. With Marjorie Weiner as editor, the CO-OP CONSUMER published Board decisions, Congress meetings, and the reports of committees and conferences, as well as area council activities such as square dances and customer surveys. Well written and illustrated articles promoted the CO-OP label, SCAN furniture and gifts, and consumer protection activities.

A "letter to the editor" from Art Danforth in the October newsletter described the new feeling:

"There's new life, new vigor stirring in our Co-op....Participation in the Leadership Development Workshops was great -- we came away enthused. There's renewed interest in consumer information: note the aggressive move on sugared cereals, the lively 'Consumer Alert' messages, the experimental Consumer Center at Capital Plaza....Yes, our Co-op has moved ahead in many different ways." This was high praise, coming from Danforth with his reputation in cooperative leadership, pamphleteering, and caustic comments about deviations from Rochdale principles.

There were encouraging happenings in many aspects of the Cooperative as 1975 unfolded.

At the annual meeting in June 1975, all past presidents of the Board were recognized and honored for contributions to the Cooperative.

At about this same time, the Board established strict guidelines for staff incentive plans. No longer would bonuses be paid exclusively on earnings, as it was felt that additional criteria would better serve the long-term interests of the organization.

Danforth put together a legal services program which would offer members recourse to a lawyer at reduced rates. The Board endorsed it and approved limited start-up financing.

The travel program got a shot in the arm when the Civil Aviation Board backed down on its threat to stop charter flights by membership organizations. However, airlines came up with more attractive price packages which reduced the margin of savings that GCS could provide. The Co-op's travel committee began shifting attention to 1-week overseas package-tour trips and to l- and 2-day local trips which became popular for members. By October more than 1,000 had taken advantage of GCS trips just in the previous 9 months. In the October newsletter, Jack Besansky, head of the Congress Travel and Recreational Services Committee, described in some detail how the Committee and the program functioned:

"Co-op is not the only organizaion that offers low-cost travel services to its members in this area....we try to focus our program on what you want and can't easily obtain elsewhere....the volunteer services of the Committee constitutes not only a membership activity but provides a way to hold costs down."

This was the year when the two credit unions finally merged. Greenbelt, the older of the two, absorbed the smaller credit union which had been developed at Wheaton.

With renewed participation in the Co-op's activities by members, there were proposals for additional member benefits. Chairman of the Board Mohn reminded members at one point:

"...many members urge our Cooperative to enter into various types of programs that would provide social benefits but would not pay their own freight. Your Board believes that it is prudent to first achieve a sound financial position, acceptable economic efficiency, and healthy growth before venturing very deeply into break-even or loss social benefit projects....[We must] make wise choices in allocating the use of resource capital between economic growth and social benefits."

On the economic growth side of the balance, management remodeled and upgraded the Greenbelt and Sherwood (Newport News, Virginia) supermarkets. On November 24, GCS opened its ninth SCAN store in the Janaf Shopping Center, Norfolk, Virginia. This was financed with a loan from the Small Business Administration. Sales at the 15,000 square foot store exceeded expectations after the first month, and Vice President Gowell declared, "It looks like we have a winner!"

Offsetting this expansion, management closed out the pharmacy division entirely, as there seemed to be no prospect for profitable operation.

GCS finished the 1974 fiscal year with a record high sales figure of $55,918,677 and net income amounting to $466,641, despite reports during the year of losses. The 6 percent increase in sales could be attributed largely to inflation and to a 53-week reporting period instead of 52 weeks. The gain in income brought the book value of the $10 shares up to $7.80, from a low of $3.12 at the end of fiscal year 1972. Cash on hand and in banks was $584,540.

Early in 1975, the Board hired an internal auditor who was supposed to report to the Board on how the accounting systems were working and any changes needed. By year's end the results were disappointing, and the appointee's services were terminated.

The Board had better luck in hiring a director for the member relations program who lasted a little longer. An enormous amount of time was spent by Board, Congress, and committees to draw up a membership program and to find a satisfactory person to run it. A major contention was whether the membership program was primarily a management concern or a Board concern, and if the head of the program, when hired, should report to the CEO or to the Board. The Board found itself divided on this issue, but the decision was made to have the head of the member relations department report to the special Membership Advisory Committee of the Board, but coordinate closely with management. This Committee would advise, work with, and supervise the person hired to run the program. After the June 1975 election, Dorothy Jacobson, former Assistant Secretary of Agriculture for International Affairs, was designated as the Board member to chair this Committee.

There was strained feeling between the CEO and the Board on the matter of control of the membership relations program. At a December 30 Board meeting, when several directors questioned why management's long-range planning report had so little reference to member relations, Waldbaum reminded them that "the responsibility for membership has been removed from operating management".

Other differences had arisen. A consumer advocate hired by Waldbaum to work with shoppers at the Capital Plaza supermarket had connections with a national consumer organization which Waldbaum thought was advantageous. Some directors, however, held a different opinion, and had expressed unhappiness with a newspaper article which played up her connection with that organization rather than with GCS. She resigned near the end of the year, feeling the pressure of criticism. Waldbaum commented that it was with extreme regret that he announced her resignation "since she is an extremely competent woman who has done a great deal in the short time she has been in the Co-op." And he further indicated his "concern about the circumstances of her leaving, hoping that the Board would reflect on how that came about".

Also: the Board proposed to hire a new attorney for GCS, especially to explore the possibilities of converting the stock corporation structure to a membership organization. Waldbaum was not impressed with the attorney's qualifications and said as much to the Board, whereupon the subject was tabled after a lengthy discussion.

The main cause of concern for both Board and management at the end of 1975 was the growing friction in their relationship. Waldbaum felt that he had "turned the Co-op around and made choices possible", but that the Board was not "facing its responsiblility to make choices and determine the direction of the Co-op". Some of the directors felt that the operating situation had become untenable: (1) the remaining supermarkets were continuing to lose money, (2) there was no assured source of supply for gasoline in the service stations, and (3) SCAN was supporting the GCS overhead. Over and beyond that, 2,400 members now had requests on file for GCS repurchase of their shares of stock.

At the very end of the year, Waldbaum submitted to the Board a "detailed and comprehensive report on the supermarkets -- history, current situation, and future possibilities". No copy of that report seems to be available.

XVII. ANOTHER TRANSITION (1976-1979)

March 16, 1976 marked another convolution in the turbulent history of the Cooperative. On the heels of the best net earnings ($618,000) in the history of GCS, the Board terminated the management services of Eric Waldbaum. This obviously calls for explanation.

Going back to the latter part of 1974, the Chief Executive Officer had formed an executive committee of operating management. In addition to Waldbaum, committee members included Bob Gowell for SCAN, Donald O'Keefe for finance, Charles Heft for supermarkets and pharmacies, William Darby for supermarket operations, and Catherine Hildeen for personnel. The committee had regular meetings and kept minutes of its meetings. Some of the directors came to view this as management by committee rather than by the CEO.

The Board had a Management Committee made up of the chairman of the Board, the vice chairman, and one other director, rotated among the other seven making up the Board. It had no final authority as any action taken required ratification by the full Board, but it helped as linkage with the CEO and his top staff between Board meetings.

In April 1975, the Board's Management Committee and management's executive committee began to meet together bi-weekly to maintain closer communication. Notes kept by Chairman of the Board Mohn indicate that in retrospect the joint meetings diminished discussion at Board meetings and also resulted in increased friction between Board and management -- exactly the opposite of what was intended. From November through the balance of Waldbaum's tenure these meetings were held only sporadically.

Interestingly, the CEO provided the Board chairman with copies of minutes of meetings of his executive committee of operating management. These reflect that decisions of management were by vote of this committee rather than having the CEO evaluate the input from all of his staff and then making a decision on what alternatives to take to the Board. Additionally, it seemed to some directors that too much top executive time was devoted to these meetings at a sacrifice of time devoted to the operation of the Cooperative. The minutes noted that the committee work became so burdensome that there was a proposal to hire a secretary for the management executive committee but a tie vote resulted in the issue being put aside.

However, in September 1975 Waldbaum employed a psychologist, Leslie Yerman-Aptekar, to assist in the processes of the management executive committee. The minutes reflect that for a time the committee appeared to spend as much time on procedures and processes as it did on substantive issues. This concerned the Board and also some of the top staff members. An excerpt from the minutes of one of the committee meetings:

"....said that many members of the Plenary Group (formed by the executive committee) think that such meetings are a waste of time....Consulting a Plenary Group is not a substitute for delegating decision making. Plenary Group meetings, he feels, are a smoke screen for not doing anything serious."

Adding to the discontent of the Board, two specific issues came up at the end of the year. Notes on meetings of the management executive committee state that Waldbaum "presented the contract draft (for his employment by the Board) to the committee for review and approval". The Board felt this was a concern for exclusive determination between the CEO and the Board without input from other members of the staff. Also recorded were occasions when the executive committee "authorized" Waldbaum to take certain actions. The Board took strong exception to such indications of confusion about who was really in charge of the cooperatives.

More cause for heartburn came from the difference of opinion about legal counsel. The Board did not have confidence in the firm which had been representing the Cooperative. At a Board/management retreat December 11 and 12, 1975, a number of problems came to a head, and among them was the lack of agreement on who should be the legal counsel. Waldbaum made it clear that he was not impressed with the Board's choice. Because he felt so strongly on the issue, the Board had a difficult time in reaching a decision. After continuing the discussion, the Board selected, by divided vote at an in camera session February 4, Jerome Weiss of Hamel, Park, McCabe, and Sanders.

In the management executive committee meeting on December 14, one of the top staff members was quoted as saying: "the legal counsel issue was just the tip of the iceberg. The issue is whether the Board is wise to make decisions directly in opposition to the opinion of operating management".

By this time the management team itself seemed to be in disarray. At an executive committee meeting on January 24, 1976, Vice President Gowell indicated he would stay with GCS only if the long range plan included sufficient growth and development of SCAN. Vice President O'Keefe "felt dumped upon" because the executive committee would not address the issue of the SCAN data processing system. Vice President Heft thought "the whole data processing approach is audit oriented rather than a management tool approach". The Board learned on February 29 that the management executive committee had requested the resignation of O'Keefe because of "repeated difficulties in getting support from Mr. O'Keefe for the executive committee".

The mixed picture of 1975 suddenly fell into focus with the start of a new year. The Board met February 14, 1976 to consider a new contract for Waldbaum as chief executive officer, to replace the one expiring May 31. Much of the discussion concerned the bonus under the current contract and the basis for a bonus in the upcoming contract. Some feeling was expressed that Waldbaum had not complied fully with three specifications in the contract and that there was criticism by some members and from some other cooperatives that the amount paid by GCS as executive compensation was excessive. Changes proposed for the new contract contained amendments concerning a bonus as well as the contentious member relations program.

When the Board met for a special in camera session on the evening of March 16, Director Jacobson read a letter from the Cooperative's general counsel to the Board regarding the employment agreement. Also read was a letter from Waldbaum to Chairman Mohn, stating that most provisions were acceptable or could be negotiated but "some of the proposed amendments were wholly unacceptable". This apparently referred to the sentence in his letter of March 9 to Chairman Mohn that a "base salary as total compensation in 1976 is wholly unacceptable to me." His letter appears to accept or indicate willingness to negotiate all points except a "discretionary bonus". Regarding the disputed membership program, his letter reads:

"I have spoken many times of the membership program as a priority and am looking forward to supporting such a program. Thus your changes, with my proposed addition seems appropriate."

The Board voted at the March 16 meeting that:

"....Whereas Waldbaum has rejected the offer by the Board of Directors, on February 29, 1976....it is in the best interests of the Cooperative that the resultant forthcoming change in management take place immediately" and "....Eric Waldbaum is hereby relieved of all responsibility and authority as Chief Executive Officer of the Cooperative immediately".

The resolution also specified that the Board would:

"....continue to fulfill all the provisions of the existing employment agreement unless Mr. Waldbaum should choose to accept a sum to be determined by subsequent Board action in return for his signed agreement to release the Cooperative from any further obligation under the existing employment agreement, such choice to be made by Mr. Waldbaum no later than March 19, 1976 and such sum to be paid upon the signing of such release".

The Board approved the separation motion unanimously and after brief discussion unanimously agreed on $20,000 as the appropriate termination payment. The Board's next step was to reinstate Donald O'Keefe as vice president, administration and finance. The Board designated O'Keefe as temporary replacement for Waldbaum for affiliated entities such as the GCS Pension Plan and the Employee Benefit Trust Retirement Plan and all partially or wholly owned subsidiary corporations.

On suggestion by Director Dorothy Jacobson, the Board extended to Rowland Burnstan an invitation to be chief executive officer of GCS for 3 months (later extended to the end of the year). Bernstan was a retired businessman, management consultant, and economist, who had served as Assistant Secretary of Commerce at one time. Burnstan was already in Washington on invitation of Director Jacobson. He accepted at $1,000 a week, plus car and some provision toward living expenses.

At the same meeting, the Board unanimously agreed to work on a list of eight priorities which included a data processing system for SCAN, new warehousing for SCAN's growing needs, establishing a SCAN retail store to replace the Aspen Hill supermarket, action on Piney Branch and Takoma Park facilities, financing, and the membership program. The Board also detailed a search committee to find a permanent CEO.

All this done, Chairman Mohn called Tony Tona, chief of security and loss prevention, to place a guard on the corporate offices to secure all records and to change all locks.

Board minutes for March 27 show that Waldbaum took issue with the Board's action and referred the matter to an attorney. The Board on advice of Jerome Weiss, the new GCS legal counsel hired at the direction of the Board, then offered $50,000 to settle Waldbaum's claim. During the next several months there were exchanges between attorneys with no settlement. On September 28, 1976, Waldbaum filed suit against Greenbelt Consumer Services, Inc., Director Bruce D. Patner, and Fairchild Publications, Inc. against GCS. The complaint was breach of contract, alleging that the Board had offered a renewal of contract on February 27, "subject to certain amendments", and that "by timely letter dated March 25, 1976, plaintiff unconditionally accepted...." Waldbaum asked for $80,000, plus $34,771 for bonuses. Against Patner and GCS, the claim was for $75,000 to compensate for alleged damages resulting from a statement attributed to Patner in a WASHINGTON POST news article saying Waldbaum's "commitment was more toward the commercial aspects of the organization than to the consumer involvement". The claim against Fairchild was for an item published in SUPERMARKET NEWS which said the Co-op "has been losing money the past year and retrenching".

The suit was finally settled in March 1977 by payment of $45,000 to Waldbaum. The Waldbaum controversy -- and the lawsuit against Checchi as well -- occupied much of the Board's time and attention during 1976, but none of this showed in minutes of the open Board sessions or in the newsletter.

Another matter which was handled in executive session was the report of furniture theft from the SCAN warehouse amounting to between $300,000 and $400,000. This apparently had been going on over several years, and suspects were being interrogated by police by the time it was reported to the Board on February 3, 1976. This was right in the middle of the Board's wrestling with Waldbaum's contract and the disarray of top management staff.

Security Officer Tona had started an undercover investigation several months earlier on learning of a complaint about a large number of SCAN delivery trucks coming and going at a house in northwest Washington, D.C. Customers came to the house and placed orders at deeply cut rate prices. Then SCAN drivers would bring the ordered furniture to the house for pickup or deliver it directly to the customers. It was a lucrative business for those involved.

During the interrogation, one of the truck drivers stated:

"I was employed by SCAN in the warehouse as a driver from May 1974 to April 1976. During that time I personally observed stealing from the warehouse constantly. On Saturday it was a free-for-all as there was only one man supervising and there were two sides to the warehouse....at least two or three full truckloads were taken each week." He named 12 others involved and knew there were more. Others corroborated this statement.

Another stated:

"The group operated with (name) in the office, the dispatchers, and drivers. The money was divided among all the people involved. Nearly all had been at SCAN for a long time and had been taking since starting. As many as 50 rugs were taken at one time and sold at one-third the value....some shipped out of state."

Recovery was minimal, because of difficulty in supplying hard evidence of the amount of the loss to the bonding company and insurance carrier. A suit against the insurance carrier yielded a paltry $29,988. Following this massive theft, holding pens were built in the warehouse, with one crew placing orders into the pens, under supervision, for individual trucks, and a separate crew, under supervision, loading from the pens onto the trucks.

Board and management agreed that a data processing system with retail inventory capacity for unit control was needed. Following a management study of system options and how they would be used, the Board approved up to $211,000 for installation of a data processing system that would provide inventory control.

There was also a substantial loss from "shrinkage" at the Penn Daw supermarket before it was closed. The same was true at Takoma Park, with additional losses there from bad checks. At the service stations in the closing periods losses were so high that management required each shift of employees to take a physical inventory and record it as the employees came on duty.

Over the years, however, losses from theft by employees and from shoplifting was less for the Cooperative's supermarkets than for the food industry in general -- about 1.2 percent against 1.8 percent on average from occasional checks.

The supermarket division continued to lose sales and operate at a loss in 1976. This trend continued and worsened, despite remodeling and a variety of experiments in merchandising and advertising. When Burnstan picked up the CEO responsibilities on an interim basis, he expressed shock at the extent of food store losses.

There was a growing realization that every time a store was closed, the newer, younger employees were released, and the older employees had to be retained under union seniority rules. This meant that the average retained employee commanded a higher salary and more vacation and retirement benefits. A business that is growing and adding new outlets does not have this problem. Chairman Mohn pointed out at the October 30 meeting of the Board that the total GCS payroll package was considerably out of line with industry standards and put the Cooperative in an unacceptable competitive position.

Earlier, and on several occasions, Director Lineberry insisted that GCS close out the supermarket division completely, because in the long-term tightening crunch the Board's first priority must be to protect the remaining assets of the member-owners.

By this time, the leaders of the Co-op and the staff people were being flooded with angry requests by shareholders to get their money back. "You have robbed me of my $10 which I paid in good faith and now you won't give it back or pay me any interest on it," wrote one woman. Some threatened to sue. Others wrote to the Securities and Exchange Commission. The explanation that the
shares of stock were an investment with risk to the owner, as well as the possibility of no dividends if the business year was not profitable, fell on deaf ears. For so many years members had the option of selling shares back to GCS for cash when they needed it, that they looked upon the Co-op as a sort of

savings bank. Many members had never understood the difference between interest and dividends.

Members in the Norfolk/Hampton/Newport News area of Virginia were especially incensed at having their money tied up with no returns on it, especially recalling that their bookstore had been closed when GCS took over Peninsula Cooperative, and now GCS was closing both food stores and one of the furniture stores.

The Sherwood supermarket was sold in June for $82,600. On July 12, the Southampton supermarket was sold to the manager, Austin Campbell, for book value less $30,000. Both stores had been losing money for a long time.

Before the sale of these two Peninsula stores, the one at Capital Plaza was turned over as of February 29 to Cooks Supermarkets, Inc. Equipment and fixtures were sold for $23,500, and the inventory was sold at 77.5 percent of aggregate retail value less $10,000. The owners of the shopping center released GCS from any further lease liability. The closing cost GCS about $40,000 but stopped the operating losses.

At a meeting January 18, the Board authorized management to close the Pimmit Hills store in northern Virginia and the Aspen Hill supermarket on Georgia Avenue in Maryland. There was some consideration of converting Pimmit Hills to a fresh produce store but nothing came of that. It closed in August. Aspen Hill was a modern facility in a good location, so Board and management agreed to convert it to a SCAN store after closing it July 26. This was done over the landlord's objections, and on November 15 it opened as the Cooperative's tenth furniture and home furnishings store.

Queen Margarethe II of Denmark and Prince Henrik visited the Van Ness SCAN store May 12, in recognition of its value to the Danish exports program. It was the Queen's only stop other than her White House and other state affairs, and it made quite a splash in the Washington papers.

Jerry Voorhis, retired head of the Cooperative League, was guest speaker at the GCS annual membership meeting on June 12, and that made a splash in the cooperative publications. "We ought to be telling the world that co-ops are different," he told the GCS members, and he reminded them that their own co-op "is a showcase because it is located near the Nation's capital".

Waiting on the SEC for approval to issue a prospectus prevented sale of stock or debentures during the year, with the result that GCS became more and more dependent upon borrowed money. And as operations continued to show deficits, the shortage of cash became acute. By October the Board had to make some hard choices about what projects could be funded and what projects would have to be set aside. Planning for two more fresh produce stores were dropped, and scheduling of a new SCAN store in the Peninsula area was postponed. The opinion was voiced that "the Cooperative has apparently lost its borrowing power". There was a consensus that the big job ahead was to restructure GCS "into a profit-making organization before considering expansion."

The SEC during these months had been asking questions about the operating losses, lawsuits, and the change of management. Early in the year the executive committee of operating management had raised the question of whether the $80,000 to $100,000 cost of filing for and issuing a new prospectus was worth the results obtained. It led to some questions about the purpose of obtaining new members, the costs of membership, and costs of capital supplied by members versus borrowed capital. Discussion of new members also involved discussion of more meaningful participation of the current membership. This sort of discussion was not new for the Co-op's leadership, but it led at this point to thinking about the comparative advantages of a membership-fee cooperative instead of the stock-holding organization that GCS had been using because of the Maryland incorporation law. Not right then, but at a later date, a GCS Board of Directors launched a drive to change the Maryland Code which then made way for a major change in the corporate structure of GCS.

The immediate membership goal for the Board was to launch a much more vital membership program with a manager who would report to the Board [for the first time in the history of GCS]. The hiring was made in April. The travel program was integrated with the other membership activities, and the membership staff was increased to seven employees. By September, though, the Board decided to have member relations report to the CEO, although Director Jacobson retained a strong interest as Board vice chairman for membership. In March 1977, the manager of the membership programs was released and Kay Hildeen, vice president for personnel, was temporarily assigned to that responsibility.

A new member benefit had developed during 1976. Art Danforth, with a background in both cooperatives and law, put together a legal services cooperative with endorsement from the GCS Board. More than 200 members signed up within 2 months to take advantage of discount rates from a panel of lawyers. By May of the following year there were 320 members. After that growth was slow. In April 1984 the Board voted to make legal services at reduced rates part of the Cooperative's package of member benefits.

Another member benefit was created by the Board in September when an option was taken for 15 vacation apartment units [later reduced to three] at Merritt Island, Florida. This was part of a cooperative apartments complex purchased by Cooperative Services, Inc., Detroit. The apartments were fitted with SCAN furniture and then rented to GCS members at rates lower than what prevailed in the area. Arrangements were handled as part of the travel and recreation program. At the Board meeting, October 30, held in Newport News, Virginia, members of the Peninsula area delegation criticized the Merritt Island project and questioned "the authority of the Board to make any investment of this type when they are unable to pay dividends".

From around two hundred inquiries for the CEO position with GCS, the Board selected Roy Bryant late in the year. He came on duty January 1, 1977, just in time to see GCS end up the year with a net loss of $462,022. Bryant brought with him 21 years of experience in the corporate food industry and nearly 4 years as general manager of the large and successful Consumers Cooperative of Berkeley, California.

Bryant requested a 3-year contract, with a salary of $115,000 per year, moving expenses, and a car. "There isn't any reason," Bryant wrote before coming to his new assignment, "why your food stores should continue to lose money if you have a proper source of supply and a realignment of staff for seven stores instead of the previous twenty-one."

When the figures came in for fiscal year 1976, sales had dropped to $48,522,820, nearly $7,400,000 less than the previous year. The cash position was worse. Members' $10 shares now had an equity value of only $5.69. Total staff was down to 588 employees. There was a lot of repair work to do. Bryant cut the staff still further after he had a good look at the job he had taken on. After 3 months in office, he had reduced general overhead by half a million dollars on an annual basis.

Next, with Board approval, he set about designing a merchandising program for each supermarket that would fit the store's market area. All seven were operating at a loss.

Guidelines for this came from a study by consultants from outside of GCS in 1976. Making up this Food Task Force were Don Lefebre from Universal Cooperatives, John Gauci who was then working for Mid-Eastern, former GCS director Lou Norwood from the Food Retail and Wholesale Division of the USDA Extension Service, and Roy Bryant and Bob Satake from the Berkeley Cooperative (this was just before these two came to GCS). There is some indication that this report covered the same ground as the one prepared by Waldbaum just before he left GCS. The study recommended continuing in the food business, with a list of specific advisories. By this time the condition of the remaining GCS markets had deteriorated to the point where one director said "it was much like rotating four worn out tires on a car".

For Eastover, on the edge of Washington's Anacostia area, management talked with neighborhood leaders about what local shoppers wanted and then renewed the lease for a year instead of closing it -- the CEO showed that closing costs would save only $30 over keeping it open in 1977. There was no membership base here. Operating results did not improve, and the store was closed in April 1978. At that time the location was up for a 5-year lease renewal. By then it was an old market which would require $200,000 to modernize. Safeway and Grand Union each had a supermarket in the shopping center offering competition that GCS could not match. Eastover was recognized as a crime-ridden locality. GCS was paying $25,000 a year for security guards. A new owner took over the market, paying GCS $3,750 for equipment and the inventory at retail price less 25 percent. Some improvements were introduced at the small Fairlington store, but this was acknowledged to be a walk-in neighborhood operation with a small but loyal Cooperative membership. It was continued on a month-to-month lease because the landlord had other plans for the location.

Bulk foods in bins and barrels were introduced at the Rockville supermarket.

The most drastic change was introduced at the large Takoma Park supermarket, where three problems had to be faced:

(1) The neighborhood had deteriorated in the years since the shopping center was built.
(2) The area delegation of members had dwindled and was without strong leadership.
(3) Sales had been down for a long time and the operating loss for a period of 36 weeks was approximately $150,000.

Bryant had told the Board in the fall:

"It is impossible to continue with our present program. You should be aware that if this [new] program does not work, there is no hope for Takoma Park as a food store."

Management closed the store for 3 days and reopened it December 1 as a "bare-bones" warehouse-type operation with no frills, reduced hours, shelf stocking in original carton bottoms, and with deep cuts in markups. Slow-moving items were removed from stock. Advertising circulars went to the houses and apartments in the area. The hope in all this was that a large increase in customers and high sales figures could offset the thin margins and put the Takoma Park investment back on a paying basis. The first week rang up $100,000 in sales, which was close to expectations. After a short time, sales again sagged and remained unsatisfactory until the store was shut down in October 1979.

The co-op information booth in the Takoma Park supermarket was moved to a position just inside the front doors, so that a membership drive could be carried on by volunteers. After long and frustrating delay, GCS had obtained from the SEC an OK to issue a new prospectus and sell membership shares again. Hildeen, head of personnel, arranged for 24 store managers and other key employees to take the Maryland examination to become security agents. That made it possible to have some one in each facility certified to sell shares. Nevertheless, sales of shares was slow. And all through this period there were members clamoring for repurchase of their holdings.

The Cooperative's leadership agonized over the complex dilemma of needing more equity capital and desiring more members on the one hand, and at the same time wanting to repurchase shares held by members who no longer lived in areas where they could use Co-op services and those held in the name of members who had died. Settlement of estates was being held up in many instances. Two additional problems: (1) quorums for meetings and voting became increasing difficult to achieve as members had to be carried on the records even after they had died or moved far away; and (2) the inflated cost of postage and printing became a burden for mailings to members who could no longer be active.

Much of 1977 and 1978 was given over to seeking a new approach to membership and raising equity capital. It was agreed that a "fair share" investment for each member ought to be about $100 but in the remaining years of GCS no way was ever found to achieve that goal. The temporary associate memberships were discontinued after SEC permitted renewal of stock sales. Board and management sought legal help in exploring options for restructuring GCS. With the help of members in the Congress, an attempt was made to have the Maryland Assembly amend the State Code to permit incorporation of consumer cooperatives. This would enable GCS to be a membership organization and not depend upon the cost and complexities of stock shares. This campaign was successful in 1978.

The membership annual meeting for 1977 included a barbecue prepared by supermarket employees under the direction of William Darby, vice president for the foods division. The event was staged in the unfinished warehouse/office building in the Corridor Industrial Park near Savage, Maryland. In August, the SCAN warehousing was moved to this new location from its three smaller storage facilities in Beltsville, and the headquarters of GCS was moved from the crowded space in Piney Branch. There was criticism, especially from some of the members in northern Virginia, about the distance from where they were located.

The CEO justified the location on anticipated annual savings of $40,000, and of reduced transportation costs from the Port of Baltimore for furniture shipments from abroad. The facility was taken on a year-by-year lease for $20,500 per month at the start. The building provided 138,000 square feet of floor space, which included 9,000 square feet for offices and another 9,000 square feet for a retail store. This facility took care of the Cooperative's needs until the furniture business was given up 12 years later.

In November, to acquaint members and the public with the new SCAN warehouse and Co-op offices, staff and member volunteers offered a Co-op Open House. There was a tour of facilities, and exhibits and co-op leaflets brought in some new memberships, but the payoff was $28,000 in sales of canned and packaged groceries by the carton, fruit, cider, cheese, electrical appliances, auto supplies, and furniture. More than 4,000 visitors and shoppers enjoyed the event and asked when it could be repeated.

Leadership and staff experimented with merchandising and services in these years of attempted recovery. The Fresh from the Crate produce market at Penn Daw proved popular but operated with only marginal financial success. Even so, another one was opened, in August 1977, in the Pennmar Shopping Center near where the former GCS supermarket had been. It was called the Co-op Green Grocer. A renewed effort was made to sign up members and form a new area council. Not much came from that try. Both the Green Grocer and Straight from the Crate were given up in September 1978. The Green Grocer had lost $19,000 in its first 4 months. These stores were sold to former GCS staff members at book value.

Working with the Board/Congress Long-range Planning Committee, CEO Bryant produced a document containing merchandising policies and goals (really procedures and practices) to improve service to shoppers and to improve the cooperative image in the remaining food stores. These were in considerable detail, including, for example:

    --Colored lights will not be used to deceptively enhance the appearance of meat or other merchandise.

    --End-aisle signs will note if a better buy is available elsewhere in the store.

    --Each fish and seafood package or tray will bear a sign saying "fresh" or "frozen" or "frozen and thawed" as appropriate.

    --No more than 10 percent of all prices will end in "9".

    --Where practical pull dates [showing shelf life] will face the shopper.

The full list was published in the CO-OP CONSUMER, filling two pages.

Vice President Darby introduced a monthly special purchase as a member benefit. The first was a smoke alarm at a price barely above wholesale. They went so quickly, that he placed a reorder for $5,000 worth. Information about upcoming special buys was carried in the members' newsletter.

For a number of years, GCS relations with Mid-Eastern Cooperative, Inc., the wholesale supplier, deteriorated. This was due to distance and a pricing system which did not favor GCS even though this cooperative accounted for more than one-third of the wholesale's business. GCS was a large stockholder in Mid-Eastern, and had votes in its board, but the GCS representatives frequently found themselves at odds with the management of Mid-Eastern on policy questions. A majority on Mid-Eastern's board permitted the small retail stores in New York to delay payment for 90 days and sometimes as much as 120 days without penalty. Outages constituted another problem. At the end of February the Board approved management's recommendation that all buying be through P.A.& S. Small at an estimated 1 percent saving and other advantages.

Vice President O'Keefe pointed out in one meeting that 90 percent of the time of the Board and the Long-range Planning Committee was occupied with food store problems. Even so, SCAN, the service stations, and real estate continued to get attention. For years, the Takoma Park Shopping Center property continued to be one of the Cooperative's biggest headaches. Another end-of- February action by the Board was approval for the sale of the Takoma Park real estate. This was reportedly a break-even deal. Closing the sale was delayed until June 1979 by a court action.

Following months of anxiety over the SCAN store at Denbigh, in the Virginia Peninsula area, the Board and management resolved to close it down and open a new SCAN in the regional shopping center of Newmarket North, in Hampton. This opened February 15, 1978. Two happenings affected SCAN sales during 1977. A plus was gained when the Board and Congress leaders agreed on appropriate credit arrangements for SCAN shoppers. There had been a strong push to make the Greenbelt Credit Union the only or at least the preferred source of credit purchases. This was modified to have the credit union one of several options. In the fall, Gowell reported that 33 percent of SCAN shoppers paid for their purchases with credit cards.

The other matter was a strike by the dock workers union in Baltimore. After a month, the cutoff in deliveries cost GCS and SCAN $400,000 in sales. Even so, the SCAN stores turned in total profits of $705,000 in the first 11 months of 1977. For the same period, supermarket losses were $580,000.

Several more SCAN notes:

   --Back in November 1976, SCAN's identity as a separate corporation was strengthened, with its own bylaws and officers, in order to avoid any legal problems in operating stores outside its existing market area. It remained a wholly owned subsidiary of the Cooperative.

275

--GCS took over the management of the two Scandinavian furniture stores in Chicago at the request of Hyde Park Cooperative.

—At the end of 1978, the gifts department was phased out, due to high labor cost per sale of such small items and also the ease with which small items could be stolen. And then the problem of keeping inventory within bounds -- this continued to cause unease because a large inventory tied up cash.

--Gowell's compensation as vice president, SCAN, was raised In July 1978 to $65,000 in salary plus bonus. Total bonus for the vice president and SCAN staff was $35,000 for 1977.

While furniture sales sustained GCS, food stores continued to be a drain. The worst was Takoma Park. In November 1978, management worked out an arrangement with the wholesaler, P.A.& S. Small, to again convert the Takoma Park supermarket. This time, with a still different merchandising program, it became the "Kash & Karry" market, with no reference to Co-op. Few members used the store by this time, but reaction was expressed by Art Danforth who asked "How kutsey kan you get?" A year later, in October 1979, board and management gave up and sold the supermarket.

Thefts and violence had made the shopping center untenable. The service station had to be closed, and in July 1981 the SCAN store also vacated the premises. That was the end of the first venture of the Cooperative outside of the town of Greenbelt, 30 years earlier.

At the start of 1978, CEO Bryant reorganized his executive staff. He made Bob Satake assistant CEO, with Board approval. Satake had worked with Bryant at Berkeley, and had come east to help with Greenbelt's problems. In California he had experience with service stations and produce departments with the cooperative and before that had been a partner in a "silk stocking" food store.

In August and September came further staff reorganization with deep cuts in personnel and some resultant savings. Vice presidents for finance and administration, for food operations, and for personnel were given separation notices, with 6 months' pay.

It may be of interest to note that while drastic steps were being taken to save money in operations and to look for means to raise cash, a variety of small expenditures continued by the Board, for example:

--$2,500 for a seminar for young families -- when only 18 persons, some of them single, signed up, it was postponed but attendance still was sparse.

--$1,200 toward expenses for the Cooperative League's biennial congress meeting in Washington, D.C., plus costs of a bus tour and dinner program for about one hundred delegates and visitors.

--$500 to send a youth to the Canadian Cooperative College at Saskatoon -- there was one applicant, the daughter of a director.

--$85 for a director to attend a dinner of the National Consumer League.

--$1,500 for a housing committee to use for legal services -- nothing came of the committee's studies about whether GCS should go into housing as an additional activity.

--$3,373 in interest from Mid-Eastern Cooperative, Inc. due GCS on a note waived because "the financial posture of Mid-Eastern is borderline". Mid-Eastern was no longer wholesale supplier to GCS.

--$50,000 unsecured loan to Cooperative Services, Inc., the Detroit housing and optical services cooperative.

--Trips for leaders. Director Tom Martin expressed his concern about sending people to places "with no real critical evaluation of benefits derived from expenditure of these funds".

Some second thoughts along this line also were raised by other directors. For many years, GCS had sent leaders and potential leaders to the summer training courses of the Cooperative Institute Association, either to conduct classes or to learn about cooperatives and leadership skills. When the Association was taken over by "new wave" co-ops and changed into the Consumer Cooperative Alliance, GCS continued to support it, but in 1978 the GCS Board decided to stop paying the tuition, room and board, and travel for 10 or 20 participants traditionally sponsored.

Quoting from the minutes of May 15, 1978:

"....it was noted that there seems to be an attempt to direct itself [CCA] into a national organization, when the original intent was to provide an educational institute for cooperatives....the new wave co-ops represented on the CCA board believe the objectives for which the original organization was established are no longer relevant, and that it needs to be a political force....it would be advisable to defer payment of CCA dues until after the 1978 meeting, when an evaluation could be made."

There were also questions about Mid-Eastern Cooperative's failure to implement services which GCS had counted on. At the same time, CLUSA was going through a crisis with Stanley Dryer leaving and some question about its very survival. GCS leadership had always recognized the need for an umbrella organization of consumer cooperatives, but along with this there was a feeling that the dues burden was heavy on GCS because of its large membership and high sales figures.

A note of caution about cost:benefit ratios was sounded by Director Earl D. Beard shortly after he was elected to the Board.
He pointed out in a Board meeting that to offset the cost of going to the SEC and issuing a prospectus, the Cooperative would need to pick up 9,000 new members.

Money -- the lack of it due to continuing losses in the supermarkets -- colored nearly all considerations at staff meetings and Board sessions. Even the unions recognized the Cooperative's plight. In their 1978 contract negotiations, employees set aside wage increases for 3 years in an attempt to help the Cooperative reestablish its margins.

Vice President O'Keefe had announced in July that GCS would have to report to the SEC that it had negative working capital. Chairman of the Board Mohn voiced at the same meeting a concern that many directors expressed over the years: "Why do we keep losing ground on the budget?" An examination of management's financial reports from Sam Ashelman to Robert Satake finds them peppered with performance figures on supermarkets that were below budget forecasts. These were accompanied with explanations about what had gone wrong and assurances that figures for the next period would be better.

The deficit position of GCS in the spring of 1978 was made even worse by a new required accounting procedure, FASB-13, which specified that certain leases had to be capitalized. The effect was to increase the deficit of GCS by $328,000 in its financial statement.

During 1978, Director Leonard Lineberry again and repeatedly proposed that the entire supermarket division be closed out. At a September 18 meeting he pointed to food store losses for the last 7 years and to a loss of $769,448 for only part of the current fiscal year. He also noted that less than 10 percent of food store patrons were members. In a long resolution he asked that management close stores responsible for the losses. The Board tabled the motion, 6-1.

Six weeks later the Peninsula area members presented the Board with a petition bearing 316 signatures requesting a special meeting of the entire membership to decide on closing the Cooperative's remaining food stores. In the office at Savage it was recognized that there was bad feeling in that area stemming from the "hasty" closing of the food stores in Hampton and Newport News in 1976. The Peninsula Area Council had expressed displeasure at continuing losses in other supermarkets still open that made payment of dividends and repurchase of membership shares impossible.

Even so, Board and management felt the cost of calling a special membership meeting was unrealistic in the face of the Cooperative's serious financial situation, even though the bylaws provided for such a meeting to be called. The member relations staff was asked to go to Hampton, Virginia and try to persuade enough petition signers to withdraw their support for the special meeting call to invalidate the request. This was done, with the promise that the question of store closings would be put on the agenda of the annual membership meeting in June 1979. Management and directors met with Peninsula members shortly after the petition was set aside, to discuss food store operations and the Cooperative's financial conditions. When the petition of Peninsula members was discused at a meeting of the GCS Co-op Congress, there was a vote of confidence for the Board's position.

When the ballots were prepared for the 1979 annual meeting, the question of closing out the food stores was included, and was substantially defeated. After that, the Peninsula Council presented a Board meeting in late June with tabulated figures on an 8-year history of food store losses. The Review and Evaluation Committee also began an inquiry into the losses estimated at $2 million over 8 years.

Despite the grave losses in the supermarkets during most of 1978, GCS finished the fiscal year in the black by $228,000. The SCAN operations, cutbacks in administrative staff, and an income tax credit for carry-forward of prior years' losses were responsible for the improved showing. Supermarket sales and earnings did improve and the food division showed a profit in the last quarter. Working capital was recorded as a negative $52,000, but book value per $10 share of stock was up to $6.02.

The following year witnessed encouraging gains; 1979 was a very successful year. Sales were up $2 million over the 1978 total to $49,720,000. Some of the recorded gain was from rising prices, but it was a solid improvement. Net income was recorded at $410,000. However, $210,000 of that came about from switching back from LIFO (last in, first out) to FIFO (first in, first out) furniture inventory, with permission from the Internal Revenue Service.

Coming back to activities and events during the year of 1979, the most important activity and/or event was the change in identity. Greenbelt Consumer Services, Inc. became Greenbelt Cooperative, Inc. on February 1. This shift after four decades was made possible by the amendment to Maryland's incorporation law which the Cooperative had been able to win through its friends in the State Assembly. For the first time it was now possible to incorporate a consumer cooperative and legally use the "cooperative" identification which had been restricted to farmer production and marketing organizations. From here on, GCS became GCI.

This was the start of a transition from a stock corporation to a membership association. It took some time, but the principal steps were authorized by an overwhelming vote at the annual corporation meeting on June 2 to make major changes in the certificate of incorporation and in the bylaws. There were 11,422 ballots cast in the largest member response in the experience of the Cooperative.

The membership votes to amend the certificate of incorporation and the bylaws set in motion a campaign to call in the $10 A- shares of stock in exchange for a non-stock voting membership. There was no change in the non-voting B shares, and GCI was pleased to report that full equity value had now been restored as a result of the improvement in operations. The July 1979 issue of the CO-OP CONSUMER advised:

"1. Anyone not now a member may purchase a non-stock voting membership in Greenbelt Cooperative, Inc. for $10. Membership will be open and available at all times.

"2. Current members may continue as members by requesting that their Series A share of stock be converted to a non-stock voting membership. By doing this, they will continue to be entitled to vote, hold office, participate in affairs of the Cooperative, and have access to benefits designed for members. However, membership will not earn dividends, nor will it be transferrable.

"3. If a member no longer wishes to continue as a member, no action is needed because at the end of a six-month conversion period (December 3, 1979) the Series A share certificate held will automatically become evidence of ownership of one share of non-voting common stock. If you wish to continue as a member of the Cooperative, we remind you that you must sign and return the Request and Authorization form."

A legal notice also appeared in the paper. By the end of 1979, 9,063 members had converted the A-share to the new $10 non-stock voting membership and 1,146 new members had joined. A hopeful indication for the future of GCI was the discovery that nearly half of the new members were in the 30-39 age bracket. The next largest age bracket was ages 20-29. This was especially important, coming on the heels of the death notices of two hardworking leaders: James Westby, Fairlington, who had headed the volunteer membership education committee, and Ernest Wolfe, Piney Branch, who had steered the Takoma Park senior citizens housing apartment to completion.

Before this and in the years that followed, there was recognition of another kind of transition. The Cooperative was losing its pioneer leaders at an increasingly rapid rate: Carnie Harper, David Scull, Si and Sarah Newman, Edie Christianson, Walter Bierwagen, Bertha Maryn, Sol Hoke, Ruth Rinehart, George and Dorothy Jacobson Art Danforth -- the list grew ever longer. And as the 1980s opened, replacing them with new younger leadership became more and more difficult. Some comments on this problem are included in Chapter XX.

The months of 1979 were especially important for the increased emphasis on improving communications with members, developing leadership, increasing member benefits, and emphasizing the fundamentals of cooperation:

--Membership cards were mailed out to all members, old and new, with a letter from Chairman of the Board Mohn. Chairmen of area councils received names, addresses, and telephone numbers of new members in their areas along with a model letter and were asked to send a letter of welcome or to telephone the newcomers an invitation to the next area council meeting.

--The monthly CO-OP CONSUMER and editor Denice Darrow received the annual Cooperative News Service Award from the Cooperative Editorial Association. This recognized the newsletter as the best in the U.S. for emphasizing cooperative values and methods to member-readers.

--An innovative and inexpensive communications tool which was started by vice president for membership, Don Cooper, which provided for education was a weekly HIGHLIGHTS mailed to each area delegate to the GCI Co-op Congress and to the directors. This was a single page on a word processor, covering developments factually and in telegraphic style, to keep the leadership informed. Key staff people were soon added to the distribution list.

--Wide distribution was given to several information pieces. One was an inexpensive "Shopping CO-OP", 4-page tabloid size on newsprint with green ink headings, about the Cooperative, CO-OP label, other cooperatives in the area, and how co-ops worked. Another was "Members' Rights & Responsibilities".

--Two additional employees were added to the membership and education department temporarily during the transition from stock corporation to membership association. One of these, John Gauci, stayed on to head the membership program until dissolution of the GCI staff in 1989. During the 1980s he put together an attractive series of brochures with related design, on various aspects of GCI, nutrition, and consumer topics.

One of the major legislative efforts of GCI leaders came to fruition in 1979 when Congress passed an enabling act for the Consumer Cooperative Bank, and this new financing entity began setting up house. The Greenbelt Cooperative later borrowed from the new Co-op Bank.

There was one important closing and one important opening during 1979.

Both the service station and the supermarket at Takoma Park were terminated in October. This left GCI with five food stores. The expansion was the tenth SCAN store which opened July 1 at Lakeforest Mall in Gaithersburg, Maryland.

Toward the close of a very successful year in operations, board and management ran into one other transition -- a painful one. Bryant's 3-year contract was coming to a close at the end of the year. The board, meeting on September 14 resolved to renew the contract with a $10,000 increase in each of the next 3 years. The minutes of the November 12 meeting indicate that Bryant asked that his assistant, Satake, be designated CEO in charge of operations and that he (Bryant) would remain as president, responsible for planning and growth. The board gave its approval by unanimous vote. There was agreement, too, on a bonus of $25,000 for 1979, and that salary for Satake would be $90,000.

At a meeting on December 26 both Bryant and Sataki met with the Board and there was extended discussion on "areas of concern". On January 19, 1980, the Board amended the employment agreement with Satake as CEO to terminate July 31, 1983. On January 30, the Board met to consider a letter from Bryant "informing the Board that he is withdrawing his employment agreement with GCI". After lengthy discussion the Board accepted "with deep regret the resignation" and directed that the amount owed to Bryant be paid in a lump sum. This was the last change in top management.

The newsletter carried a statement from Bryant explaining:

"At the time the Board made the decision to employ me...I told them I would like an agreement for at least 3 years [and] discussed things that would bring about a turn-a-round, such as a change in the Maryland law that would allow Greenbelt to become a true membership cooperative; a change in the bylaws that would allow the membership fee to be free of SEC; a change in the management structure to improve the efficiency of the staff and reduce overhead; consolidate Greenbelt's warehouses and office in to one location; develop Board committees to make recommendations for improvements; and a program to communicate all of the above changes to the membership to get their support and assistance in the turnaround. The financial report for 1979 indicates that the turnaround has taken place and the goals are completed." He described his plans to work with his church in California.

There were reorganization shifts in SCAN, and as a result of later phasing out of the petroleum and food store operations, but Satake continued as president and CEO until GCI applied for protection under Chapter 11 of the bankruptcy code.

XVIII. WITH SATAKE AND MOHN (1980-1983)

Fiscal year 1979 was so successful that the Board could set aside $50,000 for repurchasing shares of stock from people who wanted to get their original investments returned. A list of applicants for stock repurchase had been set up, and these shareholders were informed that GCI would buy back shares on the basis of date of request.

With past accumulated deficit wiped out, the Board was able to declare an 8 percent dividend on shares still being held -- the first dividend since 1971. Both the repurchase of shares and the dividend were in 1980.

Although the food markets and service stations gave no promise of net returns in 1980, furniture sales continued to be profitable enough to carry the total costs of GCI with some left over. The Board began to plan for a future patronage refund. Various record keeping methods were considered, and some alternatives to a cash return were explored. When management bought new electronic cash registers for the Greenbelt supermarket and then other stores for $175,000, there was assurance that the new equipment could provide the computing for any patronage return.

However, there were reservations about the generally optimistic picture of operations. At mid-year, it was pointed out that sales increases were at a lesser rate than inflation, so GCI figures on gains were not a valid measurement.

Sales for the year were boosted by a complete renovation of Greenbelt supermarket in August and the opening of a new one at Severna Park, Maryland on December 3. Price tag for the Greenbelt remodeling was $485,000. Improvements included a lower ceiling and other features to save on heating, cooling, and lighting costs. The renovations, with suitable local reopening publicity, provided some safeguard against competition from new chain supermarkets in the Greenway shopping complex across the Baltimore-Washington parkway from Greenbelt.

Approval of a Severna Park supermarket at 41 Baltimore-Annapolis Road in Anne Arundel County was by a divided vote, with some directors noting that the area had no Co-op membership and that there was already supermarket competition nearby. The lease was for 5 years, at $3.10 per square foot for 15,477 square feet. President and CEO Satake estimated weekly sales at $100,000. The first week did $85,000.

The Board talked about operating Severna Park as a "direct charge" store, for members only, with wholesale prices at a fixed weekly fee to cover costs. This concept, observed in Canada, was much discussed by GCI leadership but never tried. Instead, a marketing concept identified as "Co-op Cost Plus" was tried at Severna Park at the end of 1981 when sales and margins there did not respond to other merchandising efforts.

After details were worked out with the union, this store (which was outside the Washington market area) paid a lower wage and closed for 2 days during a 40-hour week. All frills such as free bags, car loading, and a store hostess were eliminated. Co-op members, showing their GCI card, were charged at the checkout counter the wholesale price plus 15 percent for orders less than $20, 12 percent on orders up to $50, and 10 percent on orders over $50. Non-members paid cost plus 15 percent, except that all senior citizens paid only 10 percent. When this proved too complicated, a straight 12.5 percent markup was substituted. Management and the Board continued to operate this Severna Park store at a loss for 2 more years.

The early 1980s was a time for intense exploration by leaders and management of the Greenbelt Cooperative -- a search for innovative ways to serve members who were unhappy with several years of cutbacks in facilities and services, and a search for ways to attract new members and additional capital. Many, many committees and ad hoc task forces were created, carefully crafted reports were prepared, numerous study retreats were held, trips were taken to see what other cooperatives were doing, and consultants were hired to analyze and advise on potential projects.

The overwhelming majority of the area council and Congress leaders were oriented toward supermarkets, service stations, and pharmacies. A few younger new members who came into the Cooperative's leadership through SCAN purchases did not stay long. Several gave "the bickering and trivia dealt with at council meetings" as the reason for leaving. One disenchanted couple wrote to Chairman Mohn: "When a council meeting devotes almost an hour in discussing whether an annual area meeting buffet should be vegetarian or serve meat it is wasting our time. We believe that Greenbelt Consumer Services should be run like a business so that it can be of economic benefit to members and shoppers."

The couple never returned even after Mohn telephoned them to explain that all kinds of people make up a cooperative. This division in understanding the objective of the Cooperative made some directors very uneasy about making hard decisions for the future direction of GCS.

The Board designated an additional director as a vice chairman for development. This was dropped after a 2-year trial and the Board reverted to four officers.

From a historical point of view, proposals for solving the Cooperative's problems and extending its benefits produced a lot of repetition. Many of the ideas were retreads, to the point where some old-timers were saying, "Let's stop re-inventing the wheel". This may have been good advice, but it also discouraged new leaders to be told, "Oh, we already tried that several years ago and it didn't work!"

One project that held promise was to use the experience of the Greenbelt Cooperative, and its position in the market place, to help "new wave" co-ops and buying clubs get started and reach firm ground. Membership and Education Director Gauci and a number of volunteer leaders worked with people in the anti- poverty program, and also with both the Cooperative League and the National Consumer Cooperative Bank in an outreach program. GCI offered wholesale grocery supply geared to the specific needs of the small buying groups and training in skills required for organizing and operating cooperatives. Some took advantage of the offer, but there was not the response that was hoped for. In talking with some of the young leaders of small new co-ops, one could sense a reticence about accepting GCI as a partner in the cooperative movement. Was there some feeling that GCI was too big, too successful to understand the problems of a real "grass roots" co-op?

Another project in response to an apparent need should have been successful. That was a credit union to serve all employees and members. Through earlier years there had been the small but successful Wheaton Credit Union, organized by local cooperative members; and there had been the large credit union that served residents of Greenbelt, Maryland. At one point, the Wheaton Credit Union changed its charter and name so that it could serve employees and members in all GCS areas except the city of Greenbelt. Later, after it ran into difficulties, it was merged into the larger, older Greenbelt Credit Union. Nothing much came of the merger, and in 1980 the branch office in the Aspen Hill SCAN was closed when it failed to provide satisfactory service.

In 1980 and 1981, a strong attempt was made to organize a new credit union with a Maryland charter to serve GCI. Director Tom Martin put this together as the Cooperative Savings Credit Union, but it was unable to begin functioning for a number of reasons. To assure that the credit union would be an integrated part of GCS, both the GCS Board and the board of the prospective credit union designated the CEO to be in charge of its management. But Satake appeared to be less than enthusiastic about the credit union. This impression discouraged several members of the Board. The forecast of subsidized costs to place the credit union into operation was a further discouragement. The nucleus of the proposed organization lingered on for a couple of years.

The biggest and most time-consuming project of 1980 was in housing. Actually there were two projects. Somewhat earlier, GCI and Cooperative

Services, Inc. of Detroit had explored a joint venture using Government loan money to build a low-cost apartment house for senior citizens in Essex, on the outskirts of Baltimore. The Greenbelt staff and Board had found that impractical, so Fred Thornthwaite and his Detroit organization went ahead with it with the help of GCI's John Brown. When Cooperative Services, Inc. ran out of cash, GCI was asked to buy the whole venture. This was a $6 million project. The investment required of the Greenbelt Cooperative was quoted at $250,000. Some directors on the Board and members of the Housing Committee pushed hard for this venture, not only to put GCI into housing for its older members, but also to bail out a sister cooperative. There were too many problems, and GCI gave up on the proposal. The Essex apartment house was offered for sale by the Detroit cooperative to the prospective residents but then retained when that co-op's finances improved.

The other venture also involved the Detroit cooperative and its need for cash during the late 1970s and early 1980s. This proposal was for the sale of the Merritt Island apartments in Florida. GCI already was leasing three units and was losing money renting them to members vacations in Florida. What followed here was sale of the apartments by Cooperative Services to their occupants. A few months later the GCI Board authorized sale of the three apartments it was leasing.

During these negotiations, the GCI Board was keenly aware that Cooperative Services, Inc. had not paid back its $50,000 loan. As a result, half had been written off already as a bad debt, although some directors hoped it might be repaid after the Detroit cooperative obtained cash on its real estate sales. And that is what eventually happened. In the spring of 1983, new officers of Cooperative Services, Inc. in Detroit arranged to repay the loan in monthly instalments but asked that all back interest be forgiven. The GCI Board agreed. The principle was eventually repaid.

Concern about the future of the Cooperative League (CLUSA) and the direction in which the National Consumer Cooperative Alliance was headed continued to command the attention of GCI leaders. The new president of CLUSA, Morgan Williams, attended a meeting of the GCI board in November 1980 to discuss his organization's future and how the Greenbelt Cooperative could help in the cooperative movement's objectives.

Regarding the newer cooperative organizations, the GCI Congress and Board resolved to maintain connections but on a low key pending a clear understanding of their objectives. Gauci had been at the helm of the Alliance for a year and hoped he had helped steer the organization into productive channels. A new member of GCI had been elected to the Alliance board and requested that the GCI board pay his expenses of $844, although he had not been designated to represent GCI. His bill was paid. He later became chairman of the new provisional area council of GCI in Columbia, Maryland, where there was a SCAN store and hope of a supermarket -- although that never developed despite extended negotiations. Some directors and members of the GCI Congress continued to have ambivalent feelings about the Alliance and its objectives. Even so, the Board continued to supply funds and send representatives to its gatherings and to NASCO, the National Association of Student Cooperatives, at Ann Arbor, Michigan, as well. GCI also helped with scholarship funds for young people who were not its own members.

Although the Severna Park store stayed open less than 4 years, a provisional area council emerged to participate in the GCI Congress. Both Columbia and Severna Park were accepted as official membership areas in May 1981. For a time both were active. The Severna Park members established a recycling project. Some Columbia members took a lead in a revision of the GCI bylaws in 1987.

The Congress had many committees at work during the late 1970s and early 1980s. Eleanor Thompson was speaker, having served in that capacity since 1977, maintaining a vigorous Congress organization before she was elected as a director on the Board. She was followed by Milton Johnson as the twelfth Congress speaker.

In an effort to encourage participation of more volunteers in the Congress, the Board came up with an incentive program and then tabled it after lengthy discussion. Later, discounts were offered to representatives to the Congress from the area councils and to active participants of committees. Eventually this incentive amounted to a 25 percent discount on SCAN furniture. Member involvement also got a boost from additional brochures in the series which Gauci and SCAN's design department developed.

The newsletter, now published twice a month as the GREENBELT CONSUMER (a name abandoned by Greenbelt city's weekly newspaper some years earlier), slipped back into one of its periods of long articles not much concerned with GCI activities. By February 1982, it was reduced to a monthly house organ. In response to high mailing costs, several thousand inactive and out-of-state members were dropped when they failed to return cards indicating a wish to continue receiving it.

The travel program was important to a segment of the membership. For some years it carried on its activities almost like a separate organization, with parties that involved folk dancing, films, and refreshments. Jack Besansky, Eben Jenkins, Gunther Sadel, Doys Shorb, Dorothy Wheeler, and Frank Kendrick were among those who provided leadership. Congress and the Board debated, in 1980, whether the program should pay its own way, and whether it should operate as a travel agency or contract for trips and accommodations through an established travel agency. Questions about the status of the program and how it should operate surfaced several times during the early 1980s before the activities just ceased in a disagreement about control.

The nine-member Board of Directors carried, during this period, a long and varied range of concerns. From a 2-day retreat in Columbus, Ohio, Chairman of the Board Mohn prepared a 13-page report dated October 13, listing 21 items to be discussed
and then went into detail about:

> --A Cooperative Savings Credit Union.
> --Reactivating the Potomac Cooperators, Inc. as a wholesaling operation.
> --Amending the Maryland cooperative law.
> --Strengthening the Audit Committee.
> --Preparing the evaluation of the CEO.
> --Reviewing the GCI staffing pattern.
> --Relationships within the consumer movement.
> --Additional member benefits.
> --Activities for Co-op Month.
> --Setting up a cooperative trust.
> --Possible survivor's patronage benefits.
> --Directions for the food, petroleum, and food divisions.
> --Housing.
> --Capital structure of GCI.
> --Insurance services.

For each item, there was an assignment of priority, responsibility, and approximate amount of time required by Board and staff.

This was followed by a 3-day retreat at Coolfont resort (owned and operated by former general manager Sam Ashelman), near Berkley Springs, West Virginia. From this came an 8-page report on:

> --Characteristics of a successful cooperative: financially viable, effectively managed, democratically controlled by user/owners, multi-service, growth oriented, and meaningful member equity.
> --Relationship with the GCI Congress.
> --What is needed in terms of business operations.
> --Priorities for Board and for management.
> --Development plan priorities.
> --Information needed for decision making.

At one point during the discussions at the retreat, Director Dorothy Jacobson stated:

"The cooperative aspect is fundamentally what makes GCI different. Is our growth as a cooperative rather than just as a successful business? Preferably because we think the members have a share, because we think we are supporting a great movement, or because we offer an alternative way of doing things."

Ben Rosenzweig, former president and at the time of the retreat a member of the Review and Evaluation Committee, inquired "whether the membership at large is going to have any input to help shape the thinking of where the whole organization wants to go."

Following a review of Satake's job performance near the end of the year, the Board adopted a position description for the president and chief executive officer, and renewed Satake's contract at $100,000 salary plus $20,000 bonus.

In January 1981, Satake named Jim Nelson as vice president and director of operations. His table of organization also called for a vice president for finance and administration, but this position was vacant until the end of 1982. Gowell had been retired as vice president for the furniture division but was brought back for a period as a part-time consultant.

SCAN sales and margins continued to carry GCI in 1981 and all through the decade until the bottom fell out in 1988. For 1981, sales for the furniture division reached $28 million and net income was $2.6 million.

Two new furniture stores were opened in 1981, and two old ones closed. Greenway SCAN, in Prince Georges County, had a preview Sunday, July 12, with the usual wine and cheese buffet and visiting dignitaries. On the next day customers flocked in, attracted by a 5-page color advertisement supplement in the WASHINGTON POST. From newly painted SCAN trucks in the parking lot in front of the new store, fast moving merchandise was sold on a cash-and-carry basis. Break-even point for this store was determined to be $25,000 per week. First week sales totaled $101,000. Rental for the 13,000 square foot facility had been projected at $113,000 for the first year. This SCAN had a highly visible location at the end of the building, and was within a few hundred feet of the Capital Beltway (I-95), the Washington-Baltimore Parkway, and the busy road to NASA.

The other opening came October 17, for a 12,000 square foot store on three levels in the very heart of fashionable Georgetown, at Wisconsin Avenue and M Street NW. The new Georgetown Park SCAN had such neighbors as Garfinkels and Abercrombie & Fitch, in a Victorian setting with fountains and gardens. Rental at this location was $18.50 per square feet (compared, for instance, to $7.34 at the Pikesville Scan on the western outskirts of Baltimore). Opening week sales came to $106,000, and then settled down at around an $80,000 average.

The two SCAN closings were at Takoma Park and at Canal Square in

Georgetown. Closeout sales brought in much needed cash. Two special events also boosted sales and income. There was a warehouse sale, with members only for the opening, which disposed of slow-moving inventory pieces. Early in the year, furniture from Israel was featured in cooperation with the Israeli embassy and Jewish food specials at the Co-op supermarkets.

Management reported that by the time the two new SCAN stores opened, the furniture division was exceeding sales and profit forecasts by about 11 percent. About 25 percent of furniture sales were cash and carry.

It had been obvious that a profitable operation like SCAN would attract competition. There were soon several imitators, like Scandinavian Collection. Although they whittled away some volume from SCAN, they never matched the quality, price, or vertical integration that were ingredients of SCAN's success. GCI was operating its furniture sales on an average markup of 40 percent and spending a low 2 percent of gross on advertising.

The two SCAN stores under GCI management in Chicago were reported by Satake to be doing well, with satisfactory earnings for Hyde Park Cooperative.

In an effort to improve performance in the service station division, the three busiest stations -- Greenbelt, Westminster, and Wheaton -- were remodeled and equipped for self-service gas pumping. All seven stations were using vehicle diagnostic equipment in servicing cars. To reinforce the Co-op image, the trade name "Exval" was dropped, and all stations carried the GCI logo.

Price competition in gasoline sales cut down GCI gross margins at the service stations from 14.7 percent in 1979 to 8.56 percent in 1981. This, along with below-budget income from auto service and repairs resulted in a division loss of $140,000 for 1981. The situation at the Piney Branch station was so bad that the CEO said GCI would lose less money by closing it and just continue paying rent on the facility. Indeed, it was closed early the next year. Gasohol, which had such a well publicized introduction by the Cooperative, lost its appeal and was phased out.

Supermarkets faced a possible strike at the beginning of 1981 when the union spokesman said GCI would have to pay the same wage scale as Giant and Safeway. Management figured this would cost an impossible increase of $1.2 million. Negotiating resulted in a contract that contained an increase of $252,000 annually.

Losses in the food division mounted and led to dismissal of the supermarkets supervisor. More than ever before, Board and management realized that competing with the big supermarket chains was a dead end impossibility. The 1981 operating results of the food stores were especially bad with losses of

$548,000 before allocated overhead.

GCI finished the fiscal year with sales of nearly $55 million and net income before taxes of $304,000. This permitted a dividend of 4 percent on outstanding shares of stock and -- for the first time since 1959 -- a patronage return, amounting to .75 percent on purchases. Book value of shares stood at the highest level ever, $15.33.

With the fee to join the Cooperative lowered to $1, there was a jump to 34,000 members. Cost of a year's membership was estimated at around $9 (membership card, mailings, newsletter, record keeping), so the increased membership was becoming a major expense. Percentage of sales to members, however, had leaped from 3 percent to 22 percent under the $1 membership fee program. This was important in meeting loan requirements of the National Consumer Cooperative Bank. It was also important to funnel any large amount of net margins back to the purchasers who were entitled to have them rather than to pay higher income taxes by retaining them as profits.

A very high portion of the Board's time during the year went into detailed examination with the CEO of the 4-week-period operating and financial reports. Chairman of the Board Mohn emphasized the necessity for directors to understand the complications of financial management in order to secure results from the growth and development plan which the Cooperative's leadership put together during the fall and winter months of 1981.

A number of special projects came out of committee reports for Board review. In addition to the proposed credit union, there was a plan favored by Rockville Delegate Ralph Golden for a cooperative home maintenance and repair service. This was in addition to his contributions to nutritional concerns within the cooperative framework. GCI did finally link up with a customer- controlled enterprise for household maintenance and repair services, but that was so near to the termination of GCI's operations that this member benefit never really took hold.

Visits were made with Recreation Equipment, Inc., a large and profitable cooperative in Seattle, Washington, with the objective of a merger or other affiliation, but action was never taken.

Director Gif Hoag, from Falls Church, headed the development of cooperative-oriented cable TV service in northern Virginia, but this, too, achieved only partial success. A similar effort was made in Montgomery County, Maryland, without much more success. Some GCI leaders, Director Anne Rollin among them, tried to revive a federation of the various cooperatives in the Washington area. This, too, failed to get off the ground.

It should be mentioned that through the years many outstanding recognitions came to some of the Cooperative's leaders. Wallace Campbell, who was a Congressman-at-large in the GCS/GCI legislative body, was elected to the Cooperative League's Hall of Fame. This honor was also bestowed upon Dorothy and George Jacobson, and upon Gif Hoag. Art Danforth, Falls Church Area Council chairman and a GCI director, received the Glenn Anderson Memorial award for his model state cooperative law among other contributions to the cooperative movement. Chairman of the Board Paul Mohn was placed on the board of the Cooperative League, and Director Anne Rollins served as deputy speaker of the newly formed CLUSA assembly. Mohn also was on the board of the International Cooperative Alliance and the board of the National Consumer Cooperative Bank, as well as president of the Association of Cooperative Educators. Warren Mathers received the Cooperative Public Service award from the National Cooperative Month Coordinating Committee. GCI had representation on the board of the Consumer Federation of America and other consumer-oriented and cooperative organizations.

The GCS Co-op Congress and the Board intended to set up a service memorial for its own outstanding leaders who died, but the years passed with names like Ernie Wolfe, Jim Westby, Carnie Harper, Walter Bierwagen, Edie Christianson being listed, but this was one of those talked-about projects that was not pushed into action.

For Board and management the first months of 1982 brought operating and financial headaches. There were questions about the way the computer system was pricing furniture inventory, and there was confusion about the reliability of the 1981 year-end net income reported. Both the CEO and the Board agreed on the need for a competent person to fill the vacant slot of vice president for finance. A search brought in someone to fill the position by the end of the year. Meanwhile the ups and downs of operating returns and cash flow provoked anxiety about the future.

The Board reluctantly approved management's urging to close the Rockville supermarket in the face of a projected loss of $175,000 in the current year. The resolution, at the end of April, cited changes in growth and traffic patterns in the store vicinity, price competition in the Rockville community, the amount of capital investment required to bring the store up to standard, and the frustration of having exhausted merchandising strategies for improved operating results.

Some of the Cooperative's leaders from time to time urged a search for new locations where a supermarket could open to serve members. The head of the supermarket division discussed the various problems of merchandising and advertising and concluded: "We are trying to find the right balance". After 40 years! Unhappily, other food cooperatives, including Berkeley, also were trying to find the right balance in the late 1970s and early 1980s.

The minutes book records what must have been obvious for several years:

"Board members expressed their concern over the possibility that the food stores might be closed one by one, followed by the closure of the service stations, leaving the Cooperative with a group of furniture stores which do not quite fit the needs [of all members]."

At this point there remained five food stores and five service stations: Greenbelt, Kensington, and Westminster supermarkets, the neighborhood food store in Fairlington, and the experimental cost-plus food outlet in Severna Park; and stations in Greenbelt, Westminster, Wheaton, Falls Church, and Penn Daw -- which was closed a few months later.

There were additional frustrations. In May, the gasoline pumps were stolen from the Greenbelt service station -- removed and loaded onto a truck in a 3-hour operation after the thieves assured a passing police car that they were making repairs. This left GCI with a $50,000 loss and its only profitable station out of service for several weeks. There was some insurance recovery. Six weeks later management fired the manager of the Greenbelt pharmacy on a charge of padding charges and pocketing between $5,000 and $11,000.

Reporting on SCAN, the CEO told the Board GCI was "definitely paying a lot more money for warehouse people, sales people, and fringe benefit costs" than competing furniture businesses paid. He cited the SCAN union contract which had provided for double pay plus double commissions for overtime, whereas competitors without a union contract paid straight time. A new contract reduced overtime to 1 1/2 pay, with a 6 percent pay increase.

By the end of 1982, management was talking about closing the New Market SCAN, in the Peninsula area. Meanwhile, a new SCAN was opened in October, in a large regional shopping center in Springfield, in northern Virginia. The chairman of the Fairfax County Board of Supervisors cut the ribbon, and there was the usual wine and cheese buffet with hundreds of Co-op leaders and other guests present.

This location was off Old Keene Mill Road, just west of I-95. It offered 1,300 square feet of floor space, including a mezzanine level, for a rental of $9 per square foot. Management estimated weekly sales at $50,000.

By the end of 1982, SCAN recorded several weekly sales figures over $1 million. The furniture division prospered so well that the Board was able to pay a 4 percent dividend on outstanding shares of stock at the end of fiscal year 1982 and a patronage refund of 1.5 percent, double the previous year and amounting to almost a quarter of a million dollars. Some of the declared refund provided cash for GCI operations, as IRA had ruled that only 20 percent of any patronage return must be paid in cash to the member/shopper. The remainder was credited in the member equity accounts. Sales for the year were $52,381,000, and net earnings $589,000.

One significant attempt to provide groceries to members took off in 1982 and looked promising on paper. This was POPS, a pre- order purchasing service that was supposed to start with 19 purchasing groups scattered around the national capital area and build up to 60 groups of 20 families at each of several depots.

The idea made good sense. It went back to the old buying club concept but it was much more sophisticated. Each month a printout of available groceries and prices, including some cheeses and processed meats, was made available to the group. Its leader who called a meeting where each member went over the listing and made out an order sheet. Individual orders were then adjusted so that the total order would be in case or carton amounts. The combined order was sent to the GCI offices in Savage. Later, on a designated date, delivery was made to a depot where the purchasers came to pick up the groceries each had ordered. They all helped with the unloading from the truck and sorting into individual orders. The leader (supposed to be rotated periodically) totaled each order on a calculator and collected payment. The total collected was then sent to the GCI office. An advance deposit provided security against failure to pick up orders.

The printout prices carried a 6 percent markup, but that did not cover costs. In October the markup was increased to 7.5 percent plus a 2 percent delivery charge. The CEO assigned supervision of POPS to Gauci as a member benefit rather than a grocery operation within the supermarket and petroleum division. By year's end it was obvious that part-time supervision of this operation on top of Gauci's schedule of other assignments was not working. Growth of the pre-order purchasing service was so much slower than predicted that a full-time supervisor could not be justified. Gauci worked up three options for the Board, none of which could put the distribution on a paying basis. To charge enough to fully cover the distribution costs would push prices so high as to make the arrangement too expensive considering how much volunteer time it required of the consumer/members.

In a January 1983 report, the estimate for POPS was 1,000 families, but at this current stage costs for administration and distribution amounted to $100 per family being served. A loss to GCI of $29,000 by the close of the year was forecast. In a determined effort to make the experiment work, a full-time manager was hired and a depot was rented at $2.43 per square foot on Viers Mill Road in Montgomery County. For the families using POPS there was an 18 percent savings compared to shopping at Giant, but only a 3-5 percent saving against prices at the Bonus stores. The POPS manager left in less than a year. The enterprise limped along until 1984 when the Greenbelt Cooperative got out of the food business completely.

Differences with Satake as CEO over two issues surfaced in the fall of 1982. These were questions about finance reporting and support for the long-debated credit union. Director and Treasurer Tom Martin had devoted countless hours to putting together the credit union proposal and felt so strongly affronted by the CEO's lukewarm position that he submitted his resignation from the Board. After some negotiating, the resignation was accepted in December. The Board resolved not to fill the vacancy until the Congress selected nominees at the end of February 1983.

Other problems caused discontent in the area councils, the Congress, and the Board. There were the usual complaints about lack of Co-op identity in the stores and stations, not enough promotion of CO-OP label items, lack of information about what was happening, lack of quorums at meetings. Only twice during the year was there a quorum at the Congress sessions. At mid-year the finance picture looked so tight that the Board discussed cutting its own budget. Directors expressed concern about the large amount of money used up in interest charges on loans. There was a disturbing shift in GCI relations with its furniture supplier, Nordiscan. There was a comment in the Board minutes that "the original concept is no longer valid" and speculation that the partnership should be dissolved.

Several directors felt that GCI's management was "not aggressive enough" and was "too quick to just cut costs". At the same time, the CEO announced he was bringing in the former comptroller from the Berkeley cooperative to advise for several weeks regarding GCI's budgeting process and internal control procedures which he felt were lacking. In opening one of several in camera special meetings, the Chairman of the Board reminded the other directors that there are matters "which the Board absolutely has to discuss...absolutely critical." Apparently several meetings were held at other locations than the Board room in Savage. Director Hoag suggested that Board and management needed to be more clear about where they wanted "to be 5 years from now".

As a base for looking ahead and planning strategies, David Cohen, active in the Penn Daw Council, urged that GCI engage a firm to make a professional demographic and marketing survey of the areas served by the Cooperative. He pushed this idea for several months, and at the end of the year the Board voted $12,250 for a firm to survey a sampling of the Cooperative's 55,000 members and report to the Board by May 31, 1983.

Despite the anxieties about operations and the financial condition of GCI during the year, final figures as of January 29, 1953 showed $52,381,000 in sales with net earnings of $589,000. This was enough for a 4 percent dividend on outstanding shares of stock and a patronage return of 1.5 percent.

The Board and management faced a dilemma on how to handle a patronage refund of $487,000 from the National Consumer Cooperative Bank in 1983. This would have to be shown on the GCI books as income and would be taxable, but there would be no cash payment. NCCB, having declared this portion of its income as a patronage refund to a member, would have no income tax liability, but would have the withheld surplus to use for its continuing operations. The statutes which created the NCCB prevented it from making cash refunds, according to the Bank's legal counsel. The impact for GCI would be a $134,000 payment to the IRS and $44,000 cash payment to its own members without receiving any cash to offset the payments.

Inquiry found the NCCB willing to redeem its paper patronage refund for 10 percent of its face value. This amount would result in a $14,000 tax payment and $5,000 cash payment as part of the GCI patronage refund to its members, leaving $30,000 addition to equity and net income for the year. The Board decided by a split vote that this result was preferable to waiting for $487,000 sometime in the indefinite future.

While considering a matter involving the IRS, it is interesting to note that at about this time IRS notified the Cooperative that it must submit to IRS the social security numbers of all its stockholders. Complying with that directive cost $25,000.

Running a cooperative the size of GCI in the 1980s had become far more complicated than when a couple of thousand members made up GCS in the town of Greenbelt.

One highly technical decision for the Board was how best to cope with the constantly changing rate of exchange between the U.S. dollar and foreign currencies, especially the Danish kroner. Even very small shifts had significant effect on SCAN furniture prices and hence sales figures and gross margins. At one point the Board had given the CEO approval to enter the forward exchange market. Hedging would have protected SCAN purchasing from fluctuations in currency exchange but by definition would have ruled out any gain (or loss) from those fluctuations. At that time there had appeared to be an advantage in buying foreign currencies under contract. It was the opinion of the new vice president for finance, however, that premiums on forward contracts for foreign exchange since that time had cost the business $1.4 million. There had been some uneasiness expressed by several directors in the beginning as to whether the Cooperative was in the furniture business or market speculation. After 3 years experience, the CEO reported that management needed full flexibility in adjusting to currency market fluctuations in order to maximize earnings. The Board found no problem with that if the purpose was a hedge to avoid large losses, but the Board was opposed to speculating.

Another complication that demanded time and money during 1983 was the necessary updating of the data processing system. In the budget approved at the beginning of the year, an increase of $136,000 was allocated to the data processing department -- this after the payroll function had been contracted to an outside firm. In March, the CEO brought in a consulting firm to review the existing system and analyze the total information system required to operate the business of GCI. The report came to the Board at its summer retreat, with a price tag of $1.5 million to implement an adequate data processing system.

The 1983 budget was ambitious. For the first time, a $1 million goal was set for net income. Other, more general goals were to improve the balance sheet and to achieve growth. Concerning SCAN there were two possibilities. One was to expand into either Chicago or Philadelphia, with the latter city preferred. The other was to go into franchising, but this involved recognized dangers.

After agreeing on a budget, the next step was to establish priorities. These included:

1. Capital structure.
2. Expansion of SCAN.
3. Food distribution alternatives.
4. A fourth earnings center (business).
5. Leadership identification and development.
6. Governance structure for the Cooperative's future.
7. Membership survey.
8. Other continuing programs (service stations, POPS, member benefits, member education, tri-partite committees including employees).

These concerns would involve Congress and staff participation as well as the Board. Leadership and reporting dates were designated for what promised to be a busy year.

Renewal of the contract with Satake as chief executive officer and president came up in March. There was agreement on $135,000 per year as base salary, but with the provision that the chairman of the Board could go up to $150,000 in the negotiation if he found that necessary.

It was in the early spring of 1983 that a critical morale situation within the SCAN staff surfaced. Complaints had come to the attention of two area councils and were reported to the Board. This was a complaint routing disapproved of by both management and the Board, but the issue demanded immediate attention.

Chairman Mohn called a special in camera meeting on March 20 with only two persons present other than the directors -- Speaker of the Congress Johnson and Chairman of the Review and Evaluation Committee Staehle. Here are quotes from the minutes:

"The chairman noted that the fundamental issue at this juncture is that the supervisory and employee relations are at an absolute rock-bottom low. To illustrate, there are more arbitrations in process than ever in SCAN's history. Particularly distressing is that the two groups that should have been aware of the problems that were surfacing and brought them to the attention of the CEO either weren't aware of them or effectively blocked them. After sifting through all the information that has been recorded, it is clear that the older SCAN managers and sales people have been in agreement; also, the younger SCAN managers and the middle and upper management have been in agreement -- creating two groups....Top management and supervisors say this is the best year SCAN has ever had. The other side is pointing out material problems. It isn't all black or white.

"....it is obvious that the employee group is determined that two people must go -- Jim Nelson and Eva Johns."

Chairman of the Board Mohn noted at the time that when the issue was brought to the Board it had reached a point where the employees would not talk about the problem with anyone in management. Satake agreed that an inquiry by the Board would be the most effective move, so Mohn appointed Directors Don Hanes and Glen Whipple to serve with him as a panel of inquiry.

Mohn described to the Board the guidelines which the inquiry panel had followed and then listed 16 issues that CEO Satake would have to consider and settle:

"1. ...schedule changes...since this is fundamentally a union responsibility, the inquiry committee stayed away from this issue even though it was the trigger that caused the employees to start going to the area councils.

"2. ...Sunday operations....a number of full-time staff do not want to work on Sunday.

"3. ...training and development seem to be deteriorating.

"4. With the change in style of management since Mr. Nelson assumed control, there has been a lack of participatory management...teamwork which was the #1 strength of SCAN operations is missing.

"5. ...quality control is slipping.

"6. ...evidence that there might be promotions based on favoritism vis-a-vis competency.

"7. Warehouse bays are not prepared for loading the trucks in the mornings and there is a lack of coordination in showing the drivers how to assemble furniture [for loading].

"8. ...safety precautions have been materially lax.

"9. Management by intimidation was brought up by a number of employees who felt that disagreement with top management would result in a reprimand of some sort.

"10. There are no procedures manuals.

"11. Disagreement about inventory levels.

"12. Advertising integrity was questioned and specific areas of concern were cited.

"13. Quality of furniture has declined....(?)

"14. There is almost no effective communication.

"15. [Some] procedures...set up without weighing the effect on store personnel.

"16. The service department is very slow to deal with the problem."

Quite a fistful of problems! And that was only the outline. There was more trouble ahead.

After the Board turned the matter over to Satake and assured him of no Board precedent to receive employee complaints through the area councils, he hired a consultant to produce a manual for employees, and then after studying the employee complaints and talking with top SCAN management he notified Nelson and Johns of their termination. He offered 1 week's pay for each year of employment with GCI as severance compensation in exchange for a "non-compete" agreement. They had already declined an offer to assign them to other positions within GCI. Their response was a lawsuit in the amount of $6 million for damages plus $8 million in punitive compensation.

The suit was against both Satake and GCI. In the bill of particulars there was a charge that Nelson and Johns were discharged "in violation of public policy because Nelson sought to require the Cooperative to comply with federal law and the public policies of the U.S. and the State of Maryland". This alleged "certain practices which resulted in the receipt of rebates from certain transoceanic carriers". In September, Satake informed the Board that GCI through its attorney had gone to the Federal Maritime Commission regarding possible infractions, and had filed a counter suit of $1 million against Nelson and Johns.

On October 6, 1983, GCI and the Maritime Commission entered into a compromise agreement under which GCI paid $30,000. This concerned "the shipping practices of ocean carriers used by Greenbelt in the importation of furniture from Denmark". Actually, Nordiscan had received rebates -- a common practice in Europe but illegal for U.S. firms. The legal fees exceeded $100,000.

While all this was going on, Chairman of the Board Mohn had emergency bypass surgery but apparently missed only two meetings.

A good many other developments occurred with SCAN during these months. Some were encouraging; a few were setbacks. The encouraging ones first. Reporting in February, Satake called the SCAN store in Loehmann's Plaza, Falls Church "an absolute gold mine and a main factor in the furniture division's profitability". The October issue of the newsletter to members carried a double-page spread on SCAN as "a 23 year old co-op success story". It made the point that prices and merchandising policies were written from the customer's instead of the seller's point of view. The feature listed 15 practices that characterized SCAN. Long-time members saw this as a return to the Cooperative's early SCAN image.

The direction was not all that clear. At mid-year Board and management struggled with a choice whether to maximize profits by easing the gross margin up to 44 percent and introducing some lower priced furniture as a mix with SCAN's traditional lines, or whether to emphasize the earlier image of high quality and lower margins. Bob Gowell, who had been brought back for a while as a consultant, discussed this issue at a Board meeting and recounted the history of SCAN for newer directors.

The Chicago furniture operation that GCI was managing for the Hyde Park Cooperative was losing money and the board of that co-op indicated a willingness to sell it. Rather than have the SCAN outpost go to some outside business and because of the GCI investment in the Chicago stores, the Board decided by a split vote in September to buy the operation for $258,000. Satake had said the decision was whether to diversify by expanding into other areas or to consolidate with stores in additional locations in the Washington-Baltimore area. The forecast for the Chicago operation was a loss of $145,000 in the first year but a net profit of $50,000 in the second year.

Following the purchase in 1983, came the question of whether to develop the Chicago SCAN as a cooperative. The decision was to incorporate it as a wholly owned subsidiary business operation. The hope for profits turned into a disappointment.

In Washington, the landlord of the Van Ness building wanted SCAN out so he could remodel for professional rather than commercial tenants. He offered $90,000 to buy back the remainder of the GCI lease, and the Board agreed, closing the SCAN store there in September 1983.

The bad news for the furniture division was more competition. A firm based in Boston, Scandinavian Design, was planning to open four or more furniture stores in the Washington area in an attempt to pick off some of the GCI SCAN market. Satake told the Board that at best the new competition would force GCI to operate more efficiently, but at worst it could put SCAN into a loss position which would be ruinous for the Cooperative.

SCAN's warehousing, assembly, and delivery operations had exceeded the original warehouse space at Savage. Some temporary nearby overflow space was being rented. The CEO authorized a consultant to make a study of the warehouse operations and ways to improve efficiency. The price tag was $32,000 for the study and $93,000 to implement the recommended changes.

The Board had its own consultant studies underway all through the year. Reports on the membership survey brought out interesting information. The Cenex firm mailed out 2,100 questionnaires in April to every 26th family on the membership list. It was intended to yield a profile of the Cooperative's members and show the extent to which they were using GCI facilities and member benefit programs. There was a surprising 79 percent return, due largely to follow-up by the member education department and Congress volunteers.

Here are some of the findings:

Sex and marital status. 55 percent women and 45 percent men. 67 percent married vs. 51 percent married in the general population.

Race. 88 percent white, 5 percent black, 7 percent other. This was way out of line with area racial figures.

Education. 70 percent of the Co-op members had college education vs. 33 percent in the general population.

Income. 80 percent of members had income over $25,000, while 56 percent of the general population had this level of income.

When asked why the member had joined the Cooperative, most newer members replied "a store employee asked me and it was only $1". Older members said they joined for patronage refunds or member benefits. Very few mentioned the idealistic reasons that had motivated most of the pioneer leaders of the original Greenbelt Co-op.

Inquiry about use of GCI facilities showed 66 percent made a purchase from SCAN, 28 percent within the previous year. Most of those who had not used SCAN lived in Westminster or Severna Park, far from the Co-op's furniture stores. For the food stores, 45 percent said they shopped Co-op occasionally, 17 percent regularly. Many more replied that they had shopped the Co-op supermarkets in the past before they closed. Co-op service stations were patronized by 18 percent of those responding. Again, lack of a station close to home or work was the reason for not using one.

Only 15 percent voted in a GCI election, and a very low 3 percent had ever attended a meeting. The GREENBELT COOPERATOR house organ was read by 76 percent of the members, and preference was for features on travel and food. Least popular were articles on GCI operations, financial reports, and calendar of events. Only 38 percent had ever taken advantage of a promotion or sale as a result of seeing an advertisement in the house organ. Of member benefits, only 8 percent used the travel program, and 85 percent had never used any member benefit. **Very sobering findings!**

Another study authorized by the Board was a management survey by Peat, Marwick, Mitchell & Company. At a later Board meeting this was defined as a marketing and strategic planning analysis. The price tag on this report was $90,000. In essence it recommended that GCI close down its loss operations. This was advice the Board had heard before. Board members expressed unhappiness with this advice, because they had expected more options to have been explored.

Outside of Board considerations, some of the area councils were active but with less than the allotted number of elected delegates. There was some realization that the membership (at $1 per member) had grown so fast and so large that communication between members and area councils no longer really existed.

The 1983 Congress election had been found irregular because several unauthorized persons voted. At a second election at the end of the summer, Ben Rosenzweig was chosen to be speaker.

The financial reports for the year were slow to be finalized, due to the Board's monumental decision of December 17, 1983 to divest the Cooperative of its remaining food stores and service station operations. Rules established by the the Financial Accounting Standards Board stated closing costs relative to divestiture must be reflected in the operating report of the year in which the decision was made. This complicated management's reporting at best. Although GCI consolidated sales were $55,361,337 for fiscal 1983, the amount restated without the food and service station figures was $33,309,000. Income before tax from continuing operations before any dividend or patronage return was $1,277,000. However, after deducting the anticipated costs for divestiture, the figure had to be restated at $334,000. No decision about dividends and patronage refunds could be made until late in the year.

XIX. FINISHING 50 YEARS (1984-1989)

The decision to take GCI out of the food and service station operations marked the end of an era. It was a traumatic action for the Board and a devastating shutting of the door for many members. Looking back, it can be seen as the inevitable end to a trend in decreasing member participation and increasing management problems going back a dozen years.

The vote on December 17, 1983 was unanimous, taken after agonized and unsuccessful search for alternatives. The Board determined that the announcement would be made January 3, but with no implementation of the closures before March 31. It was further ordered that disposal of the facilities should be made where possible to other cooperatives or to community, member, or employee groups.

Reaction to the announced divestiture came quickly and in some cases it was bitter. Protests came mainly from members who lived in the near vicinity of four of the remaining five food store: Greenbelt, Westminster, Kensington, and Fairlington.

In Greenbelt, a petition with more than 1,000 signatures asked the Board to reverse its decision or at least postpone closings for 6 months. A "Save Our Stores" group organized to hold up the closing of the supermarket or if that failed then to form a local cooperative to buy it. Jim Cassells was chairman of this group. The Greenbelt City Council, the board of Greenbelt Homes, Inc., and the Greenbelt Area Council of GCI, headed by John Webb, all took an active interest in finding an alternative to losing the anchor business and only supermarket in the community's shopping center.

There were a few who felt like Albert K. Herling, former GCS director, that:

"Little if any consideration was given to the role of the Co-op in the social and economic fabric of the community....We are all made to feel like pieces on a chess board to be moved around, discarded or surrendered at someone else's decision -- a far cry from our cooperative democracy concept....We thought we had our own enterprise -- and now it is suggested that we may be able to buy back what we believed we already owned...."

Others, especially members in the Peninsula area of Virginia who had lost their food stores several years earlier, believed with their chairman, Fred Schmidt, "There is now a hope for repurchase of shares of stock. These stores have been an awful drain on the cash flow."

Two pages of comments about the divestiture in the February issue of the

GREENBELT CONSUMER explored a fair sampling of opinions from members:

"GCI will have a difficult time maintaining its cooperative nature without retail services like food and gasoline that have frequent contact with members and that retail a necessary commodity."

"GCI represented only through SCAN will become no different than any other business, and the specialness that makes a cooperative so different will be irretrievably lost."

"It's throwing away our history and all the work of our founders."

"Where is the hint that an important meeting was about to be held?   Surely that is important news to member-owners."

"The action taken has been forced by economic necessity. The Board has finally adopted suggestions and recommendations made eight years ago."

"My anger is directed at the members who have let this happen by patronizing the larger grocery stores which have entered our area over the last several years."

"Previous closings have resulted in much higher labor costs than both our union and non-union competitors because of our preponderance of long-time employees whose rate is in the highest wage and fringe benefit categories."

"We recognize that members, councils, the Congress, Board, and management may have made mistakes in the past, but we can't turn the clock back."

Looking forward, four groups took shape to negotiate for the facilities to be divested. One of these incorporated in Maryland as Consumer Services Cooperative named long-time co-op and credit union leader Tom Martin as president and Robert Avedon, former head of GCI's petroleum division as chief operating officer. They sought to buy the four service stations that would be spun off, but they could not raise enough cash for the asking price. This group reopened the Falls Church service station 2 weeks after GCI gave it up on expiration of the lease. The single station was not viable just on its own, and the Martin group gave it up after about 6 months.

No group of members or other cooperative was interested in the Severna Park store, and it was sold. Fairlington shut down March 3 on termination of the short-term lease, and the building was torn down for replacement by an office building.

Disposal of the Kensington store was the most difficult part of the divestiture. Members of the Wheaton Area Council formed a New Consumer Co-op. In bidding for the store they found themselves in competition with three grocery firms. And all four bidders found themselves at odds with the landlord who preferred to have a drug store as a replacement on the lease. Extensions of time were given to the co-op group but it was not able to come within 10 percent of the top bid, which was the requirement set by Satake with approval of the Board. Sale of Kensington was accomplished at the end of September for $250,000 as the last in the string of divestitures except for the Greenbelt service station. Wheaton members who had organized this new co-op were left bitter at not getting the store.

Former Director Wilbur Wright led the Westminster Area Council in signing up members and raising capital to purchase that store -- including assumption of the lease. John Bixler, John Brown, Charles F. Brehm, William P. Nyce, Mildred E. Campbell, Bernard A. Sutton, Joel L. Petre, and William D. Freymen, along with Wright became the first board of directors of Westminster Consumers Cooperative, Inc. Agreement with GCI was reached on March 30, and once again cooperators in this Howard County community were on their own. By June they had 2,500 members and $80,000. Most of the cash was in transfers of member equity from GCI. The owner of the shopping center bought the service station. Many members switched to a nearby station operated by Southern States Cooperative.

The Greenbelt Consumer Cooperative, Inc. formed to purchase the supermarket and pharmacy in the city where all this started. Members of this new organization raised $80,000 by June and closed a deal with GCI. The arrangement provided that the new cooperative would lease the building from GCI, pay $250,000 for store improvements and equipment, and another $250,000 for inventory. The required cash came mostly from three loans: 80 percent jointly from the National Consumer Cooperative Bank and Consumers United Insurance Company, and 10 percent from an equity loan from the National Consumer Cooperative Development Corporation. The remaining 10 percent came from members. Most of the 4,500 GCI members in Greenbelt switched membership and equity to the new cooperative.

The first board of directors included Jim Cassels, chairman; Charles A. Sarahan, vice chairman; Richard M. Bates, secretary; Joe Timer, treasurer; Margaret H. Hogensen, Wayne Williams, and Michael Burchick. The bylaws specify that the cooperative will not expand outside the city limits of Greenbelt -- somebody evidently remembered 1950 when Greenbelt Consumer Services, Inc. decided to reach out to Takoma Park.

The new co-op did not get the service station from GCI, but later leased it from the new owner. In the 1989 fiscal year the new Greenbelt Consumer

Cooperative, Inc. racked up $6,461,441 in sales with a net margin of $58,501 and paid a 2 percent patronage refund.

In GCI the closing months for the supermarkets and service stations were painful. The personnel department, under Peter Granahan, arranged for terminal leave, severance pay, closeout of employee records, and in cooperation with the union found new positions for the men and women whose jobs were disappearing. At the stores and stations operations worsened each day as key employees left for replacement jobs and inventory was purposely depleted. Not all the depletion was intentional. "Leakage" (stealing of merchandise and failure to ring up sales for friends) cut into gross margins toward the end.

Costs for closing the stores and stations was estimated at about $240,000, but receipts from the sale of the facilities included $200,000 for the Greenbelt service station in October, the $250,000 for Kensington, and $116,000 for the other units. Management and the Board figured there was enough net gain to put $150,000 into repurchase of stock from members and former members on the waiting list.

One consequence of the divestiture was the formation of Concerned Cooperators. This was a loose group of mostly long-time members who were critical not only of losing the food stores and service stations but also of secret sessions of the Board, what they felt was a lack of information and good communication, and a fear that GCI was drifting away from being a true member-controlled, democratic cooperative. Art Danforth and Mae Gellman-Danforth were leaders in this grouping.

It was probably no mere coincidence that following notice of the divestiture of the Cooperative's last food stores and service stations there were nine candidates for the three Board positions in the 1984 elections. Two relatively new faces won places as directors. An examination of the minutes of Board meetings for the next months following the election indicates that the new directors shook things up a bit.

Mohn continued as chairman of the Board. There were 11 meetings in the first 6 months of 1984 and only eight in the second half of the year. Meetings continued to be run in three parts as they had for a number of years: an open session, an executive session, and an in camera session.

Immediately following the elections, a first assignment the revised Board got its teeth into was the evaluation criteria for the annual review of the CEO's performance. The criteria merit attention as perhaps useful for other cooperatives:

"1. Financial Performance
   Earnings
      Earnings to assets
      Earnings to sales
      Division contribution to sales
      Expenses to budget
      Sales to budget
      Unallocated overhead to budget
      Earnings to budget
      New working capital turnover rate ($ of business volume during year for each $ of working capital)
      Earning power on return on total assets (net profit margin % x asset turnover).

"2. Management Performance
      Organizational structure meets GCI's needs
      Delegates and monitors results
      Places high priority on quality of service to members
      Developed and implemented strategic plan
      Presents alternatives with probable consequences of each to Board
      Maintains sufficient management depth for key management succession
      Innovative, imaginative, and aggressive
      Is flexible.

"3. Membership
      Increased number of members
      Increased percent of volume with members
      Increased paid-in capital by members
      Places a high priority on member relations programs.

"4. Other
      Places a high priority on education and leadership development
      Public relations programs are consistent with needs of our Cooperative
      Inspires and enlists support of Board, Congress, councils, staff, and members
      Follows cooperative principles and philosophies
      Demonstrates strong overall leadership
      Is responsive to the Board."

Each director marked on his score sheet a figure from 1 to 10 in each category. Averages were then derived. A total score of 8 to 10 was considered outstanding, 4 to 7 acceptable, 0 to 3 unacceptable. An optional bonus of up to 2 percent of net margin could be added to base salary and the fixed bonus of 2 percent of net margin, depending upon the rating sheet score. No optional bonus was paid on the 1983 performance.

Satake announced two vice president appointments at mid-year: Ronald R. Frederick for finance and John Gauci for membership. These were areas of work they already had been supervising.

Early in the year Satake presented the Board with three alternative plans for management's long-range organizational structure. He echoed a concern the Board had often voiced, about assurance that the CEO could be replaced in event of an emergency. He expressed confidence that there would be in place shortly a management team that would be "a good, cohesive unit working together...a group that could continue to run the organization". He proposed to bring in a highly qualified marketing specialist within the following 2 years, and he affirmed that a good furniture division manager would emerge from within the current staff. Nearly an entire Board meeting was occupied with exploration of an optimum organization and staffing pattern. Gowell, on board as SCAN consultant, contributed to the discussion from his own experience.

Improvements in inventory control, deliveries, and billings showed as the new data processing equipment and software came into use. The Board had approved a Univac 9030 system with a price tag of $438,154 for the complete installation.

An additional 25,424 square feet of warehouse space adjacent to the one already "bursting at the seams" was leased at $18,000 for the last third of the year. This had not been in the annual budget. Another cost increase outside the budget was about $106,000 annually in wage increases coming out of negotiations with the union. More significant expenses were legal fees and payments for consultants and special reports. The fee for the business strategy report prepared by Peat, Marwick, Mitchell & Company came to $90,000 -- and the Board had been dissatisfied with it because it did not contain options they had hoped for. Legal fees had mounted to $270,000 for the previous year and were continuing in 1984.

High interest rates on GCI borrowings added difficulties in attaining net margins. A financial report in the spring showed a zero cash balance. Management had borrowed $500,000 at 11 percent to finance inventory purchases and was using a long-term loan amounting to $1,850,000 at 12.5 percent interest from the National Consumer Cooperative Bank. A short-term loan of from $300,000 to $500,000 was anticipated.

The Board's budget for 1985 was set at $90,000, with allowances for additional items. It was noted that approximately a third of that represented payments to CLUSA, other cooperatives, and consumer groups. The Board voted to drop membership in four of these, but during the year requests came in for

$2,000 annually to train leaders in new co-ops, $1,000 for a testimonial dinner, $5,000 toward a reception to help pass a model consumer cooperative bill at Annapolis, and representation at several dinners at $100 a plate. "All good causes," one director observed. Travel by directors and members of the Congress and committees was criticized by several directors from time to time but the number and cost of trips continued. The entire Board went to Denmark to familiarize the directors with the manufacture of SCAN's furniture and the people who were making it. On the other hand, compensation for a director had not been increased for several years, so there was some feeling that there was a monetary penalty for serving on the Board.

Satake informed the Board early in 1984 that he expected that using the currency futures market for the first 9 months would yield enough gain to offset operational losses. Later in the year when the matter of currency exchange rates was again discussed, Mohn observed that SCAN should be either losing or making net earnings based upon business performance and not upon vagaries of the money market.

A second SCAN for Baltimore opened February 19, 1984. This one was in Galleria shopping center at York and Seminary Roads, in Towson, Maryland. This location just north of Baltimore was selected after a lengthy market survey. Satake's presentation to the Board emphasized that this new shopping center had easy access to I-695 (Baltimore Beltway) and was in an area of young, upscale families. With more than 15,000 square feet of floor space, this 13th SCAN was the largest one yet. The capital budget provided $263,159 with a 10 percent contingency. At the pre-opening, the Danish ambassador was the guest of honor.

The two SCAN stores which had been run by Hyde Park Cooperative in Chicago and managed under contract by GCI came up for frequent discussion after GCI bought them. They were operated as a profit corporation with a Delaware charter, but it was not until October 1984 that the mechanics of the relationship were settled. In discussions with management, the Board resolved that 80 percent of any profits would be plowed back into the Chicago operation, and that 20 percent would go to GCI. The CEO proposed that two of the three directors on the Chicago board would be from management and one from the GCI Board, with the CEO controlling the stock. The Board reversed this, so that control remained within the GCI Board.

After such a traumatic year, the financial report had some bright spots. Sales for continuing operations (SCAN, that is), had climbed to $39,442,000 for 1984. Net income at a healthy $618,000 provided a patronage refund of 1.6 percent, but there was no dividend. The Board gave priority to repurchase of more shares of stock as being more important than a dividend, and authorized $250,000 toward reducing the backlog of requests. With $2,066,000 in shares outstanding, requests for redemption stood at $634,000. The book value of each share was up to an all-time record of $16.83, but that was no comfort to those waiting stockholders who could not even recover the $10 par value.

Computer data showed that more than 50 percent of sales were to members, a compliance goal for the Cooperative's loan from the National Consumer Cooperative Bank and for making patronage refunds within IRS rulings.

Other year-end data of significance: the number of members (at $1 each) pushed above 100,000; 52 percent of SCAN purchases were on credit cards; management reported a loss of $382,000 on its foreign exchange contracts on forward rates (which the Board judged to be speculation rather than hedging); the Board spent $25,000 over its budget.

All through these years, directors worried about the amount of debt the Cooperative carried. At an October 1985 meeting when the vice president for finance, Ronald Frederick, proposed opening a line of credit with the First Pennsylvania Bank and Trust Company for $2 million, it was found that management had already exceeded the $1 million limit approved earlier by the Board. This was admitted as an oversight and the limit was raised to $2 million. At this same meeting, Director David Freed took exception to the short notice for major Board decisions in some instances.

"The Finance Committee met a week ago," Freed told the CEO, "and there was no discussion of this pending matter (an additional $1.2 million line of credit). For the Board of Directors to act as a responsible deliberate body exercising its fiduciary responsibility, more than 4 days notice is needed." He said he found the unfavorable debt to equity ratio extremely worrisome.

Satake explained that the earnings picture for the rest of the year looked bleak and because of that the debt/equity ratio was "out of whack". Freed replied that "SCAN's performance hasn't matched the budget, yet financial obligations were incurred despite the fact that cash was not available to pay for it."

This exchange was similar to others that took place as part-time lay directors strove to stay on top of what had now become a fast-paced, complicated, and highly competitive big business.

At this and other Board meetings the question of total indebtedness and debt-to-equity ratio received a thorough discussion.

For the benefit of newer directors who were not yet familiar with the complexities of GCI financing, Frederick explained that the debt/equity ratio indicates the borrowed part of the funds needed to operate the business versus what comes from stockholders (members). He stated that the ideal mix would be 1 to 1, to avoid having the creditors in reality owning more of the business that the members. He went on to review briefly the history of GCI's borrowings which seldom came within even a 2 to 1 ratio which is considered acceptable in some lines of business. He noted that the ratio for GCI had been 2.5 to 1 in 1983 and 2.1 to 1 in 1984.

From here the vice president for finance explored with the directors the more exotic internal hurdle rate. He explained that this is determined by taking the profit before interest and after taxes and dividing that by the amount of capitalization.

Chairman of the Board Mohn pointed out that this offers a target to shoot for when making investment decisions. Frederick recommended an internal threshold hurdle rate of 19.1 percent to be used as a benchmark against which investments should be measured to determine whether they made sense from an investment viewpoint. It would be used as a measure for deciding on new opportunities.

At this same meeting, a 3-year renewal contract for employment of Satake as CEO and president of GCI was approved by a 3-1 vote with one abstention.

Satake stated in early spring of 1985:

"The opening of our Herndon SCAN is the beginning of an aggressive growth plan in the Baltimore-Washington area. Not only are the areas around our existing and potential sites exploding with new development, but we have an opportunity to capture new customers daily because of the transience of the area. New store development is only one of several business strategies incorporated into a new long-range plan for SCAN."

The new furniture store had 16,000 square feet of floor space with 50 room settings. It opened March 7, 1985, in the Herndon Center at 372 Elden Street in Fairfax County, Virginia.

Announcement of the Herndon SCAN and Satake's statement about the direction of GCI came in the first issue of a radically changed COOPERATOR house organ. SCAN design specialists shaped it as 12 pages on an awkward 11x11 inch format on heavy gloss paper, with full color -- quite a difference from the customary newsprint tabloid. Publication was to be four times a year instead of monthly. A useful feature in the first issue was a 11x22 inch removable insert with detailed information about the travel program on one side and listings of meetings and training courses available to members on the other side. Unhappily, the changes were made by management with neither Congress nor Board input. Unhappily, too, the publication exceeded its announced budget and drew some member criticism. Adjustments were made.

Another periodical won a better reception. LEADERSHIP -- "A Greenbelt Co-op Publication" -- was put together by Vice President for Membership John Gauci, at first as a single sheet updating information for directors and Congress representatives from the various area councils. In 1985 this became a multi-page but low-budget monthly with articles and contributions about GCI and leadership.

There was a change of leadership in 1985. Donald K. Hanes replaced Paul O. Mohn as chairman of the Board. Mohn had served as chairman 11 years, longer than anyone else in the Cooperative's 50 years. Anticipating his retirement from the Board the following June, the Board at the end of November voted $4,500 for a "substantial gift" and an appropriate event to honor him for his contributions. Because the annual meeting on June 8 failed to attract a quorum, the three directors completing their terms resigned, and the Board appointed the three candidates for election as new directors.

The Congress elected George Jones to be its Speaker for the 1985-1986 term. In the latter part of this term other interests on the part of the Speaker necessitated appointment of a 5-person ad hoc committee to plan meetings, send out agenda, and follow up on activities. This ad hoc group included: Deputy Speaker Mae Gellman-Danforth, Katherine Ott, Nathaniel K. Smith, Eleanor Thompson, and Donald Cooper.

It should be noted here that the Cooperative League of the U.S.A. (CLUSA) underwent a major overhaul during this period and emerged as the National Cooperative Business Association.

There must have been a ferment in the air, because GCI also went through months of special task force studies, a complete rewrite of the bylaws, and critical structural changes.

The area councils and Congress organizations had been falling apart for some time. During 1985, wine and cheese parties to recruit new members brought out 35 at Wheaton, 22 at Greenbelt, and 12 at Takoma Park. A dinner put on by the Falls Church Council drew 36. Three or four were new faces; the rest were old stand-bys, including a sprinkling of directors and staff. Some councils were inactive, and meeting attendance at others generally had a half-dozen regulars. So little participation in a membership over 100,000! Securing a quorum at a Congress meeting became increasingly difficult. There was now supposed to be a representative for every 1,000 members in the rapidly increasing total of $1 members.

There had been a continuing sequence of Board and Congress committees with voluminous reports. At the beginning of 1984 a Capital and Organizational Structure Committee started out with a 63-page manual of information and made several recommendations to the Board on the use of capital assets, dividends, and patronage refunds. Next was a Futures Task

Force, with Charles Hix as its chairman. This had a broad range of input with some participation at numerous meetings by newer leaders. Then came the Governance Commission. When the report from this study group came to the Board in summer 1985, it was praised as "the best one received from a task force". This report was turned over to the Bylaws Committee for amendments needed to implement the recommendations. Following 6 months of exploration and drafting by the Committee and considerable Board discussion and an open hearing, Chairman of the Board Hanes appointed a Bylaws Finalization Committee chaired by Vice Chairman of the Board Carolyn Hillier. The Hillier committee labored through the first half of 1986 and finished its job with a stack of drafts, memoranda, and meeting records 6 inches thick. The last 6 months of that year provided area council meetings, Congress meetings, and Board meetings for a relatively small number of GCI leaders to argue passionately about what the proposed rewrite of the bylaws would do to the Cooperative.

The final draft was recommended by the Board for a special membership meeting on January 5, 1987. The vote (proxies counted and announced at the meeting attended by 34 members of the Congress) was 10,357 in favor and 1,278 against the changes. Several leaders among those opposed to the changes angrily charged that the entire chain of events from the rewrite of the enabling legislation in the State capitol to the January 5 vote was a railroading action to take the Cooperative away from the members. However, the Review and Evaluation Committee, headed by Charles R. Hix, found nothing amiss. And a seven-page memorandum apparently drafted in the member relations office itemized the entire process with committees, reports, dates of meetings, and schedule of information published "to provide opportunity for any member, especially for the elected leadership, to present their ideas, opinions, and suggestions on the future governance of our Cooperative". My own opinion, as a major participant in much of this process, is that only an unfortunately miniscule portion of the membership paid any attention to what was happening.

Here are some of the changes brought about in the new bylaws:

--Three levels of association with GCI. (1) Pre-member, designated as a "subscriber", pays $1 and fills in an application form; is entitled to newsletter for 1 year, participation in any patronage refund, use of member services; may not vote or hold office; will be dropped if has not become a voting member in 3 years. (2) Voting member must have built an equity account of at least $25; is entitled to vote, hold office, participate in all member benefits; will be dropped if no participation of any kind in 3-year period. (3) Fair-share member must have built an equity account of at least $100; entitled to all member benefits for life and will receive 100 percent of any patronage refund in cash plus participation in special programs to be developed.

The need for some mechanism to relate membership to financial support through the building of equity as a demonstration of meaningful share of ownership was evident in a tabulation of how much each of the Cooperative's leaders had invested. Of nine directors, three had member ownership accounts of at least $100, qualifying them as "fair share" members. Five had between $25 and $99, and one had less than $10. Of 119 delegates and alternates in the Congress, 65 had less than the $25 required for full membership. Sixteen qualified as "fair share" members.

--Delegate Assembly will replace Congress and "shall represent and act on behalf of the membership...and shall elect the Board of Directors".

--The present area councils will be replaced by larger "Districts....the number and boundaries shall be proposed from time to time by the Delegate Assembly and approved by the Board of Directors". Districts were created for Western Maryland, Central Maryland, Southern Maryland, Federal (D.C.), Northern Virginia, and Southern Virginia.

--"The June meeting of the Delegates shall serve as the Annual Meeting of the Corporation and shall be called by the Board of Directors....There shall be an Annual District Membership Meeting for members of the Cooperative affiliated with each District."

--"Members in each District shall each year elect Delegates and Alternates who will comprise the District Council and who will represent the District Membership in the Delegate Assembly. Each District shall be entitled to have a number of Delegates in proportion of its membership to the total membership from all Districts, except that each District is entitled to a minimum of three Delegates."

--"To be a functioning representative body, a District Council must have a total of at least eight members...." and meet "at least quarterly".

--Bylaws amendments or new bylaws required "a two-thirds vote of those present and voting provided two-thirds of the Delegates are present" at the Assembly meeting. Excepted were certain Articles reserved for amendment only by "an affirmative vote of the Directors".

Note that members of GCI no longer voted for directors or on changes in the bylaws. Other changes provided for indemnification of directors, officers, employees, and agents of GCI. A Compensation Committee was specified to determine what payment should be made for directors and officers of the Board and Delegate Assembly.

A summary statement on the proposed bylaws revisions in the November/December 1986 COOPERATOR said the changes promised, among other things, (1) "a structure which places control of the Cooperative in the hands of those who use its services and have a meaningful stake in its ownership", (2) "a fair and efficient method of removing from GCI rolls subscribers who choose not to become members or members who are inactive or no longer are interested," (3) "a cost-effective means of recovering expenses incurred...in closing and servicing subscriber and member ownership accounts".

After all the thousands of man-hours and turbulent emotions that went into the revision of the bylaws, there was little opportunity to see how they would work due to events which were about to overtake GCI within a few months.

Sales turned down in fiscal 1986, and operations showed a net loss of $441,000. That was after crediting on GCI books $208,000 in income from the capital accounts of members and subscribers terminated during the year, plus $84,000 from an income tax credit. CEO Satake explained that the setback was a result of "a weakened economy prompting consumer reluctance to purchase large items such as furniture which prompted higher advertising costs", plus "the Washington area's major snowfalls occurring close to the end of the fiscal year", and "the effects of a U.S. dollar devaluated by 40 percent against European currencies". There was no patronage refund, no dividend on outstanding shares of stock, and no cash for further repurchase of shares from members anxious to unload at $10 par value shares that had a book value of $20.94 the previous year.

GCI was badly overextended financially, and a new SCAN just outside of Annapolis had opened December 5 at a cost of $350,000. As spring 1987 unfolded, GCI was in the midst of reorganizing its structure to fit the new bylaws, the U.S. dollar exchange rate was still unfavorable and worsening, competition was still a threat in the furniture business, and management was trying to trim expenses.

When about a hundred Co-op members in twos and threes approached the door of George Mason High School in Falls Church for the first annual dinner meeting of the new Northern Virginia District, they encountered a group of SCAN employees with signs and leaflets announcing a labor problem with GCI management. This was the evening of April 26, 1987 and marked the first membership awareness of disagreement over a new union contract. First mention in the minutes of the Board of Directors is this entry for an in camera session April 22: "The CEO updated the Board on the negotiations with the union."

The existing contract ran out May 1, and on the next day, Local 400 of the United Food and Commercial Workers Union had pickets in front of SCAN stores and the warehouse and office building. The strike continued more than 7 months. Because Greenbelt Cooperative was so well known, the labor dispute hit the headlines in Washington and Baltimore newspapers and even the WALL STREET JOURNAL. Labor and cooperative periodicals followed the strike story as it developed. There were many mailings to GCI leaders from both the Co-op office in Savage and from the union's headquarters in Landover, Maryland.

A letter from Local 400's President Thomas R. McNutt set forth the Union's position just before the strike:

"It is with regret that I...am writing you this letter. It concerns the current anti-union atmosphere at the Cooperative.

"Over the years Local 400 and the Cooperative, for the most part, have conducted contract negotiations with an eye toward fairness and stability. When the Cooperative Grocery Stores encountered economic difficulties, Local 400, at the request of the Cooperative, negotiated several concessionary labor agreements in an attempt to address those problems. Recently the membership of the Local, at the request of [your] management, voluntarily approved a four 10-hour day scheduling system at SCAN warehouse in an effort to reduce the Cooperative's costs, even though in some instances this resulted in a loss of income to some union members.

"While the Local and its members have continued this relationship, the Cooperative has resorted to using union-busting tactics. Recent developments in contract negotiations include Company demands for a five and one-half year contract which includes a 2-year wage freeze, underfunding essential benefits which would result in their loss, reductions in seniority rights, removals of members from the Union, elimination of daily overtime provisions and other union-busting proposals.

"I believe that the hiring of the notoriously anti-union law firm of Shawe and Rosenthal...[and other changes] created this situation....the current atmosphere can only result in...a work stoppage....Any effort you might take to return normalcy to the relationship between the parties would be greatly appreciated."

Two weeks into the strike, Chairman of the Board Donald K. Hanes mailed an eight-page memorandum to GCI leaders to "help you become better informed on the need for increasing operational efficiencies, the proposals we presented to the union and the current status of the dispute":

"Sales Commission. SCAN has operated on a flat hourly rate, which ranges from $9.00 to $10.58 per hour for full-time, and $6.00 to $10.58 per hour for part-time, plus a 3% commission pool...shared equally in proportion to the number of hours worked by each salesperson." This caused "loss of high volume salespeople as they do not see a direct relationship between reward and performance [and] feel their own performance must carry low sales performers." Also "difficulty in staffing the stores with the senior and most experienced salespersons during peak business hours and on Sundays as their compensation is based on the number of hours worked rather than on their sales volume. Therefore, we have the most experienced salespersons working when business is lowest and the least experienced working when business is at the highest."

Satake's proposal was to scrap the pooled commission and pay individual commission on each sale made. "Under our proposal, a full-time salesperson working 40 hours, without any overtime, and selling an average of $9,600 per week, which is conservative, will earn $32,656 per year. With higher sales or overtime the average will be approximately $35,000, which is what it is currently. We are not proposing to pay less."

The health and welfare issue was complicated. "Management and employees not covered by the collective bargaining agreement pay 30% of the [medical insurance] premium and GCI pays the balance or 70%. Employees who are covered under the collective bargaining agreement participate in one of four different [union] plans....the Cooperative pays 100% of the premium...even though a number of employees are fully covered under their spouse's or parent's insurance. Under the [new plan] proposed by the Union, the cost to the Cooperative would increase from $162,821 in 1986 to $351,585 in 1989, a 115% increase or $1.67 per hour per employee....we were told that [this] was a non-negotiable issue." Daily overtime was an issue in the warehouse operations. The Hanes memo said that a number of employees were working 4 days with overtime and then not showing up for the rest of the week, staying away on Saturday which was the busiest day of the week since customers prefer delivery on the weekend. The CEO proposed that overtime be paid on a 40-hour weekly basis instead of on each individual day.

Sick leave pay was another warehouse employee issue. The contract specified that sick leave should not be used as "additional annual leave", but Satake said records showed some employees were using their sick leave each month as they earned it instead of saving it for actual need. The GCI proposal was to begin paying sick leave on the second day of an absence.

The union responded with an 18-page mailing to answer the "many misrepresentations" in the Hanes memorandum and to explain that while "Local 400 tried to reach a reasonable accommodation to many issues of importance to both parties, Greenbelt never really intended to bargain in good faith".

GCI management hired personnel to replace those on strike, and brought in some from the Danish furniture factories as trainers in assembling furniture at the warehouse. The union responded by picketing the Danish Embassy in

Washington, as well as the entrance to the building on 14th Street where the GCI Board held a meeting in the offices of the National Cooperative Business Association. Pickets also appeared at the Chicago SCAN stores where union employees already had signed a contract with that GCI subsidiary.

The controversy took a turn for the worse at the annual meeting of GCI, June 6 at the Holiday Inn in Jessup, Maryland, a few miles from the GCI and SCAN offices. Delegates from the District Councils who had not arrived early found more than a hundred union members in the meeting room. No one challenged their right to attend the meeting as all those within the meeting room had presumedly paid their $1 membership fee. There appeared to be others in the hallway who were not members. The problem arose from the continuous chanting by the union members which prevented the meeting from getting under way. Many of the official delegates from the Cooperative's Districts were sympathetic with the striking employees, but some of these were provoked by what seemed an attempt to prevent or take over the meeting. The situation was complicated because the union people were calling for Bob Gowell, former vice president heading SCAN, to speak. Gowell was strongly on the side of the striking employees, many of whom he had hired and worked with over the years.

Police were called and three of the union group were arrested for disturbing the peace. After quiet was restored the meeting proceeded. Both Gowell and a spokesman for the union group were given an opportunity to make a presentation. Following this brouhaha, the union filed suit for $5 million for false arrest against Satake, the GCI Board of Directors, the acting county police chief, two arresting officers, and the county solicitor. According to a story in the BALTIMORE SUN: "The plaintiffs maintain they were handcuffed and kept in a motel laundry room for one hour by police and later charged with trespassing. Their suit contends SCAN conspired with police and the county solicitor to deprive them of the right of free speech and assembly. It also alleges false imprisonment and an invasion of privacy."

GCI and the union had met with a Federal mediator May 19 and again on June 16 with no altering of positions. SCAN hired security guards as tensions increased. There were several minor skirmishes and lawsuits filed. The union demanded access to GCI's membership list and accounts. The National Labor Relations Board received four complaints to review, one filed by SCAN and three by the union. Two were dismissed during the summer. The other two were scheduled for end of the year or later, but the strike was settled before that.

Both Satake and Local 400 claimed a victory after the settlement. The terms were close to what GCI management had offered at the end of April 1987.

Following the strike settlement, Satake contracted the consulting firm of

Morris Anderson and Associates to implement a recovery plan. Chairman of the Board Hillier obtained approval of the other officers between Board meetings for this to be done, and the other directors agreed when they met. The immediate priority was to obtain loan funds to alleviate the need for operating cash and pressure from creditors. The fee was estimated at between $35,000 and $50,000 plus 2 percent of loan funds obtained less any payment of the base amount already paid.

At this meeting, the last one in 1987, the CEO revealed that a physical inventory turned up a loss close to $1.2 million, due to damage in the warehouse, steep markdowns during the strike, and pilferage.

A month later, Michael Starshak for the consulting firm presented a plan for cash flow enhancement involving deferral of debt repayment to vendors and the National Consumer Cooperative Bank plus selling off inventory. Directors were not all convinced that the proposals would work, but agreed there was little choice.

At the February 1988 meeting the Board directed the CEO to close the Chicago warehouse when its lease expired at end of March and to sell the two Chicago SCAN stores as soon as possible. There seemed little hope of lifting operations in that city out of the red.

A special in camera conference call on March 23 produced unanimous Board action to establish a credit agreement with J. E. Ekornes A/S (a Norwegian corporation) and give a promissory note to Ekornes, as a means to avoid litigation with the Cooperative's foreign trade creditors. The note was in the amount of $810,049, at 10 percent interest. On the following day a similar conference call authorized termination of the foreign exchange line of credit with the First National Bank of Maryland in the aggregate amount of $6,500,000.

At the April 23 meeting, the Board acknowledged that fiscal year 1987 expenditures exceeded earnings and that there would be no dividends paid nor patronage refunds for that year's operations. There was a great deal of discussion about economies and reduced spending. Major preoccupation at this meeting, however, seems to have been further amendments to the bylaws. One proposed change which gained Board recommendation for the annual meeting would have permitted stock holdings by member to be counted in granting full membership rights at $25 and fair share members at $100, although the investment nature of the stock would not be affected in any way. Another amendment proposal would reduce the quorum at meetings of the Delegate Assembly (former Congress) to offset reduced attendance. After several directors pointed out that this would allow as few as 12 delegates from the Cooperative's districts to elect directors to the Board on behalf of 130,000 members, the proposal was referred back to the Bylaws

Committee for further study.

The Board gave a green light to three member benefit programs at this same April meeting: dental care, vision services, and home repairs through the American Homeservices Association.

Following the very low key annual meeting on June 4, 1988, Jeff Almen was elected chairman of the Board, replacing Carolyn Hillier. Ten days later, the reorganized Board had to grapple with the disintegrating financial situation. Inventories were low, insufficient cash was on hand for current operations, and creditors were pressing for payment. Attorneys Jerome P. Weiss and Daniel Nachtigal prepared for the Board something directors should have had years earlier: a 15-page presentation on "The Responsibilities of Cooperative Directors". This was appropriate to fit in with concern about indemnity insurance covering the officers and directors. From mid-June to mid-October, the Board faced a crisis scenario that worsened week by week.

The Board authorized Satake and Consultant D. Harris, of Morris Anderson and Associates, to examine possible courses of action and report back as quickly as possible. A priority move was an attempt to extend the termination date set by the First National Bank of Maryland on its loan to GCI and to transfer maximum funds available to that Bank. It was at this meeting on June 15 that the Board unanimously voted to have Satake prepare a petition for Chapter 11 protection under the bankruptcy laws, after consultation with the new chairman of the Board. He and Harris were also directed to explore other options: Maintain the cooperative on a scaled-down version, trade a controlling share of equity for debt, equity infusion from Danish trade creditors, sell the business outright, or liquidate the company (go out of business).

On July 8, after getting a 45-day extension on the First National Bank of Maryland loan, the Board engaged Robert Riesner to advise on "analysis of GCI's debt and capitalization restructuring and to perform such services as directed by the president and CEO with advice and approval of the Board chairman". This decision followed extended debate. Riesner's firms known collectively as PBR were well known to the First National Bank of Maryland and had done work for it.

Liquidation of SCAN Chicago assets was ratified. The Cooperative Bank agreed to defer principal repayments under its loans for a period of 1 year, which provided some cash flow relief.

There was a meeting on July 19, another on July 23, and then at a session on July 29 the resignation of Robert Satake as president and CEO was accepted with the Board chairman "authorized to negotiate earliest possible departure". The resignation of John Gauci, vice president for membership, also was accepted on August 9, with regret that there could be no separation payment.

The following weeks were extremely difficult for top staff and the Board in the efforts to search for a replacement CEO, find legal counsel for entering the Chapter 11 reorganization case, work out acceptable arrangements with creditors, fulfill legal obligations, and keep the SCAN operations together. Some furniture imports were continued on a tightly controlled basis from foreign vendors participating under Danish government guarantee programs.

At its August 27 meeting, the Board authorized continued retention of Morris Anderson and Associates as consultants, with Michael Starshak as temporary CEO, at $1,368 per diem. It also authorized closing six SCAN stores and the warehouse "with intention of paying $1.6 million over a period of 16 weeks to reduce the first secured debt and preserve the remaining value of the assets of the ongoing business of the company for the benefit of those other creditors, members and stockholders".

On September 2, Kevin McGuinness was appointed president and CEO "until the transaction with master lien participants is consummated". One of his first actions was to fax to Holger Overgaard in Denmark an update on the condition of SCAN: "Now it is an organization in crisis". While stressing the need for immediate cash, the message gave recognition to the preferability in continuing to operate the profitable stores rather than closing them to raise cash.

There was a tentative approach by one company to take over SCAN but this did not develop. There was also a proposal by the Danish suppliers that did not work out. The meeting on September 15 was a critical one, lasting until one o'clock in the morning. With payroll coming up in the next week, sales tax payments due, and funding on a day-to-day basis, Vice President for Finance R. Schwartz resigned his position, stating that as a CPA he could not continue, knowing that "before the ink is dry the Board's [proposed] agreement for financing cannot be met".

The Board had already authorized on August 27 a filing for Chapter 11 bankruptcy protection, a process that would take some weeks to prepare. Lawrence D. Coppel, of the firm of Gordon, Feinblatt, Rothman, Hoffberger and Hollander, served as legal counsel for the Chapter 11 proceedings. Daniel Nachtigal, of Sonnenschein Carlin Nath and Rosenthal, continued as counsel for GCI. The Chapter 11 case commenced on November 4, 1988.

Riesner served as President and chief executive officer for GCI and SCAN under a management agreement signed January 17, 1989, with compensation at $1,250 per day. In response to a complaint that this seemed excessive compensation, Director Joe Cohn stated "He was worth every penny of it. We would have been lost without him. I voted against hiring him, and was outvoted 8-1. His performance converted me."

Operating figures for fiscal year 1988 came to the Board through the Finance Committee late in August 1989. Assets had dropped from $12,135,000 to $6,568,000, while liabilities changed from $12,128,000 to $11,350,000, leaving an equity deficit of $4,782,000 at the end of the year. Net sales were $31,442,000 for 1988 compared with $34,510,000 in 1987, with gross margin at $8,199,000 compared with $10,370,000. Net loss for 1988 was $4,744,000, slightly above the previous year, and the accumulated deficit as of January 28, 1989 stood at $7,672,000.

At the turn of the year, the Board spent some time on such routine matters as member benefits (insurance, dental, and home maintenance discount programs), a Mission Committee, and a report of the Futures Committee. The latter was a pickup from the report of a much earlier Futures Committee report which the Delegate Assembly had approved unanimously and sent to the Board where it languished. By the end of 1989 it was too late to implement the recommendations.

There was some continuing tension between Riesner and various directors. In response to requests for operating information, Riesner pointed out that that the office was in the midst of converting the data processing to a new system. This finally was in place at the end of May. When directors raised questions about the handling of stock and membership records, about GCI relations with the National Cooperative Bank, and relations with the National Cooperative Business Association, the CEO made it clear that "my interest is in selling furniture", and reminded the Board that he had limited staff and time for anything else except preparing for the Chapter 11 settlement.

With a limit of $25,000 placed on membership activities it was not possible to send any communication to the approximately 125,000 members. The Delegate Assembly, under Speaker Basil McKinley, continued to meet. The Board kept the delegates informed as best it could about what was happening to GCI and SCAN with the eight stores which were still open.

In February, the Board obtained approval to contract with the National Cooperative Business Association to keep the membership and stock records, send out notices for the Delegate Assembly, and handle what was left of the member benefits programs. When the warehouse and office building in Savage was closed earlier, most existing records were moved to a documents storage facility, but Dorothy Reifner, long-time employee in the member relations office stored records of that office in her basement. John Gauci, who had been vice president for membership and who was at this time on the staff of the National Cooperative Business Association, picked up coordination and clearing house responsibilities at NCBA for the Cooperative.

What to do about an annual corporation meeting and election of delegates and directors was a worrisome problem for which there was no solution. The bylaws required that these be held, but no money was available for the postage and notices. GCI Attorney Nachtigal advised that "there is some support for not allowing shareholders to elect new directors when the company is clearly insolvent. In that regard, SCAN is clearly insolvent. Thus, if the Board wishes to postpone the election, there is a legal basis for doing so....Don't say you are suspending the elections; say they will be held as soon as possible." Both CEO Riesner and Lawrence D. Coppel, attorney for the SCAN bankruptcy case, cautioned that a change of directors at this stage in preparing for the Chapter 11 court hearing might have a negative effect on the attitudes of the members of the Credit Committee who have to approve the settlement plan. The Board therefore filled the two vacancies and simply let the matter of notifications for a   full-fledged annual meeting and election slide. This had the approval of the Delegate Assembly, in recognition that there was no alternative.

By April, the directors were able to get some feel for the identity of the creditors and their objectives and the kind of settlement plan that might emerge from the negotiations. Director Charles Hix asked CEO Riesner "if the Board can be provided with some clear idea of the strategies in negotiating with SCAN's creditors and some clarification of identities of the various groups of creditors and their priorities in claims".

Riesner responded that there were roughly five levels of creditors and that SCAN had to negotiate on each level. Quoting from the minutes of April 4:

"In the Danish groups there are both secured and unsecured creditors, with differing concerns and objectives. Many of the domestic creditors accept bankruptcy proceedings as a normal part of doing business and would prefer to settle for as much cash as possible as soon as possible. Danish creditors aim to be fully repaid even if that requires a long period of years, and some are willing to trade debt for equity. Riesner is trying to create a buffer between the several groups of creditors, in realization that there has to be a concentual plan in the end. The plan submitted must be an intelligent one and have feasibility for the court and debtors to agree....GCI's membership is at the bottom of the heap."

Chairman Almen emphasized that the Board must agree on a settlement decision which would fulfill its fiduciary responsibility.

The Equitable Bank in Baltimore agreed to a line of credit up to $1,250,000 at prime rate plus 2.5 percent, provided its repayment was top priority, and this was acceptable to the other creditors.

However, the Bank required that SCAN, Inc. as a subsidiary of GCI must have a set of bylaws. Riesner and Coppel brought in a draft which the Board accepted by a divided vote after some agonizing debate. Director and Treasurer Joseph Cohn requested the minutes show:

"I object to the board of SCAN, Inc. being limited to three members -- one of whom is an employee....There are also many errors in these new bylaws and not enough time for discussion."

The three directors were Riesner, Almen, and Hix. Hoag, as chairman of the Review and Evaluation Committee, advised that adoption was a formality inasmuch as SCAN, Inc. would go out of existence in a few months.

The first hard information the directors received about the identity of creditors, the amount owed to each, and what settlement terms might be expected was a tabulation brought to the meeting of April 17 by Attorney Coppel and CEO Riesner. The total owed was more than $10 million, mostly to the Danish Export Credit Council and foreign suppliers. The preliminary settlement plan proposed a spin-off of the entire SCAN operation to NEWCO, a new corporation with a board of seven directors giving control to the Danes but with GCI having representation and a minority interest. Other creditors would have to settle for a small percentage of what was owed them.

The Board demanded that Riesner and Coppel push hard for GCI to have at least two directors on the board of seven for NEWCO, that GCI have at least a 30 percent interest in the Danish-controlled NEWCO, that some funding be provided by NEWCO for the operation of GCI, and that arrangement be included for possible buy-back of SCAN by GCI if the debt to the Danish creditors could be paid by the end of 10 years.

It was recognized that there was no possibility of any repayment to stockholders or members of Greenbelt Cooperative, as there was a negative equity in millions of dollars. But the Board had Attorney Nachtigal work out a proposal which would permit equity holders to write off their losses as income tax deduction and accept a $5 membership and equity in GCI. This was adopted by unanimous vote in a meeting on August 31. But there was no way to inform stockholders and members.

The final draft of the Plan for Reorganization, accepted by all the creditors, enabled the remaining eight SCAN stores, inventory and all remaining assets to be assumed by SCAN International, Inc. with the Danish Export Credit Council and major Scandinavian creditors in control. GCI was allowed two seats on the board, given a 28 percent share in the business, a small operating budget, and a partial buy-back provision after 10 years if certain obligations would be met.

A statement on October 2 announced the U.S. bankruptcy court judge's satisfaction with the proposed Plan of Reorganization, and the Plan was sent to all creditors for acceptance or rejection. It was accepted. As of August 3, expenses for lawyers, accountants, and administration of the preparations for Chapter 11 reorganization amounted to $214,378.33.

The GCI Board named Almen and Riesner to the initial board of SCAN International, Inc. The Board seemed to have no choice about Riesner. By the November 7 meeting of the GCI Board, three directors had submitted resignations. This was the last meeting prior to the court hearing. The Board named Almen president in addition to being chairman of the Board, in compliance with Maryland legal requirements.

The Delegate Assembly met on October 21 and received information about the current situation, and planned to meet again December 11 to see where the organization would go from there.

The bankruptcy court hearing in Baltimore on December 1, 1989 activated the Plan of Reorganization.

Leaders of Greenbelt Cooperative faced the 50th anniversary free of debt, and with about 12,000 members (perhaps 50 or 60 active), some assurance of about $10,000 as operating funds, a half century of turbulent history, and a "Tentative Plan for the Future" which a committee had put together November 20 in a meeting with the Board and officers of the Delegate Assembly.

XX. PROBLEMS: HOW WE DEALT WITH THEM -- OR DIDN'T

Incorporation. Buying clubs do not need the expense or protection of a state charter. Incorporation of Greenbelt Consumer Services, Inc., was the very first step in organizing. There were going to be large sums of money handled, leases, payrolls, taxes, debts, and always the possibility of lawsuits. Incorporation protected the leaders and provided legal recognition of the Cooperative.

There were two problems. Maryland had no provision for incorporating consumer cooperatives under its Code. So GCS was chartered under the regular business section which was not appropriate for cooperatives. The solution was lobbying and persuading the State legislature to amend the State Code to permit incorporation of consumer cooperatives. The second problem was the restrictions in the original charter relating to organizational structure. The original incorporators had no idea of the amazing future growth of the Greenbelt Co-op. When it came time to amend the charter, the process was expensive and very time-consuming.

SEC Registration. When GCS decided to sell stock outside of the State of Maryland, it had to register with the Securities and Exchange Commission and issue a prospectus for each new issue of stock or debentures. This was an annual cost of $60,000 to $100,000 and involved large amounts of staff time.

The solution was to amend the charter and bylaws to convert Greenbelt Consumer Services, Inc. to Greenbelt Cooperative, Inc. -- a membership cooperative instead of a stock corporation. It was then no longer necessary to register with SEC. But that raised a new problem -- how to raise equity capital?

Equity Capital. Nearly all consumer cooperatives are undercapitalized. Greenbelt was no exception. From its initial months in 1940 and for all 50 years until the bankruptcy hearing,
GCS/GCI lacked a comfortable capital position. To borrow money it had to have a satisfactory foundation of equity capital. Issuing stock raised equity capital but it was expensive. The attempt to build membership equity (ownership) accounts simply by urging $1 members to do so failed. The leaders and management of the Greenbelt Co-op never found an answer to this crucial problem.

Operating and Financial Ratios. Fifteen years went by before Greenbelt's directors heard of operating and financial ratios as a tool for judging the condition of the Cooperative's business. Bob Morrow as comptroller and later as resident manager introduced the Board to key ratios and how to use them.

Some years later the Board was no longer getting them. Then they were available again for a time, and once more overlooked.

Key ratios are a management responsibility, and a board must insist on having 10 or 12 of them at least quarterly. They must be presented along with the norm or safe range for similar kinds and size businesses. And directors must learn how to use them effectively to be aware of trends and danger signals.

Board/Management Relations. First of all, there must be a written contract and it must set forth exactly what the board expects of the general manager or CEO. Greenbelt's first contracts were for 1 year, but after expanding beyond the original location in the City of Greenbelt, it found few qualified applicants willing to move family and household for less than 3 years, so the contract term was lengthened. With Checchi and Company on board, it was decided that a bonus was a viable incentive to improve margins. Then the Board recognized that other operations in addition to earnings were important in a cooperative. So, the Board wrote an addendum to the contract each year and specified in writing what priority goals such as employee training, leadership development, member benefits, newsletter improvement, etc. would merit a bonus, and criteria for determining the percentage bonus were included. Most important was a detailed annual performance evaluation of the general manager or CEO measured against predetermined standards. These contract devices worked very well in the years they were used.

The Board of the Greenbelt Cooperative had difficulty with some managers in obtaining the information it needed in an understandable format for making the best possible decisions. Some directors did not know what data was needed. Others asked for more than was necessary or even usable. Most general managers or CEOs were quite willing to serve up whatever the Board decided it wanted, and helped directors in learning how to use reports and operating data from management. In some years there were seminars on how to read a balance sheet, interpret key ratios, evaluate reports on operations, review leases, insurance coverage, etc. Not every top staff man was that helpful, so much depended on the ability of the directors and particularly the president or chairman of the Board.

A now-and-then problem was the quality of rapport between individual directors and the general manager or CEO employed by the Board. Some directors believed a little tension between Board and management was productive. Others came to the Board already suspicious or antagonistic. And there were boards during the 50 years that "rubber-stamped" whatever management proposed. Maintaining an even keel was difficult. There were ups and downs -- an unevenness that probably damaged the Cooperative's performance.

Bylaws. Every cooperative must have bylaws, most importantly as a protection of each member's ownership rights. And the bylaws will require amendments from time to time as conditions both inside and outside the cooperative change. But amending the bylaws can be overdone.

In the Greenbelt Cooperative, changing the bylaws became a continuing preoccupation -- a fetish that consumed too much time and energy, and sometimes did more harm than good. As the Cooperative grew in size and complexity, it became increasingly difficult for members to have input on the drafting or to understand what result would come from proposed changes. In later years, members were asked simply to vote "yes" or "no" on an entire package of changes with no opportunity to mark a choice about individual changes.

A study of Greenbelt's bylaws over the years clearly show erosion of members' rights and control. The number of membership meetings dwindled from monthly to quarterly to annual to none at the end. Quorums shrank from 25 percent to 10 percent to 5 percent. Proxy voting was not permitted at first, then became the exclusive method of voting in the last years. Directors were elected for 1 year terms, then 2, then 3 with no limit to re- election. The newsletter was published weekly, then twice a month, monthly, four times a year, and then discontinued as too expensive. Amending the bylaws required two-thirds of the entire membership at the start. This changed over the years until a stage when members were not consulted, and amendments or new bylaws required only a majority vote of some 70 delegates "qualified to vote". In 1989, the bylaws were just disregarded, as there was no money available for holding an annual meeting or election. All of this was justified, of course, because of the size of the membership, the geographic spread of the organization, or the high cost of postage.

When all is said and done, the rights of the member/owner/consumer require not only good bylaws but fair administration of them by leaders and management with a sincere dedication to the belief that the cooperative **really does** belong to the members/owners/consumers. Constant puttering around with the bylaws may serve no useful purpose.

Membership. In the City of Greenbelt, recruiting members was never a problem. New member campaigns around the Takoma Park and the Wheaton shopping centers were well planned and effective. The efforts and results around other stores varied. By the time the Kroger stores were acquired, almost no attempt was made to convert customers to members. After the first years in Greenbelt, there were three incentives: the patronage refund, dividend on shares, and member benefits. A survey in the early 1970s revealed that by then almost no one joined out of belief in the cooperative ideals. And by then operation of the facilities depended on customers rather than members, and management therefore geared operations to competing for the shopping public rather than fulfilling members' needs.

The $1 memberships were something else again, a gimmick to meet lending requirements of the National Consumer Cooperative Bank and to return earnings to customers instead of paying higher amounts in income taxes.

The area councils, Congress, and most directors were heavily concerned with the voices of the members, which resulted in some misunderstandings and differences with management's primary goal of keeping the business operating profitably. This split personality aspect of GCS/GCI became more rather than less of a problem over the years.

Meetings. There were too many. Most were poorly planned, poorly run, dull, and hence poorly attended. New members being brought into the leadership voiced dismay at the pettiness and controversy at some meetings, called them a waste of time, and did not come back after a sampling.

Executive and In Camera Board Sessions. At first, closed sessions at Board meetings occurred only for personnel matters and proposed store leases. Even these brought protests from some members. Later financial data and operations were discussed behind closed doors in an effort to avoid informing the competition. By the 1980s, every Board meeting was in three parts: open session, executive session, and in camera session. In most instances, persons who were not directors or on the Review and Evaluation Committee were invited to remain in the closed sessions if they would sign the confidentiality form pledging not to discuss outside the Board room what transpired. Another concession was the scheduling of closed sessions toward the latter part of the meeting so that visitors would not have to wait outside the room for the open session. Minutes of closed sessions were sometimes kept in a separate minutes book, but in any event, the secretary periodically presented for declassification those minutes on matters no longer considered confidential.

Policies and Procedures. In 1958, the Board began codifying its policies and its procedures to achieve consistency in its functioning. The Policies Book contained written statements agreed upon for guiding the Cooperative. The Procedures Book contained the written statements guiding the way in which the Board functioned. These were updated from time to time. Use of these guides avoided much arguing, duplication, and contradictory motions. Written policies and procedures are a must for every cooperative, small or large, in order to avoid problems. Responsibility for this fits easily into the secretary's duties.

Leadership Development. This is another success story. For the Greenbelt Cooperative leadership development was never a problem because training courses, workshops, and seminars were set up early and continued with considerable consistency throughout the 50-year history. Management, Board, and Congress worked together on in-house opportunities, and support was given to the Cooperative Institute Association, Potomac Cooperative Federation, Cooperative League of the USA, Consumer Cooperative Alliance, and National Association of Student Cooperatives for training programs. Staff people were sent to the American Management Association and various trade institutes for general and specialized training. Board retreats and Congress annual orientations introduced new leaders and potential leaders to the history and principles of cooperation, responsibilities of directors, how to be a good secretary or treasurer or committee chairman, public speaking, report writing, understanding financial reports, and many similar subjects. A specific purpose of the Congress system developed within GCS was to develop leaders and especially candidates for the Board of Directors.

Committees. Committees in themselves are not a problem. But getting them to perform effectively can be a problem. Some leaders complained that the Greenbelt Cooperative had too many meetings, but this provided participation of members and was an important way to keep the organization alive and innovative. Aside from certain basic and required committees, leaders relied heavily on ad hoc committees in response to a need which developed or to explore someone's proposal. This created committees to meet a need or the ideas of members. Over the years, however, there was much duplication. Some subjects were explored repeatedly at intervals, with little attempt to go back and use good reports that had already been prepared. It may also be noted that many excellent committee studies were never followed up. Leaders of GCS/GCI were better at appointing committees and producing reports than putting the findings into action. The most productive committees were tripartite, with representatives from Board, Congress, and management.

Reports and Studies. These came from three sources: committees (see above), management, and paid consultants. The GCS/GCI files bulge with reports and studies, some of them more than a hundred pages in length with impressive tabulations and appendices. The quality of the research and ideas is excellent in most cases. There was, however, a disheartening amount of duplication, as new studies were undertaken without reference to what was produced earlier. Many of the Cooperative's committee chairmen were employees of the Federal Government and adept at preparing reports. There was plenty of expertise within the membership, but a surprising number of consultants were hired at thousands of dollars a throw to prepare studies that were then not followed up.

Newsletter. In most years, the membership received some sort of house organ. This became a major expense as membership increased and postage rates climbed. One problem was the unevenness of format and content with the change in editors and shifts in what management and the Board wanted to accomplish through the newsletter. A second problem on occasion was control -- management or the Board or even a "free press" to be run by the editor or a committee of members. The newsletter was **the** communication link with membership. Most of the time it served that purpose well. There were periods, though, when it was little more than an advertising flyer for the stores. At other times the pages were filled with long articles reprinted from various consumer or other cooperative publications.

The unfortunate thing about the newsletter was that according to surveys taken now and then most members did not read it. No answer for that problem was ever found. It did appear, by comparing newsletter readership in rural areas, that the problem was competition for the member's available time rather than the style or content of the Greenbelt Cooperative's newsletters.

Controversy. "We had too much of it", nearly all leaders and observers agree. If the controversy was clearly a threat to the existence of the Cooperative, members would rally around. But most of the differences which plagued meetings were petty and personal. Some were power plays to seize control or prestige, some were in support of agenda of other organizations which had nothing to do with GCS/GCI. In some of the early years, there was persuasive evidence that members of extreme left-wing political groups attempted to disrupt meetings to take over or else demonstrate that cooperation as a way of accomplishing things would not work.

Dozens of intelligent new members brought to area council and Congress meetings as potential leaders turned away in disgust at criticism, un-reasonable arguments, and petty issues which sometimes prevailed. "Why can't cooperators cooperate?" was a frequent question. Well remembered are several outstanding leaders who possessed exceptional talents for negotiation and reasonableness: Dayton Hull, Sherrod East, Gif Hoag, and some others.

Legal Counsel. Some of the controversies involved management and entities outside of the Cooperative. Where these involved lawyers and court fees, they were a costly drain on the Cooperative's resources. The total cost cannot be computed with any assurance but it certainly ran into millions of dollars. No solution could be found to legal problems.

Travel. Most directors, committee chairmen, and other leaders traveled at the Co-op's expense only when it was essential to benefit the organization or its operations, they kept expenses to a minimum, and they reported in writing when they returned. There were a few, however, who abused travel funds by "representing" GCS or GCI at conferences or dinners where no real benefit resulted for the Cooperative. Several, over the years were criticized by other leaders for securing appointments as committee heads, or even setting up their own committees on paper and then requesting reimbursement for trips without holding committee meetings or completing any projects. Boards found it difficult to say "no" to directors who enjoyed travelling on missions of dubious value to the Co-op. There were rules, but enforcing them raised personal problems.

Thefts. Some of the thefts have been noted in the preceding chapters. There were many more, some by robbers who broke into stores or offices, but more by employees. Remedies were tighter inventory control, employment of security personnel, more effective check-in of merchandise, and check-out procedures for deliveries in connection with SCAN furniture deliveries. Prosecution was costly in time and money; dismissal involved the union; collecting on loss insurance ran into difficulties in establishing proof of the amount taken. There was shoplifting, which varied from store to store, but the average was less than for the industry as a whole.

Poor Follow-up on Innovations. GCS was innovative in its merchandising but weak in follow-up. The preceding chapters offer some examples and there were more. Typically the general manager and the Board would agree to try some procedure, category of merchandise, or member benefit. It would get off to a good start and appear to be workable. Some time later an inquiry would bring the answer that it had not met expectations and had been terminated. In other instances, other chains picked up the idea, promoted it as their own, and the Cooperative failed to put its own stamp of identity on it beyond its own membership: introduction of biodegradable detergents, Cornell formula bread, grade labelling, open dating on foods, unit pricing, see-through meat packaging, medical history file for prescription customers, consumer protection leaflets in the supermarkets, etc. SCAN was the exception; it had good follow-through in most of its years.

PART II

WHAT WENT WRONG AND RIGHT

XXI. WHAT WENT WRONG AND RIGHT

The growth and financial success of GCS was exceptionally spotty over the years. Numerous opportunities were by-passed and the timing of expansion moves seemed at times to be unfortunate at best. None-the-less, there was steady growth over the years until the late 1970s when retrenchment of all divisions except furniture became a necessity.

GCS did come perilously close to bankruptcy during the years 1971-1974. There was limping recovery with dramatic losses continuing in the food, service station and pharmacy divisions even with many closures of facilities including a shutdown of the entire pharmacy division. Finally, after divestment of the food and service station divisions in 1983, the future of the Cooperative was perceived as being solid with excellent opportunities for growth, profitability and services to members.

Having survived the financial crises of the early '70s, what went wrong in the late '80s? Except for the fact that the Cooperative suffered from not being able to acquire a strong financial position because of severe losses in all but the SCAN division over a period of 16 years, there appears to be no relationship between GCS's collapse in 1988 and the problems of the earlier years. They were two distinctly separate periods.

To better grasp the evolution of the Cooperative, the following analysis is presented. It is based on a combination of discussions with a number of leaders in GCS and in other cooperatives, the junior author's own observations, and an analysis made for the Cooperative's 1981 Growth and Development Plan.

A young man by the name of Dave Dunbar, a recent MBA graduate, was hired to coordinate the planning process. It was refreshing to have new perspectives in addressing the same treadworn problems and issues. Much of the analysis of GCS prior to 1981 is based upon his excellent work in putting the past of GCS in perspective. After much review by management, the Board, and elder-statesmen leaders of GCS, his analysis was accepted as fairly representing the facts of GCS' evolution.

Hindsight, obviously, is quite different from foresight. What often appears in retrospect to have been an obvious misjudgment by the Board and/or management was probably at the time, and with the known information, the best or only decision to make. Therefore, this analysis does not intend to condemn the motives, abilities, or judgment of individuals or groups of individuals. Inconsistencies, however, between stated goals or policies and actions are noted.

GCS's development can be categorized into six periods:

1. 1938-1950   Steady, profitable growth in one location
2. 1951-1959   Dramatic growth through multi-store operations
3. 1960-1969   Over extension and a crisis of identity
4. 1970-1980   Retrenchment and SCAN dominance
5. 1981-1985   Divestiture and SCAN growth
6. 1986 - 1989 Overconfidence and disaster

1938-1950   Steady, Profitable Growth in One Location

In its early years GCS was an innovative, well diversified organization with a capability of excellent earnings. The overall growth rate for the period was 20 percent. Member patronage was high and employee morale outstanding.

By 1949, however, the sale of food and associated household items had become dominant, with 68 percent of all sales and 59 percent of contribution. Several small operations, such as the movie theater, were sold. Overall growth in sales volume averages 20 percent during this period. The Cooperative was highly profitable, even by non-cooperative industry standards.

Quick growth with high profitability during this period can be attributed to:

a. The isolation of the town of Greenbelt gave the Co-op a captive market.
b. GCS was an operations innovator. It operated the first self-service food store in the country. Its self-service meat department was the first in the Washington area.
c. Member patronage was high and sales dollar per transaction was also high.
d. Staff morale was high.
e. Levels of member investment and reinvestment of patronage dividends and dividends on stock were high. This meant that adequate capital was available for upgrading and expansion, even though the after-tax cost of this capital was high.

1951-1959:   Dramatic Growth through Multi-store Operations

GCS entered into an era of large step increases in sales volume, caused by the periodic addition of retail facilities at new business locations. GCS, in fact, developed four new multi-service operations during this period and reduced its wide range of goods and services. Performance, however, was not up to industry standards.

Was this a danger signal that the Board should have pursued vigorously at that time to avoid future problems? They didn't.

In analyzing the financial data available, the Board would have found that:

a. Labor costs in the food departments were too high.
b. Overhead was too high in relation to sales volume.
c. Special purchase items—of which there was a high volume—were not priced to cover their full cost. For example, the cost of the managers' time was not included.
d. Special purchasing and similar non-core business activities diverted management's attention from normal business operations, leading to sloppy cost control and lack of incremental productivity gains.

Additionally, the Board and management were caught in a "Catch 22". To retain creditability and maintain cooperative practices, they continued to pay a regular 5 percent dividend on stock and a patronage refund. This meant that the rate of reinvestment of operating income in facilities was very low compared to competitors. In an era when medium- and long-term interest rates were in the 4 to 5 percent range, a 5 percent dividend after tax made member stock purchases twice as expensive a form of capital as borrowing. Yet, an adequate equity base was needed for borrowing.

1960-1969: Over extension and a Crisis in Identity

GCS was fighting for sales during this period of fierce competition when all the competitors were also working their hardest to retain their market share. Moreover, operating costs were out of control while management was looking at expansion. In 1960 and 1961, GCS's operating costs were 20 percent higher than the national average. This amounted to a difference of 3.6 percent of sales. In other words, GCS expenses were out of line by more than double the percentage that the average supermarket operator netted as operating income.

Another problem arose with the rapid expansion drive. GCS entered the real estate business as an amateur in a highly professional field. Two shopping center deals—Penn Daw and Takoma Park—proved disastrous and financially crippled the Cooperative for many years. The centers continued to lose money, tied up precious cash for long periods, and drained management's time and energy just when the competitive situation in food operations demanded full attention.

Management and Board attention seemed to be everywhere else except upon the rugged competitive market. The 1959 and 1960 annual reports note such activities as importing lamb from Iceland, adding a watch repair service,

341

initiating a travel service, developing a co-op mattress, and buying an independent supermarket in an ethnic neighborhood of Baltimore—a market area where the Co-op had no other dealings or interest, and, most importantly, no experience.

Problems were also created by continuing to adhere to an overly simplified management structure and a serious lack of depth of well trained managers and potential managers.

In 1962, the Board changed management. The new management—a consulting firm—appointed a resident manager who ran the day-to-day operations under the direction of the Chief Executive of the consulting firm. Immediately upon assuming management of the Cooperative, the new management presented a status report with proposals to the Board. Among the conclusions in the report:

    a. The Cooperative had grown too much, too fast, and with too few human and financial resources.

    b. The proposal for recovery was to reduce expenses, focus on merchandising, build a strong staff, and attract younger members.

    c. It was recommended that losing facilities be closed including the Penn Daw and Piney Branch stores which were losing money at a great rate. (As explained later this was not done.)

    d. It was also recommended that overhead be dramatically reduced (it was, by $200,000 annually), that the grocery warehouse be closed (it was), and that a new marketing strategy be implemented by moving to a discount operation (this too was done and all of the "Co-op" food stores became "Consumers Discount").

The cost reductions were helpful, but the marketing success of the new strategy was short-lived. The Cooperative became bland and without distinctions from its competitors. The discarding of the Co-op name along with the discontinuance of patronage refunds made many wonder whether GCS was still a cooperative.

Competitors had a cost competitive advantage in the discount game. Most were integrated backward into manufacturing and processing of a far greater array of products than were the available CO-OP label products.

The result was that the recovery of the food division was arrested in 1964, even before it had reached a level of average profitability for the industry.

By 1967, the GCS had neither the market image, the financial resources, nor the degree of operating efficiency needed to compete with the other chains.

Besides making a questionable choice of strategy, the new management and the Board failed to follow the advice in the consultant's report. Probably the most important of these related to closing losing operations. Neither Penn Daw nor Piney Branch were closed during this period. Throughout the '60s, the service station division consistently lost money, often at the level of division contribution, yet was not closed. Even with the purchase and operation of the Kroger stores (see below), (where there were basically no members to lobby to retain a store that was losing money), stores with minimal or negative store contributions were kept in the operations year after year. This non-action may very well have set the precedent for hanging on to losing operations well beyond sound business reason.

A second failure to live up to advice earlier agreed to by the Board, upon recommendation of management, had to do with new investments. Although return on investment was supposedly the main criterion for investment decisions, deals like the merger with the Peninsula Cooperative Association, the Skinker Tire acquisition, and the Kroger acquisition were made in the face of strong evidence that there was little prospect for long-term profitability. For example, only one of the 9 former Kroger stores met the store contribution standard of 4 percent.

The Kroger acquisition was a contradiction of the expansion plans that management had been espousing. The new management had recommended that any new expansion be in smaller, expandable stores in areas of market growth. Emphasis, too, was on new stores, not old ones. In acquiring the Kroger stores, GCS acquired old stores in declining areas and destroyed GCS's flexibility by tying up all available cash. As a later management report stated, "aging supermarkets are not highly regarded by shoppers."

One must recognize, however, that both Board and management in the '60s viewed GCS as a major competitor in the Baltimore-Washington food industry. They apparently did not recognize the diminished status in an ever more concentrated market place. Their strategy was the same as the other chains. Even with the Kroger acquisition, GCS had only 3 percent of the Washington market and less than 1 percent of the Baltimore market. In the world of competitive edge, or even influence, these percentages were insignificant.

The Kroger acquisition and the limited SCAN expansion used the available cash, poor operating results of the food and service stations drove down net income, and the continued payment of dividend on stock depleted reserves by nearly $300,000 from 1967 to 1971. The Cooperative was unable to maintain the food stores even in their often rundown 1967 condition, much less remodel or replace those that were most rundown. The food division was trapped in a downward spiral—it needed cash to make improvements to attract customers, but first it needed to attract customers in order to generate cash. Meanwhile, the competition was building new stores with up-to-date, efficient, and labor-saving equipment. GCS was becoming less competitive with each passing year.

1970-1980:   Retrenchment and SCAN Dominance

The Cooperative entered the '70s with great optimism. Operating results in 1969 had been phenomenal compared to the past. The 5-year plan presented to the Board by management in April 1970 envisioned 7 new supermarkets and 11 new SCAN stores during the next 5 years. Entirely new types of outlets, including retail tire stores and health and beauty aid stores, were foreseen for the other two divisions.

These plans crashed quickly. Competition in the food industry in the Baltimore/ Washington markets once again heated up and in 1970, the Cooperative's food operations suffered their worst loss in history. The next 3 years were even worse. For the years 1970-73, the food division lost over $1.5 million at the division contribution level. The cost of closing supermarkets amounted to an additional half million dollars. The service station and pharmacy divisions were also doing poorly. Only SCAN was doing well; in fact, if it had not been doing well, the Cooperative would have been gone.

Once again, in 1971, the Board made a management change. The new management and the Board faced a fundamental choice:

1. GCS could move aggressively to cut losses in the food and pharmacy divisions (at this time the service station division was holding its own) and plow SCAN's profits back into SCAN expansion, or

2. GCS could gamble on turning around the losing divisions by milking the SCAN division for the cash needed to improve facilities and cover short-term losses of those losing divisions.

As often happens, management and the Board agreed upon a course of action which embodied a little of each option rather than making a clear choice.

A survival strategy was devised for the food division. Eleven of the twenty-two food stores were closed. Both the pharmacy and wholesale tire operations were shut down. Six of the food stores received at least cosmetic remodeling and a new marketing strategy of emphasizing natural foods and consumer concerns was undertaken. In retrospect, it appears that this was a sound strategy, but it moved too slowly and too indecisively to be a success, i.e., the closings were dragged out over a 6 year period.

In attempting to re-position the food operations within the retail food market, the Cooperative probably failed because it did not go far enough or move fast enough, either in terms of substance or image. Where GCS (and other food retailers) failed, was in not tailoring operations to fit the market segment. Natural foods, the hot trend, were squeezed into the traditional supermarket format. Natural foods were sold next to soft drinks or wherever floor space was available. Rather than penetrating a small but growing segment of the market, GCS followed other food operators in skimming the extra profit margin off the natural food line.

Operationally, GCS made only minor changes to accommodate the new marketing strategy. As a result, the new approach was disappointing. Even though cooperatives were again in vogue, GCS did not change the name from Consumers Discount. By deciding not to feature the "Co-op" philosophy and name, GCS lost a key opportunity to identify with the younger people which it desperately needed to attract as customers.

As a result of the compromise approach, SCAN expansion proceeded at a slow pace, at least when supermarket losses were small enough to allow any growth. Additionally, the Board and management focused the vast majority of their time and energy on the losers rather than on the winners.

In 1975, management recommended closing the food division. Faced with the political realities within GCS—namely the area councils—that closing down the "lifeblood" of the Cooperative was unacceptable, the Board did not accept the recommendation. This was one of the several reasons why the Board changed top management in early 1976.

From 1976 to 1979 seven more food stores were closed and the division's management drastically cut. During this period GCS did not embark on any major new ventures. Rather, a cautious approach was adopted by improving (where possible) existing operations, tightening controls, paring away unprofitable operations, and disentangling itself from earlier real estate ventures.

Results were encouraging if not dramatic. SCAN sales growth had dropped to a 13 percent annual growth rate from its high of 55 percent annual rate from 1961-70. Was there still a great opportunity for SCAN growth? Yes, but there were no funds and, sadly, little attention was given those opportunities by top management and the Board.

Food store sales dropped at a rate of 8 percent per year after 1975, but losses were cut. Food stores began to contribute part of their share to overhead. The service station division was unprofitable almost every year.

The 1970s had been a traumatic decade for GCS. There had been four CEO changes in 9 years, compared with two in the previous 26 years of history. Two of its three operating divisions had become chronically unprofitable, kept alive only by subsidy from the one profitable division—SCAN. Of its 44 retail outlets in 1970, 26 were closed, including an entire division.

Nonetheless, there were reasons for optimism. GCS had survived a difficult period. The Cooperative was leaner and its chronic top-heavy administration was much smaller. Its major business was now Scandinavian furniture in which it was the leader. Finances were in reasonably good shape and with the National Consumer Cooperative Bank coming on strong, long-term, reasonably-priced debt capital was available. Most of the real estate problems which had drained management's energy for decades were ended. It was a good time to plan for the future.

1981-1985: Divestiture and SCAN Growth

Happy days did not arrive. The food division kept on losing. As stores were closed, the division costs were shared by fewer stores and across less volume. Many different approaches were tried with no success. It can be reasonably concluded that this final effort was really the culmination of earlier decisions and non-decisions.

GCS never achieved its potential in the food business for several major reasons. Included among these are:

1. Absence of a coherent and consistent financial plan for growth.
2. Failure to consistently upgrade facilities and to open new stores, such as competitors were doing.
3. Reluctance to adjust to changing neighborhoods or to "close and move."
4. Changing identity of what GCS food stores were.

At the behest of many of the area council members not to close the food division, the Board made one more attempt to find a solution by engaging still another consulting firm to conduct an in-depth analysis of the Cooperative. The report was far from encouraging. The report, coupled with the fact that neither the food nor petroleum division had come close to meeting the criteria established in 1981 for retaining them, compelled the Board to vote (unanimously) to divest the two divisions.

There were some caveats. First, that the facilities would be sold to a group which would retain the facility as a cooperative so long as their bid came within at least 10 percent of any other bidder. Second, $50,000 would be set aside for exploring other businesses (which would be more frequently patronized by members than was SCAN) for GCS to enter.

346

Finally, with the divestiture decision, it appeared that SCAN could be expanded. Earnings were high and GCS could have moved ahead. Reluctance on the part of some members of the Board to go outside of the current market area kept GCS myopically focused. Additionally, the composition of the Board changed dramatically after the divestiture decision.

The new Board members did not have SCAN expansion as one of their high priorities. Even so, new SCAN stores were opened in 1984 and 1985. In 1984 GCS's earnings matched the previous high of $618,000 and in 1985 it appeared that SCAN was on its way with record high earnings of $1.1 million.

1986-89: Overconfidence and Disaster

The Cooperative entered 1986 financially positioned for growth and stability. Working capital ($4.4 million) and equity ($5 million) were the highest in its history. Among other excellent financials were total debt to equity (1.04), long-term debt to equity (.21), and total debt to total assets (.37). Still, GCS had not recovered sufficiently to have developed an adequate reserve to withstand major traumas.

In 1986, the dollar dropped precipitously in relation to other currencies, among which was the Danish kroner. From long experience, SCAN management knew that it was not feasible to increase prices rapidly to counteract the drop in exchange rates. The decision was to try to weather the storm and to gradually raise prices so as to minimize loss of sales volume. In 1986, SCAN had its first loss since the very beginning—a loss of $441,000. Compounding the exchange rate problem was a heavy snow storm in late January 1987 (GCS fiscal year ended the last Saturday in January), which severely curtailed deliveries during a period which historically was SCAN's best.

Unfortunately, the existing labor contract expired May 1, 1987. Because of the severe drop (about 40 percent) in exchange rate, management and the Board felt that changes should be made in the labor contract to increase productivity and reduce labor costs. The union did not agree and a strike was initiated on May 2, 1987. With uncharacteristic rigidity on the part of both parties the strike continued for 9 months with disastrous results. Sales dropped from a projected $43 million to $34.5 million (about 20 percent). Legal and security costs as well as the overhead to total sales jumped materially. The bottom line became a $4.2 million loss.

National and local labor unions rallied behind the striking union. The Board and management clung stubbornly to their position as well. At the Co-op's annual meeting in June 1987, things turned ugly and precipitated a rapid decline of SCAN's image, which prior to the strike was one of the most favorable images of any business in the Washington/Baltimore market area. As a result, sales plummeted.

Sales continued their downward spiral ($31.4 million) in 1988 and the Cooperative experienced a $4.7 million loss. However, before year end (June 15, 1988), the Board had decided to seek protection under Chapter 11 of the Bankruptcy code.

Whether the strike should have been taken is a matter of opinion. However, there are many who believe that settlement of the strike should have been swift with a great deal more compromise on both sides. In previous strike-potential situations, the Board always advised management to seek prompt resolution of conflicts for exactly the reasons that occurred—loss of image over the long term and loss of sales in the short term.

GCS succeeded, however, in overcoming two decades of varying crises in three divisions and then finally closing all three. In less than three years it lost it all to an uncontrollable situation involving currency exchange and the strike, which in part could have been controlled.

After reviewing 50 years of documents, stepping back from the closeness as a Board member, and visiting with a number of older and newer GCS leaders, the conclusion of the junior author is that there were eight critical decisions and some "non-decisions" that shaped the Cooperative and eventually led to its demise.

CRITICAL DECISIONS

Eight critical decisions made by the Board of Directors of Greenbelt Cooperative materially affected the history of the Cooperative. Other decisions had an impact but, in this author's opinion, these eight, plus three "non-decisions" most affected the course of GCS:

1. June 1950, the Board approved a lease in Takoma Park. This was the first step outside of the Greenbelt geographic area. It set the cooperative into a growth mode. More importantly, it established the direction of growth as centralized vis-a-vis federated. This approach required effective strategic planning and Board decisions enhancing capital accumulation for growth. This first step was studied but does not appear to have been taken as part of a longer term written plan for growth and for financing that growth.

   In an open letter to the members carried in a newsletter, the Chairman requested that the members support the Board's plan for expansion.

Also in the newsletter was an open letter to the members from the chief executive outlining the reasons why expansion was recommended. It addressed the three issues of: "Why expand", "Why expand outside of Greenbelt", and "Why have financial and political control over new areas."

In summary, expansion would reduce per unit costs and would attract new equity. Expansion outside of the area would put the Cooperative in a better competitive position. It is essential that control be maintained in order to utilize the leadership that understands cooperatives. It is also a given that, in order to obtain financing, control would be in the hands of GCS. Thus, this decision had a positive long-run impact on the Cooperative.

2. January 1955, the Board created a Congress. This body served as a link between the members and the Board. Over time, it acquired some decision making powers and became an influence on most of the critical decisions of the Board. It served as a powerful deterrent to timely decision making by the Board. During the later years there was constant conflict between the Congress and the Board (or some of the Board) and between Area councils and Directors relating to closing of facilities. These conflicts usually resulted in trying still another approach (none of which were successful for a sustained period) to increase sales. The area councils/Congress also had a deterrent impact upon capitalizing on the early success of SCAN (late '70s, early '80s) by opposing expanding outside of the Baltimore/ Washington market area. Generally, the Congress opted for using the scarce capital for shoring up and revitalizing the food and service station divisions. The majority of the Board supported the viewpoint of the majority of the Congress. Too often these majority viewpoints were in direct conflict with the long-term, positive economic health of the Cooperative.

There was, and continued throughout, a belief on the part of the vast majority that a "furniture operation" could not sustain itself as a Cooperative, nor did they believe that a furniture operation was consistent with the very foundations of a cooperative, where there was a "frequent" contact between the "store" and the member.

Without a doubt the Congress was the key factor in the Board staying with the food and service stations as long as it did. To underline the strong feeling of the Congress, not a single director voting for closure of the food and service station divisions who stood for re-election was re-elected by the Congress after the decision to close the food and service station divisions was made by the Board.

3. <u>December 1961</u>, the Board approved the opening of a free standing SCAN store (no longer occupying space in a supermarket). It opened in April of 1962. This was the impetus which started the "real" growth of the SCAN division.

4. <u>May 1967</u>, the Board gave final approval for the purchase of the Washington Division of Kroger food stores. In the face of a 5-year plan adopted just months previously, the Board made a critical decision upon recommendation which was not consistent with the plan. This appeared to be an excellent opportunity to expand rapidly, but in a direction exactly opposite of what management had advocated—they bought worn out stores instead of new ones. Several problems immediately arose:

   a. Most of the stores were aging facilities or were in neighborhoods that were rapidly changing. This required costly remodeling in the stores and major adjustments in merchandise and merchandising practices. GCS did not take the necessary steps quickly and within 5 years most were closed.
   b. The euphoria of expansion had not been matched with the effective recruitment of members around new facilities. The Kroger acquisition overwhelmed the staff and volunteers in developing a member base of customers except by the passive approach of automatic membership through patronage refunds. This approach has never developed a true membership base.
   c. Financially, long-term debt doubled, almost a million dollars was added to inventory, working capital needs increased significantly, net earnings to sales nose-dived and the total debt to equity ratio deteriorated from .75 to 1.54. (a) and (b) above worked against any improvement in the financial situation.

5. <u>March 1976</u>, the Board made a decision to change the Chief Executive Officer. This decision established the tone of the working relationship between the Board and the Chief Executive which prevailed at least until June 1986. For those ten years there was a "balance of power" between the Board and management, each carrying out their authorities and responsibilities without abdicating them to, or usurping them from, the other.

   Slightly earlier the Board had made the decision to engage Jerome Weiss of Hamel, Park, McCabe and Saunders, as their legal counsel. This move was significant in that Weiss guided the Board through a number of legal problems including law suits, the real estate deals previously made, and filings with the SEC. The relationship between the Board and Weiss was one of trust.

6. <u>November 1976</u>, the Board approved in concept a report prepared by a Blue Ribbon Committee relating to the food division. This report's key sentence was, "The present seven food stores represent a viable base from which to establish a successful retail food division with the goal of being a leader and influential factor for the consumer in the Eastern marketplace."

This study had been undertaken after 8 years of frustrating performances of the food division. Not since 1960 had the food division covered its share of overhead costs. In fact, in only 1964, 1965 and 1974 did the food division cover any part of its allocated overhead. In light of the continual optimism, many Board members felt that "if we close stores x and y" we'll be back in the black. That never happened. Now, after closing 15 of the 22 stores owned in 1967 and 1968, the Board was at a point of wanting to know if it was possible for GCS to operate food stores successfully. The Committee said "yes". The Committee was chaired by the Assistant CEO of the Berkeley Consumer Cooperative, at that time viewed as being an exceptionally successful food cooperative. Others on the Committee included executives from the food industry—co-op and proprietary. It was a group which the GCS Board respected for their food business savvy. With one dissenting vote the Board reaffirmed its commitment to remain in the food business.[1]

Seven more years of losses in the food division followed. During this period of losses in the food division, profits in the petroleum division deteriorated even more rapidly. Since petroleum division sales were such a small part of the total, the division never received concentrated attention.

An analysis of those 7 years appears later in this chapter. It is a study in commitment according to the advocates and a study in gross mismanagement according to the critics. It is certainly one or the other.

7. <u>December 1983</u>, the Board voted unanimously to divest the food and service station divisions. In August 1983, the Board had commissioned still another study. This time it was conducted by the consulting division of Peat, Marwick, Mitchell and Co. Their charge was to examine the alternatives to staying in the food business as well as the alternative of divesting the food and service station divisions. After the report was received, the Board conducted 3 months of discussion and debate with

---

[1] This dissenting vote was by Leonard Lineberry. During his years on the Board, he consistently urged "economic common sense" by closing the divisions which were chronic "losers". He courageously defied the politics of the issues - from footnote 3. In retrospect the question arises, "what if the rest, or at least a majority, of the directors would have had the same courage?"

351

Area councils, the Congress and among the directors and management relating to the consequences of each of the alternatives. The divestiture had a positive economic impact on returns.

8. <u>May 1987</u>, the Board approved management's proposal that a hard line be taken in negotiations with the union representing SCAN employees relating to specific cost saving measures. If the union did not accept those terms, then the Board would support management in any measures necessary to deal with a strike. As it turned out the union did not accept the terms and a prolonged strike ensued, which had a devastatingly negative effect on the Cooperative.

NON-DECISIONS

The three decisions that cried out to be made, but never were, probably had as much to do with the financial roller coaster history of GCS as did any of the decisions.

1. <u>No Decision on a Comprehensive Financial Plan</u>

From the beginning the Board could never seem to come to grips with approving comprehensive capital structure and long-term financial plans. There were numerous efforts at addressing the issue, but until comprehensive analysis and recommendations of the 1979-80 Capital Structure Committee there was never a package put together dealing with equity and debt with all of their feasible alternatives.

Patchwork financing was the mode of meeting both short- and long-term capital needs. Contributed equity capital was dealt with more in terms of linkage with increased membership than in terms of equity financing. This created an uneven approach to policies regarding dividends on stock, patronage refunds, and redemption of stock. Additionally, significantly greater movement from one banking relationship to another than is usually found in mature businesses added to the Cooperative's financial disarray.

2. <u>Decision Gridlock on SCAN Expansion</u>

During the period 1974-1982, it was evident that SCAN was a proven success and that the other divisions of GCS were at best marginal and at worst real financial problems. In 1975, the Board at a planning retreat agreed that SCAN should be expanded aggressively. Over the next 10 years various alternatives were discussed, including greater saturation of the Baltimore/Washington market, expansion outside of that market area, franchising, joint ventures with other cooperatives, and joint ownership between store managers and the cooperative. Except for greater saturation in the Baltimore/Washington market, an additional store in the Virginia Peninsula area, and a management contract with Hyde Park's two SCAN stores in Chicago (replaced by GCS purchase in 1983), none of the ideas moved much beyond the discussion stage.

In the junior author's judgment there were three basic reasons why the Board did not press forward more aggressively:

a. The philosophy of the founder of SCAN, Bob Gowell, was to provide the consumer in the Cooperative's market area with real values. The notion of capital accumulation for growth outside of the Cooperative's market area was of very low priority to him. His arguments were well based given his philosophy. Margins were kept as low as possible. SCAN's gross margins of 38 to 42 percent were unheard of in the furniture industry. Members and customers benefited. Furthermore, he felt that if margins were higher the only result would be to further subsidize the losing divisions. He was probably correct. So, why not benefit SCAN's customers and suppliers instead?

    Not only did the SCAN staff during his years as head of SCAN avoid recommending expansion other than within the market area and in traditional ways, but they also argued against it. The Board kept discussing how and where to expand but never pushed beyond that.

b. Most of the Congress members and part of the Board were in total agreement with the SCAN philosophy. Many viewed SCAN as a "cash cow" to be used to support the food and service station divisions. Certainly, they felt, scarce capital should not be used to expand SCAN outside of areas where GCS members didn't live.

c. The chronic shortage of capital did not provide breathing room for undertaking a pilot effort. For example, one area that appeared to have merit was Philadelphia. To be competitive it was determined that two stores and a small warehouse would be needed. This would require a minimum of 2 million dollars for inventory, equipment, and leasehold improvements. Most would have to be borrowed. There was great reluctance to do that in light of the chronic financial weaknesses of GCS. Yet, another entrepreneur did exactly what SCAN could have done and remains successful today.

3. Postponed Action on Business Entity Failures

    As noted already, many facilities related to staying in the food business were kept open far beyond what most corporations would tolerate. At

353

one facility, Takoma Park, at least four different types of merchandising approaches were tried, plus an attempt to generate business by volunteer efforts in soliciting the dwellers of the nearby apartment buildings. None succeeded.

In reviewing the minutes, planning retreat documents, and personal notes, the evidence shows that every facility and each division closed was given a "stay" of closure of not less than 9 months and most well over a year. The three closed divisions (pharmacy, food, and service stations) were kept open many years while continuously losing money. The rationale was that in a Cooperative the objective is to provide goods and services to the members and one division supports another. In the final analysis, however, GCS was not providing competitive quality of goods and services during the waning years of those divisions.

Area councils, too, contributed to non-decisions of the Board. Before any facility was closed it was the policy to discuss the problem with the council in the area. Most times they courageously tried to drum up business. This took time and unfortunately in no instance was the effort successful over a sustained period.

The Board continually postponed tough decisions until one, two and three more approaches to achieve profitability were tried. After these approaches were tried and before any closure was undertaken management prepared a report to the Board and the affected council. This report detailed the market area including the competition, the location (age of shopping center, changing demographics, etc.), and probable market changes, such as a box store coming into the market area. Alternatives were identified with the probable consequence of each alternative.

Certainly no facility was closed without the members (particularly the leadership in the council) having been given every opportunity to assist in increasing sales. Concurrently all reasonable measures were taken to adjust the merchandising to best compete in the area. In some cases, in-store costs were increased in an effort to boost sales.

These last ditch efforts in the face of virtually certain non-success resulted in the Board postponing closure decisions far beyond what most businesses would consider reasonable. In a proprietary business it might have brought stockholder suits against the Board for nonfeasance.

SOME LESSONS LEARNED

In retrospect a number of lessons should be learned from the above historical perspective:

1. Failure to be realistic about the Cooperative's strengths and weaknesses led to the brink of disaster several times and then finally to Chapter 11.

   At several key junctures, GCS leadership failed to accurately assess the organization's ability or capacity to manage a project, or chose to pursue a strategy which was totally inappropriate to GCS's position within the competitive market. The real estate deals of the 60s, the change to a non co-op discount image in 1964, the Kroger acquisition in 1967, the Skinker Tire acquisition in 1969, and the attempt to operate SCAN successfully in the face of the 1987 strike are examples of this lack of realism.

   A more subtle, but equally important manifestation of this tendency, was the leadership's reluctance to recognize that the organization could only do a few things well. Often, GCS tried too many things, too fast, and with too few resources, even though the strategy for each separate project appeared to be sound.

   The strength of SCAN was never exploited either in terms of expansion or by using successful SCAN techniques, tactics and strategies in other parts of the Cooperative. SCAN flew in the face of tradition and carved out its own market niche within the furniture industry in the Maryland/Virginia/District of Columbia market. The other divisions of GCS tried to compete in the same traditional ways as the rest of the industry.

2. Failure to "cut bait" on losing operations greatly increased damage to the financial health of the Cooperative. Management made sound recommendations when it became obvious that a facility needed to be closed. The Board, instead of taking action, convinced (or coerced) management into "just one more effort."

   In the beginning, the opening of a new replacement store might have kept each of the divisions viable. Later, the image was so bad that even new stores probably would not have brought back the needed volume.

   The policy of subsidizing losing facilities had several deleterious effects. It diverted limited cash away from expansion and upgrading profitable units. It also drove away goal-oriented executives when their performance was not rewarded with more resources. It created a "loser" image for the Cooperative among executives, employees, members and the public. It influenced the furniture division to isolate itself from the rest of GCS; as a consequence, the other divisions learned little from SCAN's success.

3. Management, the Board, and the other leadership spent too much of their time worrying about current losing operations and not enough time on strengthening the successful ones and replacement business.

   CEO's and division vice presidents tended to take the existing mix of businesses as a given. Most planning was based on an assumption that the food, pharmacy, and petroleum divisions would simply get bigger.

   Innovation did occur, but starting in the early 70s there were almost no resources for experimentation. When GCS did anticipate trends —as it did with a coin-operated self-service car wash, natural foods, and non-food departments in supermarkets—the opportunity to become the leader was not exploited. SCAN is the exception. If GCS had developed the best ideas of managers and members, there might have been more SCAN-like success stories.

   A major lesson to be gained is that by not giving attention to successful components of a business it may very well never achieve its potential. In the junior author's view, that is what happened to SCAN. GCS management and the Board left SCAN's management to fend for itself and permitted SCAN to become isolated from the rest of the Cooperative. While SCAN management welcomed this, it was not in the best interests of the Cooperative.

4. The potential for interdependency among the businesses of the Cooperative existed, but were rarely employed. As a result, GCS's diversification remained just a latent advantage.

   While good advantage was made of GCS's diversified base up to 1965, the following years were generally characterized by a growing insulation of the component businesses. Many opportunities were passed by. In particular, the furniture division's strengths and profits were not used to further diversify or to restructure divisions with chronic losses.

5. Although planning is useful and necessary, it is counter-productive if there is no follow through. GCS (as noted in later chapters) did a lot of planning. Virtually every several years there was a new plan. Rarely were plans executed, nor were the concepts or criteria implemented or followed.

   If the GCS Board and management would have implemented the plans that were developed—and most appear to have been both sound and feasible—GCS would have been quite a different organization going into the 80s.

During the early years, management generally provided both the impetus for planning and the conduct of planning. The Board then reacted to the proposal rather than considering the alternatives with probable consequences of each alternative.

In 1974, the Board began taking a pro-active role in planning, partly as a result of a memo to the Board from the auditors. They urged that GCS develop an overall plan for the Cooperative's future. They suggested that such a plan would better enable the Board and management to review possible acquisitions and to identify future capital needs.

The first joint Board/Management Planning Committee was formed in 1975. Operating management contributed mutually in the analysis (see Appendix F). After 9 months, the Committee made its report to the Board.

Among the key points made by the Committee were:

a. Restructure the food division so that it is viable beyond the division level (this, of course, could mean some subsidization).
b. Regain the confidence of the members.
c. Continually and systematically expand SCAN both in and outside of the present market area.
d. Reorganize the capital structure.

From this point forward the Board took equal responsibility with management in initiating and participating in planning. In fact, for most of the remaining years there were continuing task forces representing management, Board, and the Congress of GCS involved in various aspects of planning. These efforts were supplemented by studies of consulting firms who were engaged by GCS.

The 1976 study was triggered by a memo which the Chairman received from an executive in the food industry who had been a GCS staffer in earlier years. This memo jolted the Board. Among the points:

a. GCS has done poorly by the consumer. Giant[1] outperforms GCS.
b. Changing the "Co-op" name to Consumers Discount and now back to Co-op was costly both in dollars and in confusion among GCS members and customers.
c. Merchandising, pricing, and advertising policies appear to be in disarray and the purchasing system is badly fragmented.
d. The uniqueness of the Cooperative has not been exploited for years.

---

[1] A competitor in food retailing in the Washington/Baltimore area. See Chapter 2.

The resultant study encouraged the Board to look favorably on the food division. Unfortunately, the criteria for evaluating progress was not followed.

Then, in 1981, another massive planning process got underway. Totally in-house, except for bringing in an MBA graduate to coordinate the effort, this effort culminated in a 3-day retreat by Board and management.

Following the retreat a Business and Growth Plan was adopted by the Board in October 1981. While this plan was much more sophisticated and included detailed strategies and tactics, it did not vary much from what was envisioned in 1976. One major difference was that stringent guidelines were set for facility performance.

For the first time, significant attention was given the petroleum division. The result was a major capital improvement program for 1981 in upgrading the stations with an investment of $325,000. Other capital budget items approved in the plan were $693,300 for SCAN expansion, but only $80,500 for the food division.

Among the goals adopted at the retreat were:

a. Increase average net earnings 20 percent annually to reach net earnings of $3 million annually by 1986.
b. Increase membership by 5,000 annually.
c. Increase member patronage to 50 percent of total sales by 1986.
d. Increase member capital investment to $4 million by 1986.
e. Develop profitable operations so that no more than 50 percent of corporate level expenses will be met by any one operating division from any one geographic area.
f. Only projects with an anticipated Return on Investment (ROI) of 12 percent after taxes, over a 5-year period or less, will be considered.
g. Operations or facilities which show a loss at the store contribution line for six consecutive periods, or for an entire fiscal year, will be divested unless reasonable projections show the operation clearing the ROI hurdle rate within 2 years.
h. The ratio of long-term debt to the sum of long-term debt and equity shall not exceed 45 percent for more than six consecutive periods.
i. Restructure the food operations.
j. Expand SCAN to the Philadelphia and Richmond areas. Pick up the pace of expansion in order to head off fiercer competition.
k. Achieve geographic diversification in the contemporary furniture business by expanding directly or indirectly into other metropolitan areas.

l. At least break even in the petroleum division.

m. And many more.

Tragically, only Goal 2 was achieved, and the guidelines were generally ignored or waived. That is a lesson that cooperatives should heed. <u>Do not make exceptions to your criteria unless there are compelling reasons</u>. For GCS there weren't, except for the politics of the organization.

Later, there were additional plans. The one by Peat, Marwick and Mitchell cited earlier provided the foundation for divestiture. Two new business plans were adopted, one each in 1986 and 1987. The plan in 1986 again set forth the intent to expand SCAN into other geographic areas and the 1987 plan focused on entering the ready-to-assemble and upholstery business.

A focused financial plan, except for the 1981 Plan which partly addressed the issue, was never set down, as can be surmised when looking at the figures and the tables.

The problems were readily identified and the few recommendations, such as those proposed by Leo Plante of Goldman Sachs in 1978, were never seriously pursued. Most of the viable solutions would have required GCS to veer from the Rochdale principles and this was not acceptable to a majority of the leadership. One recommendation was that GCS incorporate SCAN as a for-profit subsidiary with shares trading on the market. GCS would always own 51 percent or more of the shares. Today a number of cooperatives around the world are adopting the recommendations that Plante made then. Now, for GCS, it is too late.

TO SUMMARIZE: Planning is important. Planning, to be effective must be implemented and in GCS it rarely was. In retrospect, too many issues were addressed and too many ideas were directed to management to explore. That flaw diverted management's attention from critical issues.

6. Focus is as important for the Board as it is for management. From 1968 through the early 80s, GCS had far too many committees dealing with far too many diverse projects requiring both Board and management attention. It also diverted attention from the major enterprises. Part of this stemmed from a highly motivated group of volunteer leaders with a wide ranging arena of interests. For example, during one period in the mid 70s there were 24 committees, most of which included someone from the Board, the management and the Congress. True, many ideas were generated, but lack of ideas was not the problem: attention was not focused, and the ideas were rarely implemented.

Committees in themselves are not a problem, but getting them to perform effectively can be. Some leaders complained that the Greenbelt Cooperative had too many meetings, but this provided participation of members and was an important way to keep the organization alive and innovative. Aside from certain basic and required committees, leaders relied heavily on ad hoc committees in response to a need which developed or to explore someone's proposal. This created committees to meet a need or the ideas of members. Over the years, however, there was much duplication. Some subjects were explored repeatedly at intervals, with little attempt to go back and use good reports that had already been prepared. It may also be noted that many excellent committee studies were never followed up. Leaders of GCS were better at appointing committees and producing reports than putting the findings into action. The most productive committees were tripartite, with representatives from Board, Congress, and management.

What if those energies had been focused on just three of the key issues facing GCS? A planned and consistent capital plan, a means of expanding SCAN, and some innovative ways of restructuring the food division are the three areas that would have made a difference. Such a focus, however, was not forthcoming.

7. Instead of examining other alternatives to add new members, the initial decision to incorporate under the corporate laws of Maryland (since consumer cooperatives did not fall under the cooperative code), cost the cooperative hundreds of thousands of dollars. The requirement to register with the SEC cost $100,000 to $600,000 annually and took huge amounts of staff time. Membership could only be obtained by buying a share of stock rather than the usual way of just buying a membership. It was not until 1979 that GCS was able to get the Maryland law changed, which permitted a consumer cooperative to be a membership organization rather than a stock corporation.

8. A review of GCS's bylaws and other documents shows clearly the changes in the democratic process of GCS. In the early years decisions were promulgated after much input from members, resembling a town hall meeting approach. Membership meetings were held monthly where members were concentrated around a few facilities in a tight geographic area. With wider geographic expansion and more facilities, meetings were held quarterly. With the formation of area councils and the Congress in 1954, membership meetings were held annually, the norm for cooperatives and other types of corporations.

Because of a requirement of Maryland corporation laws, proxy voting was permitted. However, this was really a technicality because GCS continued to adhere to the one member one vote principle.

Originally, directors were elected for 1 year. Over the years this evolved to three-year terms with no limit to re-election. Later, a maximum of three terms was instituted.

Amending the bylaws required two-thirds of the entire membership for most of the life of GCS. In 1986, this was changed to vest the power of bylaw change to the Council of Delegates, the successor to the Congress.

9. In the early years, recruiting members was never a problem. When the Kroger stores were acquired, only a minimal attempt was made to convert customers to members. After the first years in Greenbelt, there were three incentives: the patronage refund, dividend on shares, and member benefits. A survey in the early 1970s revealed that by then almost no one joined out of belief in the cooperative ideals. By then operation of the facilities depended on customers rather than members; and management, therefore, geared operations to competing for the shopping public rather than fulfilling members needs.

   In 1981, $1 memberships were implemented so that GCS could have a sufficient percentage of members as customers to meet lending requirements of the National Consumer Cooperative Bank and to return earnings to customers through patronage refunds.

   The Area councils, Congress, and most directors were heavily concerned with the voice of the members, which resulted in some misunderstandings and differences with management's primary goal of keeping the business operating profitably. This split personality aspect of GCS became more, rather than less of a problem over the years.

10. There were far too many meetings of the Board, of the Congress, of the Area councils and of Committees. Because preparation for Board meetings was spotty, too much detail and trivia took up valuable board time. Many of the Congress and Committee meetings did not have sufficient planning and available documentation to be fully effective.

    Most Area council meetings were poorly planned, poorly run, dull, and hence poorly attended. New members being brought into the leadership voiced dismay at the pettiness and controversy at some meetings, calling them a waste of time, and did not come back after a sampling.

11. Perhaps the single most frustrating proclivity of the Board was to postpone decisions. This was particularly true when the decision would likely be politically unpopular. Closely linked was the tendency to delay until still another study was made.

WHAT WENT RIGHT

1. The most obvious thing that went right for GCS was SCAN, until the last 3 years that SCAN was part of GCS. Refer to the last part of Chapter XXII for a discussion of this "went right."

2. The stability of a Board has a significant impact upon cooperative performance. While it is the entire Board who makes decisions, most Boards reflect the leadership of the Chairman. However, GCS, as most Boards, also gained strength from others on the Board who had special skills in specific areas, in diplomacy, in asking discerning questions, in developing harmony, etc. GCS was particularly blessed much of the time with individuals who complemented one another. For the most part, the Board also worked as a team. This was particularly true in the area of financial issues, where those who were most conversant with finance and capital structure took the lead. There were only a few years where there was personal acrimony on the Board. Generally the GCS directors trusted and respected one another while at the same time voicing differences of opinion.

   Even though there are only nine persons with 10 or more years of service on the Board, the Board from 1962 through 1984 was extraordinarily stable with no changes in 1982. This was also true in 1956. Except for the years of 1964 and 1973 there were only one or two changes on the Board.

   Those serving on the Board for 10 or more years included:

Benjamin Rosenzweig	20, six as Chairman plus other offices
Paul O. Mohn	15, eleven as Chairman plus other offices
W. Gifford Hoag	14
Donald H. Cooper	12
Bruce Bowman	12
Solomon Hoke	11
L. Glen Whipple	11
Walter Bierwagen	10, all as Chairman
Robert Dressel	10, four as Chairman

   Unlike most consumer cooperatives of which the junior author has knowledge, GCS had a great deal of stability in the tenure of its Chairmen, except in the very early years and in the last couple of years. The same was not true with respect to the Chief Executives. From 1946 until 1986 there were only eight Chairmen and but seven Chief Executives (two for only one year each). In most consumer cooperatives

362

around the world the average tenure of a Chairman is less than 4 years, while the tenure of Chief Executive approaches 20 years—longer than in most proprietary corporations.

3. Another strength of the GCS leadership was that many held leadership positions in other organizations. Again, based upon the junior author's experience, there are very few Boards that have so many of their leadership in so many other organizations. Appendix C contains a listing of most of the organizations in which GCS leaders sat on the Board. In a number of organizations they rose to be an officer, including chairman.

    For the Greenbelt Cooperative, leadership development was never a problem, because training courses, workshops, and seminars were set up early and continued with considerable consistency throughout the 50-year history. Management, Board, and Congress worked together on in-house opportunities, and support was given to many organizations for training programs. Staff people were sent to the American Management Association and various trade institutes for general and specialized training. Board retreats and Congress annual orientations introduced new leaders and potential leaders to the history and principles of cooperation, responsibilities of directors, how to be a good secretary or treasurer or committee chairman, public speaking, report writing, understanding financial reports, and many similar subjects. A specific purpose of the Congress system developed with GCS was to develop leaders and especially candidates for the Board of Directors.

4. To facilitate discussion of strategies and tactics which could provide GCS with a competitive edge, the last ten years of Board meetings were held in 3 parts; regular, with any member permitted to attend, comment and ask questions; executive, which any leader who signed a confidentiality agreement could attend; and, in-camera, with only Board members, the Chairman of the Review and Evaluation Committee, and invited guests, which included management, in attendance.

    At first, closed sessions at Board meetings occurred only for personnel matters and proposed store leases. Even these brought protests from some members. Later, financial data and operations were discussed in executive sessions in an effort to avoid informing the competition. A concession was made by scheduling closed sessions toward the latter part of the meeting so that visitors would not have to wait outside the room for the open session. Minutes of closed sessions were sometimes kept in a separate minutes book, but in any event, the secretary periodically presented for declassification those minutes on matters no longer considered confidential.

5. In 1958, the Board began codifying its policies and procedures to achieve consistency in its functioning. The Policies Book contained written statements agreed upon for guiding the Cooperative. The Procedures Book contained written statements guiding the way in which the Board functioned. These were updated from time to time. Use of these guides avoided much arguing, duplication, and contradictory motions.

Obviously, there were more "wrongs" and "rights." The above gives the reader most of the highlights. However, all of the following chapters discuss other things the Cooperative did wrong or right.

EPILOGUE

NEWCO

On December 1, 1989, NEWCO operating as SCAN International, Inc., began operations as a new corporation. It is operating under a Plan of Reorganization approved by the Bankruptcy Court.

Under the Plan, a new corporation was formed, NEWCO. GCS holds 30 percent of the stock, 12 foreign suppliers (allocated in accordance to their pro rate claims) hold 21 percent of the stock, and the Danish Council (a governmental guarantor) holds 49 percent of the stock.

Over a period of 10 years, $2.4 million is to be repaid to the foreign suppliers after writing off $300,000. The Danish Council is also to be repaid $400,000 over a 10 year-period after writing off $2.2 million. The National Cooperative Bank wrote off $687,000 in exchange for GCS's accumulated patronage refund certificates. Trade creditors received 10 cents on the dollar ($3.1 million owed).

After the 10-year period and after the foreign suppliers and the Danish Council have been paid, GCS has the option of purchasing 31 percent of their stock. During the 10-year period, and after the first year, GCS is to receive not less than one half of one percent of NEWCO's total sales.

Under the Plan all members of GCS who had $25 or more in their Capital Account retained voting membership in GCS with their account reduced to $5. All shares of stock were cancelled.

NEWCO or SCAN International is, however, doing better than most furniture retailers and is opening two new stores. One is SCAN Express, a cash and carry high volume store, and the other, SCAN Clearance, an outlet type store for various discontinued and slow moving items.

GCS

Until July 1991, GCS continued to function but with no paid staff. The Board examined some business ventures that required little or no up front investment cash. Two of the board, John Gauci and Paul Mohn, sit on the NEWCO Board. The prospects are not bright unless SCAN International does well, which, as of this writing, is not the case primarily because of the economy.

In October 1991, with overwhelming agreement of the membership, GCS was dissolved and all asset and liabilities were transferred to United Cooperative Services, a new cooperative.

UNITED COOPERATIVE SERVICES

In July 1991, a new cooperative was incorporated by the Board of GCS with approval of the GCS Delegate Assembly. The purpose of the new cooperative was to facilitate the dissolution of GCS and obtain the patronage refunds (over $100,000) due GCS from a cooperative wholesaler. The refunds, under the wholesale cooperative's policies, could not be refunded to a "living" entity. The new cooperative would be the "heir" and the refunds would be available to it. Additionally, a new cooperative under the Delaware Corporate code will have more flexibility. It additionally will have a new image and the capability of serving as a quasi-holding corporation for semi-autonomous entities.

In October 1991, after the dissolution of GCS, the new cooperative received, by transfer, all of the assets and liabilities of GCS. The new cooperative has a Board of 13, the 9 members of the GCS Board plus the 4 delegate assembly officers. All previous GCS members could become members of the new cooperative by so requesting in writing; 2,212 did so.

Planning for services to be provided will begin in 1992.

XXII. THE FINANCIAL PEAKS AND VALLEYS

Greenbelt Cooperative started with a lot of enthusiasm, self confidence and limited, but adequate, capital. As with consumer cooperatives generally, the amount of equity capital was largely limited to that generated by net earnings. Willingness of members to provide contributed capital was inadequate when there was real need for infusion of equity capital for growth opportunities. None-the-less, except for 1970-1979 and the last two years, the debt/equity ratio was manageable. The lack of equity capital manifested itself more in lost opportunities and inability to keep pace with competition.

As contrasted to agricultural cooperation when the incentive to "invest" equity was both in ownership of **their** cooperative and in having a market for their products, a consumer cooperative's members were not dependent upon the cooperative for their economic well being. Also, members who "invested" through contributed equity do not benefit through appreciation of shares as do shareholders of for-profit competitors. The parallel growth of GCS its competitor, Giant Food, Inc., is herein chronicled and allows the reader sympathetic to the cooperative way of doing business to ponder "what if?"

Giant Food and GCS

Giant Food, Inc. (Giant) and GCS started their history at about the same time. In 1990, Giant was one of the most profitable and dominant regional food operations in the country with sales of $3.2 billion and net earnings of $108.4 million from 149 supermarkets. Today GCS is a paper organization with nary a store and no income.[1]

Washington's first supermarket was opened by Giant Food in 1936. The predecessor to GCS was founded and opened its first food store one year later operated by the Consumer Distribution Corporation. Giant began with food and related household products exclusively. It continued that focus well into the 50s. GCS started out as a tiny conglomerate and it was not until 1949 that food and related household products became dominant. In that year, for the first time, the food operation contributed more than 50 percent of the contribution (59%). In 1949 food operations accounted for 68 percent of the sales. During this period both organizations were highly profitable.

---

[1] In October 1991, GCS was dissolved and all assets and liabilities were transferred to United Cooperative Services, Inc., the successor cooperative which was incorporated in Delaware in July 1991.

By 1949, Giant already had 19 stores and had vertically integrated with a bakery and slaughterhouse. Only three of those stores were in Maryland when GCS made its move with the areas first shopping center in 1951 anchored by a state-of-the-art supermarket. Three years later another shopping center was opened by GCS. Its supermarket had an in-store bakery. GCS truly pioneered the concept and implementation of regional shopping centers. Giant opened its first shopping center in 1956. Giant's first in-store bakery didn't come along until eight years later.

In 1952, GCS had three stores (two were state-of-the-art supermarkets). Giant had 21. Giant over the years successfully developed an image of "consumerism". It further enhanced its image by giving five scholarships in 1954 to students who would pursue management in the food industry at American University. It did the things that proprietary businesses weren't "supposed" to do. That was the turf of cooperatives.

From the early years through the early 70s, GCS initiated consumer-friendly innovations such as "see through" meat trays, unit pricing, open data (freshness) codes, biodegradable detergents, medical listing file for prescriptions and grade labeling.

A GCS chief executive was one of the members of the food industry group operated by Super Market Institute to develop the bar codes for scanning prices at the food markets which is almost universal today. GCS was in the forefront of testimony before Congress on supporting consumer issues such as information labeling of food products and food standards.

However, which food organization was the first one to fully implement these innovations into its operations and successfully promote the ideas to the public? Not GCS. It was Giant Food, to its credit. Slowly, but steadily, it was Giant Food which was seen by the public as being the standard bearer for the consumer. With the coup of adding Esther Peterson, long a public figure in the consumer image to its staff, Giant indeed became the consumer's advocate in the eyes of the public.

In 1957, Queen Elizabeth of Great Britain visited one of Giant's food stores. It was not until 1976 that a queen visited GCS. That was the visit to a SCAN store by Queen Margrethe of Denmark.

In 1959, Giant became a publicly held company after a public offering of non-voting shares. Today Giant trades on the American Stock Exchange. A thousand dollars of shares bought then, and held, is worth well over $100,000 today due primarily to stock splits.

On the few occasions that momentum began to be generated by GCS, it was not sustained. In contrast, Giant Food sustained its momentum.

From 1955-59, GCS had growth of 80 percent, the fastest retail growth in the area. Store numbers had increased to 10 compared to Giant's 47. During the early 60s Giant surged in growth while GCS seemed to stagnate, except in its move in introducing Scandinavian furniture to Washington. It was in the early 1960s that the striking similarities of the two organizations ended.

Even though GCS was not the size of Giant at that time, it nonetheless might have generated steam and kept pace. It didn't. Why? Many theories have been discussed over the years. The ones that seem to have the most merit relate to store performance, conservative, vis-a-vis, aggressive philosophy and capital. Take your pick or take all three. The question that remains is, "WHY THE CONTRAST?"

Although N.M. Cohen (founder of Giant) had a greater capital base, GCS had a dominant market position in Greenbelt, assistance from sympathetic government agencies, and an ideology (consumer/member ownership) that appealed to many people.

Several differences between the two organizations are immediately evident:

1. Equity capital was generated quite differently.

2. Decisions were made more easily and more expeditiously by Giant. A cooperative which makes decisions in a democratic manner will encounter a lengthy and complex decision making process.

3. The operational performance in terms of net earnings to sales was more than twice as high for Giant as it was for GCS.

4. Unsuccessful ventures were shut down quickly by Giant, but ever so slowly by GCS. Over the years Giant stubbed its toe from time to time. They once had a number of super stores that carried clothing, appliances, and a full complement of electronic entertainment equipment. They also had gas stations and garden stores. When these proved unsuccessful they expeditiously closed them long before they became a major drain on the Corporation. In contrast, GCS closed individual facilities of a division one by one, placing an ever increasing burden on the remainder to carry the overhead.

   For GCS, the pharmacy division was closed down over a 6-year period of losses. The service station division contributed minimally over a 10-year period (most years sustained losses) before being closed. The food division did not cover its share of overhead from 1967 until it was closed in 1983. In only 1971 and 1975 did it contribute to overhead.

5. GCS was a much more diverse organization which required management and the Board to direct attention to three distinct types of businesses as well as many minor businesses such as travel, legal services, and perishable food operations. Additionally, management and the Board of GCS used significant energy in serving the volunteer leadership structure.

COMPARATIVE FINANCIAL HEALTH AND PERFORMANCE

Volatile financial performance began in 1964 and continued for the rest of GCS's history. This period was preceded by 25 years of lackluster performance. Figure 1, page 371, clearly shows these two periods of net earnings of GCS. Interestingly, each spanned one-half of the Cooperative's life.

During the junior author's nearly half a century of consultative experience with, and serving on boards of cooperatives, no other cooperative ever approached the wild swings of net earnings in such short time frames as did GCS.

Net earnings as a percent of sales also reflects a high degree of inconsistency of financial performance. In Figure 2, page 372, GCS's' net return on sales is compared with that of Giant Food, Inc., which shows the relative consistency of Giant in contrast to GCS. Also compared is the average for food chains, 1970-75, with less than $100 million in sales. (Table 1, page 374)

Growth of sales was steady from 1939 through 1971 (Figure 3, page 373) reaching $55.1 million. It was in 1971 that a major turning point in food store growth occurred. The first major trimming of losing food facilities was made in 1971 with the closure of five stores. This was to become the pattern for GCS's food operations. Sales recovered with the advent of a couple of new SCAN stores and increased sales in the remaining food stores. Sales in the petroleum and pharmacy divisions were never a major factor although the petroleum division did maintain sales of over $4 million (high of $6.5 million) from 1974 through 1981. The pharmacy division never reached a million dollars in sales. During the 70s sales ranged in the high $40 and low $50 millions with the highest sales reached in 1981 at $56.5 million.

In 1978, the percentage of total sales was even (45 percent each) between SCAN and the food division. From then until the food division was closed, SCAN sales as a percentage steadily rose.

The financial health of GCS, while precarious during the 1961-64 and the 1970-72 periods, was never really "life threatening" (of course, the 1986-88 crisis sounded the death knell for the Cooperative as an operating

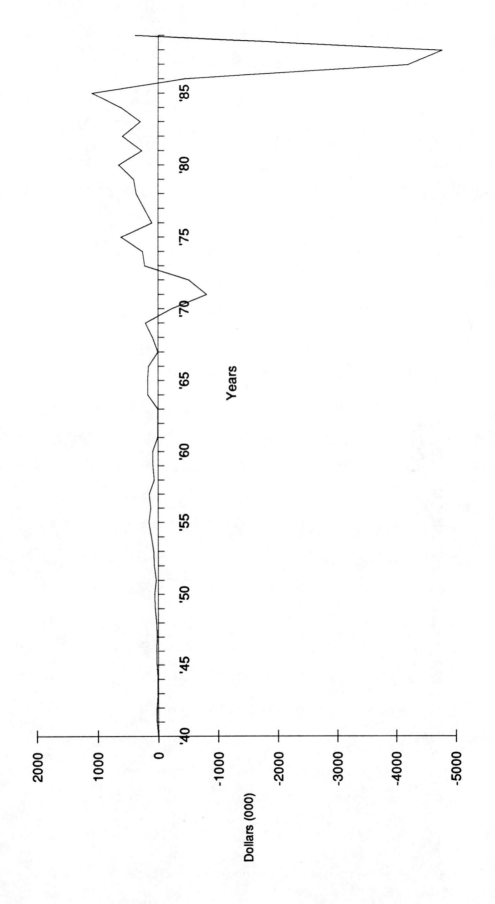

FIGURE 1: NET EARNINGS, GREENBELT COOPERATIVE, 1940-88

Dollars (000)

Years

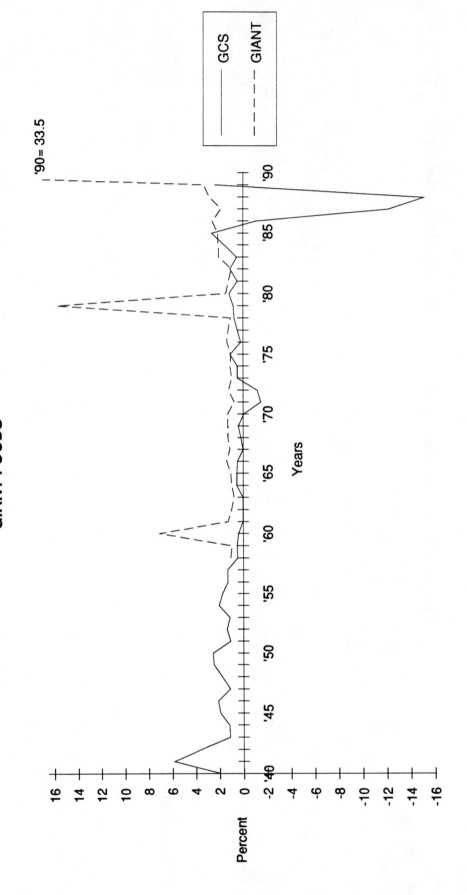

FIGURE 2: COMPARISON OF NET INCOME AS PERCENT OF SALES, GREENBELT AND GIANT FOODS

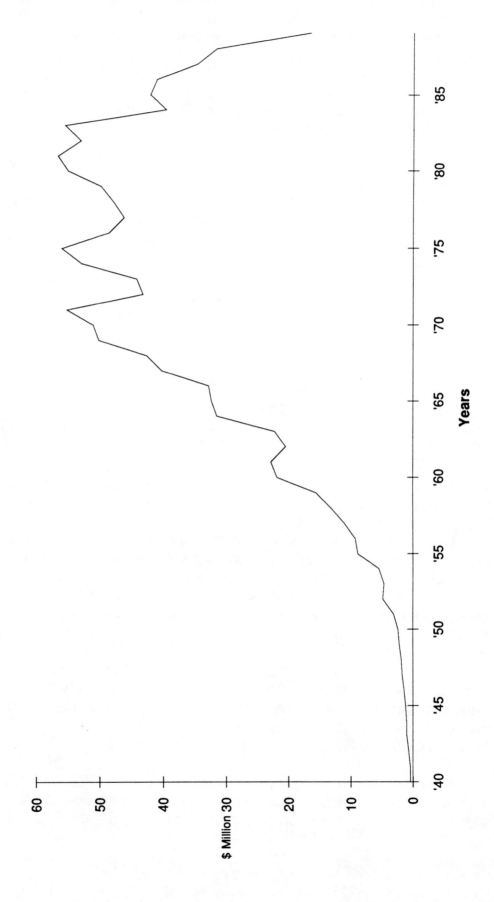

FIGURE 3: TOTAL SALES IN MILLIONS OF DOLLARS, GREENBELT

373

organization), nonetheless the Board and management were constantly seeking capital. For example, in 1969, there were 12 different sources of long-term debt ranging from subordinated debentures to mortgages to unsecured notes. In addition, there was a bank line of credit which was short-term, but because of its renewability each year it in fact became long-term borrowing.

Table 1 - Selected Operating Results of Greenbelt, Giant Foods, and Food Chains (under $100 million

	1970	1971	1972	1973	1974	1975
Gross Margin						
Greenbelt	23.46	23.98	25.93	26.16	25.63	26.28
Giant	22.98	22.87	24.37	24.99	24.63	25.10
Food Chains	20.67	21.30	20.77	20.60	19.35	19.75
Net Income						
Greenbelt	-0.03	-1.47	-1.18	0.51	0.49	1.11
Giant	1.32	0.76	1.24	.96	0.88	1.09
	1.06					
Food Chains	0.89	1.29	1.01	0.88	0.85	1.11
Net Income to Total Assets						
Greenbelt	-2.55	-10.12	-6.12	2.82	2.76	6.24
Giant	7.60	4.44	7.00	4.40	5.50	4.60
Good Chains	4.97	6.35	5.31	4.42	5.25	6.43

For the following analysis, three types of financial ratios were examined; profitability, liquidity and solvency.

The analysis of the financial information, including the comparison with Giant Food, is derived from historical data. Some of the early annual reports of Greenbelt Cooperative are missing. Some of the data has been retrieved from later annual reports and some from other sources. Another problem encountered was that the annual reports varied in the type of financial data provided and the way in which financial data was presented.

Giant Food, Inc., did not go public until 1959 and data prior to that time was not made available for this comparison. Additionally, only 10 year summary annual reports were made available as well as the latest annual report. This created gaps in some financial information where comparisons are made between GCS and Giant Food.

Another caveat, in the latter years the product mix of GCS was quite different from Giant because of the dominance of the furniture division in GCS. Nonetheless, the comparisons are useful in noting the difference in the development of two organizations which began their history at about the same time—Giant in 1936 and GCS in 1938.

Also, to give still another perspective, comparisons are made with data from a study by Wendell Earle and Willard Hunt of Cornell University of the operating results of food chains from 1970 to 1975 with sales under $100 million. Both the Giant data and the study data appear in some of the figures.

PROFITABILITY

Net Income/Total Assets

Six to eight percent return on total assets is considered minimal even for food operations. Figure 4, page 376, clearly shows GCS's lack of performance by this measure. After divestiture of the two losing divisions there was a temporary surge in 1984 and 1985. In 1986, the Cooperative was hit with two disasters. One was the forty percent decline of the dollar against the kroner and the other was a devastating snowstorm in the Washington area that prevented delivery of well over a million dollars of furniture which SCAN customers had ordered during the closing weeks of FY 1986.

Net income to total assets mirrors the dramatic swings of net earnings of GCS. There was no consistency in maintaining a minimal six percent return on the assets of GCS. Most food retailing firms believe that at least a six percent return is mandatory in order to sustain satisfactory growth. In only ten years was this goal achieved by GCS. Eight of those years were prior to 1958 and the other two were in 1975 and in 1985.

Net Income/Equity

Return to equity for retail firms, even cooperatives, is often in excess of 20 percent. Since debt capital is usually at least half of the invested capital this goal for return on equity is certainly attainable if the business is successful. In a number of years GCS met or exceeded that standard. In fact, even during years of modest net earnings the return on equity was respectable. Details can be found in Table 2, pages 377-378. Some of this success can be attributed to the relatively low equity which was a constant problem for GCS. This issue is discussed separately.

Overhead/Sales

A chronic problem which plagued GCS was overhead costs. It was an item that generated major debates between the Board and management each year

FIGURE 4: NET INCOME TO TOTAL ASSETS, GREENBELT, GIANT FOODS, AND FOOD CHAINS WITH UNDER $100 IN SALES

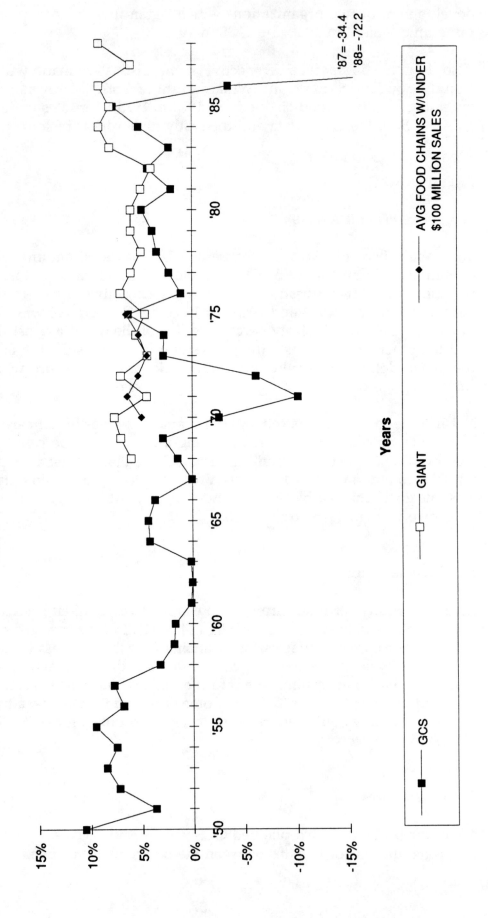

TABLE 2, FINANCIAL RATIOS, GREENBELT COOPERATIVE, 1937-89

YEAR	$000 SALES	$000 NET INCOME	% NET INCOME TO SALES	$000 TOTAL ASSETS	% RETURN ON TOTAL ASSETS	$000 EQUITY	% NET INCOME TO EQUITY	CURRENT RATIO	$000 WORKING CAPITAL	RATIO INV. TO WORKING CAPITAL	% INTEREST EXPENSE TO SALES	% O.H. TO SALES	$000 SHARES OUTSTANDING
1937	n.a.	n.a.	n.a.	n.a.	n.a.	n.a.	n.a.	n.a.	n.a.	n.a.	n.a.	n.a.	n.a.
1938	235	-6	n.a.	n.a.	n.a.	n.a.	n.a.	n.a.	n.a.	n.a.	n.a.	5.80	n.a.
1939	346	7	2.03	54	n.a.	3	n.a.	n.a.	n.a.	n.a.	n.a.	3.90	0.30
1940	377	7	1.83	59	n.a.	16	n.a.	n.a.	n.a.	n.a.	n.a.	3.90	0.70
1941	450	26	5.87	68	n.a.	20	n.a.	n.a.	n.a.	n.a.	n.a.	3.60	1.30
1942	690	25	3.58	105	n.a.	45	n.a.	n.a.	n.a.	n.a.	n.a.	2.30	1.80
1943	1,002	12	1.16	136	n.a.	74	n.a.	n.a.	n.a.	n.a.	n.a.	3.60	3.90
1944	1,036	12	1.20	135	9.20	67	18.55	1.83	49	1.37	n.a.	3.70	5.00
1945	1,163	23	1.94	179	n.a.	120	18.79	n.a.	45	n.a.	n.a.	2.90	7.50
1946	1,429	30	2.12	268	11.26	206	14.66	3.34	n.a.	n.a.	n.a.	2.70	13.90
1947	1,727	19	1.13	562	n.a.	275	n.a.	1.52	71	2.15	n.a.	n.a.	21.20
1948	1,882	33	1.78	n.a.	n.a.	308	n.a.	n.a.	n.a.	n.a.	n.a.	n.a.	22.50
1949	2,200	54	2.46	537	n.a.	361	n.a.	2.25	106	1.24	n.a.	n.a.	25.40
1950	2,399	61	2.55	577	10.59	401	22.50	2.37	130	1.11	n.a.	3.00	27.20
1951	3,064	34	1.11	921	3.70	446	7.63	1.47	127	2.29	n.a.	2.60	33.00
1952	4,834	68	1.40	942	3.61	527	19.00	1.64	172	1.68	n.a.	2.30	34.70
1953	4,629	79	1.17	935	8.46	578	13.67	1.95	195	1.50	n.a.	2.50	39.50
1954	5,450	112	2.05	1,500	7.46	692	16.17	1.55	285	1.44	n.a.	n.a.	48.30
1955	8,909	157	1.76	1,653	9.47	849	18.44	1.94	458	0.96	n.a.	n.a.	64.40
1956	9,325	123	1.32	1,808	6.82	999	12.33	2.21	752	0.66	n.a.	n.a.	87.90
1957	11,082	149	1.35	1,933	7.71	1,220	12.23	2.13	550	1.39	n.a.	n.a.	98.80
1958	13,159	67	0.51	2,063	3.27	1,402	4.80	2.40	654	0.97	n.a.	n.a.	115.50
1959	15,635	87	0.56	4,578	1.91	1,975	4.42	1.49	746	1.77	n.a.	n.a.	166.10
1960	21,860	94.8	0.43	5,390	1.76	2,271	4.17	1.56	861	1.92	n.a.	n.a.	194.20
1961	22,842	8.2	0.04	4,886	0.17	2,306	0.35	1.59	872	2.03	0.47	22.02	204.30
1962	20,463	2.1	0.01	4,467	0.05	2,136	0.10	1.60	781	1.54	0.46	22.97	n.a.
1963	22,249	6.6	0.03	3,870	0.17	2,059	0.32	1.51	626	2.15	0.31	20.66	196.30
1964	31,468	171.7	0.55	4,112	4.18	2,039	8.42	1.39	590	2.52	0.10	17.72	184.40
1965	32,295	175.8	0.54	4,048	3.99	2,127	8.27	1.51	798	2.07	0.09	18.44	n.a.

TABLE 2 (continued)

YEAR	$000 SALES	$0,000 NET INCOME	% NET INCOME TO SALES	$000 TOTAL ASSETS	% RETURN ON TOTAL SALES	$000 EQUITY	% NET INCOME TO EQUITY	CURRENT RATIO	$0,000 WORKING CAPITAL	RATIO INV. TO WORKING CAPITAL	% INTEREST EXPENSE TO SALES	% O.H. TO SALES	$000 SHARES OUTSTANDING
1966	32,758	159.4	0.49	4,347	3.67	2,214	7.20	1.56	822	2.21	0.13	18.96	184.40
1967	40,185	3.1	0.01	5,959	0.05	2,113	0.14	1.40	933	2.98	0.16	19.90	n.a.
1968	42,587	92.7	0.22	6,319	1.47	2,143	4.33	1.34	994	2.78	0.22	20.79	180.10
1969	50,122	211.9	0.42	7,310	2.90	2,622	8.08	1.35	1198	3.01	0.18	22.39	214.60
1970	50,974	-224.5	-0.03	8,799	-2.55	2,293	-9.79	1.15	914	4.40	0.23	22.43	210.80
1971	55,139	-813.3	-1.47	8,036	-10.12	1,170	-69.52	1.10	454	8.28	0.32	23.19	216.50
1972	43,122	-507.4	-1.18	8,286	-6.12	681	-74.57	1.15	692	5.63	0.35	23.35	218.30
1973	44,143	225.1	0.51	7,989	2.82	906	24.89	1.15	698	6.37	0.61	22.76	218.30
1974	52,790	259	0.49	9,387	2.76	1,133	22.86	0.99	-30		0.49	23.01	218.30
1975	55,918	618	1.11	9,908	6.24	1,709	36.16	1.14	643	7.04	0.47	23.15	218.70
1976	48,523	106	0.22	9,627	1.10	1,533	6.91	1.10	820	5.98	0.52	25.46	219.50
1977	46,124	235	0.51	10,273	2.29	1,778	13.22	1.05	838	6.99	0.55	25.30	220.60
1978	47,738	367	0.77	10,570	3.47	2,158	17.01	1.10	677	9.14	0.55	27.42	221.90
1979	49,720	410	0.83	10,530	3.89	2,586	15.85	1.31	1897	3.52	0.58	25.72	223.70
1980	54,872	654	1.19	13,323	4.95	3,041	21.51	1.45	2836	2.59	0.56	24.99	208.10
1981	56,471	274	0.49	13,152	2.08	3,127	8.76	1.60	3279	2.35	0.82	26.52	207.10
1982	52,831	589	1.11	13,568	4.34	3,575	16.48	1.59	3903	1.87	0.98	29.00	203.20
1983	55,361	297.5	0.54	12,948	2.31	3,752	7.93	1.61	4119	1.68	0.58	29.63	203.10
1984	39,442	618	1.57	11,846	5.22	3,874	15.95	1.65	3766	2.14	1.00	37.06	197.50
1985	41,948	1091	2.60	14,202	7.68	4,988	21.87	1.61	4435	2.30	0.85	35.28	173.60
1986	40,890	-441	-1.08	12,766	-3.45	4,225	-10.44	1.46	3282	2.58	0.92	38.51	164.80
1987	34,510	-4172	-12.09	12,135	-34.38	7	N/M	1.07	640	12.52	1.25	42.68	159.10
1988	31,442	-4744	-15.10	6,568	-72.22	-4,782	N/M	0.47	-5833	n.a.	1.82	40.04	159.00
1989	16,529	382.2	2.31	--	N/M	--	n.a.	n.a.	--		1.53	9.78	--

at "budget-time". GCS materially exceeded industry standards for overhead as a percentage of sales. During the 21 years (1966-87) where we have data for Giant, the overhead of GCS is higher by 2 percentage points or more in 16 of

those years. From 1978 onward it was greater by 5 percentage points and more (Figure 5, page 380).

Several times between 1971 and 1986, there were drastic overhead cuts. Decreased sales or unexpected overhead costs always seemed to push the overhead percentage back up. One theory for GCS's high percentage of overhead to sales, which has credibility, is that GCS was a mini-conglomerate without the sales volume to carry the overhead load that this kind of business requires. Besides the three divisions there were a number of undertakings of the Cooperative such as the travel program, the legal services program, the cooperative apartments, and other so-called member benefits which required more than the resources of the member services division could maintain. In addition, there was a continual stream of new pilot efforts being tried or explored both related to the three divisions and in looking at other new businesses. Together these "extra" demands on staff and equipment required more resources than what was essentially needed to operate a lean business.

There was a popular belief that a significant part of the overhead was due to the democratic structure. This was NOT the case. Even though the member relations and education programs required servicing by many segments of the staff, the cost was not high. While there are no data available for identifying this area as a percentage of sales over a substantial period, records are available for the years 1977-1984. They show that the member relations and education budget for this period averaged .487 percent of sales. The Board and Congress budgets combined, averaged .168 percent of sales. Therefore, the costs of member programs plus those of the Board and Congress were, obviously, an insignificant part of the overhead. Unlike the consumer programs of for-profit corporations geared to sales, the cost of maintaining the democratic structure of GCS only tangentially contributed to generating business. From time to time, this led to a minority of management and the Board to advocate drastic cuts for this small budgetary item.

Net Income/Sales

This measure was discussed at the beginning of the chapter. The yearly variance was extremely troublesome to the Board. Even in the years where strikes took place in some of the other chains GCS was not able to capitalize on the event beyond the period in which the strike was active. In years where there were price wars in the food or petroleum arena, GCS was severely injured.

FIGURE 5: OVERHEAD TO TOTAL SALES, GREENBELT AND GIANT FOODS

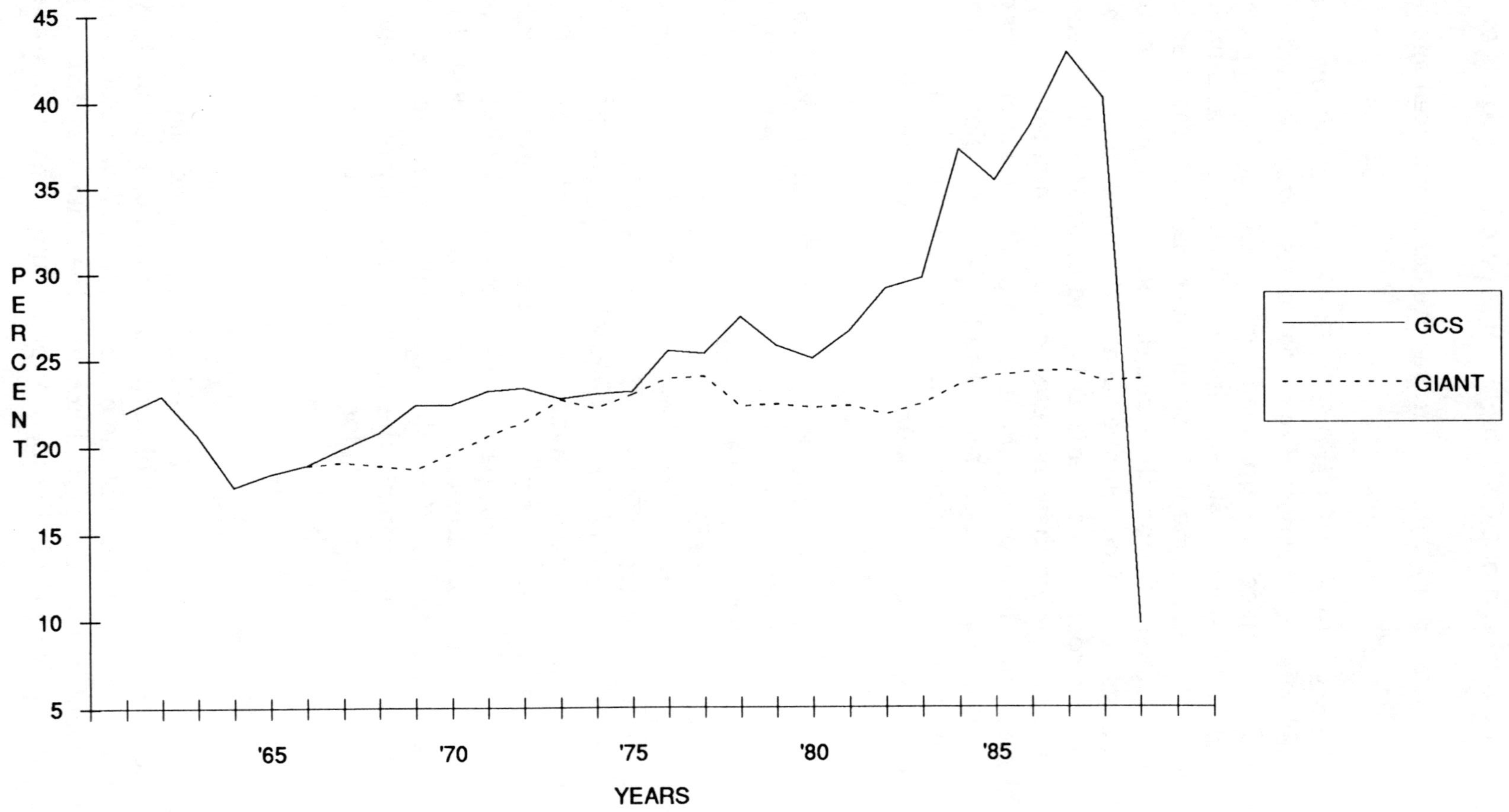

In 1976, the number of food stores was reduced to eight from the high of 23 in 1967-70. At that point the subsidy load for the furniture division became lighter and a trend of profitability began to take shape. Two years had downturns. In 1981, there was a downturn because of large losses in the food

operations caused largely by a 4-month price war and gross margins dropping from 14.7 to 8.6 percent in the petroleum division due to the oil glut. In 1983, there was also a downturn. This was due largely to the turmoil in the food and petroleum divisions as they were being divested.

Otherwise, the ten-year period was trending upwards, and with no more load to carry, the furniture operation appeared to have a bright future until the dollar dramatically weakened against the kroner in 1986 and the disastrous strike occurred in 1987. Total losses of 9.4 million dollars for 1986, 1987, and 1988 made it imperative for the Board to request Chapter 11 protection. It should be noted here that a competitor, Scandinavian Gallery, which had entered the GCS SCAN market area in 1984, also had severe losses and liquidated its entire chain of 65 stores in 1988.

LIQUIDITY

Current Assets/Current Liabilities (Current Ratio)

The current ratio varied widely during any given year. Using the year-end data, which is the only data available, the current ratio is not too shabby. After 1958, it never reached the desired, but rarely achieved, 2 to 1 level. However, as noted in Figure 6, page 382, it rarely was below 1.3 to 1. From 1970 thru 1978, the ratio hovered just above 1 to 1 and did fall to .99 to 1 in 1974. This was a grim period when attempts were made to pump new life into the food and petroleum divisions.

Inventory/Net Working Capital

The usual standard of not having inventory exceeding net working capital does not effectively apply in either the food retailing nor the imported furniture retailing businesses. However, the inventory/working capital ratio for GCS consistently exceeded even the most liberal ratio parameters. Against the safe standard of 1 to 1, the GCS ratio only fell below 2 to 1 prior to 1963 and in 1982 and 1983. Ironically, the best years (except for the very early ones) were 1979 through 1986. During the 1970s the problem of excessive SCAN inventory was legendary. Part of this was SCAN management's attempt to prevent use of funds for further forays into food operations. Table 3, page   , has the year-by-year information.

FIGURE 6: CURRENT RATIOS, GREENBELT AND GIANT FOODS

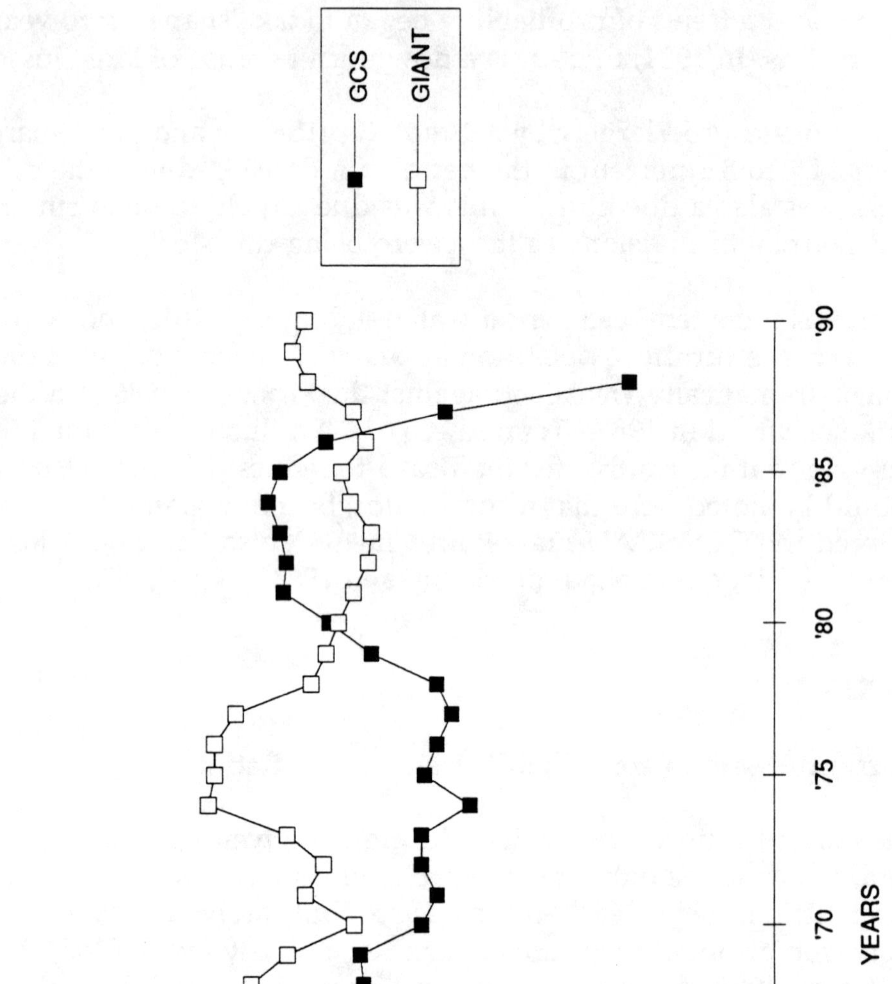

SOLVENCY

Total Debt/Total Assets

As one measure of determining the proportion of funds contributed by creditors, GCS exhibited excellent solvency during its history except for the period 1970-74 and, of course, the last two years 1987-88 (Figure 7, page 384).

Total Debt/Equity

The 9-year period 1970-79 were the only years where the debt/equity ratio was outside of acceptable norms, other than the final two years. Figure 8, page   , depicts a rather conservative approach to leveraging during the early years and from 1979 up to 1987.

Short-term borrowings, current portion of long-term debt and accounts payable plus the long-term debt , constituted GCS's total debt. The bulk of current debt was accounts payable and the line-of-credit, both of which were used for inventory purchases. These were always on the high side for furniture because GCS paid for, not only what was in the warehouse but also what was on the water being shipped. The furniture inventory was almost invariably used as the collateral for the line-of-credit.

From 1963 onwards accounts payable consistently were over 50 percent of total debt. Much of this was owed to the Danish furniture manufacturers. They in turn used these "IOUs" as collateral for their own borrowings in Denmark. Therefore, slow payment on the part of GCS materially impacted upon the manufacturers. After divestiture of the food and petroleum divisions accounts, payable dropped to the mid-forties as a percent of total debt as contrasted to high fifties and low sixties earlier. Table 3, pages 385-386.

Long-Term Debt/Equity

Long-term debt was used mostly for expansion purposes and, except for the "crisis" times, it was not used for operating capital. Figure 8, page 387, shows the same pattern for long-term debt as for total debt. One of GCS's problems was the difficulty of raising equity capital.

Long-Term Debt/Capitalization (Capitalization = Long-Term Debt plus Equity)

This is probably the strongest financial indicator for GCS. Using the industry standard of 40 percent (GCS used 45% in its 1981 Growth Plan) GCS only

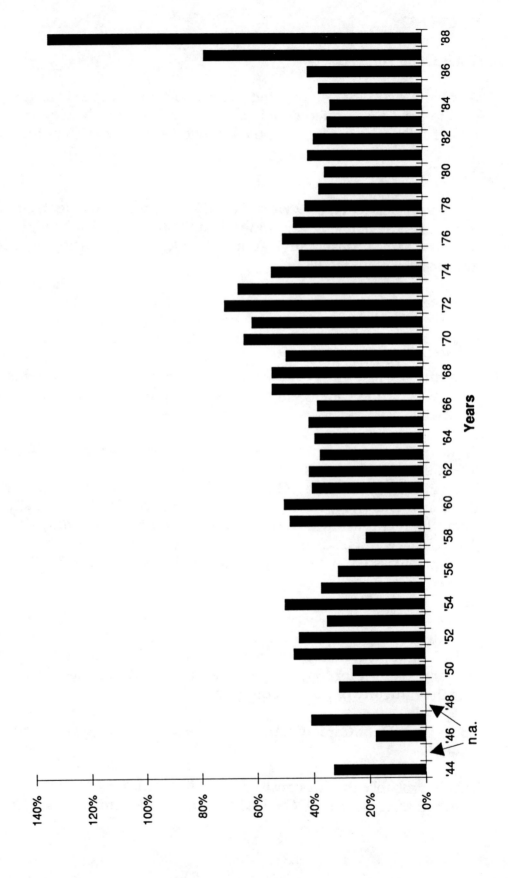

Figure 7: TOTAL DEBT AS PERCENT OF TOTAL ASSETS, GREENBELT

TABLE 3, FINANCIAL RATIOS AND FACILITIES OPERATED, GREENBELT COOPERATIVE, 1937-89

YEAR	$ MIL TOTAL DEBT	RATIO TOTAL DEBT TO TOTAL ASSETS	RATIO TOTAL DEBT TO EQUITY	% ACCTS PAYABLE TO TOTAL DEBT	$ MIL LONG TERM DEBT	RATIO LONG TERM DEBT TO EQUITY	% LONG TERM DEBT TO CAPITALIZATION	MEMBERS	EMPLOYEES	NUMBER OF FACILITIES			
										FOOD	SCAN	PETROLEUM	PHARMACY
'37	n.a.	n.a.	n.a.	n.a.	n.a.	n.a.	n.a.	n.a.	n.a.	1	--	0	0
'38	n.a.	n.a.	n.a.	n.a.	n.a.	n.a.	n.a.	n.a.	n.a.	1	--	1	1
'39	0.05	n.a.	n.a.	n.a.	0.04	9.99	92	303	n.a.	1	--	1	1
'40	0.04	n.a.	n.a.	n.a.	0.03	1.62	62	424	n.a.	1	--	1	1
'41	0.05	n.a.	n.a.	n.a.	0.02	n.a.	52	713	n.a.	1	--	1	1
'42	0.05	n.a.	n.a.	n.a.	0.02	n.a.	29	793	n.a.	1	--	1	1
'43	0.06	n.a.	n.a.	n.a.	0.01	n.a.	12	1,283	n.a.	2	--	1	1
'44	0.04	0.33	0.67	87.8	0.01	n.a.	8	1,403	n.a.	2	--	1	1
'45	0.05	n.a.	n.a.	n.a.	0.00	0.00	0	1,820	n.a.	2	--	1	1
'46	0.05	0.18	0.23	100.0	0.00	0.00	0	2,201	n.a.	2	--	1	1
'47	0.23	0.41	0.84	39.4	0.12	0.42	30	2,511	n.a.	2	--	1	1
'48	n.a.	n.a.	0.76	n.a.	0.12	0.38	28	2,506	n.a.	2	--	1	1
'49	0.17	0.31	0.46	36.9	0.09	0.25	20	2,605	n.a.	2	--	1	1
'50	0.15	0.26	0.38	38.5	0.07	0.18	16	2,678	n.a.	2	--	1	2
'51	0.43	0.47	0.97	46.7	0.21	0.48	32	3,378	n.a.	3	--	2	2
'52	0.42	0.45	0.80	48.7	0.18	0.34	25	3,547	n.a.	3	--	2	2
'53	0.32	0.35	0.56	41.9	0.15	0.26	21	4,004	n.a.	3	--	2	3
'54	0.75	0.50	1.08	48.4	0.35	0.50	33	5,503	n.a.	4	--	3	3
'55	0.61	0.37	0.72	41.6	0.32	0.37	27	6,896	n.a.	4	--	3	3
'56	0.56	0.31	0.56	48.3	0.25	0.25	20	11,027	n.a.	5	--	4	4
'57	0.52	0.27	0.42	48.1	0.23	0.19	16	12,584	n.a.	6	--	4	4
'58	0.43	0.21	0.31	76.2	0.19	0.14	12	14,026	n.a.	8	--	5	5
'59	2.04	0.48	1.04	25.8	1.00	0.49	33	19,013	n.a.	10	--	7	5
'60	2.70	0.50	1.20	20.0	1.50	0.67	40	22,496	n.a.	11	0	7	5
'61	1.90	0.40	0.84	38.9	1.00	0.45	31	23,393	n.a.	11	1	7	5
'62	1.80	0.41	0.86	37.8	0.90	0.43	30	n.a.	n.a.	11	2	7	5
'63	1.40	0.37	0.69	61.8	0.40	0.21	18	n.a.	n.a.	11	2	7	5
'64	1.60	0.39	0.79	69.6	0.40	0.18	15	n.a.	n.a.	12	3	7	5
'65	1.80	0.41	0.85	62.3	0.60	0.27	21	n.a.	n.a.	12	4	8	8
'66	1.70	0.38	0.75	57.8	0.60	0.26	20	n.a.	n.a.	13	5	8	8
'67	3.20	0.54	1.54	53.4	1.30	0.60	37	n.a.	n.a.	23	5	9	9
'68	3.40	0.54	1.58	55.6	1.10	0.52	34	27,907	923	22	5	8	6
'69	3.60	0.49	1.37	57.8	1.20	0.45	31	33,357	1010	21	5	9	5
'70	5.60	0.64	2.45	61.2	1.40	0.61	38	35,643	1061	22	6	11	5
'71	4.90	0.61	4.21	72.1	2.00	1.75	64	37,459	1023	21	8	10	5

TABLE 3 (continued)

YEAR	$ MIL. TOTAL DEBT	RATIO TOTAL DEBT TO TOTAL ASSETS	RATIO TOTAL DEBT TO EQUITY	% ACCTS PAYABLE TO TOTAL DEBT	$ MIL. LONG TERM DEBT	RATIO LONG TERM DEBT TO EQUITY	% LONG TERM DEBT TO CAPITALIZATION	MEMBERS	EMPLOYEES	NUMBER OF FACILITIES			
										FOOD	SCAN	PETROLEUM	PHARMACY
'72	5.90	0.71	8.65	52.7	2.30	3.00	77	38,411	875	16	8	10	4
'73	5.30	0.66	5.83	54.0	1.90	2.11	68	38,398	759	12	8	7	4
'74	5.00	0.54	4.45	61.9	1.10	0.97	49	38,347	771	13	8	7	3
'75	4.40	0.44	2.54	61.2	1.30	0.75	43	38,557	734	13	9	7	0
'76	4.80	0.50	3.13	70.8	1.20	0.81	45	38,592	588	8	10	7	0
'77	4.70	0.46	2.66	64.8	1.30	0.71	42	39,183	592	5	10	7	0
'78	4.40	0.42	2.04	61.2	0.50	0.23	19	40,014	524	6	10	7	0
'79	3.90	0.37	1.50	75.3	0.80	0.30	23	n.a.	n.a.	6	13	6	0
'80	4.70	0.35	1.53	73.3	1.10	0.35	26	n.a.	n.a.	6	13	6	0
'81	5.40	0.41	1.74	55.7	2.10	0.67	40	34,289	n.a.	6	13	6	0
'82	5.20	0.39	1.47	59.3	1.80	0.51	34	55,130	n.a.	6	13	5	0
'83	4.40	0.34	1.18	57.9	1.40	0.37	27	n.a.	n.a.	6	15	5	0
'84	3.90	0.33	1.01	43.0	1.00	0.26	20	n.a.	n.a.	0	16	0	0
'85	5.20	0.37	1.04	45.4	1.00	0.21	17	n.a.	n.a.	0	16	0	0
'86	5.30	0.41	1.25	40.8	0.70	0.16	14	116,018	n.a.	0	17	0	0
'87	9.50	0.78	N/M	43.4	2.00	N/M	100	116,018	n.a.	0	17	0	0
'88	8.90	1.34	N/M	61.8	0*	N/M		116,018	n.a.	0	8	0	0
'89	n.a.	n.a.	n.a.	n.a.	0.00	n.a.		n.a.	n.a.	0	8	0	0

* All became current

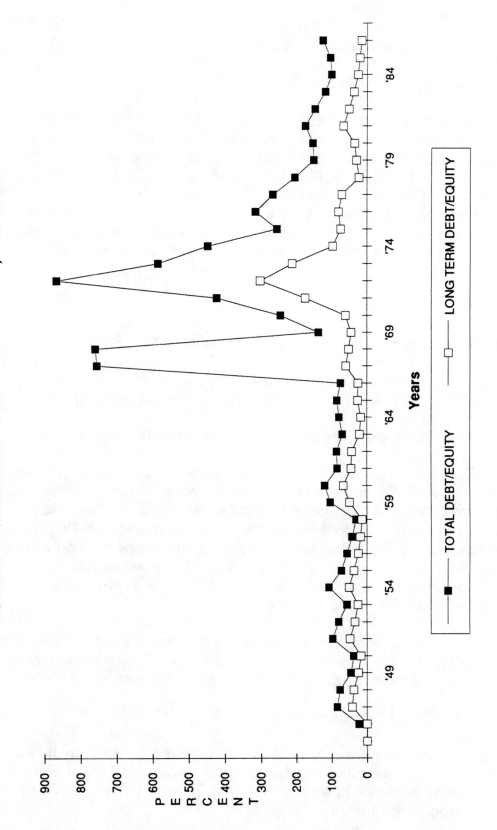

FIGURE 8: PERCENTAGE OF DEBT TO EQUITY, GREENBELT

exceeded 40 percent from 1939-41, 1971-77, and at the end, 1987-88 (Figure 9, page 389).

OTHER FINANCIAL INDICATORS

Interest Expense/Sales

There were many members attending area council meetings over the years who felt that interest expense was a major problem for GCS. In examining the data, it does not appear that interest expense, per se, was ever a problem. From 1981 it was on the high side, reaching one percent in 1984 and in 1987 and 1988 it exceeded one percent. Prior to that it rarely reached an acceptable one-half percent of sales. In fact, a far greater problem in many years was the inability, because of cash shortage, of GCS to take advantage of cash discounts. Those losses exceeded interest costs as a percent of sales. Table 3, pages 385-386, has the yearly interest expense to sales.

Member Investment

Each share of member stock had a par value of $10. Since it could not be traded on the market its value remained at $10 or below, thereby not providing real incentive to invest except as needed to vote, participate in any patronage refunds, and the possibility of a modest dividend on the stock.

Because GCS was incorporated under the Maryland regular business corporate code, to become a member/owner required an individual to buy shares of stock. This required GCS to file with the Securities Exchange Commission to register and seek approval to sell membership shares vis-a-vis a cooperative incorporated under a cooperative code that would not have shares but would only have membership fees. This was a costly process. In 1980, it was estimated that the average cost per year of the prospectus and related expenses was $82,833. To recover this cost would require selling 8,284 shares annually, a feat almost never accomplished. Table 2, pages 377-378, lists the annual shares outstanding and number of members.

The closest GCS ever came to adequate member investment after the early years was the sale of subordinated debentures. This program was quite successful during the 1970s. Of course, debentures are debt, not equity.

Dividends and Patronage Refunds

Cash dividends were paid on shares from 1939 until 1972. In 1940 and 1941 it was 3 percent and all other years it was 5 percent. In 1980, dividends of 8 percent were paid followed by 4 percent the next 3 years. No dividends were paid from 1984 onward.

388

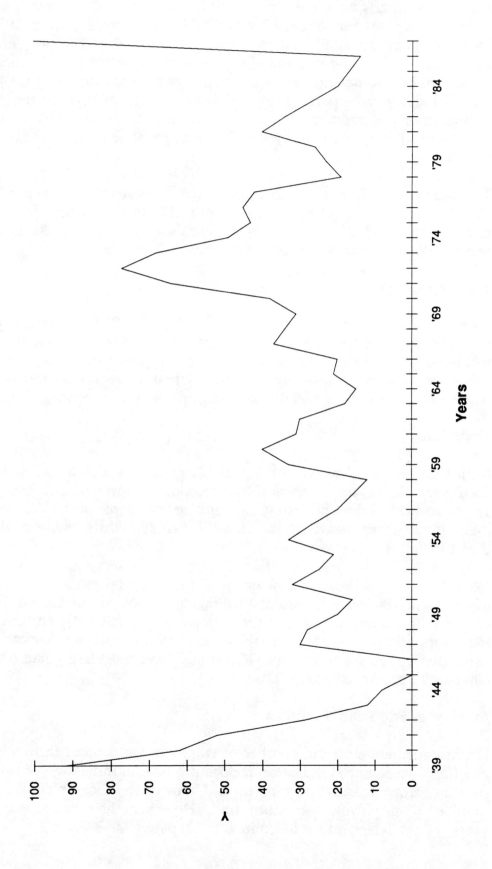

FIGURE 9: LONG TERM DEBT/CAPITALIZATION, GREENBELT

Years

389

Patronage refunds were paid in cash or in shares from 1939 through 1959. They were resumed in 1972 for 3 years, 1975 was skipped, paid in 1976, and then not again until 1981 and continued through 1985. The percentage varied each year. In the latter years the Board was faced with one of its most vexing problems, how to balance the equability of paying dividends to the long-time shareholders, paying patronage refunds to the current users of the Cooperative, and repurchasing shares from the many who had requested that their shares be repurchased by the Cooperative, effectively the only market for shares.

The issue was addressed by allocating funds each year for the repurchase of stock, setting a dividend rate of 4 percent and paying a patronage refund at a rate to be decided after the audited financials were available. This satisfied no one but did represent a compromise among all parties.

Working Capital

Working capital was a critical problem during the 1970s, making expansion decisions difficult because of the increase needed in working capital whenever a new retail facility was opened. Unfortunately this problem ran concurrently with the need for GCS to overhaul its food operations. Table 2, pages 377-378, has the annual year-end position of net working capital.

Cash Flow

Each year the Board received the monthly projected cash flow for the coming fiscal year. It was this projection that prompted approval of so many and varied sources of debt financing. It was also the source of the debates mentioned earlier regarding the SCAN inventory which many of the directors felt was excessive.

Conversely it was the cash flow generated by the retail outlets that kept GCS afloat during the crisis period of 1970 through 1979. While GCS did lose its cash discounts, the cooperative was able to keep sufficiently current with most suppliers and pay COD to the others. Without the weekly cash flow generated by the supermarkets, GCS would have most likely had to file for Chapter 11 protection at that time.

Employees and Retail Facilities

While information on the number of employees and retail facilities hardly qualifies as a financial indicator, it does provide an indication of the changes resulting from financial performance. Unfortunately, complete records of numbers of employees were not found. However, the numbers for the peak years are available and are listed in Table 2, pages 377-378.

At the peak, 1970, there were 1,061 employees. 1970 was also the peak in the number of retail facilities (45) operated by GCS (Table 3, pages 385-386). Peak facilities in each of the divisions was reached in:

1967 - 23 food stores
1967 - 9 pharmacies
1970 - 11 service stations
1985 - 17 furniture stores

BOTTOM LINE PERFORMANCE

There are many latitudes permitted (or tolerated) in a cooperative that are totally unacceptable in a proprietary business. One of those is sustained losses in one part of a business that requires major subsidizing over a long period by a successful part of the business.

Genuine differences of philosophy existed among the leadership of Greenbelt. Some, a majority during the 1970s, believed that the Cooperative must provide goods or services that kept the members in frequent contact with their Cooperative and that resulted in shopping much more frequently than would be the normal case with furniture purchases. For the most part, they saw nothing wrong with the business practice of subsidizing the food division heavily. Others believed that every effort should be made to make the food division profitable at the bottom line and if that was not possible it should be divested.

This difference in philosophy created major cleavages among the Area councils, Congress, and Board leadership. In a lesser way it also created conflict in top management.

Starting in 1964, SCAN became a highly significant factor in net earnings of the Cooperative. By 1966, SCAN was covering all of its allocated overhead and contributing over $200,00 to net income. Except for 1975, the food division never covered its allocated overhead after 1960, much less contributed to net income.

The pharmacy division also struggled, but the petroleum seemed to be a winner until the early 70s when it, too, came to hard times.

Figure 10, page 391, and Table 4, page 393, shows the contribution each division made for the years 1977-84 toward overhead and net income. The petroleum division contributed significantly to overhead in four of the years while the food division made virtually no contribution.

FIGURE 10: CONTRIBUTION TO OVERHEAD AND NET INCOME BY DIVISION, GREENBELT

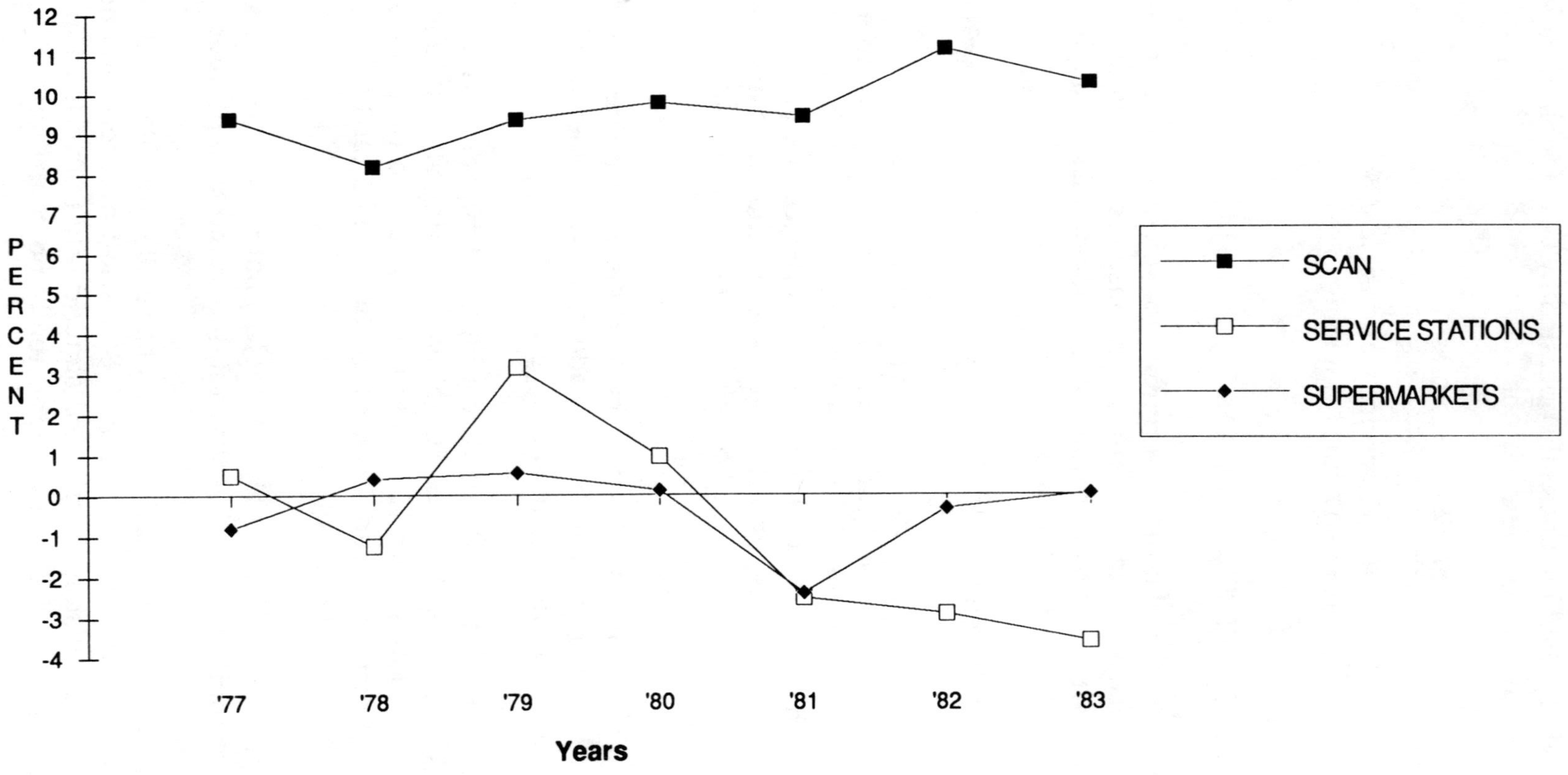

TABLE 4

Greenbelt Division Share of Sales, Contributions, and Operating Profit, 1977-84

	1977	1978	1979	1980	1981	1982	1983	1984
Percent of Sales								
SCAN	39	45	48	50	50	57	59	93
Supermarkets	49	45	41	38	40	37	35	0
Gas Stations	10	9	11	12	10	6	6	0
Scan-Chicago								7
Division Contribution								
SCAN	9.361	8.173	9.343	9.766	9.388	11.106	10.243	9.032
Supermarkets	-0.809	0.412	0.559	0.128	-2.403	-0.327	0.054	0
Gas Stations	0.493	-1.232	3.158	0.969	-2.529	-2.911	-3.588	0
Perishables	-5.138	-3.478	–					
Scan-Chicago								-26.857
Operating Profit								
SCAN	5.807	4.897	7.246	7.415	7.467	8.280	7.420	5.346
Supermarkets	-3.097	-1.929	-1.063	-1.181	-3.698	-1.531	-1.125	–
Gas Stations	-2.320	-3.695	-1.776	-0.481	-4.134	-4.459	-4.935	–
Perishables	-7.040	-5.049						

Figure 11, page 394 , shows that only SCAN covered its allocated overhead (and its interest) and contributed the only net income to the Cooperative. In an analysis computed by management for the years 1978-80, and by using three different methods of calculating ROI, SCAN ROI ranged from 22.6 to 64.6 percent

THE FOOD DIVISION

During 1960-62, there was an explosion of new supermarkets built in the GCS market area, many of which were within steps of GCS existing stores. 1961 saw the beginning of major price wars as the chains jockeyed for market share. The new supermarkets were more modern than those of GCS and GCS did not have the capital to do major remodeling in every key location. The competition took significant amounts of business from many of GCS's stores. Management countered by developing a discount program; and although the three years of 1961-63 were rocky in terms of net savings (earnings), GCS rebounded with record earnings in 1964.

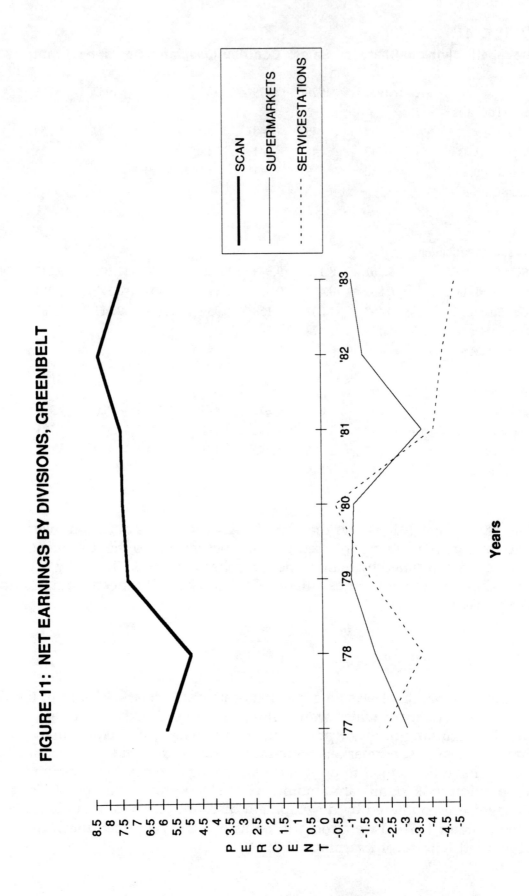

FIGURE 11: NET EARNINGS BY DIVISIONS, GREENBELT

SCAN
SUPERMARKETS
SERVICESTATIONS

Years

Warning indicators of serious problems in the food operations, however, were already flashing. Although improved, net income as a percent of sales was considerably below the industry average in GCS's market area. For example, even during the price-war years (1961-63) Giant Food earned an average of 1.03 percent on sales. GCS earned .027 percent. For the following three years, Giant earned an average of 1.14 which was only slightly above the industry average of 1.07. GCS earned an average of .53 percent even with four SCAN stores which carried a much higher gross margin than the other products sold by GCS.

In 1967, the opportunity to reach a 5-year growth objective in the food operation in one fell swoop was too much of a temptation for Board and management to resist and GCS purchased the Kroger stores when Kroger abandoned the Greater Washington market. This move increased long-term debt by 123 percent and total debt by 95 percent. While both net earnings in dollars and as a percentage of sales increased during 1968 and 1969, the amounts were far short of industry averages. The Kroger acquisition improved GCS presence in the market place, but the stores were not performing as well as expected.

The Boards from 1970-1983 were faced with an array of financial decisions, most of which focused on the food operation's survival rather than growth and expansion of the cooperative.

The Board minutes from those years show that the decisions about financing did not seem to have a consistent plan. Part of this, of course, was born of the necessity of finding sufficient working capital to meet the daily expenses to operate. Working capital during many of those years was below bare minimum and in 1974 it even was a negative figure. Cash flow emanating from the food stores and accounts payable (what was owed currently to vendors) kept the cooperative afloat.

During the years 1971 to 1983, many innovations (for GCS) were tried. Box stores, discount operations, natural foods, cost-plus (a variation of the direct charge food operations so successful in Canada), free standing perishable foods stores, pre-order programs, major and cosmetic remodeling, changed management including a supervisory service from a wholesaler, changed suppliers, and closure of the heaviest losers were all tried in an effort to "save" the food stores. Three new ones, including two perishable foods stores, were opened. All of these new efforts failed and none of the new openings ever covered even their allocated division costs.

Following is a more detailed analysis of the food division which sets forth, graphically, why some of the directors increasingly felt that the food stores should be divested.

Figure 12, page 397, gives the graphic story of the food store losses. From 1971 to 1983, $7,174,656 was lost. Perhaps even more important, the time and energy of central management and the Board was devoted to addressing the woes of the supermarket division. This left little time to address either the shaky service station division or to develop direction for a highly successful SCAN.

One director, after viewing the millions being lost, said in 1980, "Hobbies are interesting. This hobby has cost our members over five million dollars."

During the period 1977-1983, seven food stores operated at least part of that time (Table 5, see below). Figures 13, pages 398-400 and Table 6, pages 401-402, show the contribution at the store line each year and the net income after division and overhead allocations had been made. The store at Fairlington saw a net income in 1979 and 1980. The store at Kensington did the same in 1978 and 1979. Otherwise all had losses. The new cost-plus store that opened in Severna Park proved to be a disaster. Finally, as was noted earlier, the division was divested along with the petroleum division.

THE FURNITURE DIVISION (SCAN)

In sharp contract to the losses of the food division, SCAN was performing well. How much better it could have done if it would have received as much attention as did the food division is, of course, speculative. Figure 14, page 403, shows that for the 8 years 1977-84 SCAN contributed $14.8 million while GCS had net earnings of only $3.4 million.

Table 5
Number of Retail Outlets by Type Operated by Greenbelt, 1977-84

	SCAN	Supermarkets	Gas Stations	POPS
1977	11	7	7	2*
1978	13	7	7	2*
1979	12	6	7	0
1980	12	6	6	0
1981	12	6	5	0
1982	12	6	5	0
1983	17	5	4	2
1984	16	0	0	2

The rise of SCAN merits its own historical perspective, not only because of its unique nature and unprecedented success, but also because it was in many

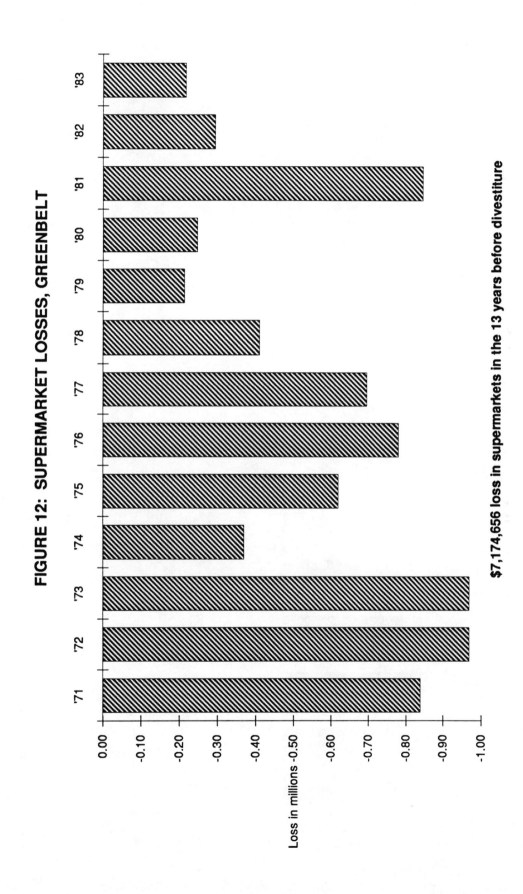

FIGURE 12: SUPERMARKET LOSSES, GREENBELT

$7,174,656 loss in supermarkets in the 13 years before divestiture

FIGURE 13: PERFORMANCE BY STORE

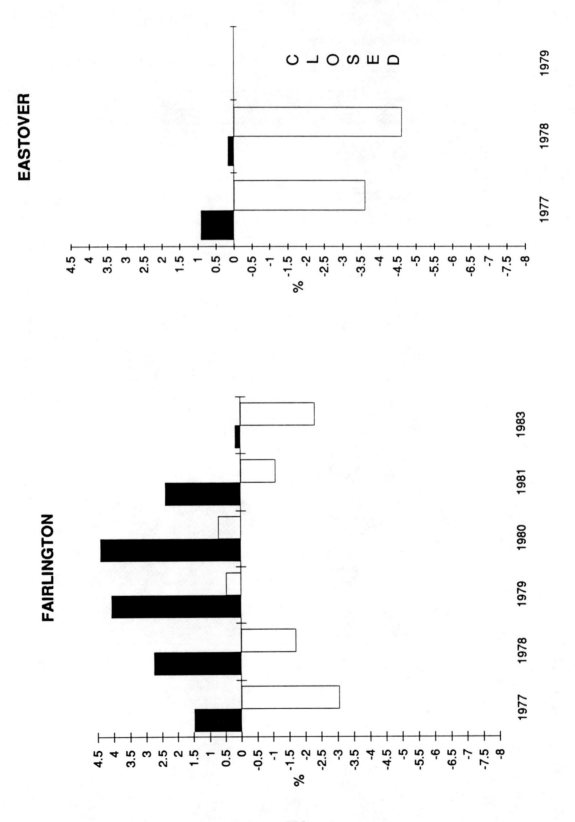

FIGURE 13 (continued)

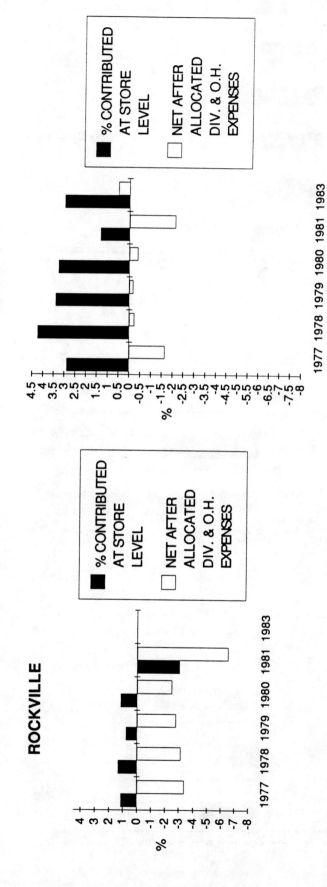

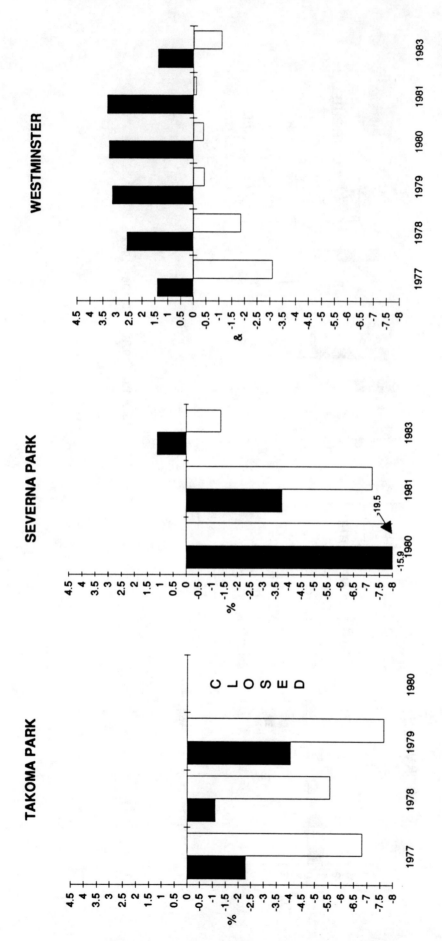

FIGURE 13 (continued)

400

TABLE 6
Store Contributions, Allocated Division and Overhead, and Net Earnings for GCS Supermarkets

	Store Contributions %	Allocated Division and Overhead %	Net Earnings %
Greenbelt			
1977	3.172	4.527	-1.355
1978	4.907	4.460	0.447
1979	4.718	3.584	1.134
1980	3.224	3.668	-0.444
1981	-3.181	3.471	-6.652
1982	--	--	--
1983	0.193	2.482	-2.289
1984			
Takoma Park			
1977	-2.290	4.527	-6.817
1978	-1.107	4.460	-5.567
1979	-4.058	3.584	-7.642
Westminster			
1977	1.420	4.527	-3.107
1978	2.602	4.460	-1.858
1979	3.159	3.584	-0.425
1980	3.280	3.668	-0.388
1981	3.355	3.471	-0.116
1982	--	--	--
1983	1.392	2.482	-1.090
Rockville			
1977	1.148	4.527	-3.379
1978	1.338	4.460	-3.122
1979	0.780	3.584	-2.804
1980	1.162	3.668	-2.506
1981	3.044	3.471	-6.515
Fairlington			
1977	1.480	4.527	-3.047
1978	2.757	4.460	-1.703
1979	4.056	3.584	0.472
1980	4.386	3.668	0.718
1981	2.375	3.471	-1.096
1982	--	--	--
1983	0.166	2.482	-2.316

Table 6 (continued)

Kensington

1977	2.882	4.507	-1.645
1978	4.239	4.460	-0.221
1979	3.414	3.584	-0.107
1980	3.282	3.668	-0.386
1981	1.345	3.471	-2.126
1982	--	--	--
1983	3.007	2.482	0.525

Eastover

1977	0.918	4.527	-3.609
1978	-0.156	4.460	-4.616

Severna Park

1980	-15.893	3.668	-19.531
1981	-3.746	3.471	-7.217
1982	--	--	--
1983	1.121	2.482	-1.361

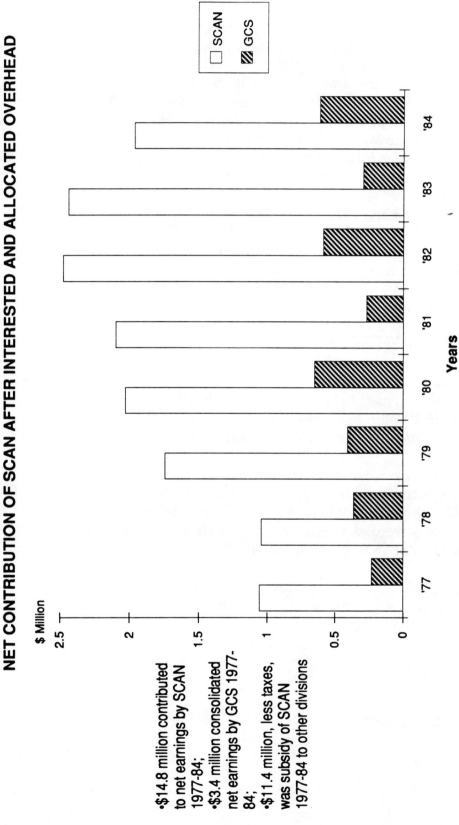

FIGURE 14: NET INCOME OF GCS AFTER INTEREST AND TAXES COMPARED TO NET CONTRIBUTION OF SCAN AFTER INTERESTED AND ALLOCATED OVERHEAD

$ Million

2.5

2

1.5

1

0.5

0

SCAN
GCS

'77 '78 '79 '80 '81 '82 '83 '84

Years

•$14.8 million contributed to net earnings by SCAN 1977-84;

•$3.4 million consolidated net earnings by GCS 1977-84;

•$11.4 million, less taxes, was subsidy of SCAN 1977-84 to other divisions

ways a separate occurrence from the rest of GCS. Certainly, its fall was largely separate and apart from what went before 1984.

As related in Chapter X, SCAN began as one of the one-time-only special purchases for which the chief executive of GCS was so well known and practiced so ardently in the late 50s. After visiting several of the Scandinavian consumer wholesale cooperatives, including their furniture manufacturing operations, he arranged to buy a large quantity of a limited number of items for sale to GCS members. He believed that the quality, design, and low cost of their furniture would appeal to Washingtonians. He was right. The initial response was wildly enthusiastic. What started out to be a special purchase program soon became a separate division (1960). By 1962, the first free standing cooperative furniture store was opened next to the co-op supermarket in the Takoma Park Shopping Center.

The SCAN name and logo were first used in 1963, the same year that a second SCAN store was opened in Falls Church, Virginia. Until 1964, SCAN's development followed the same course as the other two small divisions—pharmacy and service stations. All followed the supermarkets to new locations and were assumed to be dependent upon food-shopping members and patrons for traffic.

In 1964, SCAN broke out of the cluster pattern of expansion when a small store was opened in downtown Washington. The store was immediately successful. With but one exception, all later SCAN stores were located independent of other facilities of the Cooperative.

SCAN's separate and different development route offered GCS a means of greatly increasing the size, geographic dispersion, and diversity of its membership. It provided needed diversification at a time when GCS's other businesses were experiencing grave difficulties. From 1961 to 1970, SCAN sales grew at an impressive rate of 55 percent per year.

Although SCAN grew at a rapid rate from 1962 through 1986, the pattern of growth was very uneven as noted in the following table.

Change in number of SCAN stores, 1962-1989

YEAR	STORES OPENED	STORES CLOSED	YEAR	STORES OPENED	STORES CLOSED
1962	1		1977	2	
1963	1		1978	1	1
1964	1		1979	1	
1965	1		1980	0	
1967	0		1981	2	1
1968	2		1982	0	
1969	0		1983	2	
1970	1	1	1984	1	
1971	1		1985	1	
1972	0		1986	0	
1973	0		1987	0	
1974	0		1988	0	
1975	1		1989	0	9
1976	1				

Two imperative questions surface. First, why was SCAN not expanded during two key periods, 1965-1968 and 1971-75, when the economy was strong and the Washington market growing rapidly? From 1965 to 1981 there were only four stores added, the same number opened in only 4 years in the early 1960s. A policy of continuously opening new stores at "hot" locations could have been one important way of pre-empting competition. Many other successful retailers, from Sears in the 1920s to Seven-Eleven in the 1970s have used the approach of saturating a market area with retail outlets in order to achieve market dominance before the competition has a chance to respond.

The principal reason for SCAN's sub optimal growth rate was the lack of cash for investment in inventory and leasehold improvement. From a purely financial standpoint, the expansion of SCAN after 1966 and particularly during the 1970s was slowed markedly by the use of furniture division profits elsewhere in GCS operations. Had SCAN earnings been reinvested and the additional debt capacity used, SCAN might have more than doubled its sales and contribution.

The irony of GCS's failure to expand SCAN to its full potential was that every management plan of the late 60s and early 70s made SCAN growth the number one priority. In the 1967 plan, released only weeks before the Kroger acquisition, management stated that "the furniture division has preference for expansion." This language was echoed in subsequent documents through 1975. Yet management pushed through the Kroger deal with virtually no thought (apparently) for its effect on SCAN's growth. Again in 1969, a wholesale tire operation was purchased, a business that had only marginal relationship to the Cooperative's objectives and needs. Throughout the early 1970s, supermarkets which were chronic money losers were remodeled with funds from SCAN operating profits. By failing to exercise enough discipline to follow its own advice, management stunted SCAN's growth. Where was the Board? Both management and the Board by their decisions left GCS in a weak financial condition.

The second question is, "Why didn't GCS expand SCAN into market areas outside of Maryland and Virginia?" Bob Gowell, the long time head of SCAN, believed that SCAN should saturate the Maryland/Virginia market before expanding outside. To a degree this was probably a good strategy. On the other hand, it constrained SCAN from entering into three joint ventures with other cooperatives. Additionally, the majority of GCS Congress members felt that moving outside of the area would not be serving current GCS members. The Board was usually evenly split on the issue.

Throughout its history until 1986, SCAN had been highly successful. It met the challenge of two competitors, one a long established chain in the Washington area that began selling Scandinavian furniture and the second a chain similar to SCAN. Headquartered in Massachusetts, this chain had more stores than SCAN, and at the time was the most rapidly growing of the SCAN-type furniture stores in the country.

SCAN had been the cash cow of the Cooperative. Drained of its cash to sustain the other divisions for so many years, it did not have the reserves to withstand a catastrophic drop in the dollar's value to the kroner in 1986. That uncontrollable event plus the drawn out strike brought SCAN to the brink of extinction.

The Chapter 11 negotiations resulted in a court approved "Plan" that permits SCAN to continue to operate, albeit with a different ownership structure (see Epilogue in Chapter XXI).

SCAN's success, and indeed its existence today, is in no small measure due to the close and symbiotic relationship between SCAN and its Scandinavian suppliers. For the most part, the suppliers (the furniture makers) are small, almost like a cottage industry. Certainly at the beginning all but a couple were small, family operated factories.

Five of the factories supplying SCAN today were original suppliers. These were the furniture factories of:

1. Hundevad, founded by Aage Hundevad and later owned by his son, Bent.
2. Moller, founded by Niels Otto Moller and now owned by sons, Ole and Jonne.

3. O. D. Furniture, founded by Aage Christensen and now owned by his son Niels.
4. Tarm, owned formerly by FBD (The Danish Consumer Wholesale Cooperative) and at that time managed by Folke Palsson and now the Managing Director is Arne Kvist.
5. Vejle, owned by brothers Arne and Peder Petersen.

Two others have also been supplying SCAN for most of its history and along with those above are currently part owners of Scan International:

1. Jesper, founded by Hugo Jespersen and now owned by his son Niels.
2. Skovby, owned by Villy Rasmussen.

Jesper was SCAN's largest supplier and SCAN was Jesper's largest account. The only non-Danish supplier of note was Ekornes which began supplying the popular stressless chair to SCAN in 1975. Over $20 million of these chairs were sold by SCAN. It was founded by the Ekornes brothers.

The underpinning of SCAN's Danish connection was, and is, Nordisk Andels Export (NAE). Holger Overgaard, the CEO, began managing SCAN's affairs in Scandinavia in 1966 and continues today. This relationship alone gave SCAN a great competitive advantage. It also provided vistas of opportunities which were never exercised. Steen Hansen and Hanna Rud-Petersen are long-serving staff members who have aided materially in cementing a strong relationship between NAE and SCAN.

In 1970, a joint venture was incorporated, NORDISCAN, owned by NAE and SCAN. The purpose of NORDISCAN was to serve as the agent for SCAN in all of its transactions with suppliers from Scandinavia. This included order placement, shipping arrangements, negotiation with suppliers, management of SCAN's funds banked in Denmark, and payment to suppliers. NORDISCAN was dissolved in 1989. However, NAE continued the broad functions thereafter.

The relationship between the Danish furniture manufacturers and GCS/SCAN has always been close. Several events demonstrate that relationship:

1. In 1973, 20 manufacturers were represented at SCAN stores where their staffs explained furniture making to customers.

2. In 1973, Robert Gowell, GCS Vice President heading SCAN, was awarded the prestigious Danish Export Oscar.

3. In 1976, Queen Margrethe of Denmark visited a SCAN store for her only commercial visit while in the United States. GCS Board and SCAN

management were guests of the Danish embassy and the Queen at the Royal Danish Ballet performing at the Kennedy Center with a reception afterwards.

4. In 1982, 40 Danish furniture manufacturers attended a dinner hosted by GCS in Copenhagen during the furniture fair where the President of the Danish Furniture Manufacturers and the Chairman of GCS presented SCAN expansion opportunities.

5. In 1984, all but one of the GCS Board visited the Furniture Fair in Copenhagen and selected manufacturers.

6. In 1985, over 20 Danish manufacturers attended SCAN's 25th Anniversary celebration.

7. Since 1976, the Board Chairman of GCS/SCAN has attended the Furniture Fair in Copenhagen with but three exceptions.

8. For over 25 years SCAN staff went to Denmark to learn about quality control, manufacturing processes, and the people behind the furniture which SCAN imported. SCAN's sales force were more knowledgeable than any other sales force selling Scandinavian furniture in the United States.

9. From 1984 until 1988, SCAN awarded prizes in an annual furniture design contest. The awards were announced during the Danish Furniture Fair.

10. A special effort to generate synergism between SCAN and its suppliers was made under the tenure of Carsten Sorth's Presidency of the Danish Furniture Manufacturer Association. An untimely stroke shortened his tenure and, along with other factors, aborted some joint efforts for SCAN expansion.

IN CLOSING

The analysis in this chapter clearly shows that the decisions by the Board maintained and subsidized many "losing" operations far beyond when prudent business decisions would dictate otherwise.

Even though many of the business ratios met acceptable standards in many years of GCS's history, it appears obvious that GCS lacked a coherent financial plan. Particularly from 1976 onward, the leadership struggled to devise an effective plan to generate equity while at the same time repurchase shares from those who had requested repurchase. An acceptable plan was never found. Opportunities to expand SCAN, which would have generated equity through net earnings, were continually rejected by a majority of the board. Consequently, in years when available equity could have been more greatly leveraged, new SCAN openings did not occur.

While the financial health of GCS was not outstanding, the analysis in this chapter indicates that during much of its history, the financial health was not that bad either. GCS had every chance for success after 1983 when the food and service station divisions were divested. How decisions on marketing, pricing, labor and management might have been different following divestment can only be a matter of speculation. Those that were made resulted in requesting Chapter 11 protection.

BIBLIOGRAPHY

Arnold, Joseph L., THE NEW DEAL IN THE SUBURBS, Ohio State
University   Press, 1971.

Grout, Phil, 50 YEARS OF SERVICE, Carroll County Co-op Foundation, Inc.,
Westminster, Maryland, 1987.

Halbert, Leroy A., REMINISCENSES OF A COOPERATOR, unpublished
manuscript written in 1957.

Warner, George A., GREENBELT; THE COOPERATIVE COMMUNITY,
Exposition Press, New York, 1954.

Williamson, Mary Lou, GREENBELT: HISTORY OF A NEW TOWN, 1937-
1987, The Donning Co., Norfolk, Virginia, 1987.

ACKNOWLEDGEMENT

Tugwell Room, Greenbelt Library, Crescent Road, Greenbelt, Maryland
20770.

THE GREENBELT COOPERATOR (now NEWS-REVIEW), Greenbelt,
Maryland 20770. Published weekly by the Greenbelt Cooperative Publishing
Association, Inc., for more than 50 years without missing an issue.

Appendix A. List of Directors on GCS/GCI Boards of Directors

Directors	Elected or Appointed	From	To
Howard C. Custer	E	1-2-40	10-9-41
Sherrod East	E	1-2-40	5-21-40
Carnie Harper	E	1-3-40	8-6-41
	E	8-23-44	3-7-51
Joseph Loftus	E	1-2-40	8-7-40
Bertha Maryn	E	1-2-40	8-7-40
	A	8-3-45	6-14-46
Joe W. Still	E	1-2-40	10-9-40
Earl J. Swailes	E	1-2-40	8-7-40
Walter R. Volckhausen	E	1-2-40	8-12-40
	E	12-24-43	11-8-46
Fred L. Wilde	E	1-2-40	2-5-41
Donald H. Wagstaff	A	5-21-40	2-5-41
Lindsey Thomas	E	8-7-40	2-5-41
Denzil Wood	E	8-7-40	8-5-42
George Treiman	E	8-7-40	8-6-41
Milton Thurber	A	11-20-40	2-5-41
Charles Fitch	E	2-5-41	8-12-41
Ella Roller	E	2-5-41	2-4-42
Lloyd MacEwen	E	2-5-41	2-4-42
G. Edward Timmons	A	2-27-41	8-6-41
Clifford A. Moyer	E	8-6-41	6-3-43
Charles W. Adams	E	8-6-41	10-9-41
Francis J. Lastner	E	8-6-41	11-24-43
	E	2-27-46	9-23-49
W. Earl Thomas	A	8-12-41	2-4-42
Tessim Zorach	A	8-12-41	
	E	2-4-41	12-3-42
Harry B. Hyman	A	10-9-41	8-5-42
Lincoln H. Clark	A	10-9-41	
	E	2-4-42	2-3-43
Fred A. DeJaeger	E	2-4-42	2-3-43
Carl W. Hintz	E	2-4-42	2-16-44
Mary M. Dodson	E	2-4-42	2-16-44
Paul Dunbard	E	8-5-42	8-23-44
Dayton W. Hull	E	8-5-42	11-24-43
	E	2-28-45	1-9-48
Paul Barnhart	A	12-4-42	
	E	2-3-43	2-16-44
John Dombeck	E	2-3-43	2-16-44
Benjamin Goldfadden	A	6-10-43	11-24-43

413

Donald H. Cooper	E	11-24-43	9-26-45
	E	6-3-58	5-17-68
George M. Eshbaugh	E	11-24-43	9-27-46
Allen A. Bryan	E	2-16-48	2-28-45
James A. Flynn	E	2-16-45	2-28-45
Clarke M. George	E	2-16-44	9-30-44
Yates F. Smith	E	2-16-44	2-28-45
Allen D. Morrison	A	10-13-44	
	E	2-28-45	2-27-46
Herman Ramrus	E	2-28-45	9-13-46
Maj. Adelbert C. Long	E	2-28-45	7-17-45
Edward C. Kaign	E	2-28-45	2-27-46
Thomas B. Ritchie	E	2-28-45	6-22-45
	E	12-2-46	9-15-48
Frank E. Watson	A	7-13-45	9-21-45
Fordyce H. Merian	E	9-26-45	9-18-46
William Nicholas	A	9-21-45	2-27-46
	A	6-28-46	2-26-47
	E	8-27-47	9-15-48
Phillips M. Taylor	E	2-27-46	2-26-47
Bruce Bowman	A	9-27-46	7-1-47
	E	6-1-74	6-13-85
David Granahan	A	11-8-46	
	E	12-2-46	10-10-47
James Walsh	A	11-8-46	12-2-46
Robert F. Dove	E	12-2-46	8-27-47
Elisa East	E	2-26-47	11-28-47
Cyrilla O'Conner	E	2-26-47	2-25-48
Delbert Mesner	A	7-25-47	
	E	2-25-48	10-1-48
William A. Moore	A	11-14-47	2-15-48
Paul R. Kasco	A	1—48	2-25-48
	A	2-27-48	
	E	9-15-48	12-1-50
Benjamin Rosenzweig	A	1-9-48	
	E	2-25-48	2-15-50
	A	9-22-50	3-7-51
	E	4-1-53	6-3-58
	E	16-24-60	5-28-69
	E	9-7-72	6-7-75
Walter J. Bierwagen	E	2-25-48	5-4-58
Richard W. Cooper	E	2-25-48	8-27-48
James N. Wolfe	E	9-15-48	2-23-49
Henry R. Walter	E	9-15-48	4-1-53
T. George Davidson	A	10-1-48	
	E	2-23-49	6-12-57

Chester H. Tucker	A	10-8-48	2-23-49
	A	7-22-49	10-14-49
Charlotte M. Walsh	E	2-23-49	7-22-49
Edward W. Meredith	E	2-23-49	6-10-49
Robert T. Mitchell	A	9-23-49	
	E	11-2-49	3-5-52
Carolyn R. Miller	A	10-14-49	
	E	11-2-49	3-7-51
	E	5-26-55	6-19-59
John W. S. Littleton	E	11-2-49	9-22-50
Eleanor H. Ritchie	E	2-15-50	3-5-52
	A	6-6-52	7-18-52
Martin Bickford	A	12-1-50	3-5-52
Milton Kramer	E	3-7-51	3-5-52
Calman R. Winegarten	E	3-7-51	4-1-53
Opie Stage	E	3-7-51	3-5-52
Morris J. Solomon	E	3-5-52	4-1-53
William C. Arntz	E	3-5-52	4-1-53
	E	5-26-55	6-14-62
Harry Zubkoff	E	3-5-52	4-14-54
Sam Schwimer	E	3-5-52	5-26-55
Charles A. Bicking	E	3-5-52	6-6-52
Frank W. Lewis	A	8-14-52	
	E	4-1-53	5-26-55
	E	6-20-65	1-1-70
Bryan K. Gamble	E	4-1-53	4-14-54
Max F. Fisher	E	4-1-53	4-14-54
Larry Oosterhous	E	4-1-53	6-24-60
Robert T. Bonham	E	4-14-54	4-7-62
Robert C. Hull	E	4-14-54	6-24-60
Jack T. Jennings	E	5-12-54	5-26-55
Al Herling	E	5-26-55	6-12-57
Richard W. Barrett	E	6-12-57	1-26-62
Ruth R. Rinehart	E	6-12-57	10-10-58
Edward Wineberg	E	6-3-58	4-7-62
Solomon L. Hoke	A	10-24-58	
	E	6-19-59	6-21-61
	A	4-7-62	
	E	6-14-62	5-26-71
W. Gifford Hoag	E	6-19-59	6-21-61
	A	4-7-62	
	E	6-14-62	5-26-71
	E	6-6-81	6-9-84
George Weber	E	6-24-60	6-21-64
Aileen Newman	E	6021-61	6-20-65
Henry Redkey	E	6-21-61	6-12-63

Jack Besansky	A	4-7-62	
	E	6-14-62	6-21-64
Rev. James C. Fahl	A	7-7-62	6-20-65
Robert J. Dressel	E	6-12-63	10-11-73
Dorothy S. Wheeler	E	6-21-64	6-1-74
David H. Scull	E	6-21-64	6-12-66
John Staehle	E	6-20-65	10-11-73
Darwin E. Bremer	E	6-12-66	1-1-67
Robert W. Norton	A	3-17-67	
	E	5-25-67	9-7-72
Oscar Meier	E	5-17-68	9-7-72
Lewis F. Norwood	E	5-28-69	3-18-72
Stanley Yarkin	A	2-13-70	5-27-70
	E	5-26-71	6-1-74
	E	6-7-75	6-3-78
	A	1-3-79	
	E	6-2-79	6-6-81
Doris Behre	E	5-27-70	6-12-76
Paul O. Mohn	E	5-26-71	6-10-86
Leonard C. Lineberry	A	4-3-72	
	E	6-9-72	8-17-79
Joseph Brown	E	9-7-72	6-7-75
J. Gordon Steele	E	10-11-73	6-2-79
Wilbur Wright	E	10-11-73	4-1-77
Bruce Patner	E	6-1-74	6-4-77
Dorothy Jacobson	E	6-7-75	6-6-81
L. Glen Whipple	E	6-12-76	6-13-85
Tom Martin	A	4-16-77	
	E	6-4-77	12-11-82
Eben Jenkins	E	6-4-77	6-7-80
Earl D. Beard	E	6-3-78	1-3-79
Anne Rollin	E	6-2-79	6-13-85
Malcomb Maclay	A	8-17-79	
	E	6-7-80	6-9-84
Donald K. Hanes	E	6-7-80	6-?-87
	A	4-4-89	10-23-89
Eleanor Thompson	E	6-6-81	6-9-84
David S. Cohen	E	6-11-83	6-10-86
Lovena W. Cooper	E	6-11-83	6-10-86
David Freed	E	6-9-84	6-6-87
Carolyn Hillier	E	6-9-84	6-6-87
Martin Block	E	6-13-85	6-4-88
Arthur Danforth	E	6-13-85	5-7-87
Shekar Narasimhan	E	6-13-85	6-4-88
Floyd Agonstinelli	E	6-10-86	8-20-88
Jeff Almen	E	6-10-86	

Fred Schmidt	E	6-10-86	
Mariana Burt	E	6-6-87	6-4-88
Nathaniel K. Smith	E	6-6-87	
Joseph Cohn	E	6-6-87	
Charles Hix	E	6-4-88	
Gene Ingalsbe	E	6-4-88	
Carol James	E	6-4-88	11-20-89
John M. Wetmore	A	4-4-89	11-30-89

APPENDIX B. SOME ACCOMPLISHMENTS IN 50 YEARS

Greenbelt Consumer Serices, Inc. / Greenbelt cooperative, Inc. survived and served and grew for 50 years, during which it:

Operated 23 supermarkets
13 SCAN furniture stores
10 auto service stations
7 pharmacies
2 drugstores
2 fresh produce stores
variety store
motion picture theater (only co-op one in the U.S.)
garage
valet shop
shoe store
barber shop
beauty parlor
bakery (Ladiesburg, Md.)
radio and appliance repair shop
food warehouse
furniture warehouse
bus line
vacation apartments at Merritt Island, Florida
mail order, non-profit, direct-drug service with support from
Farmers Union and National Council of Senior Citizens.

Provided travel service and charter flights which saved $100,000 for 8,000 members in reduced air fares in first 10 years.
Paid patronage refunds totalling $823,000 on purchases in first 20 years.
Paid 5% dividend on shares of stock for 30 years uninterrupted.
Built membership up to 137,000.
Employed a staff of 1,060 at one point.
Pioneered as first food store in area to sign a union contract.
Pioneered in race relations by hiring a Japanese-American in the Greenbelt food store during World War II and by breaking hotel segregation against Afro-Americans in Frederick, Md.
Introduced see-through, prepackaged meat, and glass window meat cutting room in this area.
Introduced unit pricing in this area (Giant and Safeway followed 6 months later).
Introduced Cornell formula bread (only supplier in this area).
Introduced bulk sale of dry products (beans, coffee, rice, etc.) outside of the health food stores.
Introduced gasohol to area during oil shortage years (first station in Md. and D.C., second in northern Virginia).

Wrote and secured passage of Md. meat inspection law to conform to USDA standards.

Wrote and secured passage of a Md. incorporation law for consumer co-ops.

Secured passage of a Md. law to put a cap on consumer credit interest charges.

Helped secure passage of a Md. law to terminate to called "Fair Trade" Act which set a monopoly minimum price on a wide variety of appliances and other goods.

Secured passage of a Md. law to permit a pharmacy to operate under same roof with a food store.

Secured creation of the first consumer counsel office in Md. and appointment of a friend to cooperatives to head it.

Some of our members, with financial support from the Co-op started the consumer advisory councils in Md., D.C. and Virginia (now a function of the county and D.C. government).

Helped organize and finance the Consumer Federation of America.

Helped passage of the Consumer Co-op Bank bill in Congress.

Helped adoption of milk standards for dairies in Prince Georges County.

Helped modify IATA rules against charter flights by affiliated membership groups.

Strongly supported promotion of CO-OP label products which were the first to have content labeling and grades--and supported nutritional labeling, more realistic (less fat) meat grading by USDA, labeling of watered hams, milk grading, etc.

Largely responsible for developing and maintaining the Potomac Cooperative Federation, which arranged joint purchasing and services, as well as a legislative voice, training programs, promotional activities, recreation, and a communications forum for all kinds of cooperatives in the area.

Largely responsible for the Cooperative Institute Association by providing staffing, funding, and planning of training programs for cooperatives in the northeastern states.

Created and developed the Congress system to govern the Greenbelt Cooperative (Greenbelt Consumer Services) widespread, multi-store organization (copied by Cooperative Services in Detroit, the Berkeley co-op and others).

Experimented with the idea of using a management firm (Checci & Co.) instead of one person as general manager (CEO).

APPENDIX C - SUBSIDIARIES AND AFFILIATIONS

SUBSIDIARIES (Board seat or seats held)

GCS owned or partially owned a number of subsidiaries. These were:

1. Potomac Cooperators
2. Rochdale Cooperative, Inc.
3. Consumers Discount Supermarket, Inc.
4. Peninsula Cooperative Association, Inc.
5. Nordiscan
6. Cooperative Travel Service
7. Mideastern Cooperatives
8. SCAN, Inc.
9. Smith Bakeries
10. Takoma Park Shopping center
11. Eastern Cooperatives
12. Consumers Realty and Equipment Corporation
13. Senior Citizens Direct Drug
14. American Travel Association

AFFILIATIONS (Board seat held)

1. Agricultural Cooperative Development, Inc.
2. Cooperative League of USA (later the National Cooperative Business Association)
3. Maryland Consumers Association
4. Virginia Citizens Consumers Council
5. Consumer Federation of America
6. Cooperative Institute Association
7. Association of Cooperative Educators
8. International Cooperative Alliance (Seat on the Central Committee)

COOPERATIVE WHOLESALERS

1. Farmland Industries
2. National Cooperative Bank (Board seat held 1982-85)
3. Richfoods
4. Southern States Cooperative
5. Universal Cooperatives

APPENDIX D - HISTORICAL HIGHLIGHTS -- THE GREENBELT COOPERATIVE

Compiled by Donald H. Cooper

1937   Certificate of Incorporation issued September 1, in State of Maryland to Distribution Corp., a foundation funded by Edward A. Filene, Boston department store merchant and philanthropist.

1937   October 5. Temporary Co-op food store opened for business, with first-day sales of $11.45 to 24 shoppers.

1937   December 15. First Co-op food market opened in Greenbelt shopping center, with Robert E. Jacobsen as manager. An auto service station opened a few days earlier.

1938   April. Some of the first residents of greenbelt had experience from cooperatives in the farm areas of the Midwest, from campus co-ops at universities, from self-help groups during the Great Depression, and from neighborhood buying clubs. They formed a Cooperative Organizing Committee, with the whole town voting for leaders in the drive to form a consumer cooperative.

1938   All stores in Greenbelt Shopping Center operated by C.D.C. for the Co-op: food store, service station/garage, dry cleaners, pharmacy, lunch counter, news/tobacco shop, hair dressers, barber shop, variety store, shoe repair, theater.

1938   November. Sale of stock began with the understanding that the Co-op would take over the stores when half of the town's families became members. Initial capital was a loan of $50,000 from the Filene Foundation.

1939   March. Sulo Laakso became General Manager.

1940   January 2. First membership meeting of the new Cooperative was held, and first Board of Directors elected.

1940   February. Walter Volckhausen elected first President.

1940   February 15. First shares of stock were delivered to Greenbelt residents.

1940   September. George Hodsden became General Manager.

1941   August. Francis Lastner elected second President.

1941 - 1943   Additional "defense homes" were built in Greenbelt but no additional commercial facilities were opened except a house converted to a Co-op food store in north end of town.

1942   March. Thomas Ricker became General Manager.

1943   August. Carl W. Hertz elected President.

1944   February. Fred DeJager elected President.

1944   April. GCS supported creation of the Potomac Cooperative Federation.

1944   November. When it was learned that the General Manager was conducting   substantial business interests outside of GCS, the Board terminated his services. Sam Ahselman was hired in November as General Manager.

1945   February. Dayton W. Hull elected President.

1945   April 18. The Co-op launched a stock drive to build a new supermarket in Greenbelt. As a result of raising $53,000, it was possible to buy out Consumer Distribution Corporation thereby becoming wholly owned by local residents as a consumer co-op.

1946   GCS purchased a bus and ran a local transportation service in Greenbelt for residents.

1947   GCS converted a bus into a traveling store to tour the courts in Greenbelt until a new supermarket could be built.

1948   January. Francis Lastner elected President again.

1948   A new modern supermarket was built with the first self-service meat department in the Washington area and a bakery in the store. The Co-op pharmacy was moved to the supermarket building.

1948   Summer. Eastern Cooperative Wholesale was decentralized and a warehouse was opened in Baltimore, MD to serve GCS, Richdale (Va.), Peninsula Cooperative Association (Hampton, Va.), and Westminster Cooperative (Md.). Potomac Cooperators, Inc. was its identity but that later became the wholesale owned by GCS at Beltsville, MD.

1949   October. Walter Bierwagen elected President.

1951   August. GCS opened a new supermarket in Takoma Park, MD. on north side of New Hampshire Ave. at Ethan Allen Ave., plus a combination variety/drug store, service station, and later a shoe store. Nationwide Insurance Co. helped get this Co-op Shopping Center started with a $100,000 loan, and opened an agent's office there.

1954   December. GCS opened an even larger Co-op Shopping Center on Georgia Ave. in Wheaton, MD. for members and consumers in that area. New concept was to have produce, grocery, meats, non-food items, lunch counter, bakery, and pharmacy under one roof, with adjacent service station. Opening day drew largest crowd ever for a store opening in the Washington area as of that date, and sales were a record $127,000 opening week.

1955   January. Board created the GCS Co-op Congress to represent members in all store areas; an idea adopted from Swedish co-ops. Henry Redkey was first Speaker.

1956   September. The Co-op at Westminster, Md merged with GCS. Three years later this resulted in a whole new shopping center for Westminster, featuring Co-op as the community's largest modern supermarket, plus a service station.

1957   May. GCS opened a supermarket at Rockville, MD. to serve members and customers in that area of Montgomery County.

1957   September. GCS opened a supermarket, pharmacy, and service station in a new Co-op Shopping Center in Piney Branch, MD.

1958   GCS bought controlling interest in Smith's Bakery, Ladiesburg, MD. to secure Co-op label bread and other baked goods for its supermarkets.

1958   June. Robert Bonham elected President.

1959   February 1. Merger of GCS with Rochdale (VA.) Cooperative with its food store in Fairlington and its supermarket and service station in Falls Church.

1959   August. New Co-op supermarket and service station opened in Westminster, MD.

1959   Fall. Beltsville, MD. warehouse and office building opened at 10501 Rhode Island Ave. This new warehouse replaced an older one in Baltimore, MD. and the office staff was transferred from Greenbelt.

1960   March. GCS opened Penn-mar supermarket in a new regional shopping center at Forestville, MD.

19670 May. GCS opened a new Co-op Shopping center in Penn Daw, south of Alexandria, VA., with supermarket, pharmacy, watch repair, service station, and first SCAN furniture outlet.

1960 Jack Besansky elected second Speaker of GCS Co-op Congress.

1960 August. The N&W independent supermarket at 2825 Old North Point Road, Dundalk, MD. was sold to GCS. After one year of operation, it was converted by GCS to a Consumer (Co-op) Supermarket and became the base for a Baltimore delegation to the GCS Co-op Congress.

1960 September. GCS opened a new, large Takoma Park Shopping Center on the south side of New Hampshire Ave. with a supermarket, variety and SCAN furniture departments, pharmacy, watch repair, and Co-op service station. The older premises were subleased, in part to Group Health Association of D.C. with GCS operating its pharmacy.

1961 January. An auto club was formed for GCS members.

1961 June 24. The first charter flight for GCS members took off to Europe.

1962 February 5. Checchi and Company assumed management of GCS. Robert E. Morrow was appointed by Checchi as Acting Resident General Manager.

1962 April. The Greenbelt supermarket and pharmacy were gutted by fire during the night. Members were bussed to Takoma Park for Co-op shopping until a temporary basement store was opened.

1962 April. Benjamin Rosenzweig elected President. Robert J. Dressel elected third Speaker of the GCS Co-op Congress.

1962 April 18. The first separate SCAN furniture store opened in the Takoma Park Co-op Shopping Center.

1962 November 12. A completely rebuilt Co-op supermarket and pharmacy was opened in Greenbelt.

1963 February 19. The Fairlington store moved across the street to larger quarters with more parking space.

1963 John F. Staehle elected fourth Speaker of the GCS Co-op Congress.

1963 June. GCS opened its second SCAN furniture store on West Broad St. in Falls Church, VA. in a new building. The smaller SCAN department in the Penn Daw supermarket closed.

1963 July. Penn Daw Co-op supermarket converted to "Consumer Discount" supermarket. In November, the remaining seven supermarkets were converted to this identity.

1964 September. GCS opened its 12th supermarket, in Glen Burnie, MD. The store was formerly operated by Safeway.

1964 October. The third SCAN store opened on Connecticut Ave. in Washington, D.C.

1965 March. GCS opened a mail order direct drug service, jointly sponsored by Farmers Union and a retired citizens group.

1965 Spring. A fourth SCAN store opened in Baltimore at 404 Reistertown Road, Pikesville, MD.

1965 Irving J. Rotkin elected fifth Speaker of the Congress.

1965 Summer. GCS opened its largest pharmacy to date at 3012 Annandale Road, Falls Church, VA.

1966 May. A group of "street people" attempted a takeover of GCS. They were defeated by a vote of more than 9,000 to 17.

1966 Summer. SCAN opened a new warehouse-office building at 11310 Frederick Ave.., Beltsville, MD.

1966 December. GCS opened its eighth service station, on King ST. in Fairlington, VA.

1967 May 1. Kroger Company sold its Washington division to GCS. Nine new stores were added, giving the Co-op a total of 21 supermarkets.

1967 Paul O. Mohn elected the sixth Speaker of the Congress.

1967 October. Another pharmacy was opened in Oxon Hill.

1967 Winter. GCS acquired an Acme supermarket in Arlandria, VA.

1968 February. Peninsula Cooperative Association, Inc. affiliated with GCS. Peninsula operated Hampton and Newport News supermarkets, a Scandia furniture store, and a book store in Newport News, VA.

1968 March. Largest SCAN to date opened in Van Ness Center on Connecticut Ave., Washington, D.C.

1968   June. Robert J. Dressel elected President.

1968   December. GCS sold its Beltsville grocery warehouse and moved its offices to Piney Branch shopping center.

1968   Closed one supermarket in Fairfax, VA acquired from Kroger. Closed Oxon Hill, Wheaton, and Piney Branch pharmacies. (Leaving 22 supermarkets, 6 SCAN stores, 8 service stations, 6 pharmacies).

1969   April. GCS acquired Skinker Tires, including a Sinclair station near Van Ness SCAN, in Washington, D.C., and a headquarters and warehouse on Butler Road in Bethesda, MD.

1970   Spring. Opening of Suitland (Md.) Gasoline Center, 4626 Silver Hill Road as 10th GCS   service station.

1970   Spring. Canal Square SCAN opened in Georgetown, 1054 31st St. NW, Washington, D.C.

1970   Spring. Robert E. Morrow, President of GCS, left to become Senior Vice President of Checchi and Co. Paul C.. Nelson, assistant to Morrow, was prompted by Checchi to become Acting Chief Executive Officer of the Co-op.

1970   Fall. Lowemann's Plaza SCAN opened on Arlington Boulevard, Falls Church, VA., replacing the store on Broad Street.

1970   August. GCS introduced unit pricing to the Washington area.

1970   December. The GCS Board determined not to renew the Checchi & Co. management contract and hired Eric Waldbaum as President and CEO. (22 supermarkets, 10 service stations, 5 pharmacies, 1 direct drug service, and 7 SCAN furniture stores at this point).

1971   Bernard Easterson elected seventh Speaker of the Congress.

1971   June. Doris Behre elected Chairman of the Board.

1971   June 9. Board suspended sale of GCS stock as a result of operating losses.

1971   August. A SCAN store was opened in Columbia, MD.

1971   November. Annandale (VA.) supermarket on Little River Turnpike closed.

1972   June. Arlandria (Va.) supermarket was flooded by Hurricane Agnes, resulting in loss of virtually all merchandise and equipment. Closed.

1972   June. Dundalk and Glen Burnie supermarkets near Baltimore closed. Piney Branch closed in July.

1972   September. Fred Schmidt, Deputy Speaker, assumed office as the eighth Congress Speaker due to the untimely death of Speaker Bernard Easterson.

1972   October. Penn Daw (VA.) supermarket closed, as was the pharmacy a month later.

1973   April. Wheaton (MD..) supermarket closed.

1973   May. Wilbur Wright, Deputy Speaker, assumed office as ninth Congress Speaker due to resignation of speaker Fred Schmidt.

1973   June. Penn-mar supermarket and Suitland service station (both in MD.) closed.

1973   June. Thomas J. Martin elected the 10th Speaker of the Congress.

1973   July. Falls Church (VA.) supermarket closed.

1973   August. Fairlington (VA) and Connecticut Ave. (D.C.) service stations closed.

1973   Arlington Boulevard (VA.) supermarket closed. (Leaving 12 supermarkets, 7 service stations, 4 pharmacies, 1 direct drug service, 8 SCAN furniture stores).

1974   June. Paul O. Mohn elected Chairman of the Board.

1974   November. GCS opens Straight from the Crate, a perishables food store, at Penn Daw (VA.) shopping center.

1975   April. Falls Church (VA.) pharmacy and Takoma Park (MD.) clinic closed.

1975   October. Co-op Federal Credit Union (formerly Wheaton) merged with Greenbelt Credit Union to provide service to all GCS employees and members.

1975   November. Janas SCAN opened in Norfolk, VA.

1976 February. Capital Plaza supermarket (MD.) closed.

1976 March 16. Board appointed Rowland Burnstan CEO, replacing Eric Waldbaum who had served as CEO from January 1971.

1976 May. Sherwood supermarket, Newport News, VA., closed.

1976 July. Southampton supermarket, Hampton, VA., closed.

1976 July. Aspen Hill supermarket (MD.) closed to remodel for SCAN furniture store which opened in November.

1976 August. Pimmit Hills supermarket, Falls Church, VA., closed.

1976 November. Roy L. Bryant replaced Rowland Burnstan as CEO.

1977 Eleanor Thompson elected 11th Speaker of Congress.

1977 Spring. Legal services added as benefit for GCS members.

1977 April. GCS leased three apartments in Merritt Island, FL. from Cooperative Services, Inc. of Detroit for rental to members and employees.

1977 May. GCS contracted to manage Hyde Park Cooperative's furniture stores in Chicago. These two SCAN stores were later purchased by GCS.

1977 August 15. GCS consolidated its corporate office, SCAN office and two SCAN warehouses into a new warehouse facility in the Corridor Industrial Park at Savage, MD.

1977 August. Co-op Green Grocer, a second convenience and perishables store, opened in Penn-mar shopping center, Forestville, MD.

1978 February. Another new SCAN opened in Newmarket North mall, Hampton, VA.

1978 April. Eastover supermarket, just southeast of Washington, D.C., closed.

1978 The Co-op's two convenience/produce stores, Straight from the Crate and Green Grocer, closed.

1979 January. GCS membership reached 40,000.

1979 April. GCS introduced gasohol at the Falls Church (VA.) station as an innovation in energy conservation. A month later Wheaton was first station in Maryland to retail gasohol.

1979 June 2. At annual membership meeting, members voted amendments to certificate of incorporation and bylaws converting Greenbelt Consumer Services, Inc. to Greenbelt Cooperative, Inc., with membership no longer based on stock purchase. largest vote in Co-op's history.

1979 June. Tenth SCAN furniture store opened in Lakeforest Mall, Gaithersburg, MD.

1979 October. Takoma park (MD.) supermarket closed.

1979 December. At end of 6-month option period, 9,000 members converted their "A" share of stock to a membership, in accord with the June reorganization.

1980 March. Robert F. Satake, Assistant CEO since May 1978, appointed by Board to be President and CEO.

1980 June. Board declared 8% dividend on stock ("B" shares) and authorized repurchase of $50,000 worth of shares in the order that requests for repurchase were received. Due to financial problems this as first dividend and repurchase of shares since June 1971.

1980 August. Complete Renovation of Greenbelt, MD. supermarket.

1980 December. GCI opened supermarket in Severna Park, MD.

1981 March. Special membership meeting approved bylaws change giving Board authority to reduce membership fee (which was then set at $1). Intensive membership drive followed, with total reaching 25,000 by August.

1981 June Milton Johnson elected as 12th Congress Speaker.

1981 July. Greenway SCAN furniture store in Greenbelt, MD opens to replace the closed store in Takoma Park, MD.

1981 October. Georgetown park SCAN furniture store opened, replacing Canal Square store, Washington, D.C.

1981 Spring. Rockville, MD., supermarket closed. Piney Branch (MD.) and Penn Daw (VA.) service stations closed.

1982 October. SCAN furniture store opened in Springfield, VA.

1982 October. Preorder purchasing service (POPS) launched and ultimately served about 1,000 families with groceries.

1983 September. Van Ness SCAN furniture store in D.C. closed.

1983 September. Benjamin Rosenzweig selected as Congress Speaker.

1984 February. Another SCAN furniture store opened in Towsend, MD. at Galleria shopping center.

1984 Spring. Remaining food stores and service stations closed. In following months, Co-op members in Greenbelt and in Westminster, MD. organized their own local cooperatives and purchased the GCS supermarkets and service stations.

1984 December. GCS membership topped 100,000 (at $1 each), and 52% of SCAN purchases were made by these members.

1985 March. Herndon, VA., SCAN furniture store opened.

1985 June. Donald K. Hanes elected Chairman of the Board, replacing Paul Mohn, longest serving head of Board.

1985 June. George Jones elected Congress Speaker.

1986 GCI bylaws completely rewritten and approved in January 1987. Delegate Assembly replaced Congress; Districts replaced Area Councils; Assembly elects Board.

1986 December. A SCAN furniture store opened in Annapolis, MD.

1987 May. SCAN employees go on strike.

1987 June. Carolyn Hillier elected Chairperson of the Board.

1987 June. Basil McKinley elected Speaker of new Delegate Assembly.

1988 June. Jeff Almen elected Chairman of the Board.

1988 July. Robert F. Satake resigns as President and CEO.

1988   August 27. Board authorized filing of Chapter 11 bankruptcy.

1988   November 4. Chapter 11 case commenced.

1989   January. Robert Riesner appointed President and CEO

1989   December 1. Bankruptcy Court approved Plan of Reorganization which left GCI without assets except for a minority interest in a new corporation controlled by the Danish furniture makers and with a minority representation on the Board of the new corporation which took over the SCAN furniture stores.

1991   The Board of Greenbelt Cooperative, Inc. dissolved the corporation and relinquished its charter.

APPENDIX E. EXCERPTS FROM REPORT OF THE EXECUTIVE COMMITTEE OF THE OPERATING MANAGEMENT TO THE JOINT LONG-RANGE PLANNING COMMITTEE AND THE BOARD OF DIRECTORS OF GREENBELT CONSUMER SERVICES, INC., DECEMBER 17, 1975

[An analysis of GCS supermarkets, prepared to assist the Board in determing whether the Co-op should continue in food marketing.]

Planning. "...Estimates of the investment required to support projected expansion [of supermarkets] were unrealistic and vague...While considering new ventures, the Co-op made no plans for, nor allocated funds to, remodeling or purchase of new equipment for supermarkets then operating.

Locations. "...Co-op facilities are, as a group, older and less attractive. The oldest was built in 1947. The newest in 1965...No first-class stores in first-class locations [at present].

Membership Patronage: "...those persons who became members in the 1940s to late-1950s became Co-op's most stalwart members...Members have aged. Some have moved to other sections of the Washington metropolitan area where there is no Co-op supermarket. [For] others...needs have changed...many are couples living alone. Their children married and moved away...The heritage of Co-op philosophy is not now reflected in membership...[Of the 10 present supermarkets] Takoma Park and Rockville are stores where the surrounding areas have changed based on upward mobility of original residents and neighborhood decline. Greenbelt, Westminster, Fairlington, and Pimmit Hills are stores where members are older now with different needs. Capital Plaza, Eastover, Kensington, and Aspen Hill were Kroger stores with no customer base/members to begin with.

"...there is a small group of believers who are still committed and still shop Co-op, but they are far fewer than the number of customers needed to keep the supermarkets viable. There appears to be less than 3,000 members purchasing less than $2,500,000 worth of goods annually.

"...disaffection of members began the last year in which patronage refunds were given...the elimination of dividends in 1971, the suspension of redemption of common stock in 1972, and the closing of key membership stores, like Wheaton were also critical.

Membership Investment: "...52% of the member accounts of the Co-op own only one share [$10]. In fact, 84% of total member accounts consist of less than 10 shares. Expenses have escalated, thus the costs of maintaining membership have become even more expensive.

<u>Cash Limitations:</u> "...Supermarkets suffered as a consequence of lack of funds stemming from diversion of assets, poor investments, and a failure/inability to cut losses...dividends were continuously declared and paid, despite the absence of earnings to support them...capital stock owned by members actually declined..l.less than 15% of proceeds from debentures paid to members at maturity has been reinvested in the current offering as of December 9, 1975...At the same time these ventures [supermarkets] were causing shortages of cash for the Co-op, SCAN was growing at a rapid rate — requiring large amounts of cash.

<u>Physical Plant:</u> "Store equipment is vintage...mean age of heating, ventilation, and air conditioning is some 15 years; refrigeration...12 years...breakdowns frequent, repairs expensive, parts often no longer available...The energy crisis and sky-rocketing utility rates have triggered substantial redesign of store equipment, which Co-op has not been able to replace.

<u>Collective Bargaining:</u> "Because of the diminutive size of its bargaining unit, compared with competitors', the Co-op has not been in a position to set policy or be a major influence on the industry or unions regarding wage scales or contract conditions...It has lacked the economic power to absorb higher wage rates, while, at the same time, lacking the bargaining power to negotiate lower rates...When a food store is operating at a high volume, for its size, people working in the store are more productive. The effect is to lower the cost of labor as a percentage of sales...Since the cost of store labor represents some two-thirds of the direct cost of operating a supermarket, small differences in labor costs have great impact on earnings (losses)...With long-term employees, higher labor costs stem from higher wage rates plus additional costs for vacations and other benefits. Full-time employee benefits are costlier than those of part-time employees. Co-op, as a result of store closings with employee retention based on seniority and other contractual reasons, has more full-time than part-time employees...Without expansion, supermarkets have not been hiring new people at the lower wage rates to give comparable <u>average</u> wage rates to competition.

<u>Erratic Program Impact:</u> "Because of many shifts in supermarket merchandising programs, members have frequently been turned off by Co-op stores...Sometimes the emphasis has been on unit-pricing, consumer information, member volunteerism, and pride in the concept of cooperation. Other times, the supermarkets have de-emphasized 'Co-op' private label, consumerism, member involvement, and pride in the concept of cooperation (even to the point of changing store names).

"...Inconsistent programming does not elicit vendor confidence...Vendors have received no review, sometimes for years; suddenly, management changes and there is tough insistence on standards of performance. The

436

frequency of management changes clearly points out to vendors that there is no consistent way to deal with the Co-op...M. Loeb, Fox Grocery Company, and Richfoods have supplied Co-op in the 12 years since Co-op ceased its own warehousing.

"...Employees, too, have suffered from erratic programs. They have been barraged by pep talk after pep talk by successive management groups with different agenda...Supermarkets have been managed [in recent years] by people with little knowledge of cooperatives.

"...In the last decade, the Co-op has not had a training program.

Technological Shortcomings: Co-op has not been able to move to electronic cash registers because of lack of capital...Scanners to read the Universal Product Code symbols, which are anticipated to facilitate labor savings of up to 40% at the front end of the supermarket, will also be beyond reach...limited use of order entry devices which can shorten delivery lead time, lack of computer supported store ordering or shelf layout programs, etc.

Advertising: The cost of advertising for a small chain with wide geographic dispersion and low sales volume is prohibitively expensive as compared with major chains.

Lack of Vendor Confidence: Vendors have watched the comings and goings at eh Co-op, and many of them have simply stopped calling: insufficient volume to provide payback on their time; central warehousing purchasing outside the Washington market; poor follow-up on deals and promotions offered; lack of knowledge of who makes decisions; concern for credit risk, following substantial losses in 1970, 1971, and 1972.

Cost of Consumer Programs: "...an expense the Co-op cannot afford. While product information, recipes, consumer alerts, unit pricing, and shopping guides are important, they are not substitutes for basic shopping needs. Consumer programs are not cost-effective by themselves.

Profitability: "...Between 1971 and 1973, ten stores (half of the division) were closed. The underlying problem is best illustrated by the net loss for the remaining stores for those years, $706,654 in 1972 and $834,279 in 1973...$373,465 in 1974, $679,817 for 44 weeks ended November 29, 1975.

Member Disappointment: "...the organization does not fulfill their sense of what the Co-op should be. They want clean, beautiful supermarkets. Co-op has old stores with mediocre equipment. They want supermarkets close to where they live. Co-op has stores in areas where members lived 10-30 years ago. They want the supermarkets to make substantial savings, so they can receive patronage refunds. Co-op has a hard time keeping the stores operating at all, much less at a profit. This is hard for members to comprehend. Understandably they are angry."